Getting the Expert Edge from SAP

 Whether you are just beginning to work in R/3 System management, or you would like to improve your grasp of the subject, you will benefit from the first-hand, practical experience and information in these books.

Gerhard Oswald
Member of the Executive Board, SAP AG

Dr. Uwe Hommel
Executive Vice-President, SAP AG
R/3 Technical Core Competence

SAP R/3 Implementation with ASAP:

The Official SAP Guide

SAP® R/3® Implementation with ASAP:
The Official SAP Guide

Hartwig Brand

San Francisco • Paris • Düsseldorf • Soest • London

Associate Publisher: Amy Romanoff
Contracts and Licensing Manager: Kristine O'Callaghan
Acquisitions & Developmental Editor: Melanie Spiller
Editor: Judy Flynn
Project Editor: Rebecca Rider
Book Designer: Kris Warrenburg
Graphic Illustrator: Tony Jonick
Electronic Publishing Specialist: Adrian Woolhouse
Production Coordinator: Susan Berge
Indexer: Nancy Guenther
Companion CD: Ginger Warner
Cover Designer: Calyx Design
Cover Illustration/Photograph: Courtesy of West Stock

SYBEX is a registered trademark of SYBEX Inc.

TRADEMARKS: SYBEX has attempted throughout this book to distinguish proprietary trademarks from descriptive terms by following the capitalization style used by the manufacturer.

The author and publisher have made their best efforts to prepare this book, and the content is based upon final release software whenever possible. Portions of the manuscript may be based upon pre-release versions supplied by software manufacturer(s). The author and the publisher make no representation or warranties of any kind with regard to the completeness or accuracy of the contents herein and accept no liability of any kind including but not limited to performance, merchantability, fitness for any particular purpose, or any losses or damages of any kind caused or alleged to be caused directly or indirectly from this book.

Copyright©1999 SYBEX Inc., 1151 Marina Village Parkway, Alameda, CA 94501. World rights reserved. No part of this publication may be stored in a retrieval system, transmitted, or reproduced in any way, including but not limited to photocopy, photograph, magnetic or other record, without the prior agreement and written permission of the publisher.

Library of Congress Card Number: 98-83182
ISBN: 0-7821-2427-5

Manufactured in the United States of America

10 9 8 7 6 5 4 3 2

Software License Agreement: Terms and Conditions

The media and/or any online materials accompanying this book that are available now or in the future contain programs and/or text files (the "Software") to be used in connection with the book. SYBEX hereby grants to you a license to use the Software, subject to the terms that follow. Your purchase, acceptance, or use of the Software will constitute your acceptance of such terms.

The Software compilation is the property of SYBEX unless otherwise indicated and is protected by copyright to SYBEX or other copyright owner(s) as indicated in the media files (the "Owner(s)"). You are hereby granted a single-user license to use the Software for your personal, noncommercial use only. You may not reproduce, sell, distribute, publish, circulate, or commercially exploit the Software, or any portion thereof, without the written consent of SYBEX and the specific copyright owner(s) of any component software included on this media.

In the event that the Software or components include specific license requirements or end-user agreements, statements of condition, disclaimers, limitations or warranties ("End-User License"), those End-User Licenses supersede the terms and conditions herein as to that particular Software component. Your purchase, acceptance, or use of the Software will constitute your acceptance of such End-User Licenses.

By purchase, use or acceptance of the Software you further agree to comply with all export laws and regulations of the United States as such laws and regulations may exist from time to time.

Software Support

Components of the supplemental Software and any offers associated with them may be supported by the specific Owner(s) of that material but they are not supported by SYBEX. Information regarding any available support may be obtained from the Owner(s) using the information provided in the appropriate read.me files or listed elsewhere on the media.

Should the manufacturer(s) or other Owner(s) cease to offer support or decline to honor any offer, SYBEX bears no responsibility. This notice concerning support for the Software is provided for your information only. SYBEX is not the agent or principal of the Owner(s), and SYBEX is in no way responsible for providing any support for the Software, nor is it liable or responsible for any support provided, or not provided, by the Owner(s).

Warranty

SYBEX warrants the enclosed media to be free of physical defects for a period of ninety (90) days after purchase. The Software is not available from SYBEX in any other form or media than that enclosed herein or posted to *www.sybex.com*. If you discover a defect in the media during this warranty period, you may obtain a replacement of identical format at no charge by sending the defective media, postage prepaid, with proof of purchase to:

SYBEX Inc.
Customer Service Department
1151 Marina Village Parkway
Alameda, CA 94501
(510) 523-8233
Fax: (510) 523-2373
e-mail: info@sybex.com
WEB: HTTP://WWW.SYBEX.COM

After the 90-day period, you can obtain replacement media of identical format by sending us the defective disk, proof of purchase, and a check or money order for $10, payable to SYBEX.

Disclaimer

SYBEX makes no warranty or representation, either expressed or implied, with respect to the Software or its contents, quality, performance, merchantability, or fitness for a particular purpose. In no event will SYBEX, its distributors, or dealers be liable to you or any other party for direct, indirect, special, incidental, consequential, or other damages arising out of the use of or inability to use the Software or its contents even if advised of the possibility of such damage. In the event that the Software includes an online update feature, SYBEX further disclaims any obligation to provide this feature for any specific duration other than the initial posting.

The exclusion of implied warranties is not permitted by some states. Therefore, the above exclusion may not apply to you. This warranty provides you with specific legal rights; there may be other rights that you may have that vary from state to state. The pricing of the book with the Software by SYBEX reflects the allocation of risk and limitations on liability contained in this agreement of Terms and Conditions.

Shareware Distribution

This Software may contain various programs that are distributed as shareware. Copyright laws apply to both shareware and ordinary commercial software, and the copyright Owner(s) retains all rights. If you try a shareware program and continue using it, you are expected to register it. Individual programs differ on details of trial periods, registration, and payment. Please observe the requirements stated in appropriate files.

Copy Protection

The Software in whole or in part may or may not be copy-protected or encrypted. However, in all cases, reselling or redistributing these files without authorization is expressly forbidden except as specifically provided for by the Owner(s) therein.

To the entire Technical Core Competence Team for their effective support and helpful suggestions for improvement.
—*Dr. Hartwig Brand*

FOREWORD TO THE SAP EXPERT KNOWLEDGE BOOK SERIES

Enabling you to operate your R/3 System at a minimum cost is of the utmost importance to SAP. You can attain this *lowest cost of ownership* both by implementing R/3 efficiently and quickly with *AcceleratedSAP* and through optimized and secure production operation. *TeamSAP* exists to provide you with active and close support. TeamSAP brings together the most important resources: *people, processes,* and *products*. SAP acts as the central contact in this team and shares its knowledge with partners and customers.

To keep your knowledge up-to-date, TeamSAP conceived this book series, which offers you a detailed overview of the technical issues and concepts of R/3 System management. The books cover subjects ranging from the technical implementation project to R/3 System and database operation.

Whether you are just beginning to work in R/3 System management or you would like to improve your grasp of the subject, you will benefit from the firsthand, practical experience and information in these books. This book series also supports you in your efforts to prepare for a Certified Technical Consultant exam for R/3 Release 4.0. However, this book series cannot, and makes no claim to, be a substitute for your own experience in working with the R/3 System. The authors provide recommendations for your daily work with R/3.

With the increase in R/3 installations, there is an increased need for qualified technical consultants. Through certification, SAP has been setting high standards for many years now. Certification not only confirms whether you are familiar with R/3 System administration for a particular R/3 release, it also establishes whether you can administer one of the database systems and the extent to which you are familiar with one of the supported operating system platforms.

Upgrades to the R/3 System regularly introduce new challenges and solutions for R/3 System management. A certification can therefore only be valid for specific R/3 releases and must be renewed with every major revision.

Gerhard Oswald
Member of the Executive Board, SAP AG

Dr. Uwe Hommel
Executive Vice-President, SAP AG
R/3 Technical Core Competence

Walldorf, July 1998

ACKNOWLEDGMENTS

A book about this subject requires the participation and involvement of many gifted and dedicated people. It's amazing how much teamwork is involved and how many people worked to help me produce a book in which we can all take pride.

First of all, I would like to thank all the people in the R/3 Technical Core Competence (TCC) department at SAP. For every technical component in the R/3 System, various members of the TCC Team helped me with their many years of experience and practical solutions for implementing R/3. It makes writing seem so easy.

Next, I want to thank Melanie Freeman for translating the original German manuscript into English. I also want to thank Paul Read at SAP for his technical editing and helpful remarks regarding the translated material.

At Sybex, I interacted with various people. I want to thank all of them, especially the editors who worked on this book and made valuable changes to improve the readability.

Dr. Hartwig Brand
Walldorf, December 1998

CONTENTS AT A GLANCE

Introduction		*xxii*
Chapter 1	Introduction to the Technical Implementation of R/3	1
Chapter 2	Technology in R/3	49
Chapter 3	Project Administration	105
Chapter 4	Front-End Administration	145
Chapter 5	R/3 Instance Administration	175
Chapter 6	User Administration	213
Chapter 7	Background Processing	245
Chapter 8	Print Administration	269
Chapter 9	Database Administration	301
Chapter 10	Archiving	341
Chapter 11	Network Administration	359
Chapter 12	Software Logistics	385
Chapter 13	Interfaces	435
Chapter 14	Security	457
Chapter 15	High Availability	479
Appendix A	R/3 for Medium-Size Companies	499
Appendix B	Training Courses for the Technical Team	507
Appendix C	SAP Service & Support for the Technical Team	517
Appendix D	Glossary	529
Appendix E	Review Questions and Answers	549
Index		*568*

TABLE OF CONTENTS

Introduction xxii

1 Introduction to the Technical Implementation of R/3 1
  How Can ASAP Help You? 2
    ASAP 3
    Project Preparation 5
    Business Blueprint and Realization 6
    Final Preparation 6
    Go Live and Support 7
  How Do You Prepare the Project? 7
    Determine the Implementation Strategy 8
    Define the Project Organization 10
    Plan the System Landscape 12
    Determine the Technical Requirements 18
  How Do You Implement R/3? 22
    Create a Technical Design 22
    Set Up Your R/3 Systems 25
    Define and Set Up System Operation 29
    Define the Authorization Concept 34
  How Do You Prepare for Production? 36
    Import Data from the Legacy System 36
    Test the System Operation 38
    Perform the GoingLive Check 39
  How Can You Support Production Operation? 42
    Make Production Support Available 42
    Plan for Release Maintenance and Update 44

2 Technology in R/3 49
  Logical Services in R/3 50
    The Instance 53
  Physical Implementation of Services 54
    The Central System 54
    The Two-Tier Configuration 54

The Three-Tier Configuration	55
The Physical Parts of an Instance	56
Supported Hardware and Software for R/3	59
The Presentation Layer	60
The Session Manager	61
The SAPGUI	62
The Internet Session Manager and SAPGUI in Java	63
The Internet-Enabling Layer	63
The Application Layer	65
The R/3 Transaction	65
The Dialog Service	66
The Update Service	68
The Enqueue Service	70
The Background Service	71
The Message Service	72
The Gateway Service	73
The Spool Service	74
The Database Layer	76
The Repository	76
The SAPR3 User	77
The Database Access Agent	77
Network Architecture and Protocol	78
The SAProuter	81
Secure Network Communications (SNC)	81
Interfaces	81
Communication through Sequential Files	82
Program-to-Program Communication	84
Distributed Component Architecture	86
Business Components	86
Business Integration	88
Business Objects	89
Software Logistics	90
System Landscape	91
The Customizing Organizer and the Workbench Organizer	94
The Transport System	96
Review Questions	100

3 Project Administration   105

Define the Organization	106
Determine Your Project Team	107

Estimate the Number of Team Members Required	111
Train the Project Team	113
Determine the Procedures	116
Define the Implementation Strategy	117
Define the Implementation Standards	120
Plan the Cut Over and the Help Desk	122
Define the Strategy for Service and Support	127
Check the Project Progress	129
Prepare the Project Plan	130
Complete the Quality Check	134
Project Administration in ASAP	135
Project Preparation	136
Business Blueprint	137
Realization	138
Final Preparation	138
Go Live and Support	139
Success Factors	141
Prepare the Project Team	141
Control the Scope of the Project	141
Review Questions	142

4 Front-End Administration — 145

Define the Front-End Strategy	146
Standardize Your Hardware	147
Standardize Your Software	149
Include Office Applications	154
Install the Front-End Software	156
Install the Software Locally	157
Store the Software on a File Server	159
Consider Remote Connection to Subnetworks	160
Install the R/3 Online Documentation	162
Plan Front-End Maintenance	165
System Management Server (SMS)	165
Front-End Administration in ASAP	166
Project Preparation	167
Business Blueprint	167
Realization	168
Final Preparation	168

	Success Factors	170
	Check Requirements	170
	Train Users	171
	Ensure Network Access	171
	Review Questions	172
5	**R/3 Instance Administration**	**175**
	Determine Operating Systems and Hardware	176
	The Requirements Catalog	177
	Invitation to Tender	178
	The Quicksizer	178
	Keep It Simple	181
	The GoingLive Check	183
	Configure R/3 Instances	183
	Distribute Work Processes	184
	Define Logon Groups	187
	Define Operation Modes	191
	Monitor R/3 Instances	195
	Configure the Alert Monitor	195
	Define System Operation	199
	R/3 Instances in ASAP	201
	Project Preparation	202
	Business Blueprint	202
	Realization	204
	Final Preparation	204
	Go Live and Support	205
	Success Factors	207
	Size Hardware Appropriately	208
	Distribute System Load Sensibly	208
	Customize Alert Monitors	209
	Review Questions	210
6	**User Administration**	**213**
	Activity Groups, Authorizations, and User Master Records	214
	Activity Groups	215
	Authorizations	216
	Authorization Profiles	218
	User Master Records	218
	The Double-Verification Principle	219

	Create an Authorization Concept	220
	Plan Activity Groups	220
	Standardize Master Records	224
	Define the Logon Procedure and Password Rules	225
	Administer User and Activity Groups	228
	Implement the Double-Verification Principle	228
	Maintain Master Records and Activity Groups Centrally or Decentrally 230	
	Define System Operation	232
	User Administration in ASAP	234
	Project Preparation	234
	Business Blueprint	234
	Realization	235
	Success Factors	237
	Protect Special Users	237
	Use the Profile Generator	239
	Create User Groups	240
	Review Questions	241
7	**Background Processing**	**245**
	Create Your Concept for Background Processing	246
	Plan Requirements and Load Distribution	247
	Define Job Priorities	249
	Set Up Job Chains	253
	Consider Event-Driven Jobs	254
	Administer Background Processing	255
	Release Jobs Centrally or Decentrally	256
	Define the System Operation	257
	Background Processing in ASAP	260
	Realization	261
	Final Preparation	262
	Success Factors	263
	Schedule Standard Background Jobs	264
	Optimize Throughput	265
	Review Questions	266
8	**Print Administration**	**269**
	Plan Your Print Infrastructure	270
	Determine the Print Requirements	271

Classify and Standardize Printers	274
Define the Spool Server	277
Set Up the Print Infrastructure	282
Set Up Local Printing	283
Set Up Remote Printing	285
Consider Front-End Printers	287
Integrate the External Output Management System (OMS)	287
Monitor the Output	289
Print Administration in ASAP	292
Business Blueprint	292
Realization	293
Final Preparation	294
Success Factors	296
Use Standard Device Types	296
Optimize the Printer Throughput	297
Review Questions	298

9 Database Administration 301

Determine the RDBMS and Hardware	302
Hardware Platform	303
Storage Technology	303
Storage Capacity	307
Archiving	307
Configure the Database	308
Define the Disk Layout	308
Log (File) Mode	311
Define Your Data Backup Strategy	312
Potential Downtime Situations	313
Select Tools	315
Define the Schedule and Tape Administration	318
Back Up Very Large Databases	322
Define Your Recovery Strategy	325
Downtime	325
Monitor the Database	328
Configure the Database Calendar	329
Define the System Operation	331
Database Administration in ASAP	332
Project Preparation	333
Business Blueprint	333

Realization	333
Final Preparation	334
Success Factors	336
Size the Hardware Sufficiently	336
Test the Data Backup and Recovery	337
Protect the Special Users	337
Review Questions	338

10 Archiving 341

Archive Development Kit, ArchiveLink, and Hierarchical Storage Management	342
Archiving Run	343
The Archive Development Kit (ADK)	344
ArchiveLink	345
The Hierarchical Storage Management (HSM) System	346
Define the Archiving Strategy	346
Define the Archiving Procedure	349
Organize the Procedures	349
Define System Operation	351
Archiving Procedure in ASAP	354
Realization	354
Success Factors	355
Select a Suitable Storage Medium	356
Back Up Archive Files	356
Review Questions	357

11 Network Administration 359

Plan Your Network	360
Define the Strategy for Network Layout	361
Determine the Bandwidth	367
Assign IP Addresses in the Network	370
Set Up a Remote Connection	373
Operating Your Network	374
Integrated System and Network Management (ISNM)	375
Network Administration in ASAP	377
Project Preparation	377
Business Blueprint	378
Realization	379
Final Preparation	379

	Success Factors	381
	Configure Enough Bandwidth	381
	Use Supported Network Products	382
	Review Questions	383
12	**Software Logistics**	**385**
	Plan Your System Landscape	386
	Define the Systems and Clients	387
	Define the Implementation Strategy	393
	Define the Release Strategy	401
	Define Strategies for Customizing and Software Development	404
	Organize a Customizing Project	405
	Organize a Software Development Project	408
	Determine a Transport Procedure	411
	Maintain the System Landscape	414
	Import Patches	415
	Plan an Upgrade	418
	Software Logistics in ASAP	423
	Project Preparation	423
	Business Blueprint	425
	Realization	426
	Final Preparation	427
	Go Live and Support	427
	Success Factors	428
	Define Guidelines for Modifications	429
	Create an Authorization Concept	429
	Plan Customizing and Software Development in Detail	431
	Review Questions	431
13	**Interfaces**	**435**
	Plan the Interface Infrastructure	436
	Determine the Interface Requirements	437
	Implement the Interface Adviser	440
	Plan the Data Transfer	442
	Use the Legacy System Migration (LSM) Workbench	447
	Monitor and Restart the Interfaces	447
	Interfaces in ASAP	449
	Business Blueprint	449
	Realization	450

	Final Preparation	451
	Success Factors	452
	Define Guidelines for the Interfaces	453
	Test the Throughput	453
	Consider Open Interfaces in CCMS	454
	Review Questions	454
14	**Security**	**457**
	Define Your Strategy	458
	Control Access	459
	Secure the Network	462
	Secure the Operating-System Level	466
	Define the System Operation	469
	The User List	469
	The Information System	470
	Security in ASAP	471
	Business Blueprint	471
	Realization	471
	Final Preparation	472
	Success Factors	474
	Read and Implement Security Guidelines	474
	Train Users	476
	Review Questions	476
15	**High Availability**	**479**
	Define a Strategy for High Availability	480
	Potential Downtime Situations	481
	Encapsulate Redundant Subsystems	483
	Integrate Switchover Solutions	486
	Define the System Operation	488
	The System Operation Manual	489
	The CCMS	489
	High Availability in ASAP	489
	Project Preparation	490
	Business Blueprint	490
	Realization	491
	Final Preparation	491
	Go Live and Support	492
	Success Factors	493
	Read the High-Availability Guide	494

	List Potential Downtime Situations	494
	Conclude a Service Level Agreement	495
	Review Questions	496
A	**R/3 for Medium-Size Companies**	**499**
	Ready-to-Run R/3 (RRR)	500
	Implementation Project	501
	The Front End	502
	The Network	502
	Remote Connection	503
	Software Logistics	503
	System Operation	504
	System Administration Assistant	505
B	**Training Courses for the Technical Team**	**507**
	Management Training Courses	509
	Foundation Training Courses (Level 1)	509
	Basis Training Courses (Level 2 and Level 3)	510
	Administration	510
	Business Process Technology	512
	Integration Technology	514
C	**SAP Service & Support for the Technical Team**	**517**
	The Online Service System (OSS) and SAPNet	518
	Remote Connection	519
	Using OSS	520
	SAP Service & Support	521
	The GoingLive Check	522
	Analysis, Optimization, and Verification	523
	Requirements	523
	Data Security	524
	The EarlyWatch Service	524
D	**Glossary**	**529**
E	**Review Questions and Answers**	**549**
	Chapter 2: Technology in R/3	550
	Chapter 3: Project Administration	553
	Chapter 4: Front-End Administration	554
	Chapter 5: R/3 Instance Administration	556

Chapter 6: User Administration 557
Chapter 7: Background Processing 558
Chapter 8: Print Administration 559
Chapter 9: Database Administration 561
Chapter 10: Archiving 562
Chapter 11: Network Administration 563
Chapter 12: Software Logistics 564
Chapter 13: Interfaces 566
Chapter 14: Security 567
Chapter 15: High Availability 568

Index *568*

INTRODUCTION

This book describes the technical implementation of SAP R/3 with the efficient method called AcceleratedSAP (ASAP).

You'll learn how you can benefit from ASAP so that you can technically implement R/3 faster and more cost-effectively than you could with previous methods. In addition, this book describes how to lay the foundation during the implementation project for a more cost-effective and secure operation of the R/3 System.

ASAP

The goal of the ASAP method is to minimize the time needed for an SAP R/3 implementation project. This allows you to free up resources quickly and to realize the benefits of R/3. Therefore, ASAP focuses on how to implement R/3 based on your current business processes. The available reference processes in the standard R/3 System form the foundation. Once you have started production operation, you should create a detailed plan that describes how to run your business processes with R/3 more efficiently and how to optimize them through reengineering.

The goal of the technical implementation with ASAP is to build an R/3 production system in a short period of time and to integrate this system into an existing system landscape. To simplify reengineering after the start of production, the technical implementation should be planned as openly and as flexibly as possible. To meet this goal, ASAP recommends strategies with which you can ensure high availability with low operating costs after implementation.

Until now, SAP and its partners have relied on methods and standardized procedures. ASAP is special because it has combined the most practical solutions from consultants with the latest specialized knowledge from software developers. As of R/3 Release 4.0, all SAP customers receive a CD in the installation package that contains these collected experiences. The ASAP CD contains documents for many strategies, which enable you to shorten the consulting time or to perform many tasks yourself.

Readership

This book is of particular interest to you if you are a part of an R/3 technical implementation project. It presents the relevant technical points in the complete implementation project with ASAP. You will learn about the most strongly recommended strategies and the essential points for production operation for each component in the client/server architecture. In addition to readers who have decided on the ASAP method for their implementation project, readers who want information and suggestions for any SAP R/3 technical implementation project are addressed.

How you use the book depends on your current knowledge. Whether you are beginning an implementation project or working with the R/3 System for the first time, you should read the book as a whole. This is the best way to benefit from the information it presents. If you are interested in finding out about options for some components in the R/3 System that are new in R/3 Release 4.0, this book offers a wealth of information for reference.

Structure

The structure of this book will make it easy for you to find information about individual technical components in the R/3 System because it reflects the client/server architecture in R/3. The following table shows you which of the logical layers is covered in each chapter.

Topic	Content
Introduction	Chapter 1: Introduction to the Technical Implementation of R/3
	Chapter 2: Technology in R/3
	Chapter 3: Project Administration
Presentation layer	Chapter 4: Front-End Administration
Application layer	Chapter 5: R/3 Instance Administration
	Chapter 6: User Administration
	Chapter 7: Background Processing
	Chapter 8: Print Administration
Database layer	Chapter 9: Database Administration
	Chapter 10: Archiving
Network	Chapter 11: Network Administration
Software distribution	Chapter 12: Software Logistics
General topics	Chapter 13: Interfaces
	Chapter 14: Security
	Chapter 15: High Availability
Appendices	Appendix A: R/3 for Medium-Size Companies
	Appendix B: Training Courses for the Technical Team
	Appendix C: SAP Service & Support for the Technical Team
	Appendix D: Glossary
	Appendix E: Review Questions and Answers

The chapters have a similar structure to help you find the information about various points of the implementation easily. Each chapter begins with a section about the most practical strategies for implementing R/3. Then, efficient system operation for each component is described. The next section builds on this to show you the tasks that are part of the ASAP project plan. This is followed by a section in which you can find the essential factors for a successful implementation of R/3. At the end of each chapter, there are questions with which you can check your newly acquired expert knowledge. If your goal is to become a Certified Technical Consultant, these questions can help you prepare for the certification test.

Introduction

If you are just starting with the technical implementation of SAP R/3, the three introductory chapters are written expressly for you.

- Chapter 1, "Introduction to the Technical Implementation of R/3," explains how ASAP can help you with an implementation project. With examples based on a fictitious company, you'll learn how to prepare the implementation project, how to implement R/3, how to prepare for the start of production, and how to support production operation.

- Chapter 2, "Technology in R/3," covers the client/server architecture and thus contains the technical background knowledge for the chapters to follow.

- Chapter 3, "Project Administration," tells you how the organizational points of ASAP are different from other methods for implementing R/3.

Presentation Layer

After the introductory chapters, you'll learn, in one chapter, how to plan and realize the graphical implementation of the graphical user interface in the R/3 System, the presentation layer.

- Chapter 4, "Front-End Administration," explains which strategies are recommended for the hardware and software of the front ends. This chapter also focuses on the way the SAP front-end software can be installed and the points that can play a role in future operating costs.

Application Layer

User entries go from the user interface to the application layer, on which the entire business logic of an R/3 System runs. The four chapters on this topic show you how to provide a suitable computing capacity on this level and how to ensure its availability.

- Chapter 5, "R/3 Instance Administration," focuses on how to size the hardware resources for the application layer and how to optimally configure the available resources.

- Chapter 6, "User Administration," explains how to work together with the departments in your company to transform the job role descriptions into an authorization concept and how to organize your strategy for assigning authorizations.

- Chapter 7, "Background Processing," explains which options R/3 has for processing data in the background while you call transactions in the screen in parallel to background processing. This chapter's main focus is on how to plan your resources and how to ensure production operation from a technical viewpoint.

- Chapter 8, "Print Administration," explains which print infrastructures are recommended and how to determine the most suitable ones. This chapter also focuses on the printer types that can be connected with R/3 and which points play an important role in production operation.

Database Layer

The R/3 System stores all of its data on the database layer in a Relational Database Management System (RDBMS). The data volume can be from a few gigabytes to several hundred gigabytes. The two chapters on this topic explain, from a technical viewpoint, which resources you should schedule for the database layer and how to ensure data security.

- Chapter 9, "Database Administration," begins with how to size the hardware resources for the RDBMS and which storage technologies are recommended. Then the focus switches to the strategies for data backup and recovery because only these strategies enable you to rule out the possibility of data loss if a serious problem occurs.

- Chapter 10, "Archiving," covers the options you have for keeping your production database at an optimal size. For the long-term production operation of R/3, archiving application data is of strategic importance, and therefore, it should be taken into consideration during the implementation.

Network

The network is vital for communication between the layers in the R/3 System. In a typical R/3 System, a front-end network connects the user PCs with the computers on the application layer. Then the computers on the application layer are connected to the computers on the database layer through a server network.

- Chapter 11, "Network Administration," explains the fundamental concepts of the network topologies that are recommended for R/3 and how to estimate the required bandwidth.

Software Distribution

You'll need to adapt standard software to the requirements in your company and change the delivered R/3 software. To ensure that the changes do not interrupt the production operation of the R/3 System, SAP recommends setting up a system landscape of at least two, but preferably three, R/3 Systems. Therefore, software distribution is of central importance in a system landscape.

- Chapter 12, "Software Logistics," explains how to design a suitable system landscape for your requirements and how to implement your concept. The chapter also focuses on how to organize customizing and software development projects in an R/3 System landscape.

General Topics

The book ends with three topics that affect the entire R/3 System.

- Chapter 13, "Interfaces," explains which points must be taken into consideration when you connect the R/3 System with other systems. The focus is on how to use SAP tools to determine your interface requirements and how to transfer data from the legacy system.

- Chapter 14, "Security," focuses on potential unauthorized accesses to your R/3 System from internal and external parties. Once you understand the potential security risks, you can take appropriate measures against them.

- Chapter 15, "High Availability," explains the strategies and the tools you can use to increase the availability of your R/3 System. It includes a detailed concept for system operation, in addition to technical and organizational points.

Appendices

The first three appendices focus on the wide variety of system solutions and services that are offered by SAP and are especially relevant for the technical implementation. You'll learn which solutions SAP has developed especially for medium-size companies, which SAP training courses are recommended for the Technical Team, and which offers from SAP Service & Support play an important role in the implementation project. You'll also find a glossary of the most common technical terms and the answers to the questions at the end of each chapter.

R/3 Release 4.0

This book was developed for R/3 Release 4.0. It can be used as a foundation for other R/3 Releases and provide you with many suggestions and ideas. However, you must take into consideration that new technical developments may have been added or previously important success factors may be replaced with different ones. You should determine whether the recommended strategies are also applicable for other R/3 Releases or whether they must be expanded. The release-specific parts of the book will be regularly updated in future editions.

CHAPTER ONE

Introduction to the Technical Implementation of R/3

The quick, and therefore cost-effective, implementation of R/3 is an ambitious goal even for the experienced project manager. Experience from numerous successful implementation projects shows that a standardized implementation is possible. This standardized implementation, AcceleratedSAP (ASAP), is described in this book (which focuses on the technical viewpoint); the deciding factors for a successful project are taken into consideration.

In this chapter, you will learn how ASAP can help you. Because experiences are difficult to describe, it is easier to demonstrate by example. Based on the fictitious company Mannaberg Inc., you will be shown how to prepare the project, how to implement R/3, how to prepare the production operation, and finally, how to support operations after the start of production.

How Can ASAP Help You?

To answer this question, a typical situation in which you would use ASAP is described. From among the standard software that is available, your company management has chosen R/3. The following factors influenced this decision:

Complete R/3 integrates all business function areas and can map most of your company's business processes in the standard system.

Modular R/3 consists of modules; for example, Human Resources (HR), Sales and Distribution (SD), Financial Accounting (FI), and Controlling (CO). The modules correspond largely to the organizational divisions of your company and can be implemented on a step-by-step basis.

Scalable The R/3 client/server architecture consists of four layers: presentation, Internet-enabling, application, and database. The software on each layer can be distributed as required over various computers, thus supporting systems that have from one to several thousand users.

Open R/3 runs on common operating systems and uses Relational Database Management Systems (RDBMSs).

During the implementation of R/3, you are responsible for all technical tasks. You must set up a system landscape for your company with the following guidelines:

- The R/3 Modules Sales and Distribution (SD), Production Planning (PP), Financial Accounting (FI), and Controlling (CO) replace the existing application software.
- At the beginning, about 100 users are working at your company headquarters and about 30 users are working at your 2 European subsidiaries. In 2 years, a total of 500 users should be able to work with the system.
- The client/server architecture replaces the old mainframe architecture.
- Oracle is implemented as an RDBMS.
- Five employees should administer the system landscape.
- The system must be 99 percent available and is only allowed to fail in problematic situations for a maximum of 6 hours between 6:00 A.M. and 6:00 P.M. on workdays.
- The implementation should take six months.

ASAP

There are many different methods and tools that can help you with the implementation of R/3. But only a method such as ASAP can give you the best support because ASAP takes into consideration experiences from numerous successful R/3 implementation projects. It is the experiences collected in ASAP that help you to make decisions in your project. The experiences are documented in the *Roadmap*. You can use this Roadmap to plan an R/3 implementation without overlooking important tasks. Figure 1.1 shows how you can display the Roadmap in the *Implementation Assistant*.

FIGURE 1.1:

The Implementation Assistant

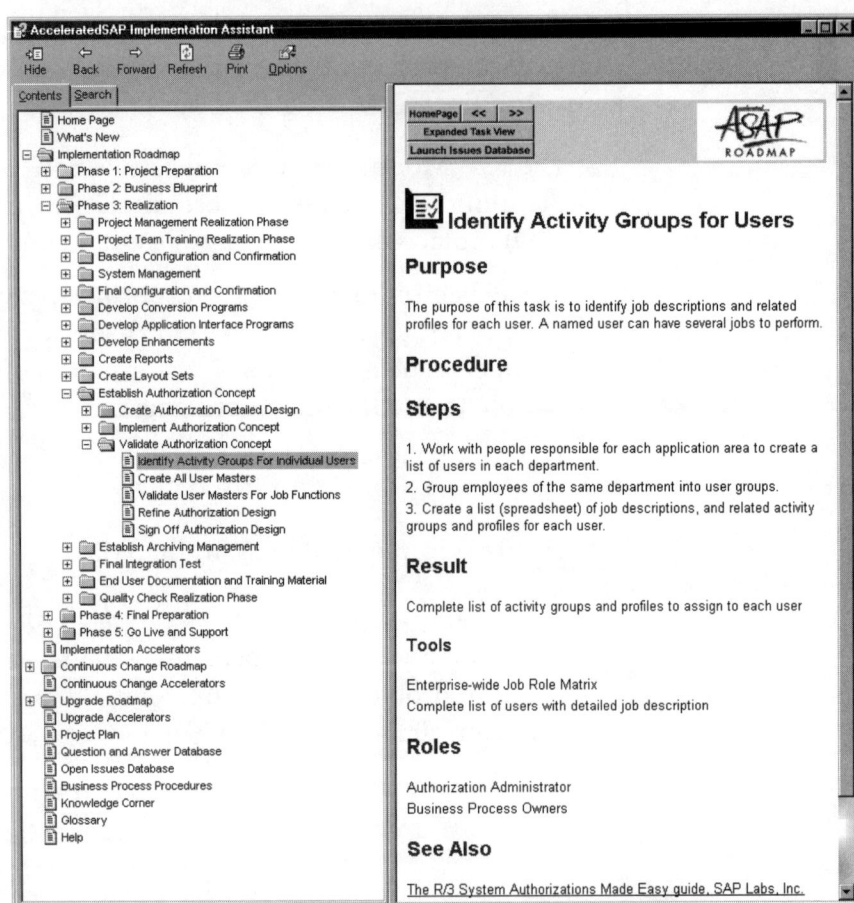

The Roadmap contains a description of the purpose, actions, results, and tools for each task, as well as the people who will perform the task. Since over 400 tasks are described, it is useful to select the tasks that are relevant to your project at the beginning of a project phase and to consider only these tasks in detail. This enables you to learn this new method in parallel to the project, even under time constraints.

ASAP connects the following three projects, which can be completed by you or your consulting partner:

- Project management
- Application implementation
- Technical implementation

The entire project takes about six to nine months depending on the complexity of the project and the available resources. In this time, you will go through the five phases:

1. Project Preparation (15–20 days)
2. Business Blueprint (25–40 days)
3. Realization (55–80 days)
4. Final Preparation (35–55 days)
5. Go Live and Support (20–24 days)

Project Preparation

Project preparation is important for the success of an R/3 implementation. It is deliberately implemented in the ASAP Roadmap as a separate phase, *Project Preparation*. During project preparation, you will determine the strategy for R/3 implementation, organize the technical project team, define the system landscape, determine the technical demands, and select your hardware and database vendors. The implementation project begins officially with the project kickoff meeting. At this meeting, the Project Manager explains the goals and the work plan. Before you advance to the next phase, the Project Manager must check the quality of the results and release the Project Preparation phase.

Business Blueprint and Realization

The Technical Team performs the essential services for the Project Team, which customizes the R/3 System during the *Business Blueprint* and *Realization* phases. At the beginning of the Business Blueprint phase, you will create the technical design. In accordance with the technical design, you should first set up the development system in which the application consultants customize the standard R/3 software for your company. At the beginning of the Realization phase, you should set up a second R/3 System to test the settings. This is known as the quality assurance system. You'll install the production system at the end of the Realization phase. For this R/3 System landscape, determine the system operation and administer each individual system. To prepare for the production operation, plan how to transfer data from the legacy system into the production system. However, you can only begin the next phase once the Project Manager has checked the quality of the results and released the Realization phase.

Final Preparation

To make the start of production easier, it is important to prepare the production operation. ASAP has a separate phase for this, *Final Preparation*. If you shorten this phase because of time constraints at the end of a project, often more problems occur than necessary in the first weeks of production operation. In this phase, you'll set up the operation of the production system and import the data from the legacy system. To start production with R/3 without problems, you must check the system settings, test the system throughput for your most important business processes, and set up a help desk. At the end of the Final Preparation phase, you should decide when you will start the production. The Project Manager checks the quality of the results and releases the Final Preparation phase.

Go Live and Support

After the start of production, you must ensure the availability of the production system. You cannot check all of the settings and the throughput of the system in detail during the Final Preparation phase. Therefore, you should monitor the important business processes at the beginning. Users have the most questions during the first few weeks. For this reason, you must set up the help desk in a way that the system administrators are not overloaded with work. You should also define your long-term release strategy at the end of this phase.

The standardized procedure in ASAP helps you create a uniform work environment for all employees in the project. New employees can be integrated more quickly into an existing project, and everyone knows the current status. Because the procedure is defined and corresponds to SAP recommendations, you will avoid unnecessary distractions. The detailed description of each task allows you to take on many of the tasks that used to be reserved for specialists. Subsequent projects will be simpler and cheaper because you are using proven standards and procedures. By assigning employees to tasks, you can better estimate your personnel and capital requirements.

How Do You Prepare the Project?

You'll prepare the project by having the Technical Team process the following essential tasks during the Project Preparation phase:

- Determine the implementation strategy
- Define the project organization
- Plan the system landscape
- Determine the technical demands

The following sections provide you with the initial view of these tasks.

Determine the Implementation Strategy

Two aspects are important for the implementation strategy. First, you must decide whether you need one or more linked R/3 Systems for the organizational structure of your company. Second, you must determine how R/3 will replace the legacy system and through which interfaces R/3 will exchange data with external systems.

System Topology

A company's strategic goals determine which tasks are important. Based on these tasks, the business processes and organizational structures are defined for the company. To map the organizational structure for the company in accordance with the R/3 organizational units, the business requirements are harmonized with the technical conditions in R/3. The system topology, in particular, must be defined.

Mannaberg Inc.

The Steering Committee of Mannaberg Inc. could choose between the following system topologies:

Linked R/3 Systems   An R/3 System is installed in every subsidiary. All subsidiaries link to the R/3 System in the headquarters through an interface developed by SAP, Application Link Enabling (ALE).

Central R/3 System   An R/3 System is installed in the headquarters. All the users in the subsidiaries work with this R/3 System on front ends through wide area network (WAN) connections.

Continued on next page

> The Steering Committee decided to implement a central R/3 System. The subsidiaries depend on the headquarters and are logically well integrated into the business processes. In this case, the linked R/3 Systems exchange more data than the front ends in the central R/3 System. The central R/3 System requires a smaller bandwidth for the WAN. In addition, the estimated acquisition and running costs are higher for the linked R/3 Systems. Therefore, the central R/3 System is more cost effective.

Migration

Initially, most companies only partially replace their existing IT infrastructure with R/3. The order in which the various R/3 modules are implemented can depend on the size of the company or the geographical limitations. R/3 almost always exchanges data with the legacy system. You must determine which system controls this data flow. To allow appropriate interfaces to be defined, a companywide standard must exist for the format of the data.

Mannaberg Inc.

Because Mannaberg Inc. had a mainframe as a legacy system, they had the following options:

Full migration (Big Bang) R/3 replaces all applications of the legacy system at one time. A permanent interface to the legacy system is unnecessary.

Step-by-step migration (cooperative operation) R/3 only partially replaces the legacy system. First, only Sales and Distribution, Production Planning, Financial Accounting, and Controlling are implemented. These applications require a permanent interface to the legacy system.

Continued on next page

> The Steering Committee decided to use the step-by-step migration. First, it protects the investment in the mainframe hardware and knowledge. Second, a full migration increases the risk of failure in the entire production because not all problem cases can be tested in advance.

Define the Project Organization

Normally, a company partially changes its existing IT organization with the implementation of R/3. If your company does not allow all tasks to be performed by the consulting partner, you must nominate your own employees and prepare them for their new tasks. Table 1.1 lists the roles you must fill to undertake an R/3 implementation.

TABLE 1.1: Roles in the Project Team

Role	Description
Steering Committee	Consists of the Project Sponsor, the Project Manager, and the SAP Consulting Manager. This committee allocates the resources and monitors the progress of the project.
Project Management	Defines the implementation strategy, obtains and administers the resources, and regularly informs the Steering Committee and the Project Team about the status.
Business Process Team	Creates the To-Be vision for the business processes (Business Blueprint), sets these processes in R/3, tests the settings, and creates the documentation for the user training.
Technical Team	Creates the To-Be vision for the technical requirements, installs and configures the R/3 System landscape, tests the settings, administers the R/3 Systems, and describes the system operation.
Training and Documentation Team	Defines the training strategy, develops training material, and trains the users.
Help desk	Processes all problems from the operation of R/3, classifies the problems, solves the simple problems itself, and passes the difficult problems to experts.

How many people take on a role depends on the size of the project. For example, if you set up an R/3 System for only 50 users, then one person must often take on multiple roles. Chapter 3, "Project Administration," describes in more detail which roles you'll require and how many employees you should assign to each role.

After the members of the new Project Team have been nominated, you can set up more rooms for the entire team. If you have an external consulting partner participating in the project, you must also provide him or her with an appropriate working environment. The team should create an initial Project Plan and work out the standards and guidelines for the entire project together. It is only when the teams can work together directly that you can avoid redundancy and, thus, unnecessary work.

Mannaberg Inc.

Mannaberg Inc. set up a new IT organization, a *Competence Center*. Five employees from the Competence Center technically implemented R/3 and administered the entire system landscape. Of these five employees, three previously had similar tasks in the company and two were freshly hired.

To ensure that the entire implementation team could work closely together, new rooms were set up for the team. The Technical Team equipped the common work area as follows:

- Each employee had a PC with a CD-ROM. The installed operating systems were Microsoft Windows NT 4 and Microsoft Windows 95.
- The installed special software for the ASAP-CD was Microsoft Project 4.1, Adobe Acrobat Reader 3, and WinZip 6.2.
- All PCs were connected to a network with access to the R/3 System.
- A printer was installed for every five employees, and a fax machine was available for all employees.

Plan the System Landscape

When you plan the system landscape, three aspects are important. First, decide how many R/3 Systems you need to adapt the standard R/3 System to the business processes in your company. Second, define how many and into which organizational units you will divide the R/3 Systems. These are known as the *clients*. Third, define how you will transport the settings from the standard R/3 System and the newly developed programs between the systems.

Three-System Landscape

If the application consultants customize your company's business processes and organizational structures in R/3, they will change the runtime environment of the R/3 System. In a system with a changed runtime environment, production operation would not be possible. Therefore, SAP recommends a *three-system landscape* with separate systems for development, quality assurance, and production (see Figure 1.2). Some companies—for example, multinational companies with productive systems in every international subsidiary—require more than the three systems recommended. However, smaller companies often choose the most cost-effective two-system landscape and do without a stable testing environment. SAP does not recommend using only one system. If you use the system for production, you can no longer use it to develop your own programs and you'll require more time for an R/3 Release upgrade. Chapter 12, "Software Logistics," describes the advantages and disadvantages of such system landscapes.

Even though you'll initially only set up one of the three systems, the development system, you must define the entire system landscape during the project preparation. In this way, you ensure that all of the settings and developments in the development system are documented and marked for transport to the appropriate systems.

FIGURE 1.2:

A three-system landscape

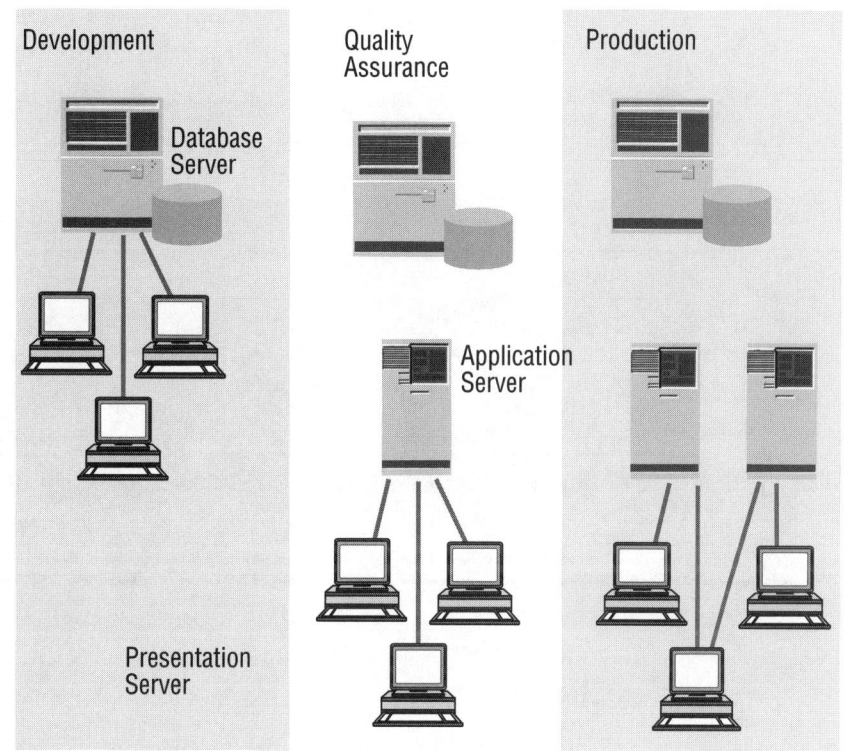

Mannaberg Inc.

Mannaberg Inc. had the following system landscape options:

Two-system landscape   The system landscape consists of two R/3 Systems. In the first system, the R/3 standard is customized, the company's own programs are developed, and the results are tested. The second system is used for production.

Three-system landscape   The system landscape consists of three R/3 Systems. In the first system, the R/3 standard is customized and the

Continued on next page

company's own programs are developed. In the second system, the results are tested. The third system is used for production.

The company chose a three-system landscape and defined the system names as listed in the following table.

Name	Description
DEV	Development
QAS	Quality assurance
PRD	Production

This three-system landscape is more expensive and more time-consuming to maintain than the two-system landscape. For the company management, the deciding factor was that they could test in a stable runtime environment in the quality assurance system.

Client

When users log on to R/3, they enter a user name and a client. From a business and organizational viewpoint, a client is an independent unit in an R/3 System. The data in a client is protected from other clients. In every system landscape, there must be at least three different clients occupying different roles: the development client, the quality assurance client, and the production client. Depending on your requirements, you can define more roles—for example, a training client (see the Mannaberg Inc. example on the next page). To run multiple independent clients in parallel in the same R/3 System, you must follow the rules and guidelines described in Chapter 12, "Software Logistics." Each client in an R/3 System can be identified by a unique three-figure combination. The standard R/3 System contains the clients 000, 001, and 066.

Even though you initially only set up the development system and its clients, the roles of the clients in the entire system landscape should have already been defined during the project preparation.

For example, the changes from one client are normally transported to the client with the same number in the target system. Therefore, you should give the same numbers to corresponding clients in the three systems between which you will be transporting data frequently.

Mannaberg Inc.

The following table shows how Mannaberg Inc. defined the clients.

System	DEV	QAS	PRD
Client	100 Customizing/Development	100 Quality Assurance	100 Production
	200 Developing Interface	200 Interface	
	300 Test	300 Training	

The Steering Committee had to weigh the developer's demands for more clients and the administrative costs for the clients. Each client in the system landscape must be set up and maintained. The more clients there are, the more time you need to administer the system.

Transport System

In the development system of a system landscape, the settings of the R/3 standard and developments are recorded into change requests. To ensure that these changes can be transported into the other systems, you must set up the *R/3 transport system* (see Figure 1.3). For this purpose, group the systems of your system landscape into an *R/3 transport domain*. To transport change requests from the development system to the quality assurance system and then to the production system, you must set up the *transport path* within the domain (see Chapter 12, "Software Logistics").

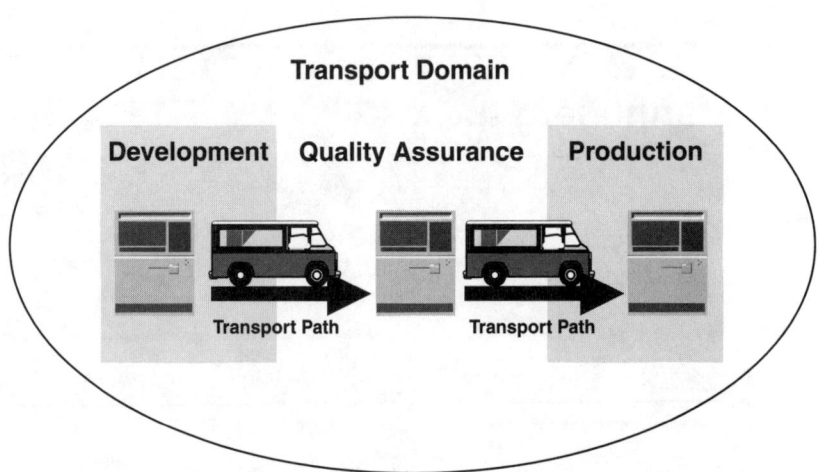

FIGURE 1.3:

The R/3 transport system

To ensure that you do not transport faulty settings or programs to the production system, you should define who transports the change request and who monitors the transport at what time. In a three-system landscape, you should transport a change request in four steps (see Figure 1.4):

1. Release the change request from the development system.

2. Import the change request into the quality assurance system.

3. Test and validate the settings and software developments in the quality assurance system.

4. Import the change request into the production system.

How Do You Prepare the Project? 17

FIGURE 1.4:
Transport steps for the change requests

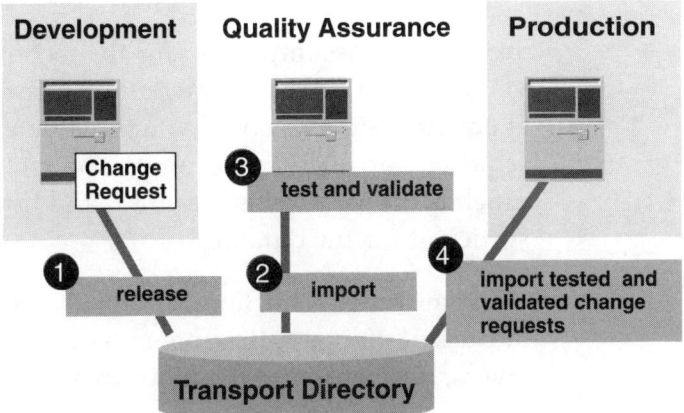

Mannaberg Inc.

At Mannaberg Inc., only the Project Manager can release change requests. No other employees have authorization to do so. Several times a day, the R/3 System administrator imported the released change requests into the quality assurance system. The R/3 System administrator checked the transport logs and notified the Project Manager if there were problems. The application consultants and developers tested and verified their work in the quality assurance system. The application consultants and developers only informed the Project Manager after a successful test. The Project Manager released the respective change requests for the production system. Once a week, the R/3 System administrator imported the released change request into the production system.

Determine the Technical Requirements

Two aspects are important for the technical requirements. First, you must define the hardware platform and the database management system. Second, you must determine the size of the required hardware; for example, how fast the CPU must be, how much main memory is required, and how much disk storage is sufficient for the database.

The multitier R/3 client/server architecture essentially consists of presentation, application, and database layers. Based on these layers, SAP supports the platforms listed in Table 1.2.

TABLE 1.2: Supported Platforms for R/3 (Release 4.0)

Layer	Platform
Presentation	Windows 3.1, Windows 95, Windows NT, OSF/Motif, OS/2 Presentation Manager, MacOS, Java
Application	UNIX (Bull, Digital, HP, IBM, SNI, SUN), Windows NT, Mainframe (IBM OS/400, OS/390)
Database	DB2 Common Server, DB2 for AS/400, DB2 for OS/390, Informix-OnLine, Oracle, MS SQL Server

You can either install the three layers of R/3 on one computer or distribute them over multiple computers. For small R/3 Systems, a two-tier configuration is often sufficient. The database and application layers run on one computer and users can access the presentation layer through a front end (see Figure 1.5). Larger systems almost always require a three-tier configuration. The database runs on the fastest computer, the application layer is distributed over multiple computers, and users can access the presentation layer through a front end.

FIGURE 1.5:

Distribution of hardware over the R/3 layers

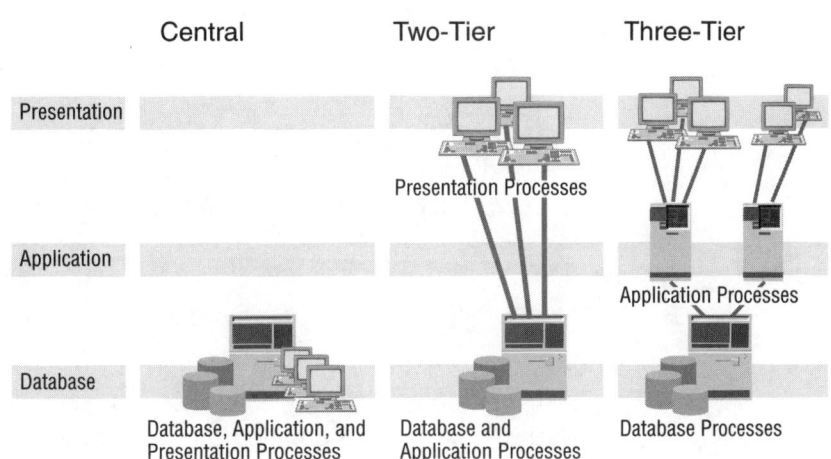

In a three-tier configuration, the front ends are linked with the computers of the application layer through a local area network (LAN) or a wide area network (WAN). Many network topologies are possible (for example, Ethernet or Token Ring). You can only connect the computers on the application layer to the database server through a LAN because a transport speed of at least 10Mbps is required. The individual layers of R/3 communicate through the standard protocol TCP/IP.

Mannaberg Inc.

Mannaberg Inc. had two options:

- Use existing technical infrastructure.
- Set up new technical infrastructure.

Continued on next page

The company management chose to largely renew the technical infrastructure when they implemented R/3. The existing mainframe architecture was replaced with the R/3 client/server architecture, and the existing infrastructure could only be replaced in certain areas. Hardware platforms from Hewlett-Packard were chosen for the database server and the application server, and the operating system was the UNIX variant HP-UX. Oracle was chosen for the database because the company had already made the strategic decision in favor of Oracle for other applications. Based on the already available knowledge about Oracle, this decision was the most sensible.

Since the existing front-end computers could not meet the requirements for R/3, all of the front ends were replaced for the presentation layer. A standard was determined for the configuration of the hardware and software for the front ends. This standard configuration for Mannaberg Inc. was implemented in the headquarters and in all European subsidiaries. Based on the standard configuration, the front ends can be administered through a remote connection, making local administration in the subsidiaries unnecessary.

Sizing

In addition to the platform and the database, you must size the hardware for your requirements. You must define the speed of the CPU, how much main memory is required, and how much hard drive capacity the database requires. The extent of your hardware requirements depends on many factors—for example, the R/3 Release, the average system load compared to the load peaks, and the number and the behavior of users. Therefore, you must determine, normally with your hardware vendor, the hardware that is appropriate for your requirements. An important criterion for hardware selection is which R/3 Release you want to use for the production system and whether the system will grow in the next one to two years. You can best protect your hardware investment if the hardware can grow with the increasing demands on the R/3 System.

The Quicksizer

You can use the SAP *Quicksizer* tool to estimate your hardware requirements. You can enter the number of users working in each R/3 module, and the Quicksizer calculates the processor speed, the main memory size, and the hard disk capacity you'll need. You can classify the users in three categories: low, medium, and high. Although the number of users is useful for a rough estimate, the exact extent of your hardware requirements depends on many more factors, as shown in Figure 1.6.

FIGURE 1.6:
Parameters for determining the hardware requirements

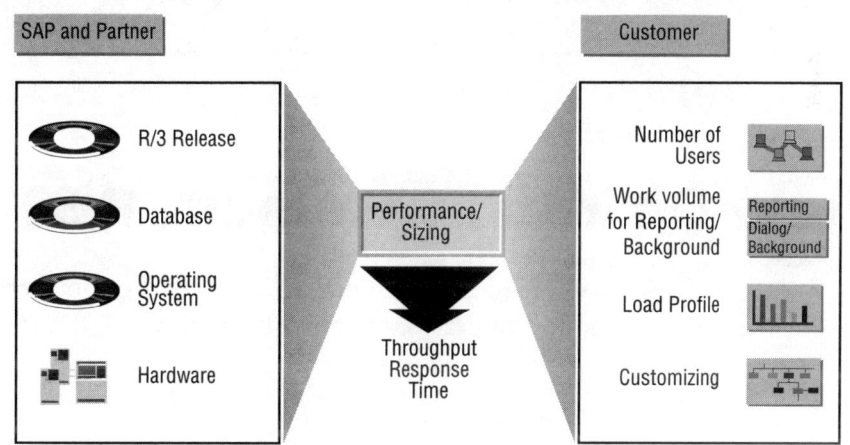

After production begins, the number of users in R/3 will often gradually increase, which means that you will need to increase your computing capacity. To protect your investment in the hardware, you should ensure that the hardware can be extended; for example, you should make sure there are sufficient slots for additional CPU or RAM.

> **Mannaberg Inc.**
>
> At Mannaberg Inc., the company management discussed the technical requirements—for example, the requirements for the operating system, hardware, database, network, and front ends—with the hardware vendor and SAP Basis Consulting. Essentially, the company will make the decision based on three criteria. First, the manufacturer must ensure that the hardware can be extended for 500 R/3 users. Second, the hardware life cycle should be long enough to protect their investment. Third, the supplier should provide favorable conditions and short delivery times for the hardware in case of error.

How Do You Implement R/3?

You should implement R/3 by having the Technical Team process the following essential tasks during the Business Blueprint phase and the Realization phase:

- Create a technical design
- Set up your R/3 Systems
- Define and set up system operation
- Define the authorization concept

The following sections provide you with an initial view of these tasks.

Create a Technical Design

Together with the consultants and specialists, you'll create a technical design in which you'll document all the technical demands on the planned system landscape. For example, you should document how to configure the hardware, how to connect the computers, how to install the software for the front ends, and how to set up the printer landscape. The design will be an important document for the subsequent phases because you can configure the system landscape in accordance with the design. The following five sections contain examples of two important components of the design: the printer landscape and the network topology.

Spool Service

The *spool service* in R/3 formats data for output on a printer or fax machine in a LAN or WAN, passes the formatted data to the spool system of the operating system, and monitors the data output. The spool service supports the most common printer types and various access methods (for example, in UNIX, the direct call from the printer through the command LP or LPR) to the printer from the spool system of the operating system.

Printer Landscape

Most companies have a *printer landscape* that can be partially used for R/3. The number of printers you must replace or acquire depends on, for example, the expected print volume, the print speed for time-critical print, and even special paper sizes. Experience has shown that the acquisition costs are only a small part of the costs of the printer landscape. The far larger part of the costs is for maintenance and monitoring. You can reduce these costs by first dividing your print requirements into categories such as, for example, time-critical or mass printing. Then you can define a printer type, which you can configure in the same way for every category. This reduces effort, costs, and the number of potential errors because, once you have configured one printer, you'll know how to configure all of the printers of the same type. Chapter 8, "Print Administration," describes how to plan a printer landscape.

> **Mannaberg Inc.**
>
> The Steering Committee at Mannaberg Inc. chose to implement mostly network printers and, only in a few exceptions, to connect a printer locally to a front end. Delivery notes and invoices are printed most frequently. To ensure that these documents are available at a specific time, they are printed every hour. Only the following printer types are implemented in the company: laser printer, color printer, ink jet printer, and line printer.

Network Topology

The various layers of the R/3 client/server architecture communicate with each other through TCP/IP. Since only a small volume of data flows between the front end and the application servers, you can connect the front end through a LAN or a WAN. However, much more data is transferred between the application servers and the database server through a network. You can only connect these servers with each other through a LAN that has a transfer speed of at least 10Mbps.

Most companies have a network they can use completely or partially for R/3. Whether you use Token Ring, Ethernet, or FDDI, and with which bandwidth, depends on the number of front ends or the available transfer speed of the connections. Chapter 11, "Network Administration," describes how to plan your network.

> **Mannaberg Inc.**
>
> Prior to the implementation of R/3, Mannaberg Inc. had for the mainframe computer a network in which the devices could communicate with each
>
> *Continued on next page*

other through Systems Network Architecture, Logical Unit 6.2 (SNA LU6.2). The company had to completely replace the existing network because the front ends, the application servers, and the database server communicate through TCP/IP for R/3. At the same time, the cable installation in the subsidiaries was standardized to ensure that a network specialist could administer the network from the headquarters. An FDDI ring was set up between the database server and the application servers. The WAN to the subsidiaries was configured redundantly. The main connection through Frame Relay with a bandwidth of 32Mbps is produced and is configured as a failover ISDN connection with a 64Kbps bandwidth. The complete network topology is displayed in the graphic below.

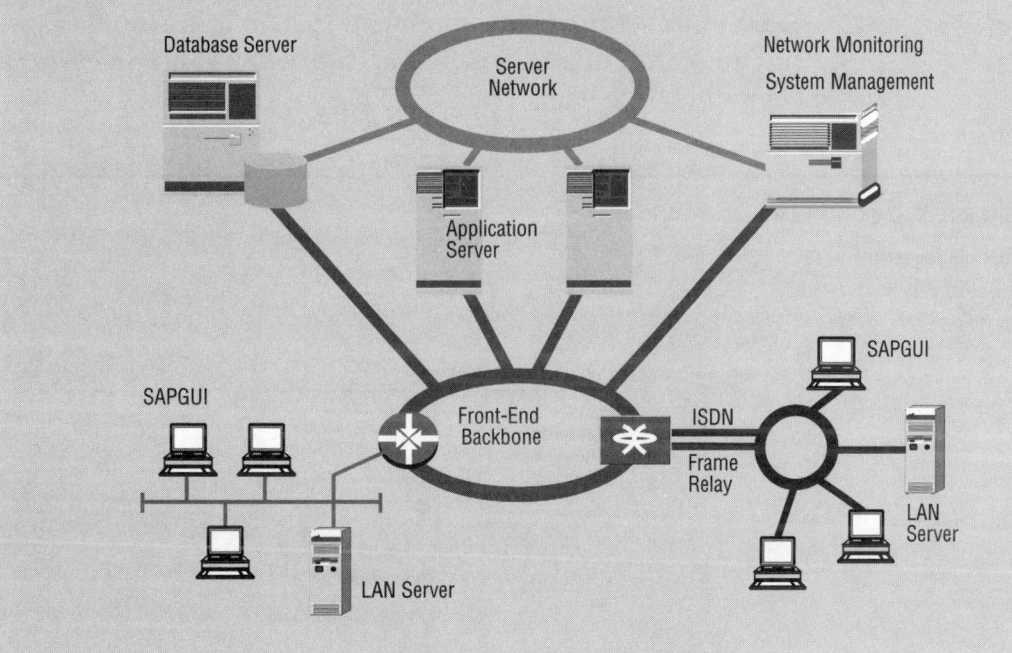

Set Up Your R/3 Systems

You should set up the R/3 Systems together with the hardware vendor and the technical consultants. Normally, you do not set up a two- or three-system landscape simultaneously; they should be set up consecutively in different phases of the project. The following three sections explain the schedule for the phases, the phase in which you set up a system, and how to set up a system.

Development

During the Business Blueprint phase, the application consultants hold interviews and workshops to determine which company structure to configure and which related business processes to customize. The consultants document the results in the To-Be vision, which is known as the Business Blueprint. The Technical Team must set up the development system to ensure that the consultants can configure the planned structures and processes at the beginning of the next phase (see Figure 1.7).

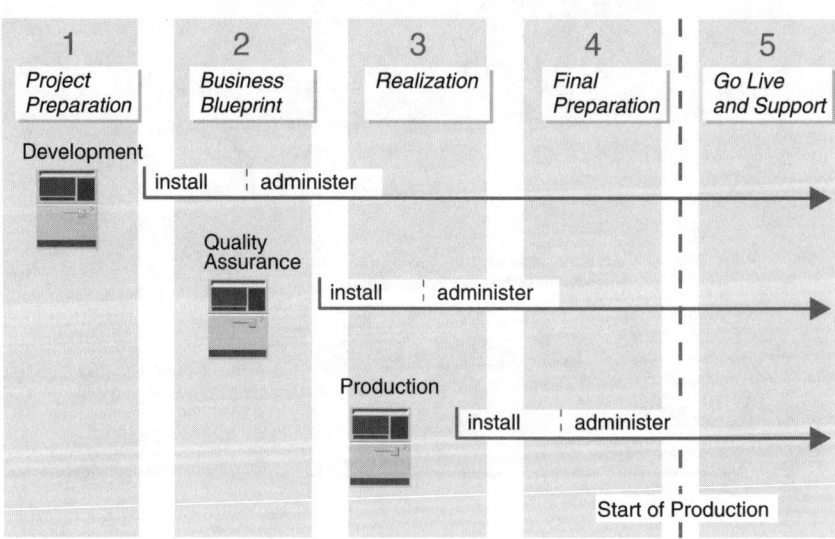

FIGURE 1.7:
A schedule for setting up a three-system landscape

Quality Assurance

In the first four to five weeks of the Realization phase, the application consultants implement a prototype of the system in the development system. In this prototype, the application consultants present the Project Management and the users with the configured business processes. Only the business processes that are essential to the company are configured. This enables you to test the concepts in the Business Blueprint early and resolve any potential misunderstandings or errors. To ensure that the application consultants have a stable test environment, the Technical Team should set up the quality assurance system during the first week of the Realization phase (see Figure 1.7). If you choose a two-system landscape, you must set up the quality assurance client in the development system at the beginning of the Realization phase, and you must not set up a separate R/3 System.

Production

At the end of the Realization phase, the application consultants finish the settings in the development system, test them in the quality assurance system, and release them for the production system. At the beginning of the Final Preparation phase, you will first transport the settings and developments into the production system, test the production system, and then take over the data from the legacy system. To ensure that this can be done directly after the Realization phase, the Technical Team should have installed and set up the production system at the end of the Realization phase (see Figure 1.7).

The life cycle for hardware is very short and the prices fall accordingly. For this reason, you should purchase the most expensive system for your system landscape—the production system—as late as possible. As displayed in Figure 1.7, the schedule takes into account the balance between *as late as possible* because of the low acquisition costs and *as early as possible* to provide a smooth start of production.

To set up an R/3 System in one and a half to two weeks, follow these steps:

1. **Set up hardware.** Your hardware vendor sets up the hardware you ordered, installs additional hardware such as printers or routers with you, and connects the hardware to the network. After the installation, the hardware vendor should test the hardware.

2. **Prepare for the installation of R/3.** A technical consultant checks to make sure the hardware has been correctly configured for the requirements of R/3; for example, the kernel parameters of the computer or the size of the swap space must be correctly configured.

3. **Install the R/3 System.** The technical consultant installs the R/3 software and the database software. The way you distribute the data files, in particular the database files, over the hard disks during the installation is a deciding factor for the data security and performance of the system. You should already have documented the hard disk layout in your technical design. An installation takes approximately one to two days. If you install more servers on the application layer, approximately two to three hours will be required for each server.

4. **Set up the front ends.** You should install and configure the R/3 front end software for the standards in your design. Chapter 4, "Front-End Administration," describes how you should define suitable standards.

5. **Set up the clients and the transport system.** In the Project Preparation phase, you have already defined the systems in which to set up the clients and how to configure the transport system. With the technical consultant, you should now implement these concepts. For this purpose, you'll use various tools—for example, the client copy or the transport management system (TMS). Chapter 12, "Software Logistics," describes this step in more detail.

6. **Create users.** In the development and quality assurance system, you should only create R/3 users for the Project Team. In the production system, you must create an R/3 user for every user. The section "Define the Authorization Concept" later in this chapter describes how to plan the authorization concept for the users.

7. **Back up the database and the operating system.** To ensure that you do not lose all the settings if a problem occurs, back up the entire system, including the files on the operating system level.

Define and Set Up System Operation

With technical consultants and specialists, you should define all tasks for the system operation of the R/3 Systems and document them in the system operation manual. For example, you should document which tasks must be performed daily, weekly, and monthly; who is responsible for which tasks; and how errors should be handled. The system operation manual is an important document for production operation of the systems because you administer and monitor the system landscape according to the specifications in it. In the following sections, you will learn from two examples about important aspects of the system operation manual, the *Computing Center Management System (CCMS)* of the R/3 System and the backup strategy for the database.

CCMS

For the technical operation of R/3, use the CCMS tools to monitor and control the system. System administrators can monitor the entire system landscape from their PCs using the CCMS graphical monitors, thus enabling them to react quickly if a problem occurs. For example, the Alert Monitor gives the system administrator advance warning of a potential problem. You can configure the Alert Monitor so that you are either notified of all the possible errors in the system landscape or only notified about special parts of the system, such as the operating system, the database, the network, or the R/3 runtime system.

Operation Modes and Logon Groups

To control the load distribution of the R/3 System, use the two CCMS tools, operation modes and logon groups. You can use the *operation modes* to change the configuration of the R/3 System without having to stop and start it. For example, you can automatically change the system each evening from a day operation mode with many users to a night operation mode with few users and many long-running programs in background processes (see Figure 1.8). You can use *logon groups* to control which users can log on to which application servers. This is especially useful for systems with multiple application servers, where you can distribute the load evenly over the application servers and increase the system availability.

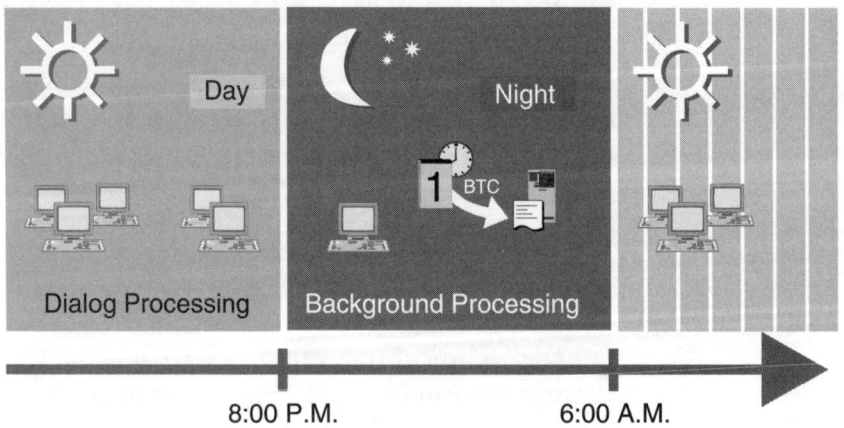

FIGURE 1.8:
Day and night operation modes

Frequently, large companies use a special tool—for example, BMC PATROL, CA Unicenter, HP OpenView, IBM Netview, or

Tivoli—to monitor all the components of their heterogeneous system landscape. You can link the CCMS with this type of application from other providers through open interfaces. Chapter 5, "R/3 Instance Administration," describes how you should plan to use CCMS to monitor and control your system.

Mannaberg Inc.

At Mannaberg Inc., five people were assigned to administer and monitor the entire system. Each person is responsible for one component of the system: the R/3 System, the database, the operating system, the network, and user authorizations. This Technical Team has written a system operation manual that defines the procedures for the system operation. For example, if an error occurs, there are instructions for error handling. These instructions define who is responsible or when and how external specialists are to be notified. The manual is divided into sections according to the system components. Each section is kept up-to-date by the administrator responsible for the corresponding component.

To control the load distribution, Mannaberg Inc. uses the two operation modes, day and night operation. They were set up based on the experiences with the legacy system. The company does not require a separate operation mode for a special system load, such as month-end closing, period closing programs, or MRP run. The Technical Team at Mannaberg Inc. set up a logon group for the users on every implemented R/3 module. Each application server belongs to only one logon group. The users use one of the logon groups for each task.

Data Backup

Companies cannot afford to lose data that was recently created or changed in the production system, such as data for delivery notes or invoices. The best way to avoid this type of loss and to have high database availability is to define a strategy for how and when to back up your database. The strategy for data backup depends on many factors, such as the size of database, the tools for data backup, and the maximum downtime for the database (that is, how quickly you must restore the database in case of failure). The database administrator plans the strategy with the Technical Team Lead and the technical consultant. The database administrator implements this strategy, checks to make sure the data backups were successful, and reacts if an error occurs.

For the database security strategy in your production system, you should

- Back up the database completely every night.
- Implement a 28-day cycle for data backup. A data backup tape is overwritten after 28 days, at the earliest (see Figure 1.9).
- Back up log files at least once between two data backups; back up log files several times between two data backups if a large volume of data is logged.
- Back up the database and log files to separate tapes.
- Back up the database and log files on the weekend, either Friday night or Sunday night. Additional backups are required if the system is processing a large volume of data in the background.
- Back up the data and structural information after each structural change to the database.

With this strategy, you can always completely restore the last four weeks worth of data in the database and prevent the log files from filling up. By separating the database backup tapes and the log file backup tapes, you can maintain two copies of the data. If a problem occurs and you find that the last database backup was defective, you can still restore the database with the previous copy. However, you must be able to import all the log files since the last error-free data backup. Chapter 9, "Database Administration," describes how you can define and monitor a suitable strategy for your demands.

FIGURE 1.9:

A data backup cycle

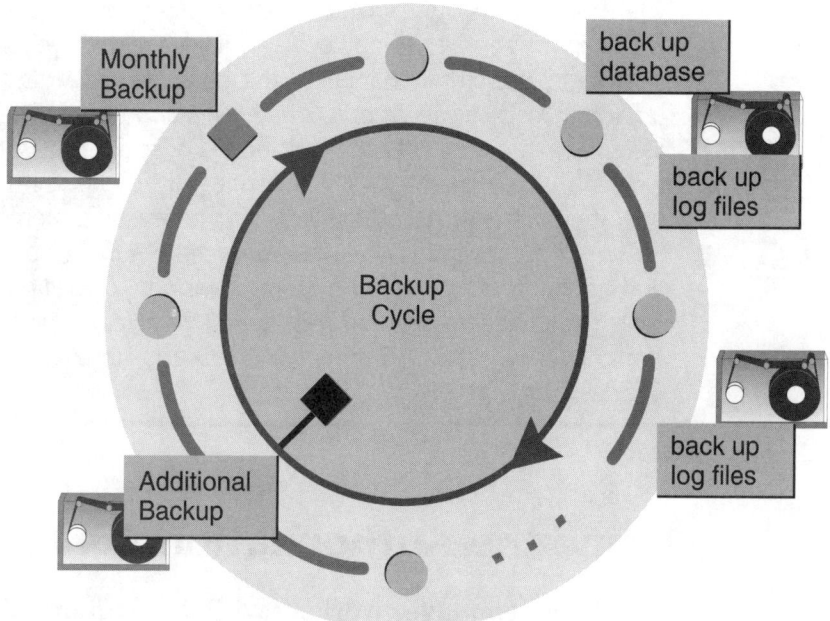

Mannaberg Inc.

The company management of Mannaberg Inc. gave the Technical Team the specification that the production system must be 99 percent available and is only allowed to fail in problematic situations for a maximum of 6 hours between 6:00 A.M. and 6:00 P.M. on workdays. The Technical Team defined a period of 4 hours for the database restore and recovery. That means that the data backup cannot exceed a maximum of 4 hours. The Technical Team decided on the hardware vendor's backup software, with which the team needs 2 hours to back up a 50GB database. The data was backed up to digital linear tapes (DLTs). A tape robot changes the tapes to ensure that no one has to be present during the backup. After a tape has been used 100 times for backups, it is replaced to avoid a failure due to wear.

Continued on next page

> The production system's Oracle database is backed up daily, and the tapes are overwritten in a 28-day cycle. Outside of this cycle, data is backed up after every structural change to the database. The data backup tapes are randomly read to see whether they can still be used. The database log files are automatically saved every half-hour. For security reasons, the log files are written to two separate tapes. Subsequently, the log files are deleted on the operating system level to ensure that the available memory space does not fill up. In approximately one half-day, the database administrator monitors and administers all the R/3 Systems in normal operation. If an error occurs that the database administrator cannot resolve, he or she can obtain help from either SAP's Local Support or the Oracle Hotline.

Define the Authorization Concept

Every employee working with R/3 requires his or her own R/3 user to be able to log on to R/3. To ensure that R/3 users can only perform the activities necessary for their work, they must be allocated an R/3 job role.

Activity Groups

In R/3, a job role is described in an *activity group*. An activity group defines the transactions that a user can call for one job role and the activities allowed within these transactions. To allocate a user to an activity group, a user master record must be created. In addition to the activities for which the user is authorized, the user master record contains, for example, the user name, password, and address.

Double-Verification Principle

In R/3, you can divide the user administration and authorization administration among three administrators. Only in a sequence can all three administrators create an R/3 user and give the user the necessary authorizations. The double-verification principle means that, within the sequence, the following administrator checks the preceding one, which rules out the abuse of authorizations.

Most companies already have an authorization concept in their legacy system. Therefore, you must first determine how much of the existing concept you can use or whether you should introduce a new concept when you implement R/3. For an authorization concept in R/3, the departments first describe the tasks and functions of the job roles. For each job role description, set up an activity group. Each additional activity group increases the administration work involved. However, there are two essential advantages for detailed job role descriptions. First, you can closely control the access to data and thus protect data from unauthorized access. Second, instead of the complete R/3 menu, each user can only see the menu for his or her job role. The user's job role menu is in the Session Manager, which is one possible *graphical user interface (GUI)* in R/3 (see "The Presentation Layer" in Chapter 2). This enables the user to navigate the menu easily. You should document all the job role descriptions and define how to administer the authorizations. Chapter 6, "User Administration," describes the authorization concept in more detail.

Mannaberg Inc.

At Mannaberg Inc, an authorization concept for how to administer the users and the activity groups was created and documented. The activity groups are set up and maintained by employees of the respective departments. For security reasons, different employees handle the user administration, for which there are two options:

Distributed user administration In every European subsidiary, the user master records are administered by one person.

Continued on next page

> **Central user administration** In the headquarters, the user master records are administered by one person.
>
> To improve security and reduce the cost of employee training, the company management decided to have central user administration. A user's department or manager must formally apply to have a user master record created or changed.

How Do You Prepare for Production?

To prepare for production, the Technical Team processes the following essential tasks during the Final Preparation phase:

- Import data from the legacy system
- Test system operation
- Perform the GoingLive Check

The following sections give you an initial view of these tasks.

Import Data from the Legacy System

From the legacy system, you will import three types of data into R/3: master data, open transaction data, and completed transaction data. Typical master data is data from suppliers, customers, accounts, or material masters. Normally, almost all the master data from the legacy system can be used for the master data in R/3 and can therefore be imported into R/3. The open transaction data belongs to business processes that are still open, such as open invoices or open customer orders. To import open transaction data, from the business viewpoint, the related business transaction or process within R/3 must be repeated until the point where the legacy system left off the transaction or process. The completed transaction data is data that belongs to completed business processes such as paid invoices or completed customer orders. All data imported from the legacy system must be up-to-date.

Batch Input, Call Transaction, and Direct Input

For every type of data, you must define how you will convert it into the format of R/3 data. For example, you can enter the master data manually if the data volume is not too large. However, it is better to import the transaction data automatically. R/3 offers three procedures: *Batch Input*, *Call Transaction*, and *Direct Input*. These procedures are described in "Communication through Sequential Files" in Chapter 2. Deciding which procedure is suitable for your requirements depends on many factors. For example, you must consider the volume of data and the period of time in which it must be imported into R/3. Additionally, you must consider the quality of the data, whether some data records from the legacy system are duplicated, or whether the data format matches that of the R/3 System. Chapter 13, "Interfaces," describes how to plan the data transfer and which procedure you should select.

Mannaberg Inc.

The Technical Team at Mannaberg Inc. determined the volume and the format of the data to be transferred from the legacy system. First, the data was exported from the legacy system and made available to the R/3 System as sequential files on the operating system level. Then, the data was imported into the R/3 System using the Batch Input procedure. The team used spot checks to make sure the data was correctly transferred. Based on tests with smaller volumes of data, the team could estimate how long the transfer would take and include this in the data transfer schedule.

Test the System Operation

To ensure that the R/3 System has a high throughput and a high availability, you must be able to rely on the procedures of the system operation. In the Business Blueprint and Realization phases, you install the R/3 Systems. At the same time, you should define the system operation and configure the systems accordingly—for example, by using CCMS, the Alert Monitor, or the operation modes. Subsequently, you should test the system operation (in the production system in particular) to make sure it is safeguarded against data loss and the system load is evenly distributed over the computers. Specifically, you should test the dependability of the data backup and whether you can restore the database within the planned time period if an error occurs.

The System Operation Manual

In the system operation manual, you have determined the procedures and tasks for each employee in the Technical Team. Now you should test the procedures to see if they must be improved or changed and make sure the employees can work with the instructions in the system operation manual. You should test the procedures and tasks many times (that is, until the desired results are achieved).

The backup and recovery of the database are among the most important tasks for production system operation. To test the procedures needed for backup and recovery, you should simulate possible situations in which the data in the database is destroyed (for example, CPU errors, hard disk errors, or users accidentally deleting data). If your company has defined a maximum downtime for the system, you should find out how long it takes to restore and recover the database from the backup tapes. The database administrator must be able to recover a database even in difficult situations. If this knowledge is not available in your company, you should hire a service provider or your hardware partner to provide this service.

Then, in the system operation manual, you must define in which error situations you want to take advantage of this type of service.

Sometimes, the people involved in the implementation project do not assume the system administration of the production operation permanently. To better prepare the employees who will handle the system administration in the future, you should have them trained on their own system by the Technical Team who planned and realized the technical implementation of R/3. All employees should test the procedures and tasks for the system operation together.

Perform the GoingLive Check

To prepare an R/3 System for the start of production, you must not only transfer the data and test the system operation, you must also check the settings and situations that could lead to problems during the production operation when there are many users—for example, incorrectly set system parameters, poor load distribution, or a poor throughput of frequently used business transactions. Optimally set system parameters or a good load distribution depends on many factors; the size of the main memory, the number and behavior of users, and the settings by the application consultants are just a few examples. The best way to check your system is to check it with experts before you start production.

To benefit from SAP's experience, you should use a special service from SAP, the *GoingLive Check.* SAP experts access your production system through a remote connection and check the system settings. The security of your data is ensured. You control the remote connection between SAP and your R/3 System. You can monitor the experts' activities on your screen and determine the password of the user who performs the GoingLive Check.

The GoingLive Check consists of three sessions: Analysis, Optimization, and Verification. These sessions are distributed, in turn, over the Final Preparation and Go Live and Support phases. After each session, you'll receive a report with recommendations for increasing the throughput of your system.

Analysis

In the first session, the *Analysis*, the SAP expert checks to see whether the production system can technically process the expected load. For example, the SAP expert checks to see whether the operating system parameters have been correctly set, whether the database was configured correctly, and whether the available hardware is sufficient for the expected load according to SAP's experiences. After the session, the SAP expert recommends which settings you should correct and whether you should possibly extend your hardware. To ensure that you can implement the recommendation before the start of production, you should hold the first session at the beginning of the Final Preparation phase, about eight weeks before the start of production (see Figure 1.10). This session is only useful if the production system is completely installed and configured.

Optimization

As soon as you have transferred the data from the legacy system into R/3, the second session, the *Optimization*, should take place. Ideally, you should have an SAP expert check a system in which you will mainly be testing until the start of production and in which the settings barely change. For this reason, you should schedule the second session in the middle of the Final Preparation phase, that is, about four weeks before the start of production. In the second session, the SAP expert checks mainly for business processes in the system that can lead to bottlenecks and for R/3 transactions that can possibly cause bottlenecks. After the session, the SAP expert makes recommendations on how you can improve certain system settings. The SAP expert shows, in particular, which bottlenecks occur and how to correct them.

FIGURE 1.10:

The schedule for the GoingLive Check

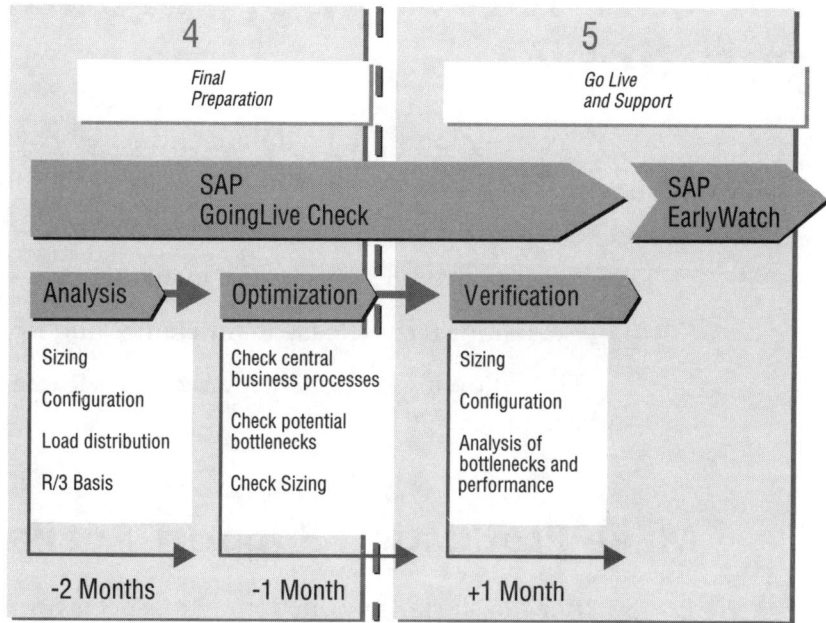

Verification

After you have implemented all the recommendations from the second session, you can begin with the production and go into the next phase, Go Live and Support. To ensure that the production system can work long-term without disruption and that the resources are used optimally, a third session is performed, the *Verification*. During operation, R/3 automatically updates statistics about the system load. In the third session, the SAP expert analyzes these statistics. The longer the period of time covered in the statistics, the more reliable results you will receive. Therefore, schedule the third session at the end of the Go Live and Support phase, that is, about four weeks after the start of production. After the session, the SAP expert recommends which settings you should correct. Appendix C describes how to take advantage of this service from SAP.

How Can You Support Production Operation?

You can support production operation by having the Technical Team process the following essential tasks during the Go Live and Support phase:

- Make production support available
- Plan for R/3 Release maintenance and update

The following sections provide you with an initial view of these tasks.

Make Production Support Available

After the start of production, two aspects are essential for production support. First, you must make a help desk available for user problems. Users have the most questions and problems in the first weeks after the start of production. Second, you must check the system performance and optimize it, if necessary.

Help Desk

The successful implementation of R/3 depends very much on how well the users can use the system and whether they receive help quickly. According to experience, users require additional guidance after the start of production for a period of a few weeks to two months. For this reason, you should have already defined (before the start of production) how problems reported by users are to be solved in your company. Normally, companies set up a help desk for this purpose. The users report problems to the help desk; they can do so via telephone, fax, or e-mail, for example. If the help desk cannot solve a problem or if the problem is classified as critical for system operation, it must be determined how the problem will be processed and who will process it. The help desk should be run by qualified employees. In the first days of the production operation, the entire implementation Project Team supports the help desk and helps ensure smooth operation. In Chapter 3, "Project Administration," you will learn how to set up a help desk for your company.

The Technical Team monitors the system as described in the system operation manual. The system operation manual should describe how the responsible employee must handle a situation in which a problem occurs that could influence the availability of the entire system. If a problem occurs that is largely unknown, the Technical Team must solve it and describe this new situation in the system operation manual. This way, the problem can be solved more quickly the next time it occurs.

The system load estimated before the start of production may only be valid for a limited period of time. For this reason, the Technical Team should regularly monitor the system resources load. Specifically in the first months of production operation, you can continually improve the system performance. R/3 provides you with tools to check the load on all system components, such as the application server, the database, or the CPU. Because R/3 updates the statistics about the system load, you can analyze the current load and the statistics of the last weeks or months. The optimal setting for the system parameters depends on many factors, and setting it is a complex task, especially for large systems with hundreds of users. Therefore, it is worthwhile for larger companies to train their own experts for this.

EarlyWatch

To help you with the performance analysis, SAP offers a special service, the *EarlyWatch Service*. As with the GoingLive Check, SAP experts access your production system through a remote connection and check your system settings. During one day, statistics about the system load are analyzed. A status report containing the results of the analysis is sent to you. In addition to the analysis, this report also contains recommendations as to how you can improve the system throughput. You should make use of the Early-Watch Service to correct problems and implement it to recognize and correct potential problems early so the availability and performance of your system remain high. How to take advantage of this service by SAP is described in Appendix C.

Plan for Release Maintenance and Update

There are two types of R/3 maintenance Releases: the *functional Release* and the *correction Release*. In a functional Release, either new business processes have been added or old business processes have been improved. Even the technical base of R/3 changes in the new Release. For example, in the functional Release 4.0A, the R/3 transport domain was implemented for the first time (see Chapter 12, "Software Logistics"). SAP only provides a functional Release on request. If you implement a functional Release, you are supported by SAP teams from Development, Consulting, and Service & Support. Together with SAP, you can verify the new R/3 software. The experiences with the functional Release then flow into the subsequent correction Release. Therefore, there are no new functions in a correction Release; instead, the quality of the function of the previous functional Release is improved. Every R/3 customer receives the correction Release without requesting it. For example, Release 4.0A is a functional Release and Release 4.0B is a correction Release. Figure 1.11 displays the schedule for the current R/3 Releases.

You must plan a Release update in detail. During a Release update, users cannot work with R/3. For this reason, an important goal for planning an update is to keep the R/3 System downtime as short as possible. Additionally, you must define when you will perform a Release update on a system in your system landscape.

For example, in a three-system landscape, you should update the Release in the development system, then in the quality assurance system, and only then in the production system. Chapter 12, "Software Logistics," describes in detail how to plan a Release upgrade.

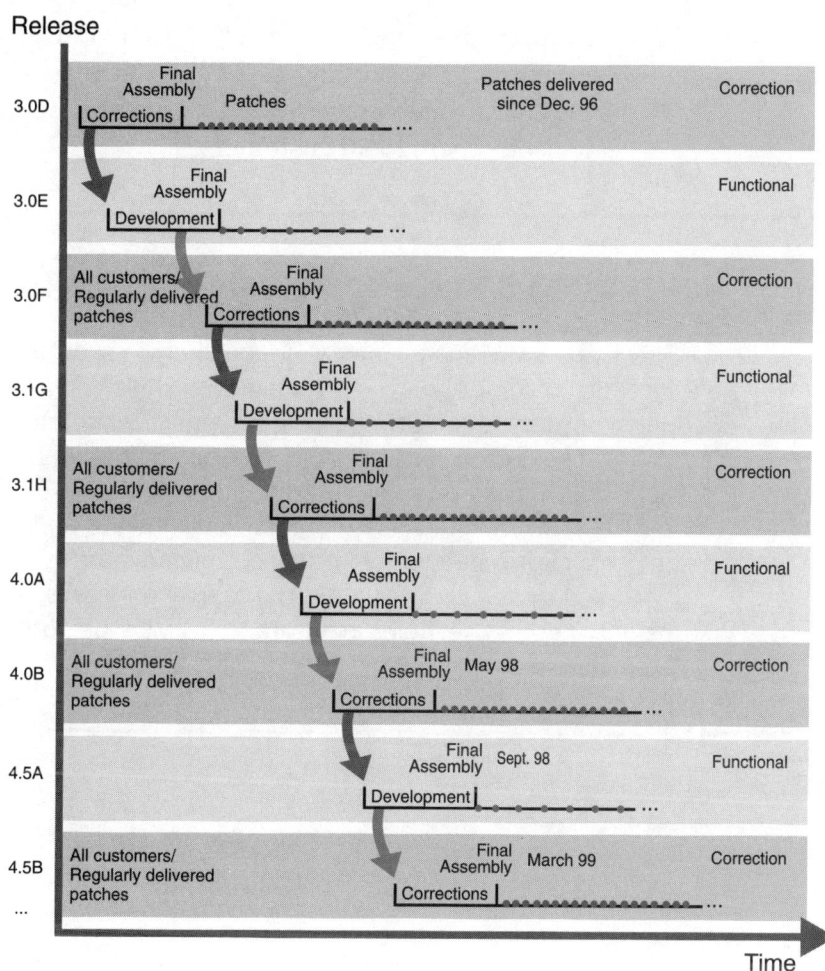

FIGURE 1.11: SAP Release planning

Patches

During the life span of a correction Release, SAP offers *patches* for Release maintenance. Each patch contains multiple corrections for one Release that are divided into different types, such as, for example, *Hot Packages* or *HR Legal Change Patches*. The patches correct the source code. You can import the patches directly into your system through a remote connection to SAP. This may take only a few minutes, depending on the size of the patches. SAP regularly groups multiple patches from a correction Release on a CD-ROM and sends them to all customers.

Mannaberg Inc.

The company management at Mannaberg Inc. determined that the R/3 Release would not be updated during the implementation project. Only the patches from the current Release were regularly imported during the project. The company wants to set up a test system for each new R/3 correction Release. A Project Team will then decide whether an upgrade is worthwhile for the company. A Release upgrade is planned as an individual project. For the project preparation, the technical requirements for the hardware and the operating system version will be checked, and if necessary, the hardware will be extended. The Release upgrade will be performed completely by Mannaberg Inc. employees.

CHAPTER TWO

Technology in R/3

As standard software, R/3 contains business applications such as Sales and Distribution (SD), Materials Management (MM), Production Planning (PP), and Human Resources (HR). So that you can adapt your R/3 System as well as possible to your technical or organizational situation, R/3 offers a client/server architecture on multiple layers. Each layer has services, which you can distribute over various computers. This means that R/3 can be anything from a computer system with a few users to a system with several thousand users. The R/3 software runs on most UNIX derivatives, Microsoft Windows NT, and a few mainframes. R/3 saves its data in Relational Database Management Systems (RDBMSs). Since networks and interfaces are based on common standards, R/3 runs in a heterogeneous landscape.

In this chapter, you'll learn which logical services R/3 offers and how R/3 physically implements them. You will also learn about the services on the application layer, which you can configure according to your technical requirements. Following that, you will be shown which network protocols and architectures are supported by R/3 and through which interfaces you can connect to other systems. The direction of R/3's technical development is explained in the section "Distributed Component Architecture." As with other standard software packages, you must set up R/3 for your requirements, and the section "Software Logistics" teaches you about which tools and methods you can use for this purpose.

Logical Services in R/3

In a standard R/3 System, users log on to various application servers from PCs through a local area network (LAN) or a wide area network (WAN). On the application servers, users run different applications, such as Sales or Production Planning. All application servers are connected to a common database, which stores all R/3 data.

The individual servers in an R/3 System provide computing capacity and storage for the following logical layers of the client/server architecture (see Figure 2.1):

Presentation Users work with the R/3 applications through the SAP Graphical User Interface (SAPGUI).

Internet-enabling Internet users connect to a Web server with the Internet Transaction Server (ITS). From the viewpoint of R/3 applications, the appearance of the Internet Transaction Server and the R/3 user through an SAPGUI is comparable.

Application The entire R/3 business logic runs on the application layer.

Database The database layer stores all R/3 data, such as the application programs and the data a company works with.

You can configure the application layer services and use them to adapt R/3 to your technical requirements. Table 2.1 lists these services and their tasks.

TABLE 2.1: Application Layer Services

Service	Task
Dialog	Processes the users' entries and performs the application logic
Update	Changes the data in the database asynchronously to the dialog service
Enqueue	Generates, holds, and releases locks on business objects in the R/3 System
Background	Processes nondialog programs
Message	Coordinates the data flow among services in an R/3 System
Gateway	Controls the communication services between R/3 and an external system (for example, R/2)
Spool	Formats and administers print requests

FIGURE 2.1:

The multilayer client/server architecture

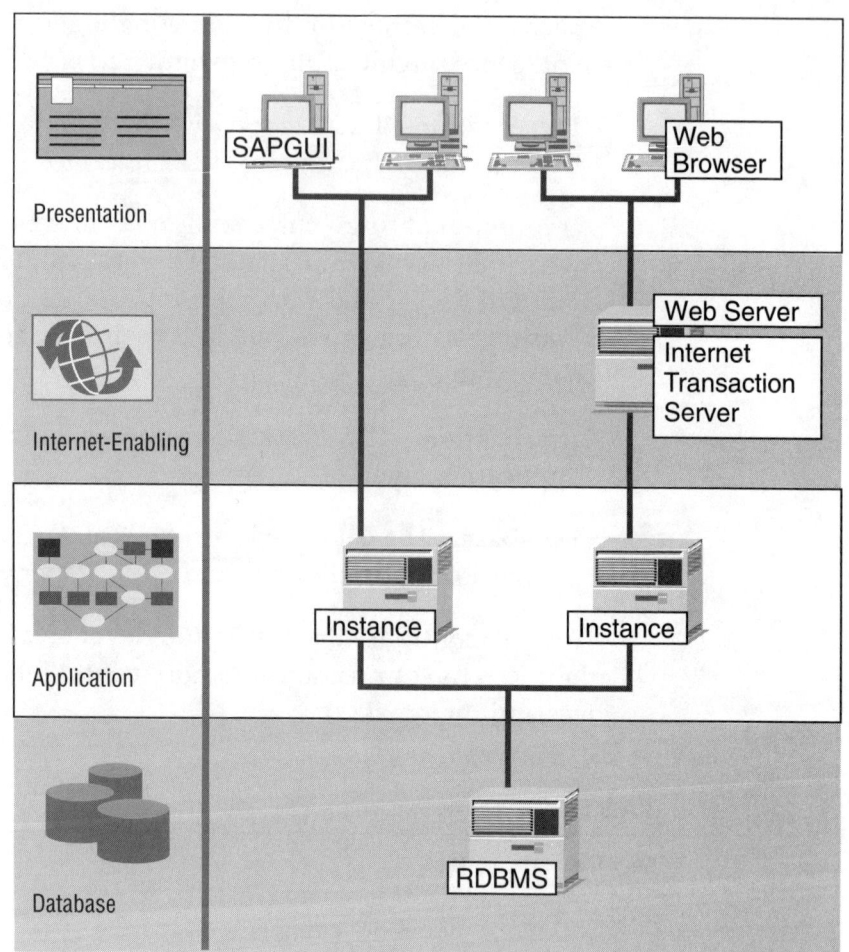

> **WARNING** There is only one enqueue service and one message service in an R/3 System. If one of these services fails, R/3 cannot function. Each of these services is called single point of failure (SPOF).

The Instance

An R/3 *instance* provides one or more services. In Figure 2.2, instance A provides only the dialog service and instance B provides primarily the background service. The services of an instance are always stopped and started together. This way, the instance combines the services into an administrative unit.

FIGURE 2.2:
The R/3 instance

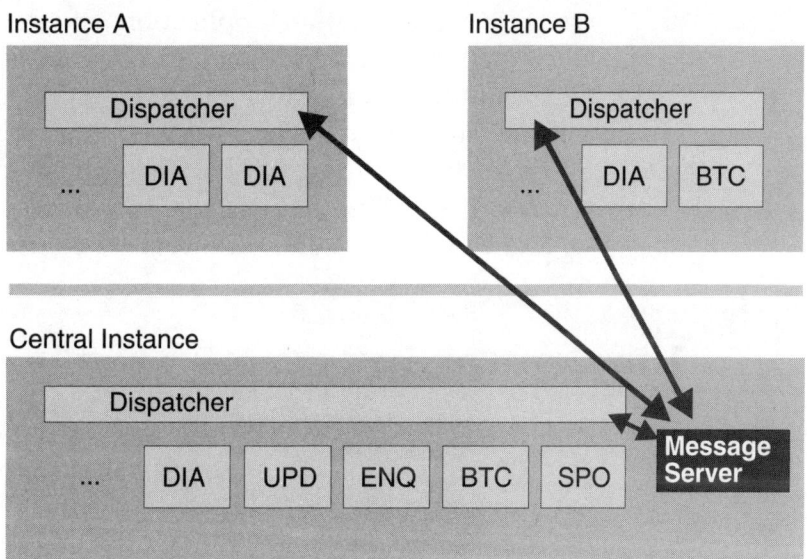

A central R/3 System consists of one instance, which provides all of the services. In a distributed R/3 System, the enqueue service and the message service are always grouped in one instance, the *central instance*. When you start a distributed R/3 System, you must start the central instance before you can start the other instances. When you stop R/3, the central instance is the last instance to be stopped.

Normally, each instance runs on its own computer, the application server. It is only as an exception that multiple instances run on the same computer. Chapter 5, "R/3 Instance Administration," describes which services you should plan for which purposes and how you should distribute these services over the instances.

Physical Implementation of Services

In the preceding section, you learned about the fundamental layers of R/3: presentation, application, and database. With the R/3 client/server architecture, you can distribute these layers over one or multiple computers and so adapt the computing capacity to your requirements. For example, you can increase the computing capacity by adding additional application servers when a large number of users cause bottlenecks. R/3 scales from systems with one user to systems with several thousand users.

The Central System

In a *central system*, one computer performs all of the work. This computer provides all of the services and the users work with X-terminals (see Figure 2.3). This type of configuration is chosen only rarely and only a few users can work with the system at the same time.

The Two-Tier Configuration

The most common *two-tier configuration* for R/3 is the *distributed presentation*. Every SAPGUI on the presentation layer runs on a front end. The application and the database run on a powerful computer (see Figure 2.3). This type of configuration is commonly implemented for customers with up to 50 users because it has lower acquisition costs and is simpler to administer than other configurations. With the *Ready-to-Run R/3* product, SAP provides

FIGURE 2.3:
Possible distribution of hardware over the layers of the client/server architecture

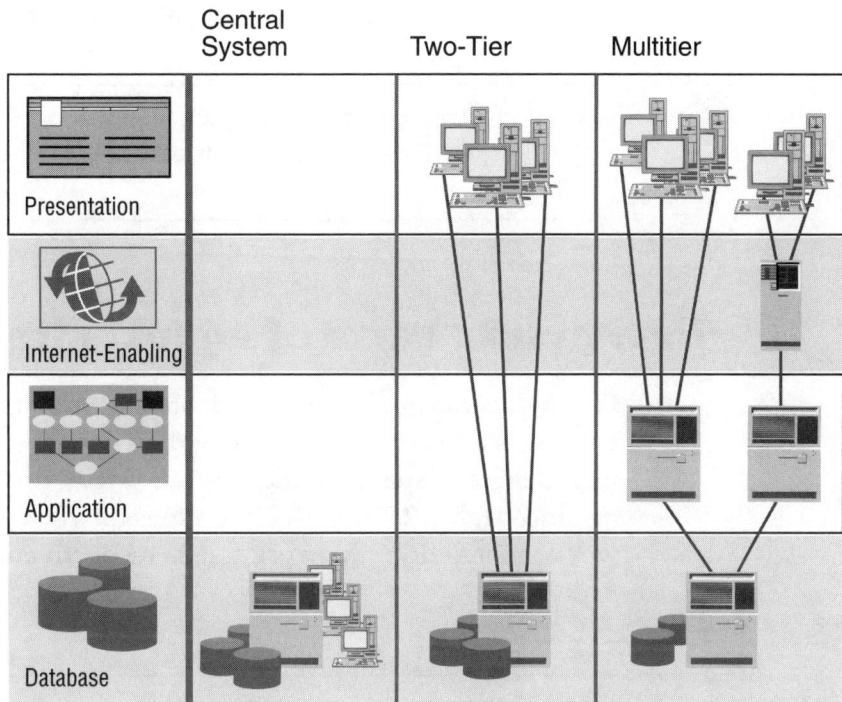

this distributed presentation especially for medium-size companies. Appendix A provides more information about this concept.

An alternative two-tier configuration is a system with powerful front ends on which presentation and application layers run. This type of configuration is only of interest for simulation or for software development. It is too expensive to provide every user with such a powerful front end.

The Three-Tier Configuration

Customers normally choose the *three-tier configuration*. Each of the three layers uses its own computer. The database and the central instance run on the most powerful computer. The application layer consists of multiple computers, each running one instance, and each SAPGUI of the presentation layer runs on a user PC.

> **NOTE** A multitier configuration is commonly implemented for customers using the ITS. Each layer consists of at least one computer, as shown in Figure 2.3.

The Physical Parts of an Instance

For the operating system, one instance consists of combined processes and the main memory they use. These processes include one Dispatcher and multiple work processes for each instance. Table 2.2 lists the five types of work processes. Each work process does the work for its respective logical service.

TABLE 2.2: Types of Work Processes in R/3

Type of Work Process	Abbreviation
Dialog	DIA
Update	UPD
Enqueue	ENQ
Background	BTC
Spool	SPO

The Dispatcher

The *Dispatcher* administers the resources for the instance. SAPGUI sends the user's entries to the Dispatcher. The Dispatcher first saves the data in a queue. As a work process becomes free, the

Dispatcher successively assigns requests from the queue. The work process processes the requests, and the results are returned to the SAPGUI through the Dispatcher (see Figure 2.4). The Dispatcher distributes the requests so that a work process spends as little time as possible processing a request. In this manner, a work process can process many requests in a short period of time and maximize its throughput. The only exception is the background work process, which is reserved for long-running requests.

FIGURE 2.4:

Physical architecture of an instance

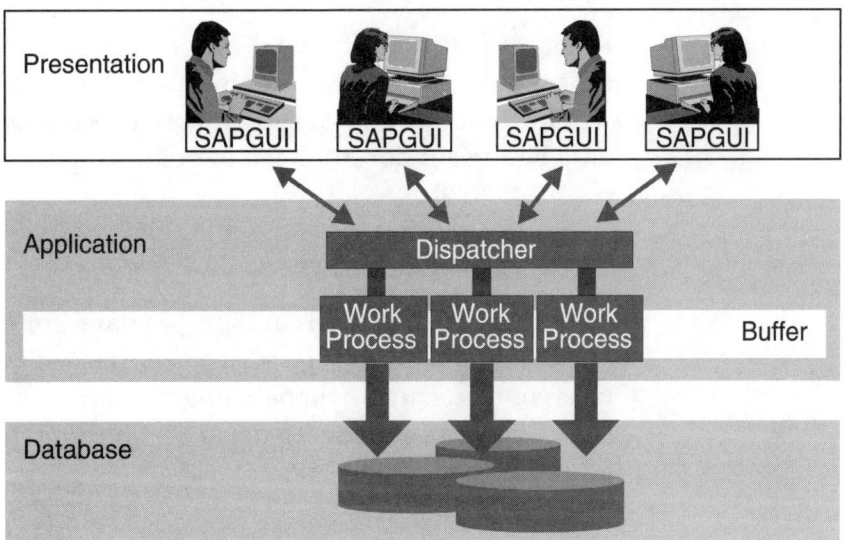

The Dispatcher assigns different dialog processes to a user over time so the dialog work processes can process a request quickly and serve many users. This is known as *dispatching*. First, a user only uses a dialog work process for the duration of the dialog step. The Dispatcher may assign subsequent user dialog steps to a different dialog work process. For a dialog work process to work for successive users, the work process is given access to specific user data at the beginning of the dialog step. This is known as *roll-in*. After the dialog step, the work process updates the user data and releases the data to other dialog work processes. This is known as *roll-out*. This technique enables 5 to 10 users to share one dialog work process.

R/3 memory management uses memory in two ways. Some memory (for example, the R/3 buffer or extended memory) is used by all the work processes, and some memory can be used by only one work process.

The Buffer

R/3 uses *buffers* to store data—for example, programs, parameters for screens, and table contents—that is frequently needed by the work processes. This allows a work process quicker access to the data because it doesn't have to get it from the database.

Extended Memory

Extended Memory contains specific data (for example, the user's authorizations) for every active user. This specific data is called user context. During dispatching, the user context is passed on from one work process to the next. This way, only the memory addresses are passed on.

Resource Requirements

For many users to be able to work with an R/3 System, it must have the appropriate resources. The following values will give you an idea of which resources are needed for standard R/3 Systems:

5–10 users per dialog work process   The exact number of users depends on which applications the users are running. For example, for the same amount of users, you'll need fewer processes in the Finance module than in the Sales module.

10–20 work processes per application server The exact number of work processes depends on the CPU power, the size of the server's main memory, and the modules being used.

1–30 application servers per database server The exact number of application servers depends on how much more powerful the database server is than an application server. The database server and the application server share the entire system load, approximately in the ratio of 1:5. That is, if the database server is as powerful as the application servers, the database server can serve approximately 5 application servers. If the database server is more powerful, it can serve up to 30 servers.

Based on these numbers, you can see that a central system with distributed presentation can serve an average of 50 users. However, a distributed system with multiple application servers can support several thousand users.

Supported Hardware and Software for R/3

For the operation of an R/3 System, you can choose to implement almost any hardware platform, operating system, and RDBMS. You can select hardware and software from among the leading manufacturers on the market, and you can also set up a heterogeneous system landscape. Table 2.3 displays the supported hardware and software.

SAP recommends a uniform hardware and operating system platform for the application server and database server as well as for the different systems in your R/3 System landscape. SAP supports heterogeneous R/3 Systems, although they involve more sources of errors than homogenous systems do and increase the amount of administration.

TABLE 2.3: Supported Hardware and Software for R/3 (Note: OSF/Motif and Apple Macintosh front ends are not supported for AS/400.)

	UNIX		Windows NT			Middleware/Mainframe	
Hardware	Bull Digital HP	IBM SNI SUN	Bull/Zenith Compaq Data General, etc.	Digital HP IBM	NCR Sequent SNI	IBM AS/400	IBM S/390
Operating System	AIX Digital UNIX HP-UX	Reliant SINIX SOLARIS	Windows NT			OS/400	OS/390
RDBMS	DB2 UDB Informix OnLine Oracle		DB2 UDB Informix OnLine Oracle MS SQL Server			DB2 for AS/400	DB2 for OS/390
Front End	Windows 3.1, Windows 95, Windows NT, OSF/Motif, OS/2 Presentation Manager (PM), Apple Macintosh, Java						

> **NOTE** Currently, the only exceptions are heterogeneous R/3 Systems with the Microsoft Windows NT operating system for the application server and a UNIX derivative for the database server.

The Presentation Layer

For the presentation layer, R/3 provides the Thin Client. The Thin Client does not have any application logic. It receives only data from the application, presents the data to the user, and transfers the user's entries to the application.

For the R/3 presentation layer to run on your front end, the Thin Client needs only the data that is necessary to process the screen and to check the user entries. All other data for the application logic is transported only from the database to the application server. This enables you to connect front ends to the R/3 System through a WAN because so little data flows between the front end and the application server.

As you saw earlier in this chapter, you can connect an application server with 10 dialog work processes to anywhere from 50 to 100 front ends. If the number of users grows, you can increase the number of front ends on each application server until you reach the maximum number of front ends on each server. It is only then that you have to consider an additional application server.

The R/3 presentation layer is suited to the requirements of different user communities. There are separate graphical user interfaces for the following:

Occasional users   An occasional user should work with R/3 through a Web browser, the Internet application component.

Professional users   The professional user can access R/3 through the Session Manager or the SAPGUI.

The Session Manager

Through the *Session Manager*, you can log on to multiple systems simultaneously and have multiple screens open during a session. This enables you to switch quickly and easily between various screens of different R/3 Systems. The Session Manager allows easier navigation to the functions within the menus than the SAPGUI allows. You can store your most frequently used transactions in the user-specific part of the Session Manager window and see only those transactions that you are allowed to use. Figure 2.5 displays how the Session Manager may appear on your front end.

Using the Session Manager, a user is logged on simultaneously to three R/3 Systems: TC2, TC3, and TC4.

FIGURE 2.5:

An example of the Session Manager

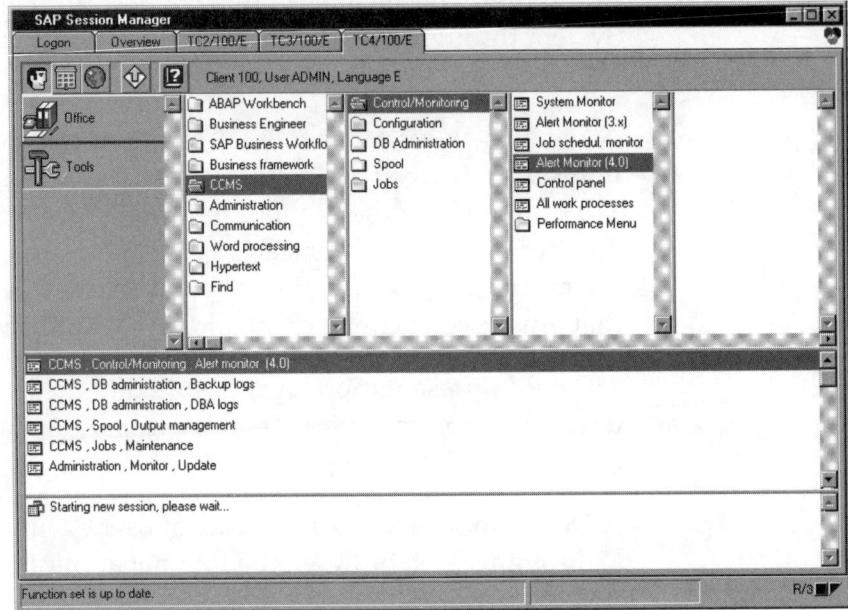

On the operating-system level, the Session Manager is a program that runs locally on the front end. The Session Manager logs the user on to the selected R/3 System and displays every open session in an overview. It saves the latest settings (for example, the user name) for the different systems. The next time you log on, you only need to enter your password.

The SAPGUI

The SAPGUI is intended for users who mainly work in a single R/3 System. Through the SAPGUI, you can log on to an R/3 System and perform the desired functions. To work simultaneously on different functions, you must open additional windows.

The Internet Session Manager and SAPGUI in Java

Java has established itself as a new hardware-independent and easy-to-use platform in the Internet. With the implementation of the standard user interfaces Session Manager and SAPGUI in Java, you can also access all R/3 functions through the Web (see Figure 2.6). By using Java, you can also use previously unsupported hardware platforms as front ends. This includes all platforms with Java-enabled Web browsers—for example, the reasonably priced NetPCs or network computers (NCs). By implementing the Internet Session Manager and SAPGUI in Java, you no longer need to perform any front-end administration of R/3 software. The required software is taken from the Web server; there is no need to install SAP-specific software.

The Internet-Enabling Layer

As of R/3 Release 3.1G, you can implement business processes through the Internet. From a technical viewpoint, you need a special server for this, the Internet Transaction Server (ITS). Figure 2.7 displays how the ITS is divided into two components, the Application Gate (A-gate) and the Web Gate (W-gate).

The A-gate exchanges data with R/3 applications like an R/3 user would through an SAPGUI. As a result, the A-gate is like a normal R/3 user for R/3 applications. R/3 sends the data to the A-gate in the format of the SAPGUI protocol, and the A-gate inserts the data into HTML templates and sends it through the W-gate to the Web server. From there, the data is transferred to the customer's Web browser through the Internet.

From a business point of view, you can use the *Web transactions* through the ITS. The Web transactions are mapped to R/3 transactions, which select and change data in the R/3 System. The Web transactions are selected so that they are easy to use and therefore users do not need training. You can set up the display of your Web transactions with the standard Internet tools. Which Web transactions you can use and how to program your own Internet applications are explained in the R/3 online documentation.

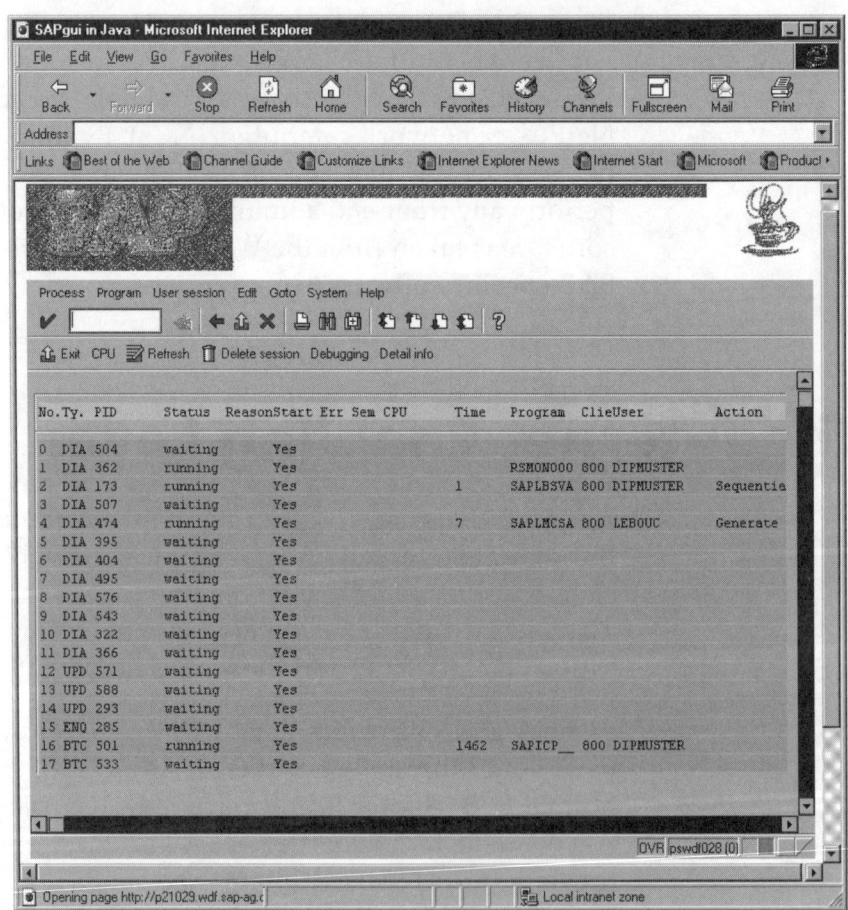

FIGURE 2.6:

An example of SAPGUI in Java

FIGURE 2.7:

The architecture of the Internet Transaction Server

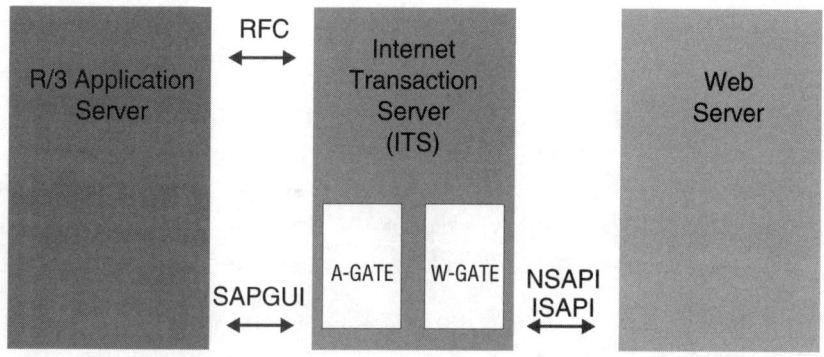

The Application Layer

The application level processes and coordinates all R/3 business processes. A business process normally consists of multiple business transactions. A business transaction combines processes that only make sense from a business point of view if they are performed together. For example, a credit and debit posting is a business transaction. The debit posting by itself would lead to incorrect data.

The R/3 Transaction

An *R/3 transaction* normally consists of multiple dialog steps and is also known as an SAP Logical Unit of Work (SAP-LUW). If the user switches from one dialog step to the next, a new screen is displayed. A screen is sometimes known as a Dynpro, which stands for Dynamic Program. You enter data in each screen, and it is stored temporarily and not written directly to the database. From a business viewpoint, only the complete R/3 transaction (not each individual screen) changes the information in a meaningful way. To ensure that the data in the database is always permissible, an R/3 transaction is either completely performed or not performed at all.

R/3 transactions are performed by the R/3 runtime environment and are programmed in Advanced Business Application Programming (ABAP), a fourth-generation programming language developed by SAP. A dialog step of an R/3 transaction is processed by a dialog work process. Because of dispatching, different dialog work processes normally process a complete R/3 transaction.

For the database, each dialog step in an R/3 transaction is a database transaction. If a database transaction corresponded to an R/3 transaction, the database transaction would contain the time it takes for a user to enter data in addition to the processing time. Because it frequently takes several seconds to enter data, an R/3 transaction would occupy the resources of the database for a long time and would considerably reduce the throughput. Since each database transaction releases its lock at the end of the transaction, an R/3 transaction must have its own locking mechanism. You will learn how this works in "The Enqueue Service" later in this chapter.

To ensure that an R/3 transaction is completed as quickly as possible for a user on SAPGUI, the dialog and the update of the data input occur asynchronously. During the dialog with the user, R/3 collects the input. After the transaction has ended for the user, R/3 changes the data in the database using the update service. In this way, an R/3 transaction divides into dialog and update processes (see Figure 2.8). You will learn how the update service works later in this chapter.

The Dialog Service

As you learned in the preceding section, the dialog in the R/3 transaction consists of several dialog steps. The dialog service

FIGURE 2.8:

The R/3 transaction

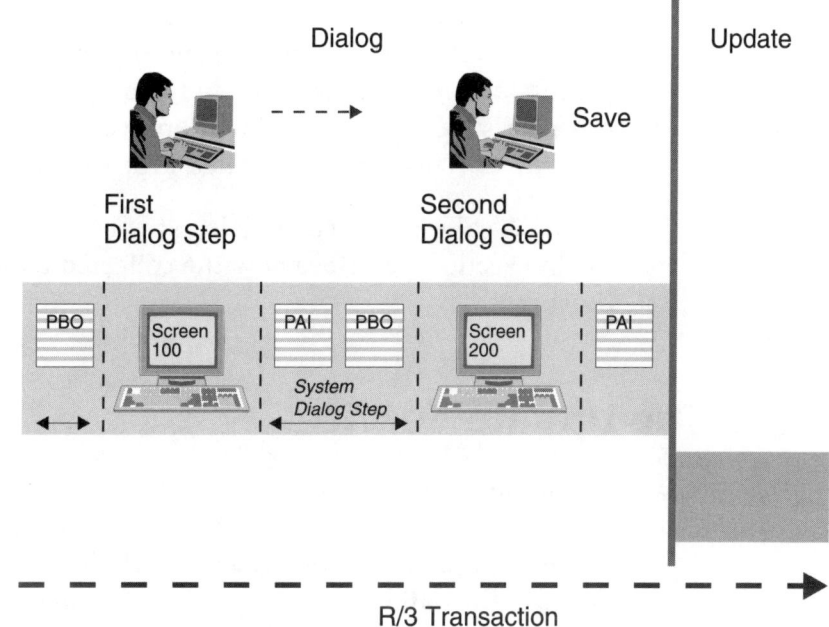

handles the processing of the dialog steps. The dialog service requires multiple dialog work processes and main memory. In a distributed system, each application server provides the dialog service.

Process after Input

After you enter data through SAPGUI, the work begins for the dialog service in the form of a dialog step. The data you enter is sent through the Dispatcher to a dialog work process. Then the work process accesses the user data in the main memory and processes it, which is known as the *roll-in*. This process is called Process after Input (PAI).

Process before Output

The dialog work process then prepares the next screen and sends the data to the SAPGUI. At the end of the dialog step, the work process updates the user data in the main memory and releases this user-specific data to all work processes, which is known as the *roll-out*. This process is called Process before Output (PBO).

Data is collected in each dialog step of a transaction. The following section describes how the collected data is updated in the database.

The Update Service

The update service allows you to work quickly in dialog, and you can control the database load caused by the update. The update service requires multiple update work processes and storage space in the database. In a distributed system, you can distribute the update work processes as you require. For four dialog work processes, you should schedule one update work process.

A dialog step in a transaction marks the data for the update. The dialog service writes an update record to a table in the database. This update record contains the data to be updated and the names of the programs that will later update it. The last dialog step in a transaction completes the update record, and the dialog service transfers the update record to the update service with the ABAP statement COMMIT WORK. By doing so, the dialog service passes the locks (which it set at the beginning of the transaction) to the update service (see "The Enqueue Service" later in this chapter). For example, if the user interrupts the transaction, no data can be changed in the database. For this reason, in a case such as this, the dialog service does not pass any update records to the update service.

The update service selects an update work process (see Figure 2.9). The work process reads the update record and updates the data from the update record in the respective tables in the database. Next, the update service deletes the update record, releases the now redundant locks, and ends the R/3 transaction.

FIGURE 2.9:

The update service

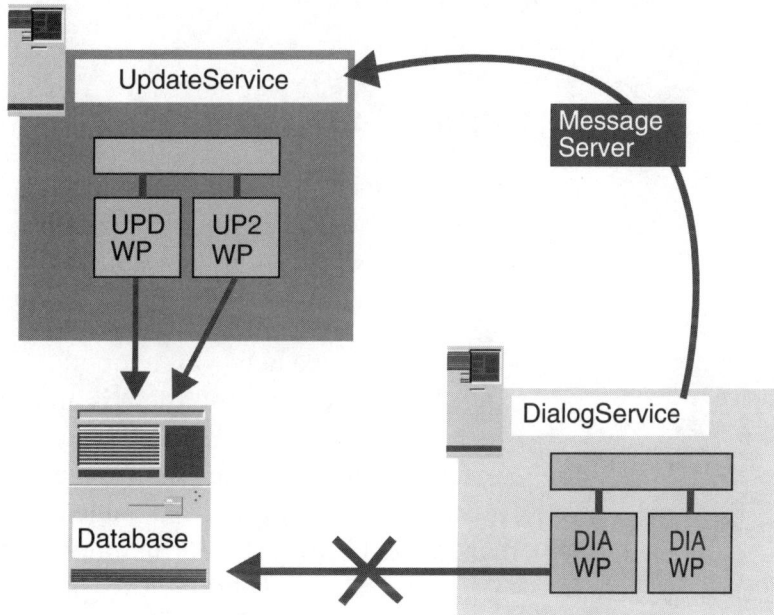

An update record has multiple update modules. Important and time-critical data is in the *V1 components*. All other data (for example, statistical information) is in the *V2 components*. You can reserve an individual work process for the V2 components (the UP2 work process displayed in Figure 2.9). You should schedule a type UP2 update work process for 12 dialog work processes. If you do not reserve a type UP2 work process, the normal update work processes (UPDs) update the V2 components.

If, for example, the update service cannot update the data because of a database problem, it interrupts the update and resets the database changes that were already made. The update record remains intact and is given the status *Error*. The update service releases the locks and notifies you of the interruption with an express message. Once the R/3 administrator has resolved the problem, you must decide whether or not to repeat the interrupted R/3 transaction.

The Enqueue Service

To prevent inconsistencies, business objects cannot be changed simultaneously by different users. Since an R/3 transaction is not the same as a transaction in the database, R/3 uses its own lock management. This is called the *enqueue service*.

The enqueue service needs an enqueue work process and a lock table. In a distributed system, there is an application server—the enqueue server—where the enqueue work process runs and where the lock table is located in the main memory. All of the enqueue work processes can access the lock table directly. All work processes for other servers access the enqueue work process through the message server, and the enqueue work process enters the lock in the lock table (see Figure 2.10). The enqueue server work processes lock in less than one-tenth of a millisecond. The other work processes require between 20 and 80 milliseconds.

If an object has been entered in the lock table, it is locked for other users. If a user wants to access the already locked object, the enqueue service notifies the application that the desired operation is not possible at that time. Once a lock is set, it is either released directly by the application program or it is released by the update program if the lock has been passed to the update service.

FIGURE 2.10:

The enqueue service

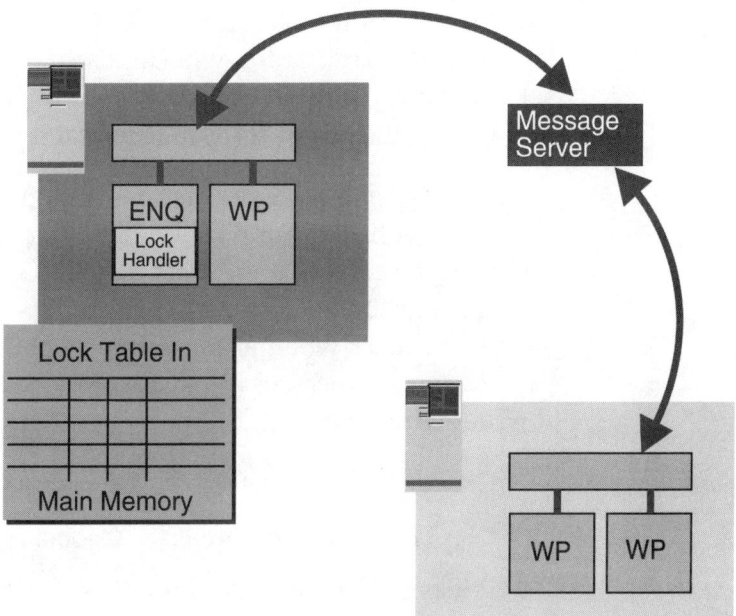

The Background Service

The background service processes programs without dialog; that is, when you are online, you do not need to enter data or select options. This service can be used, for example, for periodic tasks or for automatic data transfer from an external system.

The background service processes programs in the form of SAP jobs. A job consists of one step or multiple steps that are performed successively. A step is either an ABAP report or an external program that is performed on the operating-system level. The background work processes process the jobs.

In R/3, you can schedule a job to start at any time. For example, you can start a job immediately, at a specified time, or only on workdays. Often, jobs must be started periodically. For example, the system control jobs run in set cycles in the R/3 System. To run jobs in a preferred order, you can use the *job classes* A, B, and C to set a priority for each job. To run jobs on a specific computer, you can specify the target computer for each job.

The *background scheduler* ensures that jobs run at the desired start time. A background scheduler runs periodically on each application server with at least one background work process. Each background scheduler works independently and during each run checks whether jobs must be processed and which background work processes are available. The jobs run according to the following rules:

1. Class A jobs run before class B jobs.
2. Class B jobs run before class C jobs.
3. If jobs are in the same class, those with a specified target computer run before those without a specified target computer.
4. If jobs have the same authorization according to the preceding criteria, the job with the longest wait time runs first.

If background work processes are available on multiple application servers, then the job runs on the server that first activates its background scheduler.

The Message Service

The message service requests or releases locks, starts updates or jobs, and saves data about system performance. In a distributed system, the message process runs on an application server. This is known as the *message server*. This application server is the central point of communication with the other application servers. The enqueue work process should also run on this application server because the message service and the enqueue service should be able to communicate as quickly as possible.

Logon Load Balancing

Users can log on to the R/3 System with the SAPGUI or the Session Manager through the *logon group*. With a logon group, you can group multiple application servers logically to one server. Instead of logging on to an application server directly, you can log on to the message server through the logon group. The message server knows all of the application servers that belong to each logon group and logs you on to the server that has the lowest load. This is called *logon load balancing*.

The Gateway Service

The gateway service connects networks with various protocols; for example, it can connect a network that uses TCP/IP with one that uses Logical Unit 6.2 (LU6.2). This enables a program-to-program communication in heterogeneous networks—such as between an R/2 System (which is a mainframe system) and an R/3 System (see Figure 2.11). This service is based on the Common Programming Interface-Communication (CPI-C) protocol and is also known as the CPI-C Handler.

The CPI-C protocol is implemented in the ABAP language in both R/2 and R/3. Only a small part of the protocol is supported in the CPI-C Starter Set. For CPI-C communication with external programs, SAP delivers the CPI-C libraries. Since the protocol is included in X/Open Standard, external programs can also be connected to R/3 by other implementations of the CPI-C protocol.

The message service is used to exchange short messages between application servers within an R/3 System, and the gateway service is used to exchange larger volumes of data.

On the operating-system level, the gateway service consists of the gateway reader processes, the gateway work process, and the gateway monitor. In a standard installation, these processes run on each application server.

FIGURE 2.11:

The gateway service

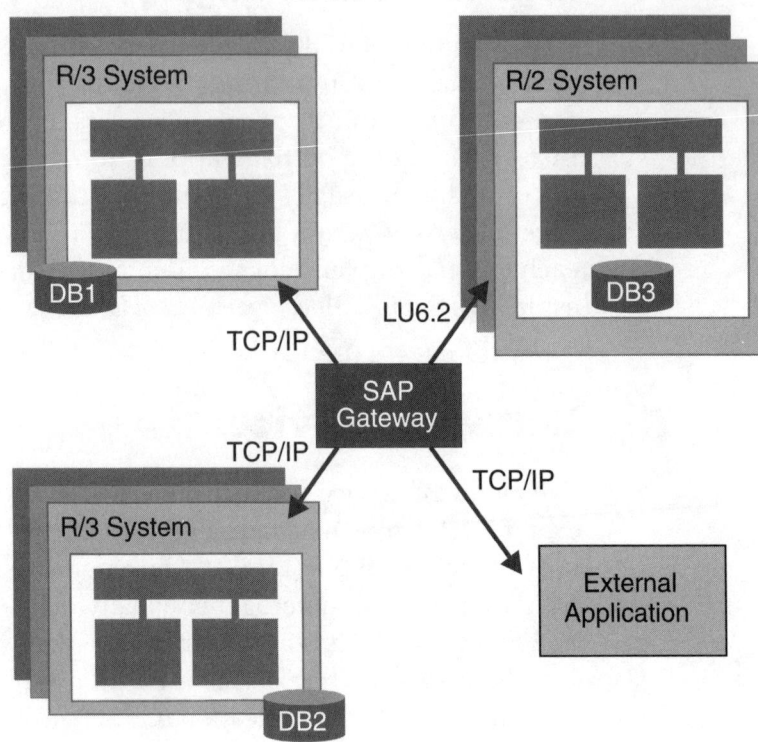

The Spool Service

The spool service formats data for output on printers or fax machines in LANs or WANs, passes on the formatted data to the spool system of the operating system, and monitors the data output.

As of R/3 Release 4.0, you can configure the spool service of an instance with multiple work processes the same way you can configure the dialog, update, and background services—in this case, with multiple spool work processes. In up to and including R/3 Release 3.1, only one spool work process can be configured on an instance.

Spool requests are generated during dialog or background processing. A spool request only specifies to which printer the data should be sent and which print format was selected for the printout. R/3 stores a spool request in tables in the database. However, R/3 saves the data to be printed within the Temporary Sequential Objects (TemSe), as illustrated in Figure 2.12.

FIGURE 2.12:

The spool service

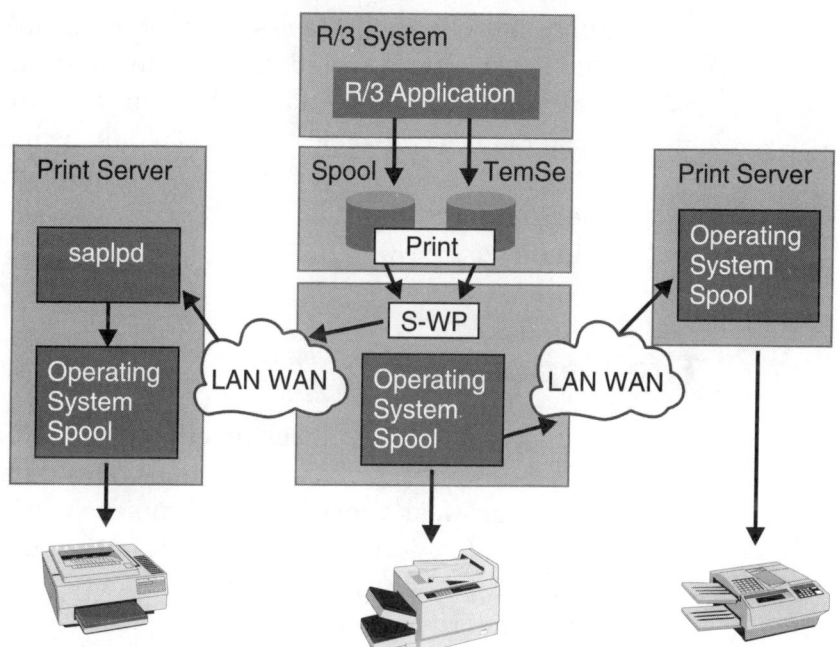

Before the data is printed, the system generates a print request for the spool request. The spool work process processes this print request, formats the data from the TemSe for the printout, and passes the print request to the spool system of the operating system (see Figure 2.12). The operating system spool administers the queue for the printer and sends the data to be printed to the printer.

The Database Layer

In the integrated R/3 client/server architecture, all of the services in the application access a central database. This ensures that all services can read the same information. R/3 only uses an RDBMS for the database service. The database stores both data (and information about the structure of the data) and all R/3 programs. Currently, all data and programs are distributed over the database in approximately 13,000 tables. Most of these tables are transparent; that is, the data is stored unencrypted and can also be read and interpreted by an external application. The other tables are pool or cluster tables. The table content can only be interpreted by using R/3 services and consists mainly of administrative information. See *SAP R/3 System Administration: The Official SAP Guide*, by Liane Will (Sybex, 1998).

The Repository

The database stores all customer application data, which is produced during the system operations. This data causes the database to grow, and therefore, it occupies the most space in the database. In addition to the customer data, the database contains the *R/3 Repository*, which is the most important component of an R/3 standard installation and occupies many gigabytes. As shown in Figure 2.13, the Repository objects are divided into the ABAP Dictionary and R/3 application. The ABAP Dictionary describes the structure and the relationship of all data. With the information from the ABAP Dictionary, R/3 interprets and generates the application objects, such as the programs or screens. The Repository describes the R/3 runtime environment centrally and free of redundancy. If you, as a customer, implement R/3, you can adapt the runtime environment to your requirements. The methods and tools that you need to do so are described in "Software Logistics" later in this chapter.

FIGURE 2.13:
Data stored in the database

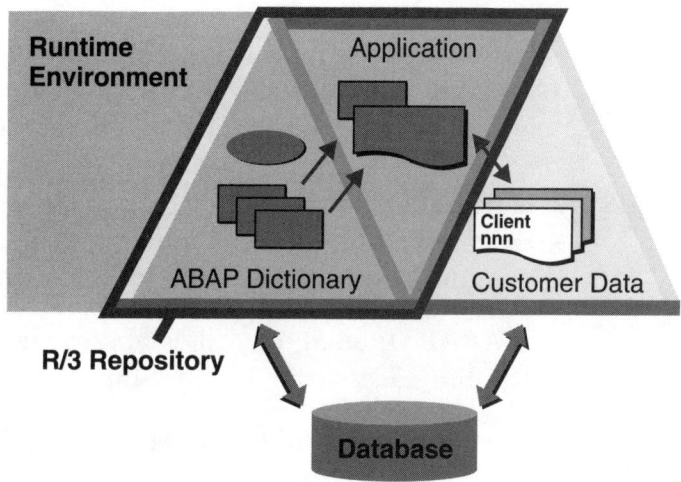

The SAPR3 User

An R/3 user cannot access the data in the database directly; he or she must access it indirectly through a work process. When you start R/3, each work process logs on to the database as database user SAPR3. Therefore, a work process does not have to log on again if the dispatcher allocates it to another R/3 user. The database user SAPR3 can access all R/3 data. The database management system does not decide which data can be read or changed by which R/3 user; instead, it is the R/3 authorization concept on the application layer that decides (see Chapter 6, "User Administration").

The Database Access Agent

Data is defined and manipulated with the Structured Query Language (SQL). Although SQL is largely standardized, there are manufacturer-specific dialects. To ensure that the application can work with different databases, each work process has a database-specific interface. This is called the *database access agent*. The database access agent connects the work process with the database, supplies the database with the desired data or Repository objects, and closes the connection to the database. In addition, the agent controls the transaction in the database and synchronizes the table buffers of the R/3 instances. The agent communicates with the remote or local SQL interface of the database and uses the manufacturer's SQL dialect. In R/3, you have two SQL dialects:

ABAP Open SQL   All databases are supported when applications access the database through ABAP Open SQL.

ABAP Native SQL   ABAP Native SQL expands ABAP to the manufacturer-specific SQL dialect. Applications that only access the database through ABAP Native SQL only run on the manufacturer-specific database.

When the Open SQL statements are interpreted, the R/3 database interface checks the syntax of the statement and, if possible, uses the SAP buffers, which are located locally in the main memory of each application server. To ensure that the database does not need to be accessed for reading, the applications store frequently used data in the buffers. Data such as ABAP programs and screens and ABAP Dictionary information should be buffered only if it is frequently read, but it should be changed rarely. When the ABAP Native SQL statements are interpreted, the R/3 database interface checks neither the syntax of the statement nor the SAP buffers. The statements are passed directly to the database. In R/3, ABAP Native SQL statements are only used if the function is specifically for the database.

Network Architecture and Protocol

The goal of the network architecture in an R/3 System is to connect the computers and to distribute the resources—such as data from the database or application logic from the application servers—around the network. To ensure that individual components of the network can be exchanged easily, the architecture is based on a layer model, known as the *communication layers*. This approach arranges the computer network in hierarchical layers; the hardware layer is the foundation and the application layer is located on top of the hardware layer. The transfer logic between two computers is called a *protocol*.

R/3 communicates through a multitude of protocols in a network with other R/3 Systems, R/2 Systems, or non-SAP systems. In a distributed R/3 System, the front end, the application servers, and the database server always communicate through the standard protocol, TCP/IP. For other R/3 Systems, R/2 Systems, or non-SAP systems, SAP supports the TCP/IP and Systems Network Architecture, Logical Unit 6.2 (SNA LU6.2) protocols.

Above the network layer, R/3 supports the communication interfaces Common Programming Interface-Communication (CPI-C), Remote Function Call (RFC), and Object Linking and Embedding (OLE) Automation for application programming.

In a typical R/3 System, the database, application, and presentation run on different computers. The front ends exchange data only with the application servers and the database server communicates only with the application servers. Figure 2.14 shows the network divided as follows:

Front-end network For each screen change, approximately 1.6KB of data flows between the front end and an application server. This volume of data increases if you print locally from your front end, load graphics, or work with office applications. The front ends can be connected to the application server through a LAN or a WAN. All network topologies are possible—for example, Ethernet, Token Ring, FDDI, or ATM. The data should be transferred with at least a rate of 9600bps.

Server network For each dialog step, approximately 20KB of data flows between the database server and the application server. Therefore, the server network can only be a LAN and should have a transfer speed of at least 10Mbps. Systems with multiple application servers require a powerful network, such as an FDDI with 100Mbps.

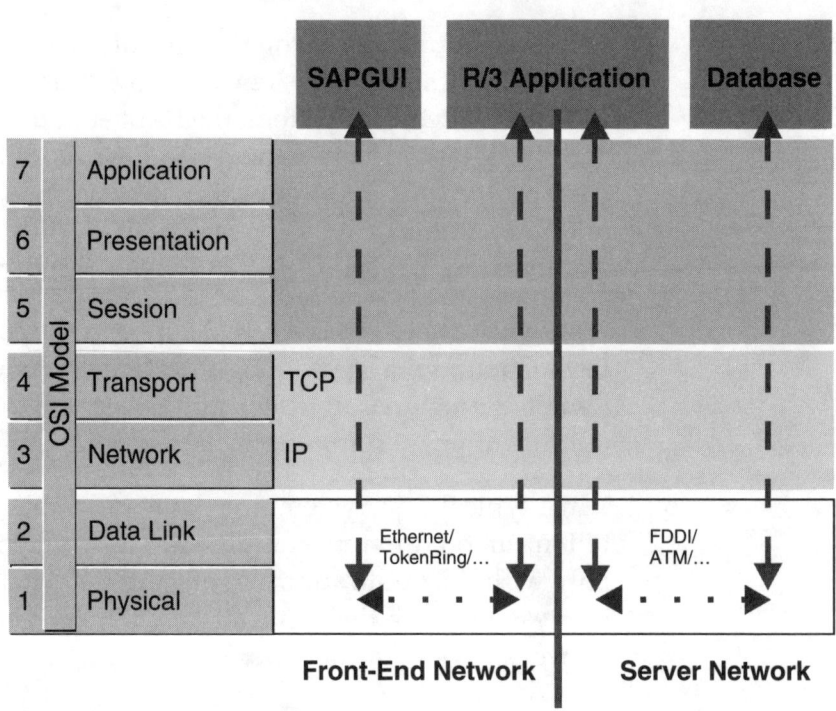

FIGURE 2.14:
Network architecture for a three-tiered R/3 System

In Chapter 11, "Network Administration," you will learn how the bandwidth of the front-end network is configured for your requirements. You should configure the important connections in the front-end network twice. This way, a damaged connection can be bridged quickly, and the front ends remain connected to the application servers.

The SAProuter

In addition to a physical network security, you should use the *SAProuter*, an SAP software product, to control the external connections to your network. The SAProuter is an intermediate node in a network connection between R/3 Systems. Each SAProuter has its own Route Permission Table, which determines which routes can be used and which passwords are necessary for access. This enables you to reduce the number of access points. Additionally, you can use the SAProuter to make your firewall computer more secure against undesired external connections. Chapter 11, "Network Administration," explains where you should implement the SAProuter in the network.

Secure Network Communications (SNC)

To protect the network data flow from undesired access, you can integrate the front-end network in a network security system. SAP offers the *Secure Network Communications (SNC)* functions. The SNC functions start security products that have implemented the standardized interface GSS-AP1 v2 and those services that are available in the R/3 System in the form of a shared library or DLL (see Internet RFC 2078; you can find RFCs at `http://www.rfc-editor.org`).

Interfaces

Normally, you must integrate R/3 into an existing landscape of different systems. If multiple systems are involved in a business process, they exchange data with each other. For this type of communication, R/3 has interfaces that support the common international standards.

In the following sections, you will learn how to communicate through sequential files and which program-to program communication is possible.

Communication through Sequential Files

You can transfer data to the R/3 System by means of communication through sequential files. For example, the data can be from an external system, which is replaced completely or partially by R/3. During communication through sequential files, the systems are loosely linked, which means that a system can fail without impeding the other systems in their essential tasks.

First, the external system writes the data to sequential files. Then, the sequential files are transferred to directories in the operating-system level in R/3; from there, they are imported into the R/3 System. For this import, you can choose from three procedures: *Batch Input*, *Call Transaction*, and *Direct Input*.

Batch Input

First, the Batch Input procedure saves the data to be imported as Batch Data Communication (BDC) tables in a file. This file is called the Batch Input Session. As displayed in Figure 2.15, the Batch Input Session is then processed. The Batch Input Session is passed to the appropriate R/3 transaction. The dialog steps of the transaction run as they do for a user during online operation and store the data in the database. To create a Batch Input Session and an import program, you can record the order of events in a transaction online in R/3. See the R/3 online documentation or *SAP R/3 System Administration: The Official SAP Guide*.

Call Transaction

The Call Transaction procedure is an alternative to the Batch Input procedure. After the data record has been entered into the

BDC table from the sequential file, the transaction is called directly (see Figure 2.15). This procedure is therefore faster because a Batch Input Folder does not have to be written or read.

FIGURE 2.15:

Batch Input, Call Transaction, and Direct Input

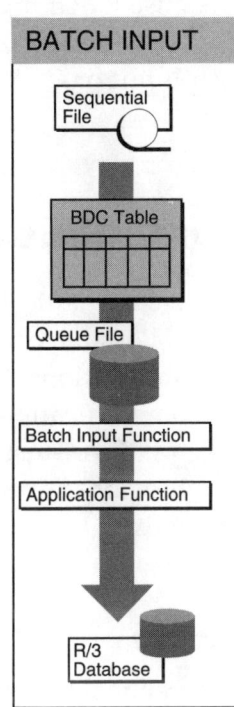
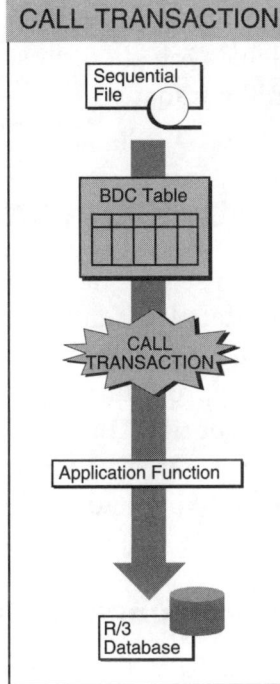
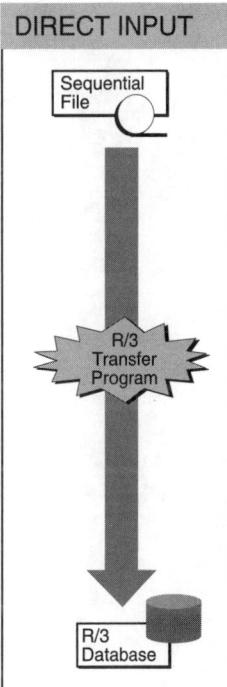

NOTE Batch Input and Call Transaction use R/3 transactions. Therefore, the data is subject to the same integrity tests they are subject to in dialog mode before they are imported.

Direct Input

The Direct Input procedure writes the data directly to the database without using transactions in R/3 (see Figure 2.15). Therefore, the programs must check the integrity of the data. This is difficult to program because a transaction in R/3 checks the data thoroughly. A Direct Input procedure is useful if you want to import a lot of data very quickly.

For some applications, R/3 maintains standardized procedures for data transfer; the procedures use Batch Input, Call Transaction, or Direct Input. If there are no standardized procedures available, you should use Batch Input or Call Transaction to program the transfer.

Program-to-Program Communication

You can use program-to-program communication to import and export data from the R/3 System. Possible communication partners are R/3, R/2, and external applications. You can only implement the program-to-program communication if SAP supports the appropriate interface for the platforms used. Frequently used interfaces in the R/3 System are Remote Function Call (RFC) and Object Linking and Embedding (OLE).

Remote Function Call (RFC)

RFC is based on the Common Programming Interface-Communication (CPI-C), but it offers more functions than CPI-C and is easier to use. However, the technical requirements for RFC are the same as the CPI-C requirements. The R/3 System supports three types of RFC calls: synchronous RFC, asynchronous RFC, and transactional RFC.

Synchronous RFC

During a *synchronous RFC*, the calling program does not continue to run until the called program is finished processing data and makes the results known to the calling program.

Asynchronous RFC

During an *asynchronous RFC*, the calling program continues to run and does not wait for the results from the called program in the target system. The only condition is that the target system is running at the time of the RFC call.

Transactional RFC

A *transactional RFC* combines multiple programs in a business transaction. In the target system, the programs are processed in a predetermined sequence. If one of the programs is interrupted, the entire transaction is interrupted and any changes made by the other programs are reset. During transactional RFCs, the target system need not be available at the time of the RFC call. You can also configure the query interval and frequency to the target system individually.

To ensure that you can call an external program through RFC or that an external program can call a program in R/3 through RFC, R/3 is delivered with an RFC-Software Development Kit (SDK), which contains the C-library to link to external programs.

Object Linking and Embedding (OLE)

With OLE, you can link R/3 to office applications that have OLE2 Automation, such as Microsoft Word or Excel. This way, you can use R/3 through the front-end environment that you are familiar with. The R/3 System can be used as an OLE client and an OLE server.

If R/3 is an OLE client, you can call the office application from an ABAP program. OLE commands from the ABAP program are transferred to the front end through the SAPGUI as RFC. The SAPGUI maps the RFC calls to OLE commands for the office applications.

If R/3 is an OLE server, you can call the ABAP program or Business Application Programming Interfaces (BAPIs) from an office application (BAPIs are described in "Business Objects" later in this chapter). OLE commands are sent to the SAP automation server. The automation server converts the OLE commands to RFC calls and sends them to the R/3 System. The R/3 System triggers ABAP programs or BAPIs, which send their results back through the SAP automation server to the office application. Since both ABAP programs and BAPIs are located within R/3, the office application must first log on to the R/3 System. You can use the internal R/3 authorization concept to control which ABAP program or BAPIs can and cannot run an office application.

Distributed Component Architecture

For existing applications, SAP is introducing step-by-step business objects—for example, customers, materials, and orders. An application appears to other applications as comprising only business objects with appropriate methods. Before the business objects were developed, the R/3 application shared access to a common database. This common database is divided up step-by-step into components, which can also be distributed across a network. SAP calls this open architecture that is based on components the *Business Framework*.

In the following sections, you'll learn about the advantages offered by the architecture of the business components, how R/3 integrates the individual components from a business viewpoint, and how the basic interface, the business object, is composed.

Business Components

Large companies in particular want to implement their applications decentrally and in different time zones. Additionally, R/3 should be simpler to link to products from third-party vendors or to your own solutions. Business processes should be able to extend over multiple components. The goal of the SAP business components is to let you set up and run heterogeneous, companywide, distributed applications systems. The stable interfaces let you quickly integrate new components and equip the individual components independently from one another. This simplifies the implementation and maintenance of a complex, companywide system landscape.

The R/3 System is developing into a family of components. As of Release 4.0, Human Resources is an independent R/3 kernel component with its own Release cycle. In future Releases, Finance and Logistics will also be independent components. You can link the R/3 kernel components with industry-specific components from, for example, commerce or the oil industry. Additionally, components will be developed that support your business decisions or your Internet applications.

With these business components, R/3 has another scaling layer. Now you can run multiple databases in parallel, but the separate data management is transparent from the business-management standpoint. This ensures that you have the following configuration options for your system landscape:

Central system with a database This system enables you to run small systems simply.

Distributed components with multiple databases This system enables companies that work decentrally to distribute their individual applications. You can maintain the components separately.

Central system with multiple databases This system enables companies with geographically separate subsidiaries to distribute their entire R/3 System. In each branch office, the users work in R/3 through a LAN and not through the slower WAN.

In a distributed environment, the individual components exchange data that are linked, from a business viewpoint, to the business process. Frequently, a business process spans over all components in a system landscape. The way you synchronize the communication between components is important for the integration of components in a business system. You will learn the necessary method for this in the next section.

Business Integration

Suppose you disconnect the application system because of technical, organizational, or economical conditions. However, the components remain interconnected through business processes. To integrate the applications on the business process layer, R/3 offers the following two methods:

Application Link Enabling (ALE)   Through ALE, you can exchange business messages between disconnected applications.

SAP Business Workflow   Using the SAP Business Workflow, you can structure and automate business processes that span over multiple components.

IDocs

To divide a system into components or to add a new component to a system, you must first determine which application runs on which systems and which business objects are exchanged by the applications. Technically, R/3 uses Intermediate Documents (IDocs) to exchange data.

An IDoc is an SAP standard that determines the structure and the format of the data to be electronically transmitted. The IDoc standard was developed from the EDIFACT and ANSI X12 standards.

IDocs are uniquely identified with a control record. The data records from the applications form the core. The status of an IDoc on its path from the application to the business partner and back is recorded in status records.

To send the data from one application to another, the sending application first generates a message, which is called the *Master IDoc*. Next, the message is passed to the ALE layer, where it is prepared to be sent. From the business viewpoint, the ALE layer decides what subsequently happens to the message, which user is notified, and which steps are to be performed and when. The communication layer then transfers the Master IDoc and starts processing the message in the receiving system.

Through ALE, you can connect R/3 Systems with each other, R/3 Systems with R/2 Systems, and R/3 Systems with external systems. You can also connect R/3 Systems with different Releases. Even after a Release upgrade, data exchange will normally continue without maintenance.

NOTE ALE does not necessarily need an RFC connection. You can also transfer the IDocs from one system to another as files. In this way, communication through sequential files is also possible for ALE. You can implement communication through sequential files if the RFC connection is not supported for your system environment.

Business Objects

A company's business processes can change over time. The application software must be able to cope with such changes. As opposed to a business process, the business objects (for example, orders or customers) barely change. With this type of business object, you can program durable and stable interfaces.

Until now, there was no recognized standard for business objects. SAP therefore uses the step-by-step approach to object technology. As of Release 3.0, R/3 contains SAP business objects, which are documented in the SAP Business Object Repository (BOR).

Business objects are the components for communication on an application-related network layer. For example, the R/3 Internet capability or the connection to office applications can be implemented through these components. Business objects provide business functions, which are called methods. For example, an object called Customer has the methods Create customer or Display customer. The descriptive names lead to transparent and simple programming.

The Business Application Programming Interface (BAPI)

External applications can access business objects through standardized, platform-independent methods—the Business Application Programming Interfaces (BAPIs). The BAPIs use the business methods of the business objects. You can access the BAPIs using DCOM from Microsoft, CORBA from OMG, or Java. Together, the SAP business objects and their BAPIs form an open, object-oriented view of the business processes and data in the R/3 System.

Software Logistics

Software Logistics includes all methods and tools with which you customize R/3 and develop ABAP programs for your purposes. When you customize or develop programs, you change R/3's runtime environment. Make sure you test your changes before you use them in your production system. Preferably, you should develop, test, and produce in three separate R/3 Systems.

This section teaches you why an R/3 System landscape should consist of more than one system, how to perform a customizing and development project, and how to transport your settings from one system to another.

System Landscape

When you log on to R/3, you must enter your user name, your password, and a client. The client has its own users and its own data in the database. Data is only visible in the client in which it is created. The data can neither be changed nor displayed from another client through application functions. Therefore, a client is generally an independent unit from a business and organizational point of view. All R/3 data is divided into:

Client-dependent data   For example, user and application data

Client-independent data   For example, ABAP programs or ABAP Dictionary data

With R/3, SAP delivers three clients: client 000, client 001, and client 066. Client 000 has special functions for maintaining R/3. An R/3 upgrade supplies new functions to this client. You may neither delete client 000 nor change its data. Client 001 is a copy of client 000. You may change this client. Client 066 is a special client in which only technical system monitoring can be performed. SAP's EarlyWatch Service and GoingLive Check can use client 066 to check your system through a remote connection. The business data for the other clients is not visible from client 066, which ensures the security of your data from unauthorized accesses. You may neither delete client 066 nor change its data.

The IMG and the ABAP Workbench

Before you can start production with the R/3 System, you must adapt it to your company with the Implementation Guide (IMG)

and ABAP Workbench tools. With the Implementation Guide, you can set the business parameters, such as articles or periods for each business year. Most settings in Customizing depend on the client, although there are settings that are valid for all clients—settings that modify the Repository, for example.

With the ABAP Workbench, you only change the Repository. You can develop your own programs, expand on programs delivered from SAP, or modify SAP programs. Client-independent objects are always changed with the ABAP Workbench.

If you change the Repository through Customizing or development, the runtime environment of your R/3 System changes at the same time. Information is only recorded once in the Repository. All recorded or changed information is automatically available to every application. The work process interprets a *runtime object*, which is essentially generated from the source code of an ABAP program. If the source code has been changed since the last generation, runtime objects are regenerated before they are implemented.

Three-System Landscape

You cannot run any production applications in an R/3 System when Customizing and software development is taking place because the R/3 System's runtime environment is changed. To ensure a stable runtime environment and continue to develop at the same time, you must have at least two R/3 Systems. SAP recommends three separate R/3 Systems. You should distribute the roles of these R/3 Systems as follows:

Development system In this R/3 System, you can develop programs and customize the R/3 System. Changed objects are collected in change requests and released for transport into other systems.

Quality assurance system   In this R/3 System, you can import the released change requests from the development system. You can test and validate the Customizing and software changes. You can release error-free Customizing and software changes to the production system.

Production system   In this R/3 System, you can import the released change requests from the quality assurance system. You can use the tested Customizing and software changes to run your application in the production system.

Two-System Landscape

The basic disadvantage of a three-system landscape is the high cost of hardware and the increased effort to administer an additional system. The two-system landscape is less expensive, particularly for smaller systems. In this type of landscape, you should distribute the roles as follows:

Development and quality assurance system   In this R/3 System, programs are developed and the R/3 System is customized in one client, which is called the development client. Changed objects are collected in change requests and released. You can copy the released change requests into another client, which is called the quality assurance client. In the quality assurance client, you can test and validate the Customizing and software changes.

Production system   In this R/3 System, you can import the released change requests from the quality assurance client. You can use the tested Customizing and software changes to run your application in the production system.

WARNING   SAP does not recommend a one-system landscape. If you use only one system, you cannot continue to develop programs after the start of production. In addition, you can no longer work in the production system during an update.

In the following section, you will learn how to coordinate Customizing and software development with the Customizing Organizer and the Workbench Organizer.

The Customizing Organizer and the Workbench Organizer

While you are customizing or developing programs in the development system, you should have R/3 automatically display all changes or settings. This way, you can import your changes into other systems. Since a Repository object is only available once in the system, you must also check the version of an object to ensure that you can return to an older version if you have problems. The Customizing Organizer (CO) and the Workbench Organizer (WBO) support you in these tasks.

The Customizing Project

At the beginning of a Customizing project, the Project Manager creates a *change request* and assigns the Project Team members to it. The Customizing Organizer then generates a *task* for every Project Team member. When a Project Team member calls a Customizing transaction and changes the R/3 standard, R/3 automatically records that member's settings in the task. At the end of the project, the task contains all customizing that the Project Team member made for this project.

When a Project Team member's work is completed, he or she releases the task. No further settings can be recorded in a released task. If all Project Team members have released their tasks, the Project Manager can release the change request. This ensures that the change request contains all customizing that was implemented or changed in the Customizing project by the Project Team members.

The Development Project

The procedure for a development project is similar to the procedure for a Customizing project. The Project Manager creates a change request, assigns the Project Team members to it, and is responsible for releasing the change request. This ensures that the changes can be imported to the other systems. The Workbench Organizer administers all of the change requests that contain client-independent objects—for example, ABAP programs, changes to the ABAP Dictionary, or general Customizing settings. Only Project Team members can change objects that are in the change request. This enables those assigned to development projects to work independently from one another without fear of changing the same program.

If you create Repository objects (for example, an ABAP program), you allocate this object to a *development class.* All objects in a development class belong to one field and are transported to other systems through the same path. Especially in large projects, you can divide the developed programs, for example, into classes that correspond to the appropriate application.

If the project leader releases a change request in the Workbench Organizer, R/3 creates a complete new version of the changed Repository objects in a Versions Database. For the old version, only the differences from the new version are stored in the database. With the help of this stored information, R/3 is able to rebuild the old version, if necessary. This enables you to follow the history of your development and return to an old version.

The Workbench Organizer links each Repository object to the name of the system in which it was generated. For example, all Repository objects that SAP delivers belong to one system called SAP. This ensures that you know which system the original object is stored in. All other systems can only contain a copy of the original, even if you transport the objects into another system with change requests. You should configure your system landscape in a way that your Repository objects are only changed centrally in a system and the copies in other systems cannot be changed so you can avoid having different versions of a program in different systems.

> **NOTE** Because of the integrated runtime environment in R/3, you should perform Customizing and software development simultaneously in one client. By doing so, you can ensure that the Customizing settings and software developments are compatible within a client.

The Transport System

R/3 writes released change requests to a transport directory on the operating-system level, thus creating transport requests. You can use the transport system to transport and monitor transport requests from one R/3 System in your system landscape to another.

The R/3 System Name

To ensure that the transport system can differentiate between the sender and recipient of a transport request, all of the names of all R/3 Systems in the system landscape must be different. The name of an R/3 System consists of three characters. For example, you can use the following names for a three-system landscape:

DEV Development system

QAS Quality assurance system

PRD Production system

You should determine the name of an R/3 System during its installation. You cannot change the name after installation. Therefore, you should have already determined all of the names before you set up a system landscape.

In a three-system landscape, requests are transported as follows:

1. You release your change request in the system DEV.
2. R/3 exports the change requests in a transport directory on the operating-system level. This way, the change requests become transport requests. The other systems can also access the transport directory.
3. You import the transport requests into the QAS system by using the Transport Management System (TMS).
4. You test and validate the settings and developments in the QAS system.
5. You import the transport requests into the PRD system by using the TMS.

For the transport to run as described here, you must connect the systems physically and logically.

The Transport Directory

You can physically connect the system through a common transport directory on the operating-system level. After a standard installation of R/3, the path to the transport directory is:

UNIX   /usr/sap/trans

Windows NT   \\<*name of computer*>\sapmnt\trans

All computers you transport between should be able to directly access this directory on the operating-system level. However, there are situations in which you cannot set up this type of directory. For example, because of a high level of security, other systems may not be able to directly access the operating-system level of the production system. In this case, you must copy the files in the transport requests to the appropriate transport directory. This procedure is described in further detail in the R/3 online documentation or in *SAP R/3 System Administration: The Official SAP Guide*.

> **NOTE** A background work process processes parts of a request's import or export. To display the status of each change request, the dialog work process requires information from files in the transport directory. In a distributed R/3 System, each of the available background and dialog work processes must be able to perform these tasks. For this reason, all application servers must be able to access the transport directory.

The Transport Domain

You can connect the systems logically through an R/3 transport domain. In a transport domain, you can include R/3 Systems with roles such as development, quality assurance, or production. In a two- or three-system landscape, you can group all systems in one domain. In a complex system landscape with many systems, multiple domains may be necessary, although requests are never or rarely transported between the domains (see Figure 2.16).

The Transport Group

R/3 Systems with a common transport directory form a transport group. One transport domain can contain multiple transport groups. In a two- or three-system landscape, the systems normally have a common transport directory, which ensures that only one transport group is available in one transport domain. If, for security reasons, you do not want to connect the production system with the other systems, you can have two transport groups in one domain (see Figure 2.16).

FIGURE 2.16:

Transport domains and transport groups

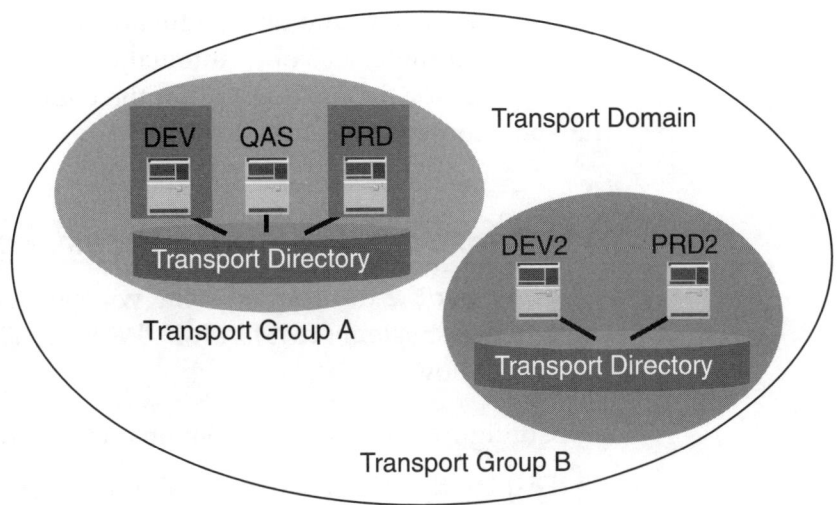

The TDC and BDC

You can administer a transport domain centrally from an R/3 System by using the transport domain controller (TDC). You can set up your transport system for the TDC, and all other systems are sent a copy of the settings. If the TDC fails, you cannot change the settings of the transport system. Therefore, you should additionally set up a backup domain controller (BDC), which can take on the tasks of the TDC. For example, in a three-system landscape, the production system should be a TDC and the development system should be the BDC.

The Transport Route

A transport domain only determines the systems between which transport requests can be transported. This enables, in principle, a released change request from the development system to be imported into every other system in the domain. To ensure that this request is transported first into the quality assurance system and, only after this, into the production system, you must set up the transport route. R/3 only automatically marks a released transport request for the next system in the chain of systems if the transport route has been set up.

The Transport Management System (TMS)

To administer the transport system, you can use the Transport Management System (TMS) in R/3. With the TMS, you can perform the following tasks:

- Configure the transport domain and the transport route
- Display the import queue of all the systems in the transport domain
- Import transport requests from the queue into its respective system
- Monitor the transport system

NOTE Once you have set up your transport system, you do not need to change any settings unless you add another system to the system landscape or you change the role of one of your systems in an existing system landscape. You must make the new settings centrally on the TDC and copy them to the other systems in the transport domain.

Review Questions

1. Which work processes exist in R/3?

    A. Dialog

    B. Update

    C. Message

D. Enqueue

E. Background

F. Gateway

G. Spool

2. Which statements are correct?

   A. The update service allows users to work more quickly in dialog.

   B. Each dialog work process requires its own update work process.

   C. A dialog step in a transaction marks the data for the update.

   D. The update service requires the necessary locks from the enqueue service so that no other user can change the same data.

3. Which work processes have direct access to the lock table?

   A. All work processes

   B. All work processes on the enqueue server

   C. Only the enqueue work process

   D. All dialog work processes

4. Which statements are correct?

   A. A job consists of one or more steps. Each step is scheduled to start automatically at a specified time.

   B. A job consists of one or more steps. Each step calls either an ABAP program or an external program.

   C. The background scheduler starts the scheduled jobs automatically. A background work process processes a job's steps.

D. Only special ABAP programs can be scheduled as jobs. For example, ABAP programs that generate large lists cannot be scheduled as jobs.

5. Which work processes log on to the database when R/3 is started?

   A. All work processes

   B. All work processes except the enqueue work process

   C. Only the work processes of the central instance

   D. Only the dialog, background, and update work processes

6. Through which protocol do front ends and application servers communicate?

   A. UUCP (UNIX to UNIX Copy Protocol)

   B. IPX/SPX (Internet Packet Exchange/Sequential Packet Exchange)

   C. TCP/IP (Transmission Control Protocol/Internet Protocol)

   D. NetBIOS (Network Basic Input Output System)

7. Through which protocol does an R/3 System communicate with an R/2 System on an MVS/VSE Mainframe?

   A. SNA LU6.2

   B. TCP/IP

   C. DCAM

8. Which statements are correct?

   A. A client has its own users and its own tables in the database. You can change them from other clients through application functions.

B. All R/3 data is divided into client-dependent and client-independent data.

C. A client has its own ABAP programs and ABAP Dictionary data.

D. A client is an independent unit, from a business viewpoint as well as from an organizational viewpoint.

9. Which statements are correct?

A. At the beginning of a Customizing project, the Project Manager creates a change request and assigns the Project Team members to it. Tasks are only generated for the assigned team members.

B. To correct errors, you can reverse the release of a task and change your settings in the old task.

C. Employees with developer authorization may change all ABAP programs in a development system.

D. Each Repository object is linked with the name of the system in which it is generated. For example, all Repository objects that SAP delivers belong to one system called SAP.

CHAPTER THREE

Project Administration

In an R/3 implementation project, different teams work toward a common goal: to implement R/3 as quickly and as successfully as possible. Essentially, the teams are divided into the application consultants and the Technical Team. The application consultants create the Business Blueprint. The Business Blueprint is used to map the company structure and customize the business processes. The Technical Team sets up and administers the required R/3 Systems for the application consultants' plan. At the same time, the Technical Team plans and sets up the entire system environment for the production system. The production system must be able to process the load generated by the users and be available as planned.

Often, personnel costs make up the largest part of the entire cost of the R/3 implementation. Experience shows that you can save money with simple strategies for personnel organization and procedures. This chapter covers aspects of your project administration and explains how to do the following:

- Define the organization
- Determine the procedures
- Control the course of the project

Define the Organization

The implementation of R/3 in your company takes place over a limited period of time. If you were to implement R/3 using only your existing organizational structure, your company management would be overburdened. Because your existing organizational structure would not be optimally suited to the implementation project, it would be better to set up a separate organizational structure for the duration of the project. For the project organizational structure, describe the project areas that must be accounted for throughout the project and the roles necessary to implement R/3.

In this chapter, you will learn about the essential aspects to consider for your own project organization. You'll learn which roles to assign to a Project Team and how many team members you'll need. The section "Train the Project Team" describes the training service that SAP provides for the Technical Team.

Determine Your Project Team

The success of a project not only depends on the methods you use, it also depends on the people involved. If employees are assigned to the Project Team according to their aptitude and abilities, you'll save time and money. To ensure that the team members can work together effectively and to avoid unnecessary work, you must define each task and decide what aspect of the implementation each team member is responsible for. During the implementation of R/3, the Project Team is typically divided into Project Management, Business Process, Technical Implementation, Quality Assurance, Production Support, and Training and Documentation.

To prepare the project, use an organization chart to describe how you want to organize the Project Team. Define the necessary roles for the technical implementation and allocate these roles to the Project Team members. Describe the tasks and responsibilities for each role. In ASAP, the following seven roles are recommended for the Technical Team (see Figure 3.1):

Technical Team Lead The Technical Team Lead appoints the Technical Team, leads it, and schedules the team resources. Together with the Project Manager, the Technical Team Lead plans the technical requirements and the size of the R/3 System landscape, organizes the invitation of tender for the hardware (that is, solicits for bids from different hardware vendors), collects the offers, and selects vendors. In some projects, the Technical Team Lead is also called the System Architect.

R/3 System administrator The R/3 System administrator is in charge of the application layer. (See Chapter 2, "Technology in R/3," for more detailed information on all layers of the R/3 System.) The R/3 System administrator configures the R/3 instances, monitors daily system operation, and resolves potential technical problems.

Database administrator The database administrator is in charge of the database layer. He or she configures the Relational Database Management System (RDBMS) and monitors the daily database backups and growth in the database.

Network administrator The network administrator is in charge of the network and the presentation layer. He or she sets up the network and updates the Release for the SAP front-end software.

Operating System administrator The operating system administrator is in charge of the operating-system level of the R/3 System, from the front ends to the database server. He or she installs the operating system, backs up the data on the operating-system level, and administers the hardware.

Authorization administrator The authorization administrator is in charge of user and security administration. He or she creates the security strategy for the company and generates the appropriate authorization profiles in R/3. This role is a subset of the System Administration function. Chapter 6, "User Administration," describes the related tasks in more detail.

Technical consultant The technical consultant provides you with expert knowledge about all aspects of R/3 technology. During the implementation of the R/3 Systems, the technical consultant can help you create a strategy for data backups and practice database recovery in case of error. Depending on the size of the project, the technical consultant is either a full-time member of the team or only works by request.

> **NOTE** SAP recommends integrating consultants from SAP or certified consultants from SAP partner companies into the ASAP implementation project.

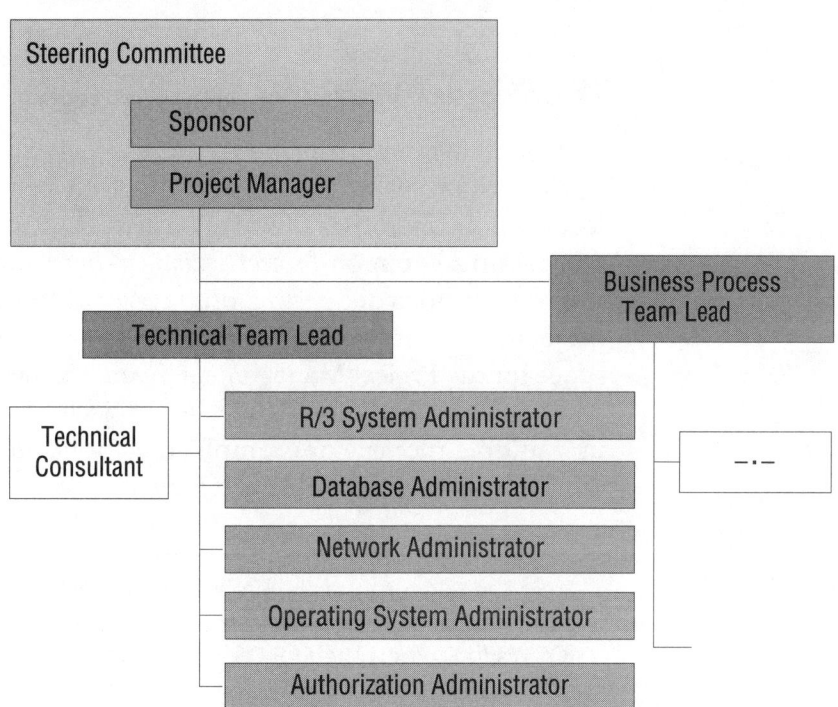

FIGURE 3.1:
Organization chart for the Technical Team

If you have decided to have a service provider perform some of the tasks, only assign the provider roles that are needed less frequently for production operation. For the Technical Team, roles that are needed less frequently are network administrator, operating system administrator, and authorization administrator. However, you should have your own employees occupy the roles of R/3 System administrator and database administrator. These two roles comprise important daily tasks for the operation of R/3, such as monitoring system operation and backing up the data in the database. Ideally, employees in the Technical Team should have at least two years of experience administering R/3 and know the company's existing (legacy) system environment. The number of team members you'll need for each role depends on how complex your R/3 System is from a technical viewpoint (see "Estimate the Number of Team Members Required" later in this chapter).

The Project Working Environment

The team members must be able to contact each other at any point during the project. At the beginning of the project, you should locate all the members of the team close to one another physically and set up a common *Project Team working environment*. There are different options depending on the size of the project. For smaller projects, the ideal project working environment provides sufficient space for the Project Management Team, the Business Process Team, and the Technical Team. For larger projects, you may need to set up multiple rooms. For example, the application consultants and the Technical Team could each have their own room.

NOTE From the beginning of the project, the Project Team must be able to access the SAP online services, such as SAP Online Service System (OSS) and SAPNet. The SAP OSS can be accessed from the R/3 System with transaction code OSS1, and SAPNet is at `http://sapnet.sap.com`. To provide access, you'll need a remote connection with the appropriate security (see Chapter 11, "Network Administration").

Communication and Escalation

For Project Teams within a complex organization, you should define the *communication* and *escalation paths* in great detail at the beginning of the project. For example, to define the communication paths, determine which team members are invited to which meetings, who is informed about which decisions, and who deals with external suppliers and service providers. During the implementation project, the Technical Team must ensure the availability of the development system and the quality assurance system.

If serious errors occur, the escalation paths help you quickly notify the person responsible and immediately correct the problem. For the escalation paths, define who has to notify whom in which problem situations and which external specialists or service providers can help in which situations.

Estimate the Number of Team Members Required

The number of team members required for the Technical Team depends on the complexity of the project. For very complex projects, most roles are full-time positions for the entire length of the project. However, for less complex projects, some roles are part-time positions or are only required during special project phases. To estimate your requirements, you must first determine the complexity of your project. Table 3.1 lists the categories of complexity for an R/3 implementation.

TABLE 3.1: Categories of Complexity for an R/3 Implementation

Complexity	Modules	Number of Sites	Number of Users	Technical Criteria
Low	FI, CO, SD, MM, PP	Up to 5; only domestic	10–100	Up to 5 standard interfaces; no development work; data transfer (master data, low volume of transaction data); downtime from errors possible
Medium	FI, CO, SD, MM, PP, HR Up to 2 special modules	5–14; up to 4 countries	100–500	More than 5 standard interfaces; some development work; data transfer (master data, transaction data); short downtime from errors possible

Continued on next page

TABLE 3.1: Categories of Complexity for an R/3 Implementation *(Continued)*

Complexity	Modules	Number of Sites	Number of Users	Technical Criteria
High	All	More than 14; more than 4 countries	over 500	Noncertified interfaces; large volume of development work; data transfer (master data and transaction data with large data volumes); no downtime from errors possible

> **NOTE** To keep the calculations simple, some technical aspects have been omitted from Table 3.1. For example, an R/3 implementation becomes more complex the more heterogeneous the hardware platforms and operating systems are. In addition, the complexity and the heterogeneous character of your network also play a role. The aspects that were not included can cause the team member requirements for the implementation project to deviate from the information in Table 3.2.

After you have determined the category of your project, refer to Table 3.2 to determine the approximate number of team members required for the Technical Team. In projects with low or medium complexity, one person takes on multiple roles. The last row of Table 3.2 shows the (approximate) total number of team members required for each level of complexity. If you distribute the roles among the team members, consider the individuals' strengths, experience, and time available for the project.

TABLE 3.2: Team Member Requirements for the Technical Team during the Implementation

| Role | Complexity | | |
	Low	Medium	High
Technical Team Lead	Part-time	Part-time	Full-time
R/3 System administrator	Part-time	Full-time	Full-time
Database administrator	Part-time	Part-time	Full-time

Continued on next page

TABLE 3.2: Team Member Requirements for the Technical Team during the Implementation *(Continued)*

Role	Low	Complexity Medium	High
Network administrator	Part-time	Part-time	Full-time
Operating system administrator	Part-time	Part-time	Full-time
Authorization administrator	Part-time	Part-time	Full-time
Number of team members	Up to 3	3 to 6	Over 6

> **NOTE** Often, not all of the criteria of a category suit your company or you may have more requirements for the project than are listed. To more accurately estimate your team member requirements, you should consult with an SAP Consulting Manager or an SAP partner company.

Train the Project Team

The most successful projects are performed by team members who have specialist R/3 knowledge. If not all team members already have this knowledge, you must train the Project Team in the early stages of the project. The training courses in SAP's International Training Center are designed for the Project Team and address both R/3 applications and R/3 Basis. SAP has an extensive training offering for the entire Project Team. For the Technical Team, the offering is made up of the following:

Management training courses These one- to two-day management training courses teach you about the planning and realization of the technical implementation of R/3. The training courses address decision makers, data processing managers, and Technical Team Leads.

Introductory training courses: (Level 1) These one- to two-day introductory courses provide you with conceptual knowledge about the technology of the R/3 System and an overview of SAP's Service & Support. The courses address the entire Technical Team.

Basis training courses: (Level 2 and Level 3) The three- to five-day Basis training courses teach you details about, for example, administering R/3 and the database. Level 2 courses inform you about the basics. Level 3 courses expand on the basics and have the respective Level 2 courses as a prerequisite. The Basis training courses address the entire Technical Team.

> **TIP**
> You can find the current training schedule and more information either in the OSS (within OSS, use transaction code BNSC and select the appropriate event category) or in SAPNet (http://sapnet.sap.com/training4.0).

Refer to Appendix B to determine which training courses are recommended for each role. Plan to attend the training courses for Management, Level 1, and Level 2 at the beginning of the implementation project. You should schedule Level 3 training courses three to eight weeks after the Level 2 training courses.

Following a course, you can reinforce your knowledge with the SAP media R/3 Basis Knowledge Products and SAP TechNet. The next two sections include a more detailed description of these media and where they are available.

Basis Knowledge Products

R/3 Basis Knowledge Products inform you about all of the topics in the R/3 Basis training courses. They are available on CD-ROM and use various media—for example, videos, HTML documents, and Microsoft Word documents—to present the information. There are Knowledge Products available for most Basis training courses, and every participant of a Basis training course receives a CD. You can find the list of available R/3 Basis Knowledge Products and how to order them in the OSS (within OSS, choose R/3 Note 61675, "Information on the R/3 Basis Knowledge Products") or in SAPNet (at http://sapnet.sap.com/EducationServices, choose R/3 Knowledge Products).

SAP TechNet

SAP TechNet is an online Internet service for SAP customers and partners. You can find TechNet at http://sapnet.sap.com/technet. It informs you about current topics on R/3 technology and about technical aspects of the applications. SAP TechNet is divided into Knowledge Base and Forum. In the Knowledge Base, SAP regularly publishes articles; for example, there are articles about current developments and recommendations from SAP about administering an Oracle database (see Figure 3.2). TechNet covers the following topics:

- Software Logistics
- System Management
- System Monitoring
- Technical SD, CO, PP
- SAP Database Administration
- ABAP Development Workbench

You can join an online discussion with other SAP customers and partners in a forum. The forum discusses issues and questions and considers future developments of training courses and Knowledge Products. The forum is moderated by SAP.

FIGURE 3.2:
SAP TechNet for customers and partners

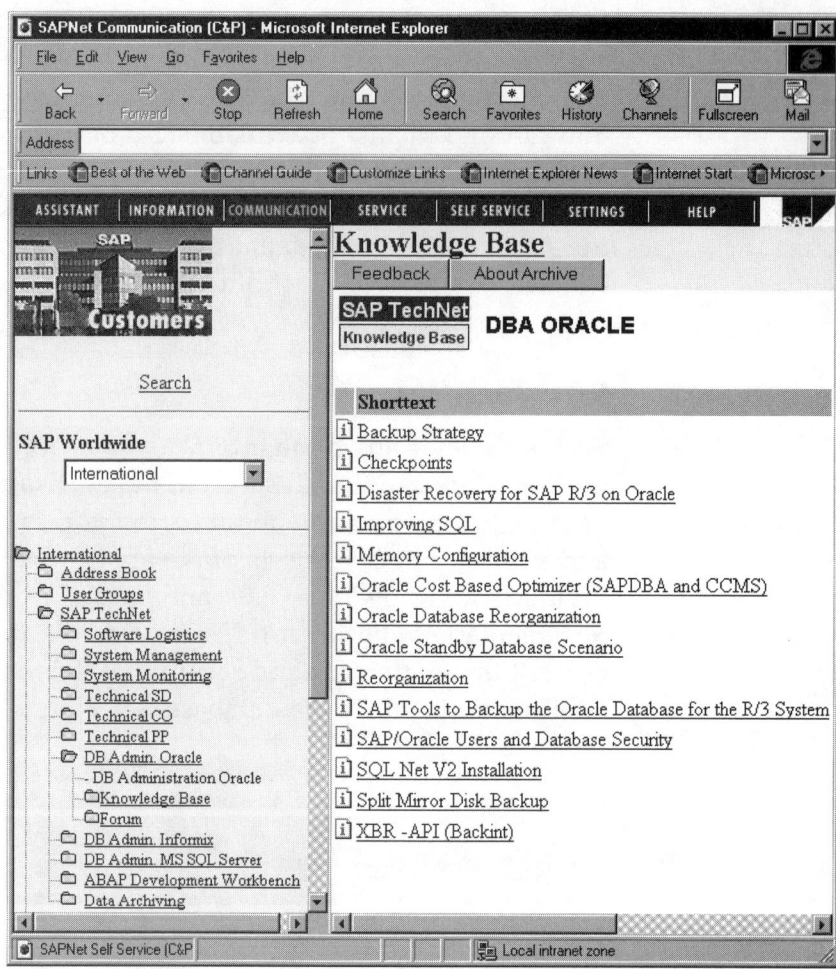

Determine the Procedures

At the beginning of your project, you should define the basic processes and procedures that will be required to complete the project. For example, you need to decide whether you want to implement the modules of the R/3 System step-by-step or whether you'll start production with all modules at the same time. These processes and procedures will help you avoid unnecessary work and help you create a consistent schedule for the tasks. The following sections explain how to:

- Define the implementation strategy
- Define the implementation standards
- Plan the Cut Over and the help desk
- Define the strategy for service and support

Define the Implementation Strategy

You should define the implementation strategy during your project preparation. Your strategy must be in harmony with your company's long-term R/3 goals. During the technical implementation, consider the benefits of R/3 technology over the software technology you are currently using. This helps you define and realize your most important goals. For example, R/3's open client/server architecture allows you to choose your hardware from different leading hardware vendors. You can choose computers ranging from slower computers to the fastest computers available, depending on how critical the system's speed is for your company. You should work together with your hardware partner to size your hardware. Chapter 5, "R/3 Instance Administration," describes this task in detail.

NOTE The goals for the implementation of R/3 must be clearly defined and verifiable. When you define the goals, you are laying the foundation for the project plan, which defines the tasks, time, resources, and budget (see "Prepare the Project Plan" later in this chapter).

Two points are essential to the Technical Team for the implementation strategy. First, you must define at an early stage whether you want to implement all of the planned R/3 modules at the same time or gradually with a step-by-step implementation. This influences the way you should size the hardware. Second, you must determine the course of the implementation, known as the *roll out*, in the departments or subsidiaries. This influences when you will configure the network and the front ends.

Step-by-Step Implementation

With a *step-by-step implementation*, R/3 modules or SAP business components are implemented consecutively rather than simultaneously. The advantage is that you can continually change your system landscape and distribute the acquisition costs over a longer time period. The Project Teams for the implementation are smaller and therefore easier to coordinate. If you decide on a step-by-step implementation, you must plan the initial hardware, from a technical viewpoint, in a way that the hardware can grow with the step-by-step implementation of additional modules (see Figure 3.3). You should have your hardware partner confirm, or perhaps even guarantee, the ability to expand to the planned final size of the system.

> **NOTE** The size of the system is always defined in advance for an R/3 Release. If the Release is updated during the step-by-step implementation of R/3, you must modify the system size to the demands of the new Release.

During the step-by-step implementation, legacy systems are run in parallel. Often, the business processes run on all of the systems so they can exchange data with each other. For this reason, you'll normally have different interfaces for every step of the step-by-step model. You should determine which system controls the interface, how much data is transferred, how communication is restored if an error occurs, and how the strategies for data backup in the systems have to be harmonized. Chapter 13, "Interfaces," describes what you need to consider.

FIGURE 3.3:

Hardware growth for the step-by-step model

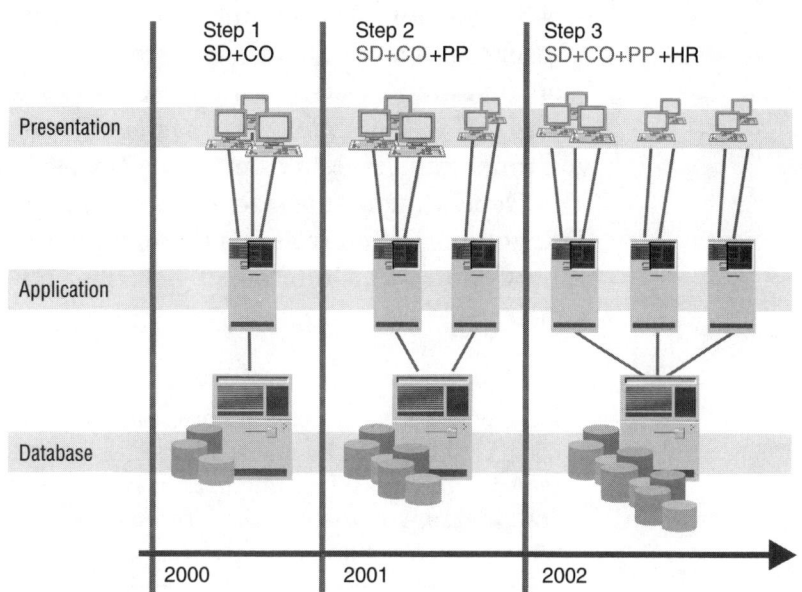

The Roll Out Strategy

In the *roll out strategy*, you should define the implementation procedure for the individual departments or organizations within the company. At the same time, you must consider possible geographical limitations. For example, in medium- to large-sized companies, you must often include subsidiaries or plants in the front-end network. The following questions are essential for the roll out strategy: In which order is R/3 released for the users? After the start of production, should all users immediately be able to work with R/3 or will R/3 be implemented on a step-by-step basis?

From a technical viewpoint, the deciding factor is whether you have the resources to make the front ends available to all users simultaneously. In larger companies in particular, you must ensure a simultaneous release for several hundred users, and you must ensure that you have trained all the users and that a help desk is available. The advantage of a simultaneous release is that all users can enter data in one system. If you release R/3 for the users on a step-by-step basis, some users enter data in R/3 while others still work in the legacy system. During the entire roll out, you must transfer data from the legacy system into the R/3 System. Depending on the size of the company, this can mean a high data volume each day and is therefore not feasible in a large company. Chapter 13, "Interfaces," describes how to realize a data transfer.

> **NOTE** If multiple R/3 projects are running within a company, dependencies could exist between them. Each respective Project Manager must consider the possible effects the roll out can have on the other projects. For example, you should have a companywide standard for the data formats to ensure that the interfaces can be determined accordingly.

Define the Implementation Standards

During the Project Preparation phase, you should define standards and procedures for the implementation. All team members must understand the basic procedures and follow them. For the Technical Team, the following questions are essential:

- Who is allowed to change the technical system configuration and when?

- How are R/3 extensions and modifications approved, released, and documented?

System Configuration

To configure an R/3 System, you have two options. First, you can use system parameters to adjust R/3 to your hardware resources (for example, you can adjust the number of work processes in an instance, or you can adjust the size of the buffer). The values of the system parameters in R/3 are set and changed in profiles. Second, you can change the configuration of R/3 through the operation modes. This way, you can switch R/3 from day operation to night operation with a higher requirement for background processing (see Chapter 5, "R/3 Instance Administration").

A change to the system configuration affects all users. You must therefore define who is authorized to change the system parameters or the operation modes and when. You should document each change in a system operation manual. This gives you the ability to restore the previous configuration if an error occurs. In the system operation manual, you must also define who approves changes to the configuration, who configures the system, who must be informed of the changes, and which naming conventions exist.

Modification

Depending on your requirements, you can modify programs in the standard R/3 software. These modifications are specific to each respective R/3 Release. If you upgrade your R/3 System Release, you must adjust your modifications. To do so, you must know exactly why the program was modified, whether the standard must be modified again in the new R/3 Release, and who is responsible for modifying the program.

> **TIP** SAP recommends using the standard R/3 software without modification where possible. If you must modify the standard, keep the number of changes as low as possible.

If modifications are necessary, you must define a procedure to approve the changes, to check the quality, and to release the changes for production operations. It is essential for Release updates that the changes are documented. During the implementation, you'll frequently have external consultants perform the changes. Generally, the consultants are no longer in the company at the time of a Release update. Therefore, you only have the documentation with which to decide whether you must modify the standard again or not.

Plan the Cut Over and the Help Desk

The period of time between the deactivation of the legacy system and the start of production of the R/3 System should be as short as possible. Despite time constraints, the R/3 System should have unlimited availability after the start of production. In addition, users should be helped quickly if they have problems or questions about using R/3. You can only fulfill these typical management expectations of the Technical Team if you plan the Cut Over and the help desk at an early stage.

The Cut Over

At the end of the Final Preparation phase, you'll switch from the legacy system to the R/3 System. This period is called the *Cut Over*. At the beginning of the Cut Over, you'll transport the released Customizing settings and Repository objects from the quality assurance system to the production system. Then, you'll transfer the master records and transaction data from the legacy system to the production system. The Cut Over ends when you have signed off the production system and released the start of production (see Figure 3.4).

If you have a detailed plan for the Cut Over, you can switch smoothly from the legacy system to the R/3 System. In a Cut

Over Plan, you should define how to transfer data from the legacy system and how long you'll presumably need to do so. You should document all the tasks needed for the Cut Over and assign each task the necessary resources (for example, who performs the task). The Cut Over Plan should contain a checklist to use as the basis for the approval. You can use the checklist to make sure the necessary preparations for each task have been performed.

FIGURE 3.4:
Flow of the Cut Over before the start of production

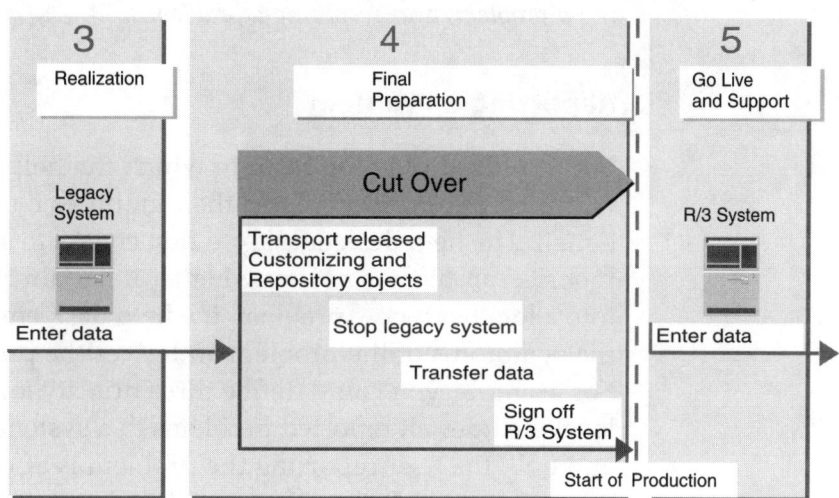

TIP To solve possible problems, schedule a pause of at least one day between the end of the Cut Over and the start of production. Since the Cut Over normally happens on a weekend, you must have a list of people who can help you if problems occur.

The Help Desk

The help desk receives all user inquiries centrally. It supports the users' technical questions and helps solve problems with the front end or with the R/3 System. With a well-organized help desk, you can lower the costs of operating R/3 and improve user acceptance for the new system. You should plan the procedures within the help desk during the Realization phase. Especially in larger companies, the complexity of the setup and procedures in a help desk are often underestimated. The earlier the help desk reflects your company structure, the more effectively it can support the work procedures in individual departments. Essentially, user inquiries go through three steps at the help desk: *reporting a problem, processing a problem,* and *resolving a problem.*

Reporting a Problem

You should define the form in which the help desk receives inquiries. Often, users report their inquiries by telephone or by e-mail. The help desk employee first checks to see whether the reported problem is new or whether it has already been entered into a log. For a new problem, the help desk employee documents the symptoms of the problem and gives the problem a priority. For example, you could define three priority levels. A low-priority level includes all reported problems in a system that is still running and only the user reporting the problem is affected. A medium-priority level includes all reported problems in a system that is still running and multiple users are affected. A high-priority level includes all reported problems in a system that is down or when a large number of users are affected. Plan your infrastructure and resources for reporting in accordance with the number of users.

Processing a Problem

You should define who processes which problem and how to solve a difficult problem. A deciding factor for quick processing of a problem is the different levels in the help desk (see Figure 3.5). Especially in larger companies, there are frequently three levels. In the First Level, problems are received and the less serious problems are immediately solved. In the Second Level, there are specialists for the various system components—for example, specialists for different modules or R/3 technology specialists. The specialists solve most problems that are passed to them from the First Level. In the Third Level, there are experts and technicians. The experts frequently have other important tasks in a company and should therefore only have to solve the most serious problems.

FIGURE 3.5:
Help desk flow

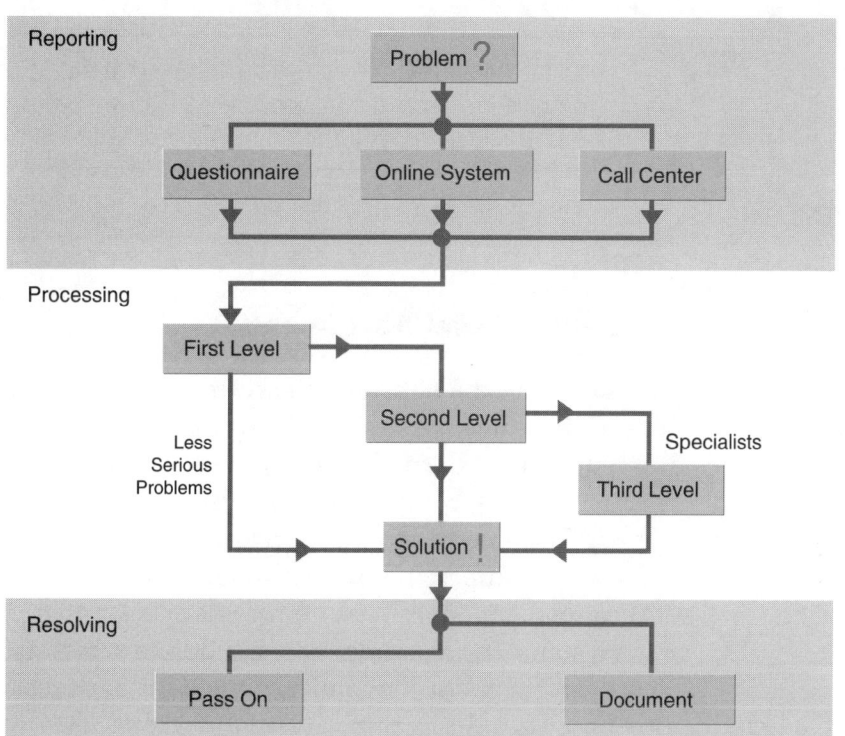

NOTE If the help desk cannot solve a problem, then SAP, the consulting partner, or the hardware partner can help you; you should define the situations in which the Second and Third Levels pass the problem on.

Resolving a Problem

You should define who passes the solution on to the reporting user and who documents the solution. To improve their knowledge, members of the First Level should document the solutions found in the Second Level and pass them on to the reporting users. You should proceed in the same way between the Second and Third Levels.

> **TIP** At the help desk, there is no procedure that works optimally for all situations because the procedures are driven and changed by each event. Therefore, you should plan the organization and procedures of the help desk in a way that you can expand on them and update them, especially in the test phase.

Service Level Agreement

Based on the nature of the future organization of the R/3 help desk, you can define in detail the *Service Level Agreement* internally and externally. This agreement states that the Technical Team is a service vendor in your company. Internally, the Technical Team comes to this agreement with the company management and the affected departments. From a technical viewpoint, the agreement covers your entire network and all layers of your R/3 System. For example, you can define which work areas the help desk covers or how quickly the help desk reacts to an inquiry and processes it in a normal situation. If serious problems occur, you can solve them more quickly if you have defined special escalation procedures in a Service Level Agreement for this type of situation. In the external Service Level Agreement, consider how you can include the services of partners in daily system operation and in solving serious problems (the procedures for solving serious problems are called escalation procedures). The next section explains which services and support are offered by SAP.

Define the Strategy for Service and Support

During the implementation and the production operations of R/3, SAP R/3 Services can help you with certain tasks. SAP has set up a worldwide R/3 Service & Support network that is available around the clock and includes SAP partners. To benefit from this network, you need a remote connection to SAP. R/3 Support is your contact for all questions about R/3 and can support you from the onset of project preparation. In addition to R/3 Support, SAP offers consulting services provided by specialists. The following services are especially useful for the implementation project (see Figure 3.6):

On-Site Consulting If you require consulting directly in your company. SAP specialists come to you and, among other things, help you with your technical design for the R/3 System landscape or with the configuration of the R/3 System.

Remote Consulting If you require consulting on short notice. SAP specialists answer your questions over the telephone or via video conferencing. If necessary, and with your approval, the experts access your system through a remote connection—for example, to perform system settings with you.

GoingLive Check To plan the start of production after the implementation of R/3. SAP experts ensure that you can go into production smoothly.

These services can improve the quality of the implementation project and the production operation of R/3.

FIGURE 3.6:

Integration of R/3 Services in ASAP

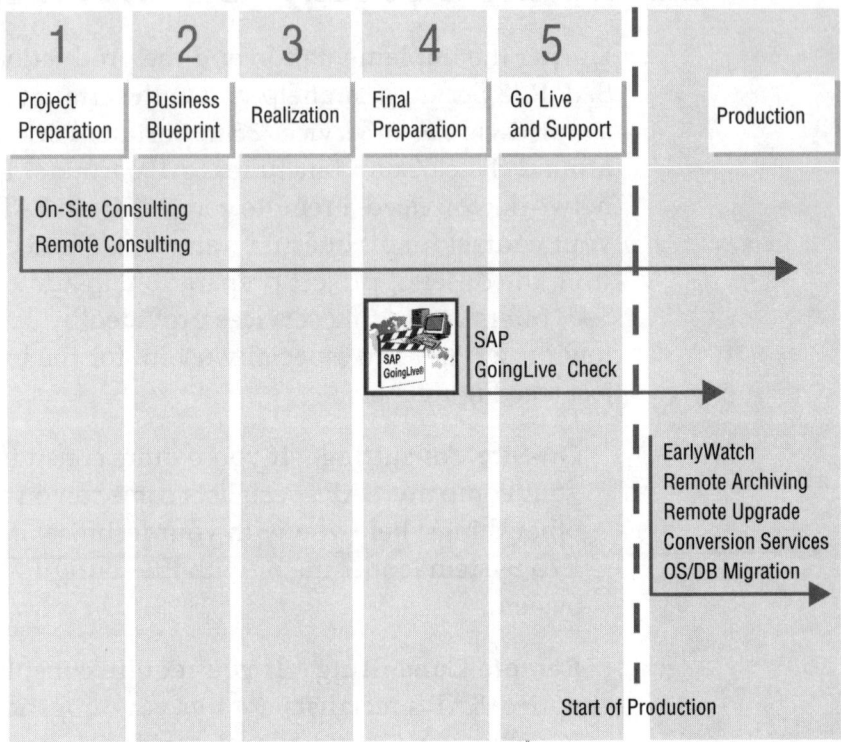

The following services are suitable to ensure smooth productive operation and to take on special maintenance tasks after the start of production (see Figure 3.6):

EarlyWatch   To find potential bottlenecks in the performance of your R/3 System. Before bottlenecks can have serious effects, SAP experts check your system through a remote connection and recommend ways to optimize performance.

Remote Archiving   To archive the R/3 System data. Before the growth of the database leads to performance problems, experts archive the SAP data from your database. See Chapter 10, "Archiving," for more detailed information.

Remote Upgrade   To upgrade the R/3 Release in your system landscape. Normally, SAP experts access your system over a remote connection and upgrade your system's current Release. This allows you to minimize the time and costs associated with running R/3, and you do not need to make any resources available. See Chapter 12, "Software Logistics," for more detailed information.

Conversion Services   To adjust an R/3 System after the start of production to settings that are specific to your business and have been changed. For example, a currency conversion can be performed to adjust the currency to the EURO, which will be the new currency of the European union in 1999.

OS/DB Migration Service   To migrate to another RDBMS or hardware vendor.

> **TIP**
> Because SAP continually improves and expands the R/3 Services, you can find the most current information and how to order the services in SAPNet at `http://sapnet.sap.com/SupportServices` or `http://sapnet.sap.com/ConsultingServices`. Alternatively, you can contact SAP Local Support at the SAP office in your country.

Check the Project Progress

The implementation of R/3 is a time-restricted project. After purchasing R/3, you'll want to start your production operation as quickly as possible. Therefore, you are under great time constraints during an implementation project. You can only meet these expectations with a detailed task plan and a schedule with the appropriate distribution of resources. Throughout the entire project, you must make sure you have accomplished the tasks in the allotted time and that resources aren't missing. In the following sections, you will learn how ASAP supports your project plans.

Normally, R/3 should be implemented quickly and the production system must meet the guidelines of your company's management as much as possible. Throughout the entire project, you must monitor the quality of your results. Often, some components are checked too little or forgotten because of time constraints. In ASAP, you can only advance to the next phase if you have checked the quality and signed off the results of the phase you've just completed.

Prepare the Project Plan

Project planning is an ongoing process that you monitor and, if possible, improve. Good project planning includes a detailed project plan. The methods you'll use to determine and check the progress of the project are defined in the project plan. You should document when all tasks begin and their duration, both planned and actual. Each task should be allocated the necessary resources (for example, the person responsible and the equipment needed). Additionally, you must set up a budget plan, which you can use at the beginning of the project to plan the financing. During the entire project, you can compare your actual costs with the planned costs. This way, you can recognize deviations early on and take decisive action.

During the project preparation, set up the first project plan to steer the project in the desired direction. Preferably, you should define the tasks and the schedule for the first two phases, Project Preparation and Business Blueprint, right at the beginning. For the other three phases, Realization, Final Preparation, and Go Live and Support, set up an approximate plan. Chapter 1, "Introduction to the Technical Implementation of R/3," includes an in-depth discussion of the five phases of the ASAP project plan and their purposes. Before you begin a phase, define its tasks and schedule in detail. Over the entire project, make sure the guidelines are followed. Most projects deviate somewhat from the initial plan, and you must be able to revise the plan and adapt to any changes if necessary.

Project Management Tools

To follow a project plan and to be able to monitor the progress of the project, you should use a *project management tool*, such as MS Project. With these kinds of tools, you can create a task plan with an appropriate schedule. You can define the milestones and customize the dependencies between tasks. For example, you should have set up and tested the data backup in the development system before the application consultants start the Customizing in the system. You can use the project plan in ASAP, which uses MS Project, as a template (see Figure 3.7). The tasks in this plan are identical to the tasks in the Roadmap (see Chapter 1). Additionally, the schedule is already set up in advance with empirical values for the duration of each individual task. Dependencies between tasks are taken into consideration. In accordance with your requirements, you can add new tasks to or remove old tasks from this project plan.

A project plan consists of three subplans:

- The work plan and schedule
- The resource plan
- The budget plan

The Work Plan and Schedule

In the work plan and schedule, define which tasks are to be processed, how long the processing takes, and when you expect to begin and end the project. For the status of each task, you should define more than just when the task begins and ends. Table 3.3 lists four recommended status levels.

FIGURE 3.7:
The ASAP project plan using MS Project

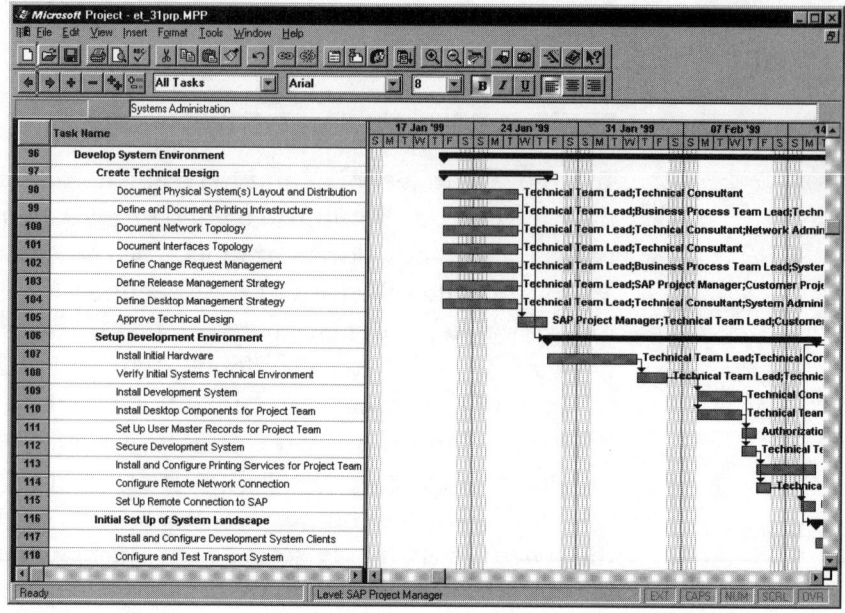

TABLE 3.3: Recommended Status for the Tasks in the Work Plan

Status	Description
Being processed	The task has been started; document the date the task begins.
Completed	The task is completed for the processor only when its results are documented; document the date of completion.
Check	The results of a task are verified; if necessary, errors are corrected.
Quality checked	The results of the task correspond to the quality requirements and are released for use; the task is considered completed in the project plan.

Critical Path Tasks

In the schedule, you must consider the order in which the tasks are performed and the *critical path* tasks. For example, time delays occur if you do not buy the hardware, order the network connections, or plan training courses in time, so these tasks are considered critical path tasks.

The Resource Plan

In the resource plan, define who processes the task and at which point resources are needed. In this plan, you should consider the internal team members and the external consultants. You will require some of the team members to work full-time during the entire project. You'll only need some of the other team members (for example, the technical consultant) for a limited period of time. For each resource, state the tariffs and other costs so you can inform the Project Manager at any time which costs occurred for which tasks.

> **TIP** Do not schedule a 100 percent workload. It is better to plan for an 80 percent workload. Experience has proven that the workload is always underestimated and therefore the schedule can no longer be implemented.

The Budget Plan

In the budget plan, define which combined costs are caused by the implementation project. Essentially, this includes the following:

- Personnel costs for internal team members and external consultants
- Hardware costs; for example, database servers and application servers, PCs, printers, a network addition, and so on
- Software costs
- Training costs, internal and external at SAP or partners

To plan the financing for the implementation of R/3 exactly, calculate all potential expenses into the budget. By comparing the actual incurred costs, you can define how well the budget is administered. This enables you to prevent a potential rise in costs early on.

Complete the Quality Check

Before you advance from one phase to the next, you must check the quality of the completed phase. Only after you have achieved the predetermined goal of one phase should you advance to the tasks of the next phase. Within a phase, a task is only completed when the quality is good. At the end of each phase, the results of the quality check should be presented to the Project Manager. It is important that both the person responsible for the phase and the Project Manager check the results of a phase again because partial results can negatively influence other project areas. The Project Manager then decides whether the quality was achieved. The Project Manager releases the phase and the project can advance to the next phase.

During the implementation project, the Technical Team sets up the entire system landscape and ensures the availability of each individual system in this landscape. Table 3.4 lists the important results for each phase in ASAP, where quality is the deciding factor for releasing the phase.

TABLE 3.4: Important Quality Checks for the Technical Team in ASAP

ASAP Phase	Result
Project Preparation	System landscape strategy complete.
	Sizing of the system landscape determined (standardized SAP front ends, CPU, main memory, hard disk memory for application server and database server).
	Remote connection to SAP established.
	Project administration set up.
	Project Team trained (Management training courses, introductory courses).

Continued on next page

TABLE 3.4: Important Quality Checks for the Technical Team in ASAP *(Continued)*

ASAP Phase	Result
Business Blueprint	Creation of technical design completed. Project Team trained (Basis training). Development system set up. System administration set up.
Realization	Quality assurance system set up. Production system set up. Authorization concept created. Interfaces for data transfer developed. Test plans defined. Service Level Agreement designed. System operation defined and documented in the system operation manual.
Final Preparation	Cut Over plan created (transition from legacy system to the R/3 System). Analysis and Optimization session of GoingLive Check completed. User training completed. System operation of the production system set up. System operation tested. Production support plan created. Help desk set up.
Go Live and Support	Verification session of GoingLive Check completed. Final inspection of the production system takes place.

Project Administration in ASAP

In the previous sections, you learned what factors to consider for project administration during the implementation of R/3. In ASAP, these points are distributed over the individual phases in the project. The following describes when to perform certain tasks.

So that you can follow the status during the entire implementation project, create a detailed project plan at the beginning and update it regularly by holding weekly status meetings. Each Team Lead tells the Project Manager which tasks were completed, which are being processed, and whether problems have occurred. Using this information, the work plan and schedule are updated. The necessary resources and the budget depend on the progress of the project. In the status meeting, the individual Team Leads learn about the progress of the entire implementation and discuss possible problem situations that could influence the scheduled dates for milestones or the start of production. If tasks are delayed, you may allocate additional resources to these tasks so they can be completed. Notify all team members regularly about the project status. As mentioned earlier, before you advance from one phase to the next, the Project Manager must check the quality of the results and release the phase.

Project Preparation

To prepare the project, first define the strategy for the implementation of R/3. Together with your consulting partners, check your strategy and work it out in detail. The goal for the implementation must be described in detail and match the long-term goals of your company. From the company's goals, you can determine whether you'll require the most powerful hardware that is currently available or whether you must expect a high data volume for the database. You should also define in your strategy whether you will implement all the planned R/3 modules simultaneously or step-by-step. You can define the course of the implementation in the departments or subsidiaries of your company in a roll out strategy. If you perform multiple R/3 projects simultaneously, you must schedule possible effects they will have on other projects, especially in the roll out.

In addition, project preparation requires that you determine the project organization structure. Define the organization for the project, determine the roles of the project, and assign the roles to the team members. In a Project Team transition meeting, present the organization structure and the results of project planning. Each team member can contribute to the project in the subsequent discussion. After this meeting, each team member should understand the extent and the goals of the project.

Ensure that the members of the Project Team can work together directly. For example, you could set up one or more project rooms for the whole team so team members can be notified quickly about changes in the project and can solve problem situations together. The Technical Team is responsible for the technical equipment in the project rooms. To ensure that the Project Team can use the R/3 Service & Support network, you must set up a remote connection to SAP.

The team members must prepare for the project by attending the introductory training courses in the first weeks of the project if possible. You should create a training plan in which you determine which team members attend the training courses at the SAP training center or the courses of other training providers. The team members must attend the training courses early on to avoid the possibility of a delay caused by fully booked courses. If you plan training courses at your company's site, include additional resources such as a training room and an R/3 System on which the employees can practice.

Business Blueprint

In the second phase, Business Blueprint, the Project Team attends the Level 1 and Level 2 training courses in the SAP training center or at other providers' locations. After a training course, decide whether the desired knowledge was communicated and evaluate the training course. Based on this evaluation, the Project Manager can decide whether more courses are required. The Project Manager should attend the management training courses earlier than the rest of the team attends their course. Appendix B, "Training Courses for the Technical Team," describes which training courses are recommended for each role of the Technical Team. The team can also deepen and expand their acquired knowledge with R/3 Basis Knowledge Products and SAP TechNet.

Realization

In the third phase, Realization, prepare the production support and the Cut Over. In a Cut Over Plan, define how you will switch from the legacy system to the R/3 System. You must plan this early to ensure that, prior to the Cut Over, all preparations are completed and the team members are available at the scheduled time. The Cut Over Plan is checked by the Project Manager and approved by the company management. The help desk is an essential component of the realization plan because the new R/3 System users will need support once the system goes live. You must plan the help desk infrastructure early—in particular, how to report, process, and resolve problems. At the same time, the Project Team attends Level 3 training courses at the beginning of the Realization phase.

Final Preparation

At the beginning of the fourth phase, Final Preparation, refine the Cut Over Plan and the plan to support production. Based on the temporary plans from the previous phases, update the plans and determine the tasks, the schedule, and the resources in detail. During the final preparation, you must train all users, test the system operation, perform the GoingLive Check, check the business processes in the production system, and completely import the data from the legacy system. The Project Manager, together with the company management, approves the start of production of the R/3 System and releases the Go Live and Support phase. At the end of this phase, the Cut Over takes place and you can release the production operation.

Go Live and Support

During the fifth phase, Go Live and Support, determine your long-term strategies for production support and a possible Release update. For production support, define your plan for long-term support of users' questions and problems and how to ensure good performance of the system. Consider also how to train new employees. At the same time, consider how to plan and implement technical changes to the production system. For the Release update, define the requirements for upgrading a Release. Here, an important goal is to keep production system downtime as low as possible.

Before you finish the implementation project, evaluate the results of the project and confirm the completion of the project in a formal sign-off. To evaluate the success of the project, compare the results with the goals set in the Project Plan at the beginning of the project. You must especially evaluate whether the desired business advantages were achieved. Based on this, you can continue to optimize the business processes over the long term and continue to expand on the business advantages.

Table 3.5 lists the tasks in ASAP that are associated with project administration. Each task is displayed in the phase in which it occurs, and the team member who performs the task is listed.

TABLE 3.5: Phases and Tasks for Project Administration in ASAP

Phase	Phase Name	Task	Role
1	Project Preparation	Review and refine implementation strategy	Project Manager, Business Process Team Lead, Technical Team Lead
		Determine project organization	Project Manager, Business Process Team Lead, Technical Team Lead
		Establish Project Team working environment	Project Manager, Business Process Team Lead, Technical Team Lead
		Prepare project plan	Project Manager

Continued on next page

TABLE 3.5: Phases and Tasks for Project Administration in ASAP *(Continued)*

Phase	Phase Name	Task	Role
1	Project Preparation	Create Project Team training plan	Project Manager, Business Process Team Lead, Technical Team Lead
		Define system problems and error handling process	Project Manager, Business Process Team Lead, Technical Team Lead
		Conduct quality check	Project Manager
2	Business Blueprint	Agree on the project status	Members of the Steering Committee, Project Manager, Technical Team Lead
		Conduct Project Team training	Project Manager, Business Process Team Lead, Technical Team Lead
		Conduct quality check	Project Manager
3	Realization	Agree on the project status	Project Manager, Business Process Team Lead, Technical Team Lead
		Perform initial planning for production support and Cut Over	Project Manager, Business Process Team Lead, Technical Team Lead
		Conduct Project Team training	Project Manager, Business Process Team Lead, Technical Team Lead
		Conduct quality check	Project Manager
4	Final Preparation	Agree on the project status	Project Manager, Business Process Team Lead, Technical Team Lead
		Plan the Cut Over and support in detail	Project Manager, Business Process Team Lead, Technical Team Lead
		Conduct quality check	Project Manager
5	Go Live and Support	Verify long-term plans	Project Manager, Business Process Team Lead, Technical Team Lead
		Review the project	Project Manager, Business Process Team Lead, Technical Team Lead

Success Factors

To successfully implement the project administration, you must give particular consideration to the following aspects:

- Prepare the Project Team
- Control the scope of the project

The following sections describe these aspects in more detail.

Prepare the Project Team

The experiences and leadership quality of the Project Manager are often deciding factors in the success of a project. The following are requirements for effective decision making:

- The right team members are involved.
- The team members are informed.
- The processes for making decisions and solving problems are defined.

The Project Teams meet regularly. In status meetings, the individual Project Managers discuss possible problem situations. You must ensure that decisions are made and the employees in the Team are notified if a problem occurs. Usually, status meetings take place once a week. Only when problems occur or you must change the scope of the project should you hold status meetings more frequently.

Control the Scope of the Project

Good project planning means that you determine the tasks in as much detail as possible at the beginning of the project, which enables you to define the scope of the project. During the project, you should control the scope of the project as much as possible. The further your project progresses, the less the scope of your project can change.

To prevent a delay in the project and greater expense through unnecessary changes to the scope, you can define an approval procedure. Each change must be formally applied for, and you must explain why each change is necessary. Afterward, you should estimate how the changes influence the schedule and the budget plan. After the Project Manager has considered the costs and benefits, he or she approves the changes or rejects them.

Review Questions

1. Which roles must be occupied in a Technical Team?

    A. Operating system administrator

    B. Technical Team Lead

    C. Training Manager

    D. Network administrator

    E. R/3 System administrator

    F. Database administrator

    G. Authorization administrator

2. Which consulting service helps you find potential performance bottlenecks in your R/3 System?

    A. Remote Archiving

    B. EarlyWatch

    C. Remote Upgrade

    D. Conversion Service

3. When do you begin planning the Cut Over?

    A. During the Project Preparation phase

    B. At the end of the Business Blueprint phase

    C. During the Realization phase

CHAPTER FOUR

Front-End Administration

Users work with the R/3 applications through the SAP Graphical User Interface (SAPGUI) or Session Manager (which also has a graphical user interface). For a user's PC to become an R/3 front end, the PC must be able to access SAP front-end software locally or through a network. The PC must also be connected to the R/3 application layer through the network. Using the TCP/IP protocol, R/3 transports the data between the front end and the application.

Front ends make up a substantial part of the total costs of the system because, even in smaller R/3 Systems, there are more front ends than application servers and database servers. Experience shows that you can save money with simple strategies for purchasing and maintaining front ends. The costs increase if you want to ensure high front-end availability. To include these two aspects in front-end administration, this chapter shows you how to perform the following tasks:

- Define the front-end strategy
- Install the front-end software
- Plan front-end maintenance

Define the Front-End Strategy

The total cost of front ends is only a small part of the cost of hardware and software. The larger part of the cost is incurred by maintenance and monitoring. To lower the cost, you must define a front-end strategy at the beginning of the implementation project. In this strategy, you should take technical requirements and user needs into consideration.

The following sections explain the essential aspects that make up an efficient standardization strategy. First, uniformly configure your front-end hardware; second, standardize the front-end software;

and third, include commercially available office applications—*office applications* refers to applications typically used in office environments (word processing, spreadsheet, and database applications).

Standardize Your Hardware

There are several efficiency concepts for standardizing hardware: homogeneity, grouping resources into pools, and standardization of configurations.

Homogeneity

To administer front ends with as little work as possible, and therefore cost-effectively, in ideal circumstances you would use hardware of the same type for the entire installation. This way, you and your hardware partner can define a standard PC. It is easier to administer 200 identical computers than it is to administer 200 computers of various types in various configurations and requiring varying support. In a network of identical computers, you can also be sure that, if a selected hardware or software configuration will work for one computer in the network, it will work for every computer. At the same time, you can solve hardware problems more easily if you can compare a computer that isn't working properly with a computer that is similarly equipped and configured and works without problems.

Having homogeneous hardware is easier to implement for new companies than it is for companies that already exist and have computers of various types. However, often companies replace their old hardware during the implementation of standard software to improve the return on investment. To migrate from heterogeneous to homogeneous hardware, there is an efficiency concept: grouping resources into pools.

Grouping Resources into Pools

It may not be practical to use the same front-end hardware throughout your entire company because it is expensive to upgrade or replace all the front ends at the same time. Often, you already have user PCs in your company that you can use for the R/3 System. For this reason, you should consider grouping the front ends into three or four pools. A pool consists of computers of the same type. If your front ends are grouped into pools, you can upgrade or replace a pool independently from other pools and therefore distribute the cost of upgrading or homogenizing over a longer time period. Experience shows that administering the front ends is simple and cost-effective even with four different types of hardware.

A standard PC must have a certain speed for the R/3 front-end software. Table 4.1 lists the system requirements recommended by SAP for the supported operating systems. You can find current information in the SAP Online Service System (OSS) within R/3 Note 26417, "System request for frontend wk centers/SAPGUI."

TABLE 4.1: Recommended System Requirements for Front Ends (as of October 1998)

Operating System	CPU	Main Memory	Disk Storage	Graphics Card
Windows 3.1/3.11	Pentium 133MHz	32MB	40MB; 140MB (complete)	800×600, 256 colors
Windows 95	Pentium 133MHz	32MB	40MB; 140MB (complete)	800×600, 256 colors
Windows NT 4/3.51	Pentium 133MHz	48MB	40MB; 140MB (complete)	800×600, 256 colors
OS/2	Pentium 133MHz	32MB	50MB	800×600, 256 colors
Apple Macintosh	MC68020, MC68030, MC68040; PowerMac: P601, P603, P604	32MB	40MB	800×600, 256 colors

SAP recommends a graphics card with at least 1024×768 pixels for graphics applications, such as SAP ArchiveLink or the graphics Screen Painter in R/3.

> **NOTE** In addition to these recommendations, consider the recommendations of the operating systems' vendors. If you want to include office applications, also consider the requirements of each program.

Standard Hardware Configuration

In addition to using standardized hardware, you should ensure that the hardware is configured in accordance with a single standard as much as possible. For example, you can use similarly configured network, graphics, and sound cards in every front end. If you have grouped the front ends in pools, set them up identically within each pool. Often, you can also configure computers with different hardware to a uniform standard. You can use the same ports on all computers with a network card even if the computers and network cards are from different vendors.

Define standards for the settings that are identical for different types of hardware. After you have configured the hardware for one computer, you'll know how to configure it for all other computers of the same type. This helps you avoid extra work and makes the configuring process less susceptible to errors. At the same time, it makes troubleshooting easier. For example, based on the standard, you'll know the network card settings and can use them constructively to investigate problems quickly.

Standardize Your Software

Ensure that you standardize the front-end software and that it is uniformly configured. By doing so, you can simplify the administration and make troubleshooting easier. It is easier to administer a network when the same SAPGUI release is installed on all your computers and configured as a network than it is to maintain a network in which different releases of SAPGUI are used.

User Groups

Unlike the front-end hardware, the front-end software may not need to be the same for all the users in the company. For example, some users work with R/3 daily and use many different functions, and others only use a few functions even though they too work with R/3 daily. Therefore, you should consider dividing the employees into user groups and configuring the front-end software identically in each group. Table 4.2 lists the user groups that are currently conceivable in R/3.

TABLE 4.2: R/3 User Interfaces for Different User Groups

GUI	User Group	Description
Internet Application	Occasional user	R/3 is used through Web browsers. The Internet applications do not contain all of the R/3 functions and can be used without training.
SAPGUI/SAPLOGON	Regular user (SAP standard menu)	Single-system, single-task work environment. Through the SAPGUI, you can perform all R/3 functions; each user navigates with the SAP standard menu
Session Manager	Regular user (user-specific menu)	Multisystem, multitask work environment. Through the Session Manager, you can perform all R/3 functions. Each user navigates with his or her own menu that only contains the functions for which the user is authorized

Supported Platforms

The front-end software from R/3 Release 4.0 runs on all front-end platforms that are also supported by Release 3.0 and Release 3.1.

As shown in Figure 4.1, SAP is planning to divide the platforms into Windows, Java, and standard browsers with future R/3 Releases. The advantage of this solution is that all platforms are supported.

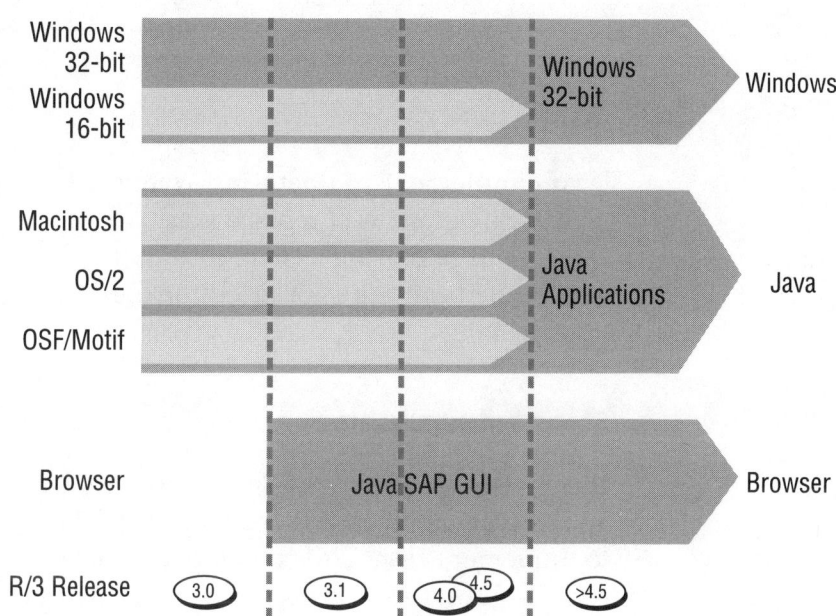

FIGURE 4.1: Supported front ends

Windows

R/3 Release 4.0 continues to support 16-bit Windows platforms. However, it also includes new technology that SAP has developed for the user interface, and the new technology is often only available for the 32-bit platform. For example, on a 32-bit Windows platform, you can use the new SAPscript Editor. Therefore, you should take into consideration the new features for 32-bit Windows when you are choosing your front ends. As displayed in Figure 4.1, after Release 4.5, R/3 will not continue to support 16-bit platforms.

> **NOTE** To use the Windows options on other operating systems as well, some customers use Windows emulations or MultiUserNT systems. Currently, there are no special versions of SAPGUI supported or planned for these products. For this reason, SAPGUI's functions may be limited on Windows emulations or MultiUserNT systems, depending on which products are implemented.

Java

If you implement an operating system other than Windows, pure Java applications will replace your Apple Macintosh, OS/2, or OSF/Motif operating system in the future. Table 4.3 displays which functions are supported for these operating systems with Release 4.0.

Standard Browsers

As of Release 3.1, R/3 has a Java SAPGUI. Here, SAPGUI is a Java applet that can be displayed by a Web browser. This enables you to implement front ends on all platforms that support the Java-enabled browser—for example, NetPCs or network computers (NCs). However, with a Java SAPGUI, you can only use the R/3 functions for which you do not require other applications (such as office applications) on the front end.

Table 4.3 displays all of the operating systems for front ends that are supported by R/3 Release 4.0. You can find the current information in OSS within R/3 Note 66971, "Supported frontend platforms Release 4.0/4.5."

TABLE 4.3: Supported Operating Systems for Front Ends (as of October 1998)

Operating System	Available	Remarks
Windows 3.*x*, Windows NT 3.51	As of 4.0B	Release 4.0B of SAPGUI for Windows 3.*x* or NT 3.51 can be used for R/3 Release 4.0A and supports all functions for Release 3.1 of SAPGUI. SAP recommends that you migrate to Windows 95 or Windows NT 4.
Windows 95, Windows NT 4	As of 4.0A	Full support.
Apple Macintosh	As of 4.0A	Release 4.0A of SAPGUI for Apple Macintosh supports all functions for Release 3.1 of SAPGUI.
OS/2	As of 4.0B	Release 4.0B of SAPGUI for OS/2 can be used for R/3 Release 4.0A and supports all functions for Release 3.1 of SAPGUI.
OSF/Motif	As of 4.0A	Release 4.0A of SAPGUI for OSF/Motif is available on the supported hardware platforms for UNIX by R/3 and supports all functions for Release 3.1 of SAPGUI.
Java	As of 4.0A	Support depending on Java environment implemented.

NOTE You should only implement network products that are supported by SAP. The document *SAP System Requirements for Networks, Frontends and Communication Interfaces*, provided in every R/3 delivery package, displays which products you can currently use with which release. This document tells you, among other things, which TCP/IP products you can use to connect to the R/3 System. You can receive this document in advance through SAPNet at `http://sapnet.sap.com` or through the sales department at SAP.

Include Office Applications

In addition to SAPGUI, R/3 users normally use multiple office applications, such as word processing, spreadsheet, and database applications. Many employees have a good command of their office applications and have tailored the applications to their needs. To benefit from this knowledge and the many office application functions in R/3, you should include the applications in the R/3 front end. For example, you could process letters and faxes to your customers or employees with the word processing program, and the data can be held in the R/3 database.

Object Linking and Embedding (OLE)

As of R/3 Release 4.0, you can include OLE-enabled applications (such as Microsoft Office, Lotus SmartSuite, CorelOffice, StarOffice, and Visio) in R/3 through Advanced Business Application Programming (ABAP) objects. You can start the functions of the office applications from R/3 or react to the results of the office application in R/3. For example, you can open, save, or print documents within office applications from R/3, where the office application can be a part of SAPGUI (see Figure 4.2). The documents are administered through the R/3 memory and OLE. For this technology, you'll require more main memory than was necessary prior to R/3 Release 4.0. An advantage that countermands the memory demand is that you decrease the runtimes with this technology. In the previous procedure, data was downloaded to the local front-end file system, which could lead to bottlenecks.

Requirements

To connect an office application to the R/3 System through ABAP objects, you'll need the following:

- R/3 Release 4.0 and SAPGUI 4.0

- Microsoft Windows 95 or Windows NT 4
- An office application with an OLE2 interface

The section "BC Office Integration" in the R/3 online documentation describes how to connect an office application to the R/3 System.

FIGURE 4.2:

An example of a spreadsheet in R/3

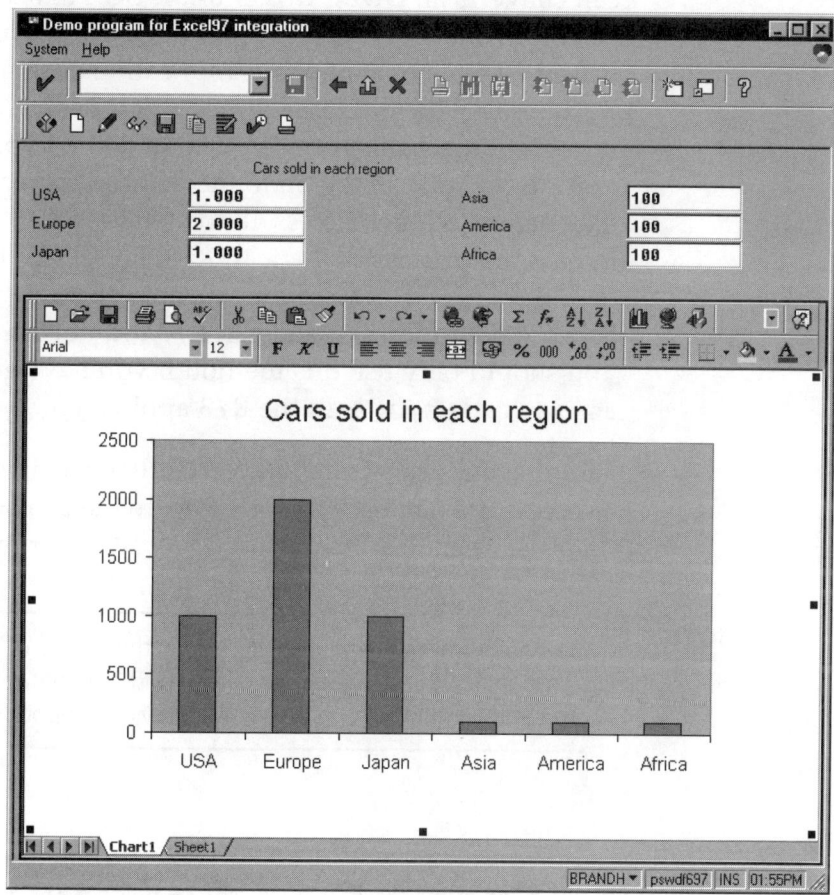

Open Database Connectivity (ODBC)

To access the R/3 data in the database from within an office application, you can use either the Structured Query Language (SQL) interface from your vendor or the Open Database Connectivity (ODBC) interface. ODBC is an SQL dialect from Microsoft and is supported in the R/3 environment by the majority of Relational Database Management System (RDBMS) vendors. The ODBC call converts an ODBC driver to the SQL dialect of the database. To use ODBC, you must install the ODBC driver. You must also use an ODBC-enabled office application such as Microsoft Access. By accessing the database directly, however, you'll bypass two important mechanisms in R/3. First, you'll bypass the authorization check. You can log on to the database directly with a database user name and then access all the tables in R/3. Second, you'll bypass the processing logic in R/3. For example, you can enter data through ODBC and thus destroy the integrity of the database because the processing logic in R/3 did not check the entered data. You should only use this method if you have good reason to not access the data through the R/3 application.

To prevent users from inadvertently or deliberately using ODBC to access the database directly, secure the password of the relevant database user. See Chapter 14, "Security," for more on this subject.

> **NOTE** SAP recommends read-only access to the tables of the R/3 database through ODBC. If you have destroyed the database with a write access through ODBC, SAP cannot provide support.

Install the Front-End Software

Because the SAP software must be installed on a large number of front ends for an R/3 production system, you must find the easiest installation and update procedure for your requirements. SAP delivers the front-end software for R/3 on a CD, and you can install the software on each front end directly from the CD. However, this procedure is too time-consuming for more than 10 front ends. The installation and future maintenance is easier if you perform these tasks from a file server through a network.

To install the software, there are two alternatives. First, you can install the software locally on each front end by distributing it from a central file server in the network. Each time a user calls the front-end software, the front end loads it from its local disk into its main memory. Second, you can install the front-end software only on the file server. Each time a user calls the front-end software, the front end loads it from the file server through the network and into its main memory. In the following sections, you learn about the advantages and disadvantages of both procedures. The subsequent sections explain how to distribute the front-end software in a WAN and how to make the R/3 online documentation available for users.

Install the Software Locally

To install the R/3 front-end software locally on every front end in a LAN, each front end must be able to access the installation package. Either the front ends access the installation package on the CD directly from a common CD-ROM drive, or you can copy the installation package to a common drive. As displayed in step 1 in Figure 4.3, you call the installation program from each front end to install the software locally. During the installation, you can decide whether you want to install the software completely or install only selected components for each front end.

Disadvantages

One disadvantage of this procedure is that you need additional disk space for every front end. A full installation requires about 140MB. Also, the software must be installed on every front end.

Normally, you should not leave the installation process to the users. Instead, you should have experienced and trained employees perform the installation. Only then can you ensure that the software is installed in accordance with your defined strategy.

FIGURE 4.3:

Installing front-end software locally

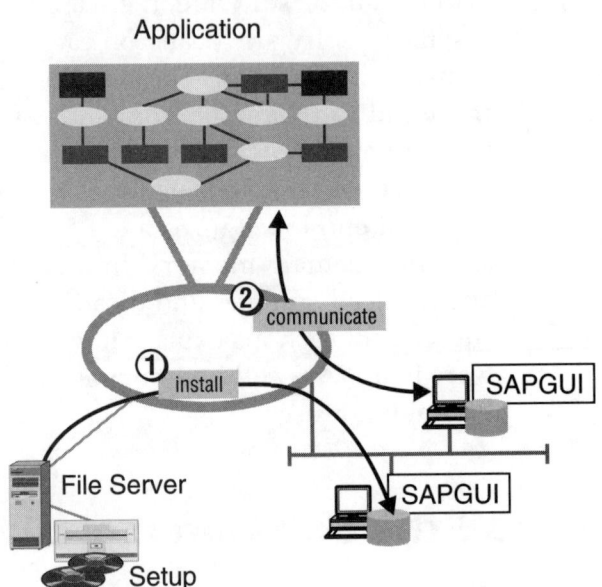

Advantages

With a local installation, the front-end software is available on every PC. This ensures that the availability of R/3 does not depend on the availability of the file server. Also, you'll have an additional load on the network only during installation because the software is only loaded once from the file server. As displayed in step 2 in Figure 4.3, you only need to set up your network for the data stream between the front end and application server. Chapter 11, "Network Administration," explains how to set up your network.

Store the Software on a File Server

To install the R/3 front-end software locally on a file server in a LAN, every front end must be able to access the software at any time. For example, if a user starts SAPGUI on a front end, the front end accesses the file server in the network and loads the SAPGUI software into its main memory. As step 1 in Figure 4.4 shows, you can access the installation package from the file server. You can install all the software or only selected components. To ensure that the users can access the software from their front ends, you must set up a program group on each front end. You must also set up configuration files (for example, FRONT.INI or SAPLOGON.INI). The configuration files allow you to customize your front-end software. See *SAP R/3 System Administration: The Official SAP Guide*, by Liane Will (Sybex, 1998).

FIGURE 4.4:
Installing front-end software on a file server

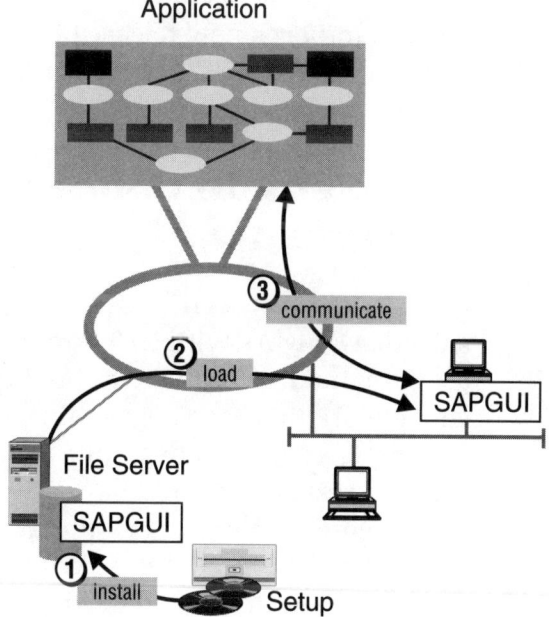

Disadvantages

One disadvantage of this procedure is that the load on the network is increased. As step 2 in Figure 4.4 shows, each user must load the software through the network. This is especially not advisable for WAN connections. Also, users cannot work with the R/3 System if the file server fails. To ensure that R/3 is always available, you must also ensure that the file server is always available with, for example, an alternative computer. This means additional costs and increased administration.

Advantages

There are two advantages to installing the software on a file server. First, you only have to install the software once, centrally, on one computer. This saves the time you would have spent installing the software on each front end. Second, you can control the release and the components of the software centrally, which ensures that you can import a new release of the software without having to import it to every PC in your company.

Consider Remote Connection to Subnetworks

Often, users such as field service employees or employees in the subsidiaries work with R/3 through a WAN connection. If you are going to distribute the front-end software in a WAN, each subnetwork that is connected through the WAN should consist of a separate administrative unit. To simplify the administration of subnetworks, you should have at least one file server in every subnetwork. You can install the front-end software according to one of the two procedures described earlier. That is, you can install it locally on each front end from the file server, or the front ends can load the software directly into the main memory from the local file server through the network.

However, to ensure that all the connected subnetworks have the same software release, central administration is advisable. For central administration, you must set up a file server in the main network so the file server will control all other file servers in the subnetworks. From the file server in the main network, you can ensure that the most current software release is always available. Then, you can distribute the current release to the file servers in the subnetworks and from these file servers to the front ends (see Figure 4.5).

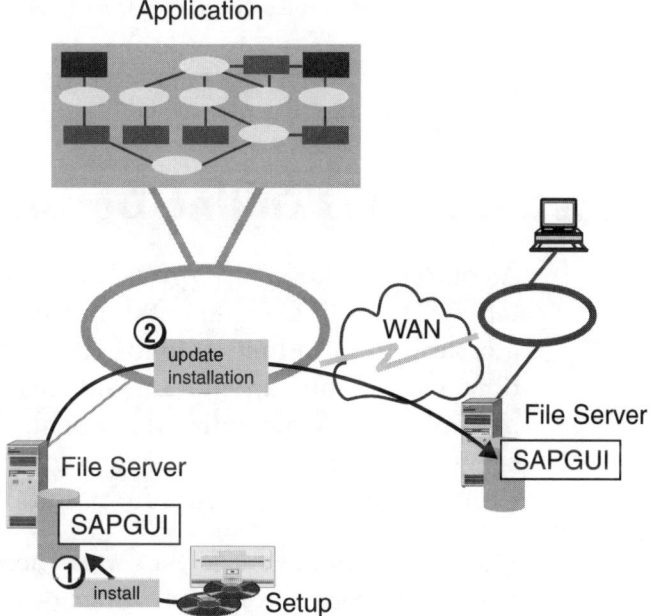

FIGURE 4.5:

Installing front-end software through remote connections

Often, field service employees work with R/3 on their laptops through slow WAN connections, such as telephone lines. If you want to import a new front-end software release to these laptops, you must often transfer between 10 and 40MB. Table 4.4 lists the most common procedures for installing SAP front-end software through remote connections.

TABLE 4.4: Procedures for Installing SAP Front-End Software through Remote Connections

Procedure	Remarks
WAN link	Software is loaded from the file server through a remote connection. The complete installation package is loaded from the file server by using FTP. Then the software is installed locally. A WAN link is only advisable if the connections can transfer data with at least 19.2KBps.
Local installation	Front ends have CD-ROM drives. The software is installed locally from the CD. A local installation is only advisable if you can quickly provide each employee with the CD.
Temporary LAN link	The front end is temporarily connected to a subnetwork if an employee works in the subsidiary. A temporary LAN link is the quickest and easiest method.

Install the R/3 Online Documentation

As of Release 4.0A, SAP provides HTML-based online documentation. The online documentation includes the R/3 Library, the glossary, an introduction to the R/3 System, the Release information, and the Implementation Guide (IMG). Figure 4.6 shows an example of how the online documentation is displayed in a Web browser. You can use this technology to display the online documentation on all supported front-end platforms.

To ensure that every R/3 user can access the R/3 online documentation from a front end, you should store the HTML files of the online documentation either on a Web server or on a file server in the front-end network. To ensure even R/3 users in complex front-end networks with subnetworks can reach the online documentation, each subnetwork should have at least one Web browser or file server from which you can make the HTML files available.

FIGURE 4.6:
Online documentation with an excerpt from BC Office Integration

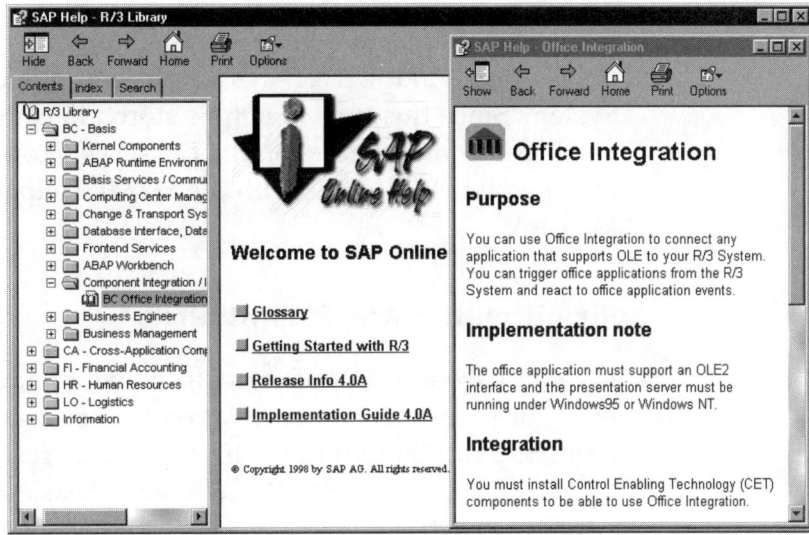

Types of Help

You can choose between three types of help: PlainHtmlHttp, PlainHtmlFile, and HtmlHelpFile. Table 4.5 displays the different file formats and types of access for the three types of help.

TABLE 4.5: Types of Help in the R/3 Online Documentation

Type of Help	File Format	Access	Platforms	Required Disk Space
PlainHtmlHttp	Standard HTML	Web server	All	About 600MB for each language version (for Windows NTFS)
PlainHtmlFile	Standard HTML	File server	All	About 600MB for each language version (for Windows NTFS)
HtmlHelpFile	Compressed HTML (HTML Help)	File server	Windows 95, Windows NT 4	About 700MB for German and English together

HtmlHelpFile

SAP recommends that you use HtmlHelpFile if you only use Windows 95 or Windows NT 4 as a front-end platform for your R/3 System. Since this type of help is stored in compressed form, you need less memory space on the file server. You can display the compressed HTML files with the HTML Help application from Microsoft.

PlainHtmlHttp and PlainHtmlFile

If you use front-end platforms other than Windows 95 or Windows NT 4 for your R/3 System, SAP recommends using either PlainHtmlHttp or PlainHtmlFile. If you already have or want to set up a Web server, PlainHtmlHttp will be the easiest to use. If you do not have a Web server or you don't want to set one up, you can use a file server as an alternative and make the PlainHtmlFile available on it.

Depending on the platform, the Web browser must meet specific requirements or limits. Table 4.6 lists the browsers you can use on each operating system platform.

TABLE 4.6: Web Browsers for Online Documentation (as of Release 4.0B)

	MS Internet Explorer 3.02, HTML Help 1.1	MS Internet Explorer 3.02 (or higher)	MS Internet Explorer 3.03 (16-bit)	Netscape Navigator 3 (or higher)
Windows 3.x	No	No	Yes	No
Windows NT 3.51	No	No	Yes	Yes
Windows 95, Windows NT 4	Yes	Yes	No	Yes
Apple Macintosh	No	Yes (3.01)	No	Yes

Continued on next page

TABLE 4.6: Web Browsers for Online Documentation (as of Release 4.0B) *(Continued)*

	MS Internet Explorer 3.02, HTML Help 1.1	MS Internet Explorer 3.02 (or higher)	MS Internet Explorer 3.03 (16-bit)	Netscape Navigator 3 (or higher)
OS/2	No	No	No	Yes (2.02)
OSF/Motif	No	No	No	Yes

> **TIP** The guide called *Online Documentation Installation* describes how to install the online documentation. This guide is contained in the installation package. If problems occur, you can find an overview of the possible causes in OSS within R/3 Note 101481, "Collective Note: Extended Help and R/3 Library."

Plan Front-End Maintenance

Normally, the software installation is controlled from the front end. In large companies with many front ends, front-end maintenance is difficult if new software or new software versions can only be installed directly on each front end. To reduce costs, ensure that the front ends can be maintained through the network. To maintain front ends through the network, you need a special system management tool—for example, Microsoft's System Management Server (SMS).

System Management Server (SMS)

As of R/3 Release 3.0, the R/3 front-end software installation program has an interface for SMS. You can use the SMS interface to distribute the software over the network in SMS packages. An administrator can decide which front-end software components to install for the individual user groups and bundle the appropriate SMS packages. The administrator also determines when a new release should be installed. There are two options. First, the software is installed completely without dialog at a fixed time. Second, the user is notified that a new release of the software is available, and the user can decide when to install the new software.

You can use this system management tool to administer your front ends centrally and thus reduce the amount of time it takes. These tools also enable you to implement and control the standards for software centrally. This way, you can configure the software on the front ends identically and avoid problems that occur because of, for example, different software releases or incorrectly installed versions. To administer front ends centrally, even in complex networks, you should consider each subnetwork as a separate administration unit. As described earlier in this chapter, each subnetwork should have at least one file server. The file server in the main network controls all of the file servers in the subnetworks.

NOTE When you maintain the front-end software, you must ensure that the latest release of SAP front-end software is compatible with all of the older R/3 Releases, not vice versa. Therefore, SAP recommends that you use only one R/3 front-end software release for all front ends. The R/3 front-end software release must be at least as new as the latest R/3 Release in the system landscape.

Front-End Administration in ASAP

In ASAP, front-end administration is distributed over the separate phases of the project. The following sections explain which tasks in ASAP are planned for front-end administration and in which phase.

Project Preparation

During the first phase, Project Preparation, you should describe the technical requirements for the entire R/3 System and the front ends. You can use the results from the kickoff meeting and the suggestions from your hardware vendor for the most cost-effective hardware. You should also consider the suggestions from your technical service provider (for instance, a network service provider) if you have one. Since you are now defining your front-end strategy for the next few years, ASAP recommends that you check your decisions thoroughly. Ensure that the front ends can meet the current requirements and, as far as possible, the future requirements of the R/3 front-end software.

Business Blueprint

In the second phase, Business Blueprint, you should define your strategy for front-end maintenance. The more front ends you use, the more thoroughly you must plan the procedure. For the time period of the implementation project, create a schedule that details when the existing front ends must be adapted to the R/3 standard. You must determine how to upgrade the R/3 front-end software when you upgrade the R/3 Release, particularly after the implementation project is complete. You must also take into consideration the possible remote connections to subsidiaries or field service employees. Ensure that you include all of the existing interfaces on the presentation layer in your strategy.

To ensure that the Project Team can work with the development system, you should install the front-end software during the Business Blueprint phase. If you have a large Project Team, it is worthwhile to set up a help desk for its members. At the same time, you should plan the user training. Before you can start production operation, all users must be trained for their individual tasks. If you upgrade front-end platforms for the users during the implementation of R/3, the users must be trained for the new platforms. SAP recommends that the users have a direct contact person for questions and problems during production operation. You should identify an individual employee in each department as a contact person. They work as a member of the Project Team during the implementation project and help users with questions about performing R/3 transactions after the start of production.

Realization

ASAP recommends that you configure the front-end network for the production system and install the front ends for the users during the Realization phase. This is the best way to prepare for the Final Production phase because your production system setup is almost complete. As soon as you have set up the front ends, make sure they are set up as planned for all users and test the settings of the SAPGUI or the Session Manager. If you want to have an external service provider take over the front-end maintenance, it is preferable that you make sure the service provider fulfills the Service Level Agreement before the Final Preparation phase. This allows you sufficient time to discover and correct any omissions.

Final Preparation

As you prepare for the start of production, you should train the users. Depending on your requirements, you can use an external training course, an internal training course on your system, or a combination of both. If you train the users internally, the Technical Team equips the training rooms and ensures the continuous availability of the R/3 System during the training courses. Often, users are trained on the quality assurance system. This ensures that the training system is similar to the future production system and the final preparation of the production system is not impeded by the training courses. The best way to prepare users for their daily work is to give them access to the company's master data and transaction data. Transfer this data from the legacy system; if you have already transferred it from the legacy system to the production system, copy it to the quality assurance system.

Table 4.7 lists the tasks in ASAP that are related to the implementation of front-end administration. The table lists the phase in which each task is performed and the person who performs it.

TABLE 4.7: Tasks for Front-End Administration in ASAP

Phase	Phase Name	Task	Role
1	Project Preparation	Define system infrastructure requirements	Technical Team Lead, R/3 System administrator
		Check system sizing results	Technical Team Lead, technical consultant
2	Business Blueprint	Define management strategy	Technical Team Lead, R/3 System administrator, technical consultant
		Install front-end components for Project Team	Technical Team Lead, R/3 System administrator
3	Realization	Install front-end hardware and components	Technical Team Lead, R/3 System administrator, technical consultant
		Install and configure network environment	Technical Team Lead, Network administrator
4	Final Preparation	Set up environment for user training	Project Manager, Technical Team Lead, Trainer
		Transport training data into training environment	Project Manager, Technical Team Lead, Trainer

Success Factors

To successfully implement front-end administration, you must:

- Check requirements
- Train users
- Ensure network access

The following sections describe these aspects in detail.

Check Requirements

You can only install the R/3 front-end software if the front ends meet the minimum requirements for hardware and software. During the Project Preparation phase, you should define the standards for your front ends. You must consider the demands that R/3 places on the front ends and which platforms are supported. Table 4.8 lists important notes from the SAP Online Service System (OSS). These notes inform you about the current status of system requirements and installation of front ends.

TABLE 4.8: R/3 Notes about Front-End Hardware and Software Requirements

Note No.	Short Text
26417	System request for frontend wk centers/SAPGUI
66971	Supported frontend platforms Release 4.0 / 4.5
86895	Additional Info: Upgrading to 4.0x PC Inst.

Before you begin installing the front-end software, make sure your front ends meet all the requirements. To do so, you'll need two documents. First, read Note 86895 from OSS (see Table 4.8). This note contains the latest installation information. Second, the

R/3 software package contains the Installation Requirements: Frontends checklist. In this checklist, the hardware and software requirements are described for the supported platforms. There is also a short description of how to check the requirements for each platform.

Train Users

In many companies, the old front ends are often replaced with new front ends when R/3 is implemented. This means that all users must be trained to use the new devices and interfaces. If your company switches from a mainframe to the R/3 client/server architecture, users must learn how to use R/3 and how to use the new operating system platform.

Often, users accept a new system more easily if they are well trained and have individual instructions available. You should write separate instructions for your company's most important R/3 transactions. The best way to illustrate the essential steps is with screen shots of your R/3 System. This enables even inexperienced users to learn how to use R/3 quickly and easily, and they make fewer mistakes from the beginning.

You should group the company-specific instructions for the applications in a system operation manual. At the same time, you can also document procedures for potential problem situations in the system operation manual. These procedures explain to the users how to proceed in certain situations or who they should notify.

Ensure Network Access

If a front end cannot access the R/3 System through the network, a user cannot work with R/3 even if the application server and the database server are working without problems. Therefore, before you install the front-end software, make sure you can connect from the front end to the application server through the network and also on the operating-system level. After the installation, make sure you can use SAPGUI to log on to an R/3 System in your system landscape (see *SAP R/3 System Administration: The Official SAP Guide*).

You should plan the network topology so it provides a fail-safe system that is sufficient for your requirements. For example, alternative lines are often set up for WAN connections. If the main connection fails, the network immediately switches to an alternative line to enable users to continue working with R/3. Chapter 11, "Network Administration," describes how to plan a network topology.

Review Questions

1. Which operating systems are supported by SAP for SAPGUI Release 4.0?

    A. Microsoft Windows 95

    B. Microsoft Windows NT 4

    C. Unix/Motif

    D. OS/2

    E. Linux

    F. Windows emulations

    G. Windows NT (Alpha Processor)

    H. Apple Macintosh

2. Which statements are correct?

    A. As of R/3 Release 4.0, you can include OLE-enabled office applications through ABAP objects on all supported platforms.

B. You can start an office application from R/3 or react to the results of the application in R/3.

C. You can directly access the tables of the R/3 database from office applications through the ODBC interface. SAP recommends read-only accesses to tables through ODBC.

D. You can bypass the authorization check in R/3 and the processing logic in R/3 with the office applications that are integrated through ABAP objects.

3. Which options do you have to install the front-end software?

   A. Install the software locally on the front ends.

   B. Install the software centrally on a file server.

   C. Install all components of the front-end software without selecting individual options.

   D. Install the software on the front ends without dialog using system management tools.

4. Which statements are correct?

   A. As of Release 4.0A, SAP has HTML-based online documentation.

   B. The HTML files in the online documentation must reside on every front end.

   C. For the installation of the online documentation, you can choose between two types of help: PlainHtmlFile and HtmlHelpFile.

   D. You can use a Web browser to display the HTML-based online documentation on all supported front-end platforms.

CHAPTER FIVE

R/3 Instance Administration

The application layer in an R/3 System runs on one or more application servers, depending on how much computing capacity your production operation requires. The services on the application layer are grouped into administration units known as R/3 instances. Normally, there is one instance per application server, but there are exceptions in which there are multiple instances on one server. For example, for a UNIX-based application server with more than four CPUs and much more than 2GB main memory, it is sensible to configure multiple instances because of performance reasons and limited address spaces due to a 32-bit architecture.

When you choose your application server, you must balance between the desired processor speed and your budget for hardware. You should work together with your hardware partner to size your hardware. The following section describes the important points you must consider. To ensure that your hardware resources are optimally set and available, the subsequent sections show you how to perform the following tasks:

- Configure the R/3 instances
- Monitor the R/3 instances

Determine Operating Systems and Hardware

You can select your operating system and hardware platforms from different vendors. As described in Chapter 2, "Technology in R/3," R/3 instances run on most UNIX derivatives, on Windows NT, and on IBM mainframe platforms. SAP supports all the platforms equally and does not give preference to any particular vendor. Table 5.1 lists the R/3 Notes about the operating system versions for R/3 Release 4.0.

TABLE 5.1: R/3 Notes about Operating Systems for R/3 Release 4.0

Note No.	Short Text
85838	Released operating systems R/3 4.0x/4.5x ORACLE
85840	Released operating systems R/3 4.0x/4.5x INFORMIX
85841	Released operating systems R/3 4.0x/4.5 ADABAS
85842	Released operating systems R/3 4.0x/4.5X DB2/CS
85844	Released operating systems R/3 4.0x/4.5x DB2/390
85845	Released operating systems R/3 4.0x/4.5x AS/400
85846	Released op. systems R/3 4.0x/4.5x MS SQL Server

NOTE You can find additional Notes about other R/3 Releases in SAP Online Service System (OSS) under the component XX-SER-SWREL (Release planning).

The Requirements Catalog

To help you select the best platform for your requirements, you should create a requirements catalog. You can use it to request offers from your hardware partner. Before you create your requirements catalog, record and document the current status of your system landscape. Using the current status as a base, define the target status in your catalog. In your target status, consider your company's long-term strategy for information technology. For example, you should consider whether to replace an existing mainframe architecture with the client/server architecture or whether to implement standard software for the entire company for the first time. Consider the following important points when you are choosing the hardware for your R/3 System:

- Which R/3 Release and how many users are going live?

- How many users work on each R/3 module?
- How many transactions do the users call daily?
- What is the data volume created by the users daily or weekly?
- What is the availability you must ensure?

Often, companies work together with consulting firms or systems resellers who have specialized in the company's industry to create the current and target status. This enables you to save time, and it compensates for the potential of not being up-to-date with the rapid innovation cycles for hardware and software.

Invitation to Tender

Your next step is to start an invitation to tender by sending your hardware partners your requirements catalog. Based on the requirements catalog, the hardware partners submit a quotation. The quotation contains the hardware partners' suggestion for the hardware configuration (see Figure 5.1). This process is known as hardware sizing. There is no simple rule for sizing. Since you have many options for setting up R/3 and mapping your business processes in R/3, individual systems vary greatly in their resource requirements. The hardware partners make their suggestions for your configuration based on their experience with many customers and benchmark tests.

The Quicksizer

Together with the hardware partners, SAP developed the Quicksizer to help you estimate the sizing and to support your initial budget planning. The Quicksizer is an online service in SAPNet that customers and partners can access through the Internet (see Figure 5.2). You use the Quicksizer to calculate which resources you will need for the CPU and the main memory of the application servers. The Quicksizer also calculates the anticipated size of the database. This enables you to estimate the net capacity for the hard disks of the database server. The results apply to the most current R/3 Release.

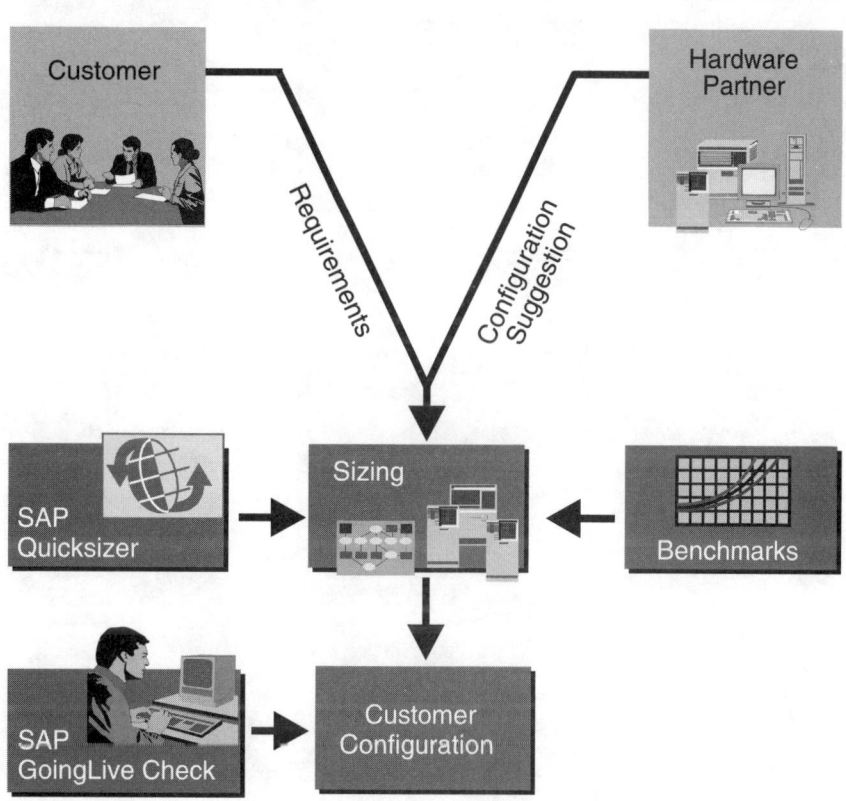

FIGURE 5.1:
Sizing procedure

> **NOTE** You can find the Quicksizer in SAPNet at `sapnet.sap.com/sizing`.

FIGURE 5.2:

The Quicksizer (sapnet.sap.com/sizing)

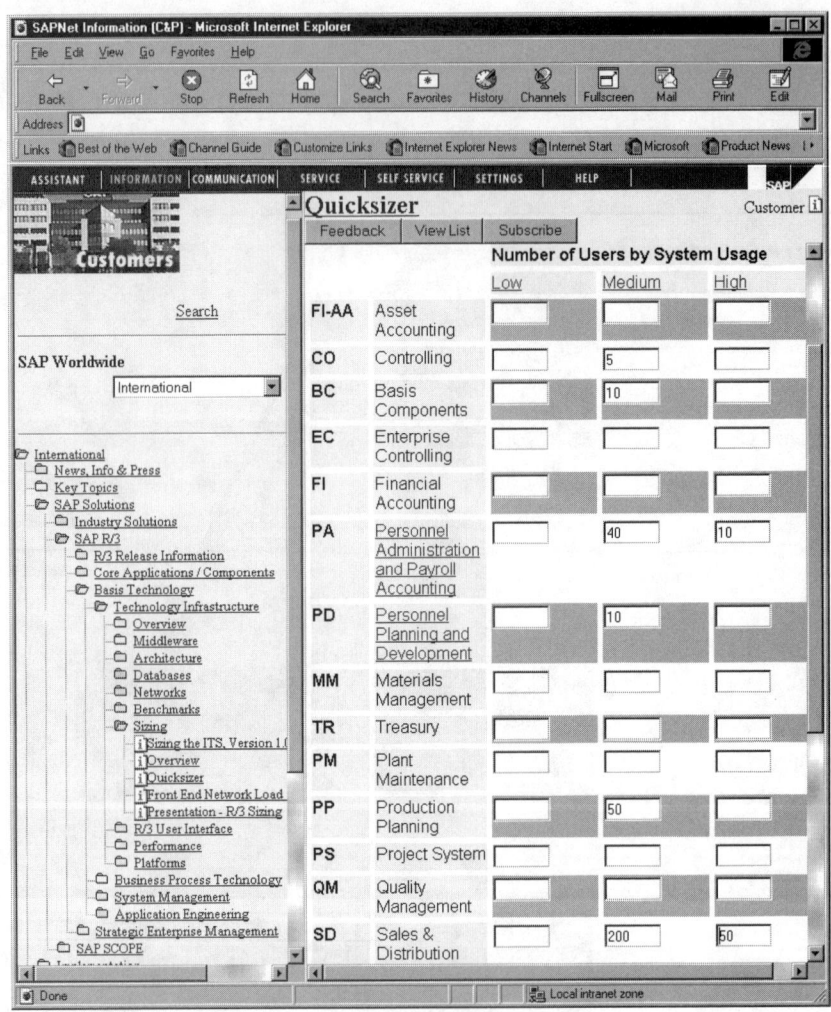

As shown in Figure 5.2, you can use the Quicksizer to calculate the resources needed based on the number of users on each module. To do so, divide the users into three categories: low, medium, and high. Allocate the users to categories in accordance with the criteria in the Quicksizer documentation. The calculations based on the number of users are only approximate. For example, they do not take into consideration the size of the system load due to background processing. For this, you must include more variables in the sizing, such as the number of invoices or delivery notes that are changed or displayed by users each day. To take these aspects into consideration, the Quicksizer has another option. You can enter the numbers for the most important business objects in each module, and then the resources required are calculated based on a quantity structure. These numbers can only be determined together with the departments. Often, consultants or hardware partners can help you with this.

> **TIP** Map the sizing for the load peaks generated by the users so the throughput is ensured, especially when the users work most with the system. Normally, there are two load peaks in a workday: in the morning between 10:00 and 11:00 and in the afternoon between 2:00 and 3:00.

Keep It Simple

After you have received the quotations with the suggestions for your configuration, you can select your hardware vendor. When you select your platform, ensure that you are using a uniform operating system platform for the R/3 instances and the Relational Database Management System (RDBMS). SAP does support heterogeneous R/3 Systems, although it is recommended that you use homogeneous systems. Currently, the only exceptions are heterogeneous R/3 Systems with the Windows NT operating system for the application servers and a UNIX derivative for the database server. If you require multiple application servers in a heterogeneous system such as this, it is preferable that you use the same hardware for the application servers and configure it identically. In comparison to a heterogeneous system with different platforms, it is easier to install and administer the R/3 instances, adapt the system parameters, and upgrade the Release on a homogeneous system. In particular, you should ensure that you use similar operating system platforms within an R/3 System and for the entire two-, three-, or multiple-system landscapes. This way, you'll keep the number of possible error sources low and your system landscape simple. The following criteria are also important for hardware selection:

Scalable hardware Ensure that you can expand the computing capacity and the main memory in the servers. Additional users or newer R/3 Releases occasionally require additional resources.

The hardware life cycle The best way to protect your investments is to buy your hardware at the beginning of its life cycle. However, if you do not need the newest generation of processors, it is most cost effective to buy one of the two previous generations.

Quick expansion of hardware Ensure that you can expand your hardware quickly and cost-effectively when necessary. Shortly before the start of production in particular, bottlenecks can occur that you may only be able to resolve with additional hardware.

Service Level Agreement with your hardware partner Arrange your Service Level Agreement in a way that you can adapt your requirements to the availability of your system. For example, if a problem occurs, your system is only allowed to fail for a maximum of four hours on a workday. In the case of a hardware failure, the hardware vendor must be relatively quick to provide the necessary service.

> **NOTE** Depending on the volume of your orders, you should make a preliminary selection of two to three hardware vendors based on the critical criteria. You should then discuss the hardware configuration in detail with them and possibly check the performance with a test installation.

The GoingLive Check

During the Project Preparation phase, you should sign a contract with your hardware partner and begin with the installation of the development system. The production system is set up at the end of the Realization phase. During the Final Preparation phase, you should test the system to make sure it can handle the load generated by the users. To benefit from SAP's experience with start of production, you should use a special service from SAP, the GoingLive Check. The SAP experts check the configuration of your R/3 System to see whether it can process the planned load. If necessary, the SAP experts recommend that you correct certain settings or expand your hardware in accordance with this analysis. Appendix C describes how to take advantage of this service by SAP.

Configure R/3 Instances

For the operating system, an R/3 instance consists of processes that work together and main memory that is used by the processes. The processes include Dispatcher and multiple work processes for every instance. The work processes perform the work for the logical services: dialog, update, enqueue, background, and spool. Frequently, an instance has 10 to 20 work processes configured, which enables about 50 to 200 users to work on one instance.

To configure the instances, you need to be aware of three important points. First, through the work processes, you should control which services an instance provides and with how many resources. Second, through the logon groups, you should control which users log on to an instance so you can distribute the load over the instances. Third, through the operation modes, you should control whether more resources are available for dialog or background processing during certain time periods. This way, you can distribute the load over a day.

Distribute Work Processes

How many of each type of work process can run on an application server depends on the type of CPU the computer has, how much main memory is available, and which programs are called by the users. You should discuss this with your hardware partner because he or she can judge (from experience with other customers' configurations) how fast the CPU is and how many work processes this CPU can handle.

The best configuration does not use 100 percent of the resources. There should always be a free work process available for each service. You should consider two points regarding the number of work processes you should run: If too few processes of one type are configured, requests have to wait for free work processes, thus increasing the response time. If too many processes are configured, the CPU is overloaded and too much main memory is used. The resulting operating system paging increases the response time.

> **NOTE** A maximum of 40 work processes should run on one application server for two reasons. First, the Dispatcher can become a bottleneck if there are more than 40 work processes. Second, the CPU capacity is normally completely exhausted with 40 work processes. If the number of work processes is too high, it can lead to considerable bottlenecks because the work processes mutually prevent each other from accessing the resources. If you require more than 40 work processes, it is easiest to install another application server to distribute the load. The R/3 Note 9942, "Max. number of work processes is 40 due to events," informs you in detail about the maximum number of work processes you should run.

There is either a maximum or a minimum number for almost all types of work processes for each instance or for each R/3 System. Table 5.2 lists the rules for the number of work processes allowed.

TABLE 5.2: Rules for the Number of Work Processes Allowed

Work Process	Number for Each Instance	Number for Each System	Remark
DIA (dialog)	Minimum 2	Minimum 2	To give users the ability to log on to an instance at all times, a minimum of two work processes must be running.
UPD (update)	Free	Minimum 1	UPD work processes can be distributed over all the instances.
UP2 (update V2)	Free	Free	If there are UP2 work processes, then V2 updates are only possible in these processes. If there are no UP2 work processes, the UPD work processes handle all of the updates. At least one UP2 work process should run in the system.
BTC (background)	Free	Minimum 1 (minimum 2 during upgrade)	From the BTC work processes, work processes for job class A can only be reserved by using operation modes (see Chapter 7, "Background Processing").
ENQ (enqueue)		Exactly 1	More than one ENQ work process is only useful in special cases and should never be set up without permission from SAP.
SPO (spool)	Free	Minimum 1	As of Release 4.0, multiple SPO work processes can run on one instance.

You can define the number of work processes through the system parameters. When you start R/3, the system parameters are set. Therefore, you should write the values for the parameters in an instance profile. If you change the system parameters during system operation, the changes are first visible after you have stopped and restarted the R/3 System. The R/3 online documentation and *SAP R/3 System Administration: The Official SAP Guide*, by Liane Will (Sybex, 1998) describe how to change system parameters.

Example: Figuring the Minimum Number of Work Processes

Using the rules from Table 5.2, you must configure at least the number of individual work process types in the following table for the instances.

Instance	DIA	UPD	UP2	BTC	ENQ	SPO	Sum
Central instance	2	1	0	1	1	1	6
Dialog instance	2	0	0	0	0	0	2

As long as you consider the rules in Table 5.2, in principle, you are free to schedule however many update work processes you need for the number of dialog work processes you are using. However, SAP's experiences show the following typical relationships between the number of work processes:

One UPD for 4 DIAs Four dialog work processes require approximately one update work process to write the data to the database.

One UP2 for 12 DIAs Twelve dialog work processes require approximately one update work process of type V2 to write statistical data to the database.

One BTC for 4 DIAs Four dialog work processes require approximately one background work process to perform the normal tasks of the applications in the background.

Previous experiences have shown that these relationships are valid for most R/3 modules, for example, FI, CO, SD, MM, or PP.

Example: Figuring Typical Relations for the Number of Work Processes

Based on the typical relationships between the number of work process types, the following table lists two examples.

Instance	DIA	UPD	UP2	BTC	ENQ	SPO	Sum
Central instance	12	3	1	3	1	1	21
Dialog instance	12	3	1	0	0	0	16

NOTE In the first weeks after the start of production, you must make sure you have configured sufficient work processes. You must also specifically check to see that you selected the appropriate relationships between the number of work process types.

Define Logon Groups

A logon group collects multiple R/3 instances logically in one instance. If a user logs on to the R/3 System through one logon group, his or her request goes first to the R/3 message server and not directly to an R/3 instance in the logon group. Then, the message server logs the user on to the instance of the logical group that currently has the lowest load and, thus, a medium response time. This procedure is called *logon load balancing*.

The essential advantage of the logon group is that you can control the user logon centrally from the application layer and simplify maintenance. For example, if you exchange or add an instance, you'll only change the related logon group. You do not need to change the settings on every front end. At the same time, you'll increase the availability of R/3. As long as at least one instance is active in a logon group, users can log on to R/3 through this group. You'll also simplify the load distribution. R/3 distributes the load evenly over the instances of a logon group. A user does not need to check for the instance on which a request can be processed most quickly. You'll also increase the quality of the R/3 buffer. R/3 can process user requests most quickly when the ABAP program called by the users is in the buffer of the instance. To ensure that the programs from the various R/3 modules do not displace each other from the buffer, you should define a separate logon group for every module. As Figure 5.3 shows, this is how the instances are harmonized with the corresponding module.

> **NOTE** In the standard R/3 System, a user can log on through any logon group. During a logon, the system does not check to see whether a user is allowed to use the selected logon group or not. For example, in Figure 5.3, users from group FI can log on through the group SD and vice versa.

To centrally control user logons through logon groups, you can use one of two approaches. The optimistic approach is to allow users to select the applicable logon group. Leave the standard settings in R/3 unchanged and tell each user which logon group to use. The pessimistic approach is to check during a logon to see whether the user is authorized to use the selected logon group. To do this, you have to extend the logon function in the standard R/3 System. In the logon procedure, include a separate program with which to check the logon group for every user using a user-exit. R/3 online documentation explains which user-exits you can use for this.

FIGURE 5.3:

Increasing buffer quality using logon groups

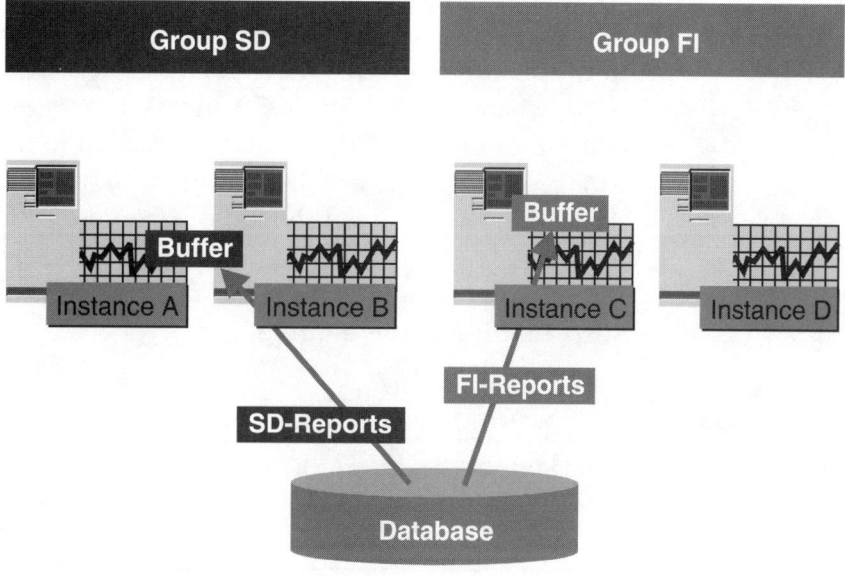

> **NOTE** As an alternative to the user-exit, you could configure the front ends in a way that the user can only select one logon group by using an icon. However, this way, you control the logon decentrally from the presentation layer instead of centrally from the application layer. Maintenance is more difficult if you have a large number of logon groups.

One Logon Group

If your system only has one to three instances, preferably, you should configure only one logon group. This allows the best load distribution and increases the availability of R/3. If you set up a logon group for each instance, the users of one group are tied to an instance that may become overloaded. Another disadvantage of logon groups with only one instance is that users cannot switch to another instance of the logon group if their instance fails during logon. You'll have to change the group manually more often to enable the users of the affected group to log on to another instance.

Multiple Logon Groups

If your system has many instances, it is preferable to configure multiple logon groups. Each logon group should consist of two or more instances. As Figure 5.3 shows, the users of a logon group should call reports in R/3 that are related to the same R/3 module (for example, Sales and Distribution (SD) and Financial Accounting (FI)). This allows the load of one logon group to be distributed over two instances. If an instance fails, the users of the group can log on to another instance. The buffers of the instances are also adapted to the module in use.

> **NOTE** You can set up and maintain logon groups in the Computing Center Management System (CCMS) in the R/3 System. To call this R/3 transaction directly, you can use the transaction code SMLG (see the R/3 online documentation for instructions on using transaction codes).

Example: Setting Up Logon Groups

The following two tables represent two R/3 Systems, each with a different number of instances, to show how many and which logon groups should be set up. The first table shows that there is only one logon group for an R/3 System with three instances.

Instance	Logon Group
app1_C11_00	All users
app2_C11_00	All users
app3_C11_00	All users

Continued on next page

The next table shows that two logon groups are set up for an R/3 System with six instances. Four instances are scheduled for the users in the Sales and Distribution (SD) module because they require more resources than the other modules. Accordingly, only two instances have to be scheduled for the Financial Accounting (FI) and Controlling (CO) R/3 modules.

Instance	Logon Group
app1_C11_00	FI/CO users
app2_C11_00	FI/CO users
app3_C11_00	SD users
app4_C11_00	SD users
app5_C11_00	SD users
app6_C11_00	SD users

Define Operation Modes

Using operation modes, you can dynamically switch between the types of work processes without having to stop and start R/3. On the one hand, you use an operation mode to define how many work processes a service in the instance can use. On the other hand, you can determine the time period in which an operation mode should be active, as seen in Figure 5.4.

NOTE When you switch operation modes, R/3 does not terminate a running program in a work process. More often, an occupied work process is marked for the switch. The marked work process is switched only after the program has ended and the work process is free.

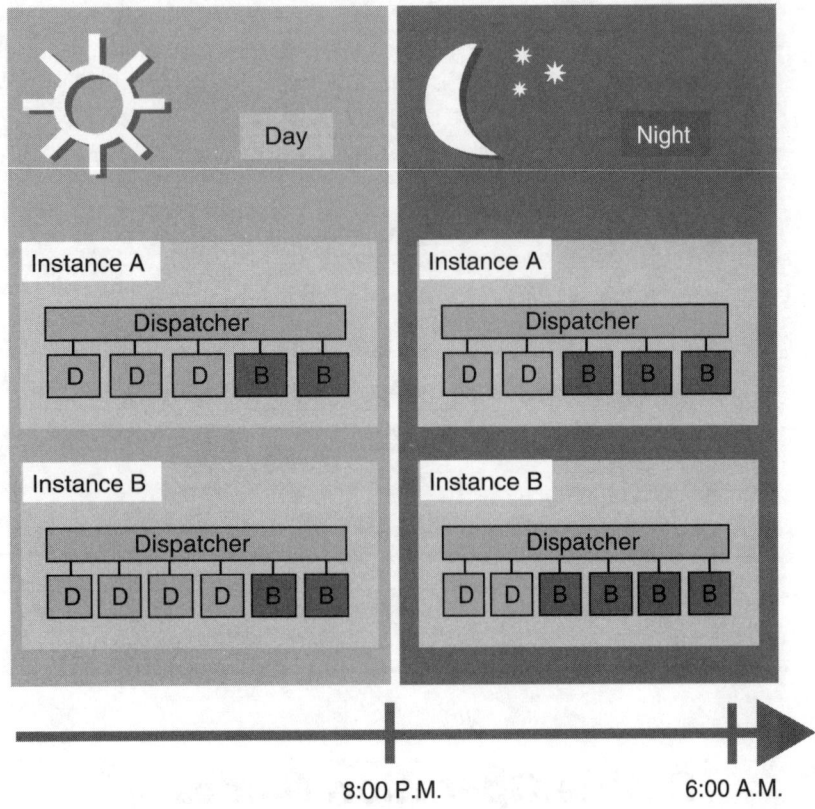

FIGURE 5.4:

Using operation modes to switch the distribution of work process types

There are two advantages to using the operation modes. First, you can dynamically adapt the resources of the instance to the load distribution over a day. During the day, you can configure more work processes for the dialog service and during the night, more work processes for the background service (see Figure 5.4). Second, the quality of the R/3 buffer is almost completely retained during an operation mode switch. If you could only switch the type of work processes by changing the system parameters, then to switch the operation mode, you would have to first stop the R/3 System and start it again with the changed parameters. After restarting the R/3 System, the buffers are only partially returned to their previous state, and thus, their quality is lower. Then, users must wait longer for the responses to their requests. The R/3 online documentation and *SAP R/3 System Administration: The Official SAP Guide* describe how to set up operation modes and what you must take into consideration to do so.

> **TIP**
> The sum of the work processes in an instance cannot be changed through operation modes. Similarly, the number of enqueue and spool work processes cannot be changed through operation modes. You can only reserve background work processes for the job class A through operation modes (see Chapter 7, "Background Processing").

Day and Night Operation

If your system mainly processes user requests in dialog during the day and performs background processing during the night, you should configure two operation modes, day and night operation. Doing so enables you to adapt the distribution of work process types of one instance to the load distribution during the day without difficulties. If you were to set up only one operation mode for the entire day, the dialog work processes would not be fully occupied at night. However, you would not be able to perform any more background jobs at night than you could during the day.

24-Hour Dialog Operation

If your system is used by dialog users 24 hours a day, you should configure only one operation mode, 24-hour dialog operation. In this case, background processing can run on a special instance because the system load is evenly distributed over the entire day.

> **NOTE**
> You can set up and maintain the operation modes in CCMS in the R/3 System (transaction code RZ04).

Example: Setting Operation Modes

The following table shows the operation modes of an R/3 System with a central instance and a dialog instance. For R/3 Systems with varying loads, two operation modes are defined. During the day, there are many dialog work processes; during the night, there are many background work processes.

Time	Operation Mode	Instance	Dia	Bp	BpA	Spo	Upd	Up2	Enq	Sum
7:00 A.M.– 5:00 P.M.	Day operation mode	App1_C11_00	12	3	1	1	3	1	1	21
		App2_C11_00	12	3	-	2	3	1	-	21
5:00 P.M.– 7:00 A.M.	Night operation mode	App1_C11_00	3	12	1	1	3	1	1	21
		App2_C11_00	3	12	-	2	3	1	-	21

Exception Operation

In addition to normal operation with a 24-hour cycle, you can define an exception operation. With an exception operation, you can schedule a special distribution of work processes for exceptional load on your system. At the end of the month in particular, your system can be overloaded by month-end closings or period closing programs. For example, you can make the required resources available by setting up an operation mode with which you can switch to the maximum number of background work processes for your system.

Monitor R/3 Instances

To ensure maximum availability and performance in your R/3 System, you must regularly monitor the R/3 instances. The Computing Center Management System (CCMS) has the tools with which you can monitor the technical operation of your R/3 System. You can check the system status and the operation modes, recognize potential problems in advance, and monitor system performance.

To ensure that you put the tools in the R/3 System to optimum use, the following sections show you how to perform the following tasks:

- Configure the Alert Monitor
- Define the system operation

Configure the Alert Monitor

CCMS has a graphical Alert Monitor with which you can continually monitor your entire R/3 System landscape and, in particular, the runtime environment in the R/3 instances. The Alert Monitor is a warning system that warns you of potential problems in advance. For example, alerts are displayed if a work process does not work correctly or if a problem message is displayed in a system log. If an alert is displayed, you must resolve the error that triggered the alert. Only then does R/3 automatically remove the alert.

The Monitoring Object and the Monitoring Attribute

Figure 5.5 shows that the monitoring objects to be monitored are grouped in a tree structure. There is a separate tree structure for each system in your system landscape. Each monitoring object has at least one monitoring attribute. The monitoring attributes receive the data to be monitored (for example, the value for the buffer quality or the value for the CPU load). In accordance with methods and rules, R/3 maps the data in three alert conditions. R/3 displays the alert status in the colors red, yellow, and green. Table 5.3 lists the meaning of the colors.

FIGURE 5.5:

The Alert Monitor structure

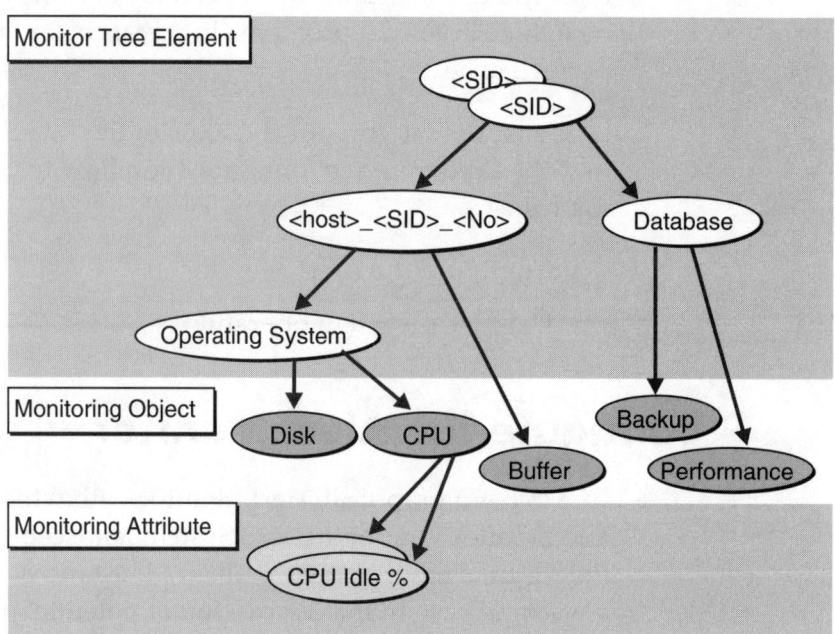

TABLE 5.3: Alert Colors and Their Meanings

Alert Color	Meaning
Red	Error
Yellow	Warning
Green	Everything okay

Monitor Tree Elements

The alert status is registered by the monitoring object and is displayed upward on each level on the tree structure. A node in the tree structure is called a *monitor tree element*. A monitor tree element collects all of the alerts registered and passes the alert with the highest status upward. If the top node in the tree structure displays a red alert, there is at least one monitoring object in the entire tree that has a red alert.

The Basic Monitor

In the Basic monitor, you can display the complete tree with all of the monitoring objects in the standard R/3 System. The example in Figure 5.6 shows that you can branch to the alert of the monitoring attributes in the System TC4 tree structure. Experience shows that the complete tree structure with all the monitoring objects is too large to check the system for problem situations daily. For this reason, you can cut out partial tree structures from the entire tree. You can then adjust them optimally to your system. For example, if you have filled your Project Team with the recommended roles for ASAP, you should create a separate Alert Monitor for each role. Ensure that the partial tree structures continue to represent the original entire tree structure; otherwise, administrators could miss an alert. R/3 online documentation and *SAP R/3 System Administration: The Official SAP Guide* describe how to create separate monitors and how to maintain the threshold values for the alerts.

As soon as you have set up an R/3 System during the implementation project, you must set up the Alert Monitor for your requirements. You should set up the monitor for the development system first because it is the first system you'll set up. Since you can monitor the other system from one system with the Alert Monitor, you can adapt the development system's monitor for any new systems in your landscape accordingly. The disadvantage is that your monitors are not available if the development system fails. Since the production system has the highest availability requirements, you should set up all of the monitors for your system landscape in the production system.

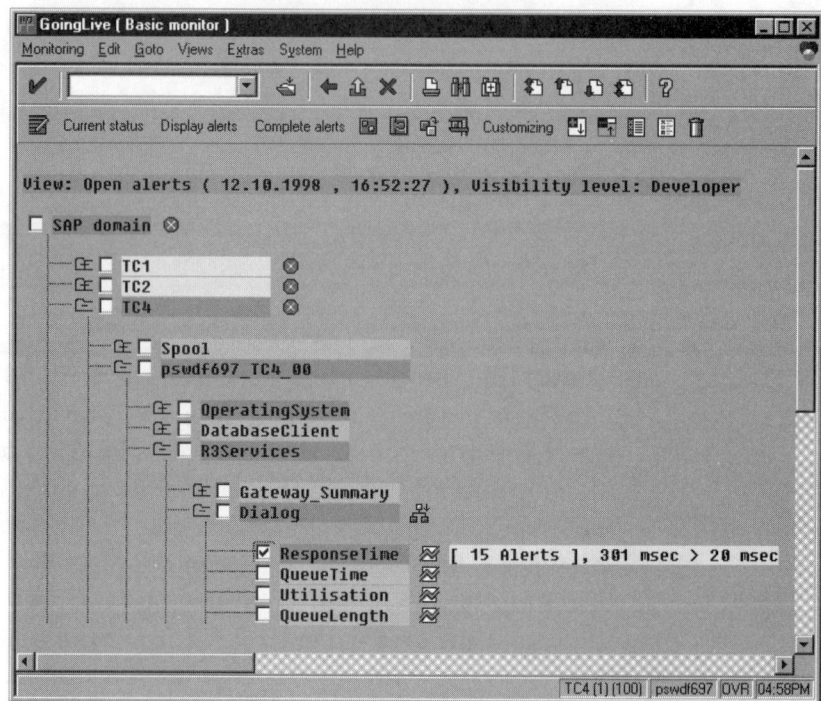

FIGURE 5.6:

The Alert Monitor's Basic monitor

> **NOTE** In CCMS, there are various open interfaces to which you can connect applications from third-party vendors for an integrated system and network management. Chapter 13, "Interfaces," covers this topic in more detail.

Define System Operation

The Technical Team must ensure the availability of the production system as well as the other R/3 Systems in the landscape. During the Realization phase in particular, the development system and the quality assurance system are the production systems for the application implementation. When data is lost or throughput is poor, productivity is reduced, which may postpone the start of production. From the time you set up the development system, you should work together with technical consultants and specialists to define the system operation for the R/3 instances. An R/3 System administrator should then document it in the system operation manual. During the Realization phase, while the application consultants perform Customizing work in the development system, you can document experiences with the procedures of your system operation and adapt the manual to the procedures that may have changed. These experiences flow into the system operation of the other systems.

The system operation is divided into nonregular activities and regular activities; for example, checking the Alert Monitor is a regular activity. In the system operation manual, you should define how often certain activities should be performed. Table 5.4 shows the important daily activities for monitoring the R/3 runtime environment and describes the important considerations for each one.

TABLE 5.4: Daily Activities for Monitoring the Runtime Environment

Activity	Transaction Code	Remarks
Alert Monitor (4.0)	RZ20	If a red or a yellow alert is displayed, there is a problem.
System Monitor	RZ02	All R/3 instances must be active and in the correct operation mode. If an instance is inactive, there is a problem.

Continued on next page

TABLE 5.4: Daily Activities for Monitoring the Runtime Environment *(Continued)*

Activity	Transaction Code	Remarks
Process overview	SM50 SM66	In normal operation, the status for work processes cannot be stopped or ended or have a long runtime.
System log	SM21	Warnings or error messages in the system log must be analyzed.
Update	SM13	The update processes must always be active. Terminated update records should not occur in the production system.
Dump analysis	ST22	ABAP dumps should not occur in the production system. In the development system and quality assurance system, dumps can occur.
Lock entries	SM12	Old lock entries should not occur in normal operation.

If you discover a problem during daily monitoring, you must analyze, correct, and document it. Solutions to simple problems may already be in the system operation manual. For difficult problems, you should define whom to notify and which specialist can help in this type of problem. The transactions listed in Table 5.4 are described in more detail in the R/3 online documentation. *SAP R/3 System Administration: The Official SAP Guide* describes the problems that can occasionally occur and how to analyze them.

> **TIP** For these daily activities, SAP recommends keeping a logbook. In the logbook, you can keep track of when a component was last checked, by whom, and whether any problems occurred. This enables you to reconstruct the history of a problem situation, and in the future, you can either recognize this type of problem more quickly or avoid it altogether.

In addition to these regular activities, the R/3 administrator also has many R/3 maintenance tasks to perform. Table 5.5 shows the important activities and the important considerations for each one.

TABLE 5.5: Activities for Administering R/3 Instances

Activity	Role	Remarks
Starting and stopping R/3 instances	Technical Team Lead, R/3 System administrator	Before you stop an R/3 System, all the active users must be notified, all running jobs must be terminated, all planned jobs must be reset, and all existing interfaces must be stopped.
Maintain system parameters	Technical Team Lead, R/3 System administrator	To change system parameters, use only the CCMS profile maintenance tool.
Maintain logon groups	Technical Team Lead, R/3 System administrator	Users should only log on through the logon groups on R/3.
Maintain operation modes	Technical Team Lead, R/3 System administrator	During a standard R/3 installation, no operation modes are created, so you must create them directly after the installation.

To avoid downtime and poor performance in the R/3 System because of unnecessary changes, you can define procedures for approval for every activity in Table 5.5. In particular, you must formally apply for changes to the system parameters, logon groups, or operation modes. Each time you make a change, you must explain why it is necessary. After the Technical Team Lead has considered the work and the usefulness, the changes are either accepted or rejected. Each change is documented in the system operation manual.

R/3 Instances in ASAP

In the previous sections, you learned the important considerations for administering R/3 instances during the R/3 implementation. In ASAP, these points are distributed over the individual phases of the project. The following sections describe when to perform certain tasks.

Project Preparation

During the Project Preparation phase, you'll define the required technical infrastructure for your system landscape. The technical infrastructure depends on the R/3 Release you use for production operation. There are two important aspects for the infrastructure. First, you must select the hardware platform and the RDBMS. Second, you must determine the extent of the hardware you'll need. For the application servers in particular, you should work with the hardware partner to define how fast the CPU should be and how much main memory is required. To select the hardware that is appropriate for you, first create a requirements catalog. Based on this catalog, collect the quotations from the hardware partners and choose one of them. When you make your decision, ensure that the hardware sizing is sufficient for your needs. To protect your investment in your hardware, you must be able to expand the computing capacity and the main memory of the server. R/3 is scalable from one to several thousand users, and the computing capacity must be able to grow accordingly.

Because you'll set up the development system at the end of the Business Blueprint phase and the quality assurance system at the beginning of the Realization phase, you must order the hardware for these two systems early in the Project Preparation phase. In ASAP, the production system is set up before the Final Preparation phase. This enables you to test the system extensively during the entire Final Preparation phase. You should consider the hardware delivery time when you order the production system. To implement the R/3 System in six months, you should order your hardware for the production system at the end of the Project Preparation phase. If you plan for a longer implementation, you can order your hardware accordingly so it will be cost effective.

Business Blueprint

At the end of the Business Blueprint phase, you'll set up the development system. In the development system, the application consultants customize the standard R/3 System for your company. The Technical Team is responsible for the availability of this system to ensure that the application consultants can work without interruption. All downtime or data loss costs you money and can postpone the start of production. For this reason, the procedures for the system administration in the development system must be already defined, especially the tasks of the R/3 System administrator. With the technical consultants and specialists, you should define all of the activities for the system operation in the R/3 Systems and document it in the system operation manual. For example, you should document which task have to be performed daily, weekly, or monthly; who is responsible for which tasks; and how to handle error situations.

As soon as you have set up the development system, you should configure the system's CCMS. This allows the R/3 System administrator to monitor the entire system landscape from his or her workstation with the graphical monitor in CCMS and to react quickly in case of error. For example, the R/3 System administrator can change the settings for the Alert Monitor so that only specific parts of the system are displayed, such as the operating system, the database, the network, or the R/3 System. System administrators can then test and learn about the procedures of the system operation in regard to the future production system. If there are any innovations on this topic, you should document them in the system operation manual.

You must check some of the components in the R/3 instances regularly. The higher a system's availability needs to be, the more frequently you must check certain components. For example, you should check to see whether the work processes are overloaded or whether there are problems registered in the system log. Each of the R/3 Systems in your system landscape has distinct requirements. In the development system and the quality assurance system, the R/3 System administrator checks some components only once a week, whereas all of the components of the production system are checked daily. In the system operation manual, list all the activities and define how frequently the activities must be performed for each R/3 System.

Realization

At the beginning of the Realization phase, you'll set up the quality assurance system. The application consultants need this system to check their Customizing and development efforts. As with the development system, the Technical Team must also ensure the availability for the quality assurance system. The requirements for the system administration procedures are the same as they are in the development system. As soon as you have set up the quality assurance system, you should configure the CCMS in the system so the R/3 System administrator can monitor both systems of the system landscape from his or her workstation with the graphical monitors in the CCMS.

At the end of the Realization phase, you'll set up the production system. To prepare for administering the production system, you should define the procedure and roles in accordance with your experiences with the development and quality assurance systems. These procedures are tested during the Final Preparation phase, which is why you should develop appropriate test procedures in this phase. For example, you must be certain that an alert is displayed if an error occurs. If some of the alert threshold values are set too high, you will not be warned by an alert in advance and will therefore not be able to react early.

To document this procedure precisely, you should create the first version of the system operation manual for the production operation. This manual is an important document for the production operation of the systems because the Technical Team administers and monitors the system landscape in accordance with its guidelines. The manual is divided according to the components in the system. The R/3 System administrator is responsible for the R/3 instances and maintains the manual for these components.

Final Preparation

At the beginning of the Final Preparation phase, you'll set up the production system. As you did with the two other systems, you must then configure the CCMS for the system administration. You already defined the guidelines on this topic in the preceding phase.

To ensure that the R/3 System has a high throughput and a high availability for production operation, you must be able to rely on the system operation procedures. In the previous phases, you have already collected many experiences with the system operation for the development and quality assurance systems. However, you should still assume that the production system has considerably high demands on availability and data security. For this reason, within ASAP, it is recommended that you extensively test the production system. For example, you should test the R/3 instances to determine whether sufficient work processes are running, whether the logon groups are well chosen, and whether the operation modes switch over without problems. In all, you should test and check the R/3 instances for all the tasks of the R/3 System administrator. Ensure that the administrators can perform all the necessary steps in accordance with the system operation manual. If necessary, have the experienced employees from the implementation project train the administrators on your future production system.

Go Live and Support

After the start of production, you'll run the production operation in accordance with the defined procedures. In addition to these administration tasks, you must supervise the R/3 users. The users have the most questions and problems in the first weeks. The more users who accept and can effectively use the system, the more successful your R/3 implementation will be. The deciding factor is not only whether users have been sufficiently trained, but how quickly a user is helped if problems occur. While you are preparing production, you should set up a help desk that receives all of the requests from users. The Technical Team members are the specialists for technical problems. The help desk should only pass serious problems to the Technical Team to avoid overloading the administrators with more than their daily activities.

During the production operation, the R/3 System administrator regularly monitors the load on the resources for the instances. You can constantly improve the throughput in your system, especially in the first months. In particular, take into consideration how the users load the production system, when the load peaks occur, and whether all the instances are fully loaded. These experiences allow you to better harmonize the operation modes and logon groups with your requirements. To optimally customize the system parameters (for example, the size of individual buffers of an instance), you'll need special knowledge and experiences. SAP provides support with a special service, the EarlyWatch Service. Appendix C describes this service and how to request it.

Table 5.6 lists the tasks from ASAP that are related to the implementation of the R/3 instances. Each task is described in accordance with the phase in which it is performed and the person who performs it.

TABLE 5.6: Tasks for Administering the R/3 Instances in ASAP

Phase	Phase Name	Task	Role
1	Project Preparation	Determine technical requirements	Project Manager, Technical Team Lead, R/3 System administrator
		Acquire hardware	Project Manager, Technical Team Lead, R/3 System administrator
2	Business Blueprint	Define system administration for the development system	Technical Team Lead, R/3 System administrator, technical consultant
		Configure CCMS for the development system	R/3 System administrator, technical consultant
		Check the functions of the system administration	R/3 System administrator, technical consultant
		Define the periodic processes of the system administration	Technical Team Lead, R/3 System administrator, technical consultant

Continued on next page

TABLE 5.6: Tasks for Administering the R/3 Instances in ASAP *(Continued)*

Phase	Phase Name	Task	Role
3	Realization	Define the system administration quality assurance system	Technical Team Lead, R/3 System administrator, technical consultant
		Configure CCMS for the quality assurance system	R/3 System administrator, technical consultant
		Define the system management for the production system	Technical Team Lead, R/3 System administrator, technical consultant
		Create the system operation manual	Technical Team Lead, R/3 System administrator, technical consultant
4	Final Preparation	Configure CCMS for the production system	R/3 System administrator, technical consultant
		Perform system tests	Project Manager
5	Go Live and Support	Make the production support available	Technical Team Lead, technical consultant
		Optimize the system utilization	Technical Team Lead, technical consultant

Success Factors

To successfully implement the administration of the R/3 instances, you must give the following points consideration:

- Size the hardware appropriately
- Distribute the system load usefully
- Customize the Alert Monitors

The following sections describe these points in more detail.

Size Hardware Appropriately

You should work with your hardware partner to determine two components for the hardware of the R/3 instances. First, you should determine the required computing capacity and, along with it, the type of CPU. Second, you should define the size of the main memory. You should plan the performance of the hardware for the load peaks and not for an average load. This way, user requests can still be processed when the system is being heavily used.

> **NOTE** Normally, different R/3 Releases need different resources for the hardware. Therefore, determine the sizing for the R/3 Release with which you want to run your production system.

You already sized the hardware during the Project Preparation phase. If the extent of the production system changes during the project, and with it, the number of users or implemented modules increases, you must adapt the sizing accordingly.

You can test your production system to make sure it can process the planned load only during the Final Preparation phase. If the tests find a bottleneck, you'll have to increase the hardware accordingly. To avoid having to postpone the start of production because of delivery times, you should secure a special Service Level Agreement with your hardware partner for the Final Preparation and Go Live and Support phases.

Distribute System Load Sensibly

Good distribution of the system load is a deciding factor for an optimal throughput and high availability. To distribute the system load efficiently, use both of the following options:

- Logon load balancing
- Operation mode switching

Logon load balancing is particularly worthwhile for systems with multiple instances. Users do not have to check to see which instances are available and which instance can process a request the fastest. For logon load balancing, it is essential that users log on to R/3 exclusively through the logon groups.

Operation mode switching lets you adapt work process daily load profiles by using dialog and background processing. You must make sure the selected distribution of the work processes is optimal for your requirements, particularly in the first weeks after the start of production. Take particular care to ensure that your critical background processing jobs have sufficient resources.

Customize Alert Monitors

Optimally customized Alert Monitors are often the deciding factor for an advance warning of problems. Experience shows that the complete tree structure in the Alert Monitor is too large to check the system daily for problem situations. Therefore, you should create a separate Alert Monitor for each role in the Technical Team. Each administrator adapts the Alert Monitor to his or her requirements.

Some alerts in the Monitor require threshold values. As soon as the threshold value is exceeded, the R/3 Monitor triggers an alert. For example, you could set the threshold value for the quality of a buffer in a way that a quality under 90 percent triggers a red alert. SAP does deliver with predefined threshold values, but they are not optimally adapted to your configuration. For this reason, you should make sure all problem situations are correctly displayed by the Alert Monitor, particularly during the Final Preparation phase and in the first weeks after the start of production.

> **TIP**
>
> If a threshold value is set too low, a red alert is always triggered, even if there is no problem. In this case, you must increase the threshold value gradually.
>
> If a threshold value is set too high, no red alerts are triggered, even if problems exist. In this case, you must decrease the threshold values gradually.

Review Questions

1. What are the important things to consider when you select your hardware?

    A. The minimum hardware requirements must be met.

    B. You must be able to expand your hardware.

    C. The instances in an R/3 System should run on different hardware platforms.

    D. Hardware sizing is the same for all R/3 Releases.

2. Which statements are correct?

    A. At least two dialog work processes must run on each instance.

    B. At least one enqueue work process must run on each instance.

    C. Only one spool work process can run on each instance.

    D. At least one update work process must run in each R/3 System.

3. Which statements are correct?

   A. You can only monitor the R/3 instances with the Alert Monitor.

   B. You can divide the entire monitoring object tree structure into partial tree structures.

   C. You can monitor all the systems in your system landscape from one system with the Alert Monitor.

   D. The Alert Monitor only displays two statuses for a monitoring object: a red alert for an error and a green alert if everything is okay.

CHAPTER SIX

User Administration

Every user logs on to R/3 with a user name, a client name, and a password. The user name allows R/3 to determine, for example, which transactions a user can perform. R/3 denies all transaction calls for which the user does not have authorization. In R/3, the authorizations are collected in groups. These authorization groups each describe a job role in R/3. You can allocate multiple job roles to one user or one job role to multiple users.

R/3 provides two approaches to securing access to data by using authorizations. The optimistic approach allows you to give users authorizations that allow them to perform all actions in R/3 with only a few exceptions. The pessimistic approach allows you to give users authorizations that only allow them to perform the tasks in R/3 that are necessary for their job roles.

Even in smaller systems, several dozen users work with R/3. The way you assign authorizations to users and the way you administer users affects each R/3 System in your company. This chapter explains the most important aspects of the authorization concept in R/3. You will learn how to create an authorization concept for your company and which options you have to administer user and activity groups.

Activity Groups, Authorizations, and User Master Records

An authorization allows a user to perform a specific activity in the R/3 System. It must be entered in the user master record of the user. You must first enter an authorization in the authorization profile, not directly in the user's user master record. You'll then allocate the authorization profile to the user master record. In R/3, you can give users the necessary authorizations in two ways:

Manually You can create individual authorizations, group them in an authorization profile, and allocate the profile to a user. To do so, you need detailed knowledge of the authorizations available in the system and their interdependencies.

Automatically   You can generate authorization profiles through the Profile Generator and allocate users with these profiles through the activity groups. The Profile Generator allows you to create an authorization profile for a job role description more quickly and easily than you could if you used the manual procedure.

The following sections explain activity groups, authorizations, authorization profiles, and user master records. The section "The Double-Verification Principle," later in this chapter, describes how to distribute the tasks for the user and authorization administration among three administrators.

Activity Groups

In an activity group, you should define the transactions and activities permitted for a job role and which users can perform them. For example, if you need a job role description for an accountant, first use the Profile Generator to create the activity group fi-ledger in R/3. To find out more about the Profile Generator, use transaction code PFCG (see the R/3 online documentation for instructions on using transaction codes). From the menu tree within the Profile Generator, select the transactions that the accountant will be authorized to perform (see Figure 6.1). You can set up the menu tree for your company beforehand in the *company menu*. To create your company menu, you can simply copy the menu paths that you can use in your company from the menu in the standard R/3 System. The Session Manager displays the company menu. The Session Manager allows you to navigate through the menu tree more easily than you can navigate through the standard R/3 System because the paths in the standard R/3 System that you don't need are not displayed.

FIGURE 6.1:

Selecting transactions for an activity group for an accountant from the company menu

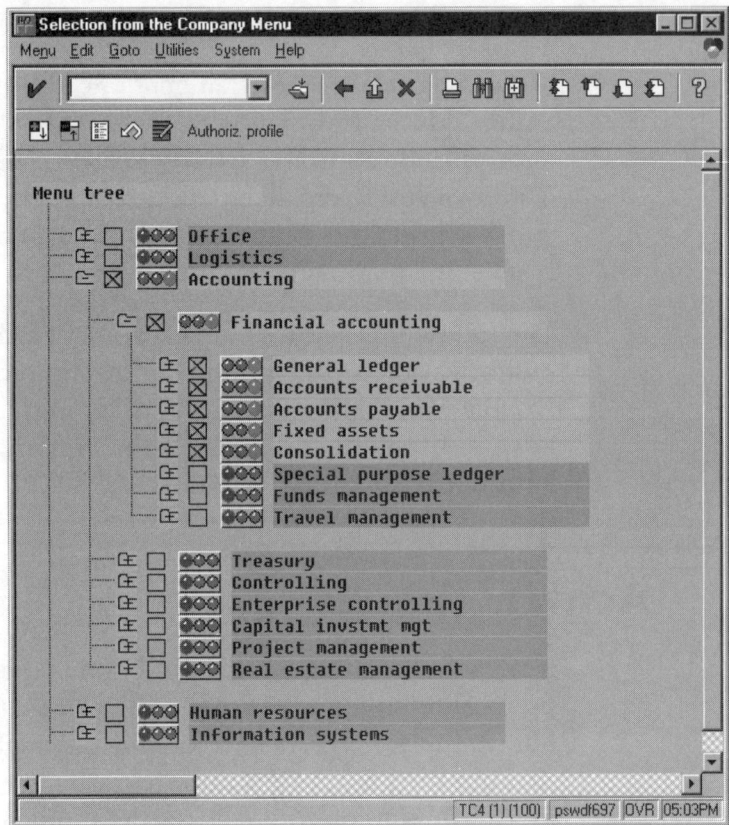

Authorizations

The Profile Generator only searches for the required authorizations for the transactions selected and no more (see Figure 6.2). Each authorization uses one authorization object as a template. An authorization object consists of multiple authorization fields and has a unique name. The object name indicates its purpose. To generate an authorization from an authorization object, you must define the values for the authorization fields. The Profile Generator has default values for most authorizations, and for the others, you can select the appropriate values. For example, Figure 6.2 shows that the Archiving authorization object has three fields: Activity, Application Area, and Archiving Object. An accountant would need different values in the Archiving Object field to be able to archive different types of accounting documents. The Profile Generator proposes multiple authorizations, each with a different value in the Archiving Object field, for example, FI_MONTHLY and FI_SCHECK, as shown in Figure 6.2.

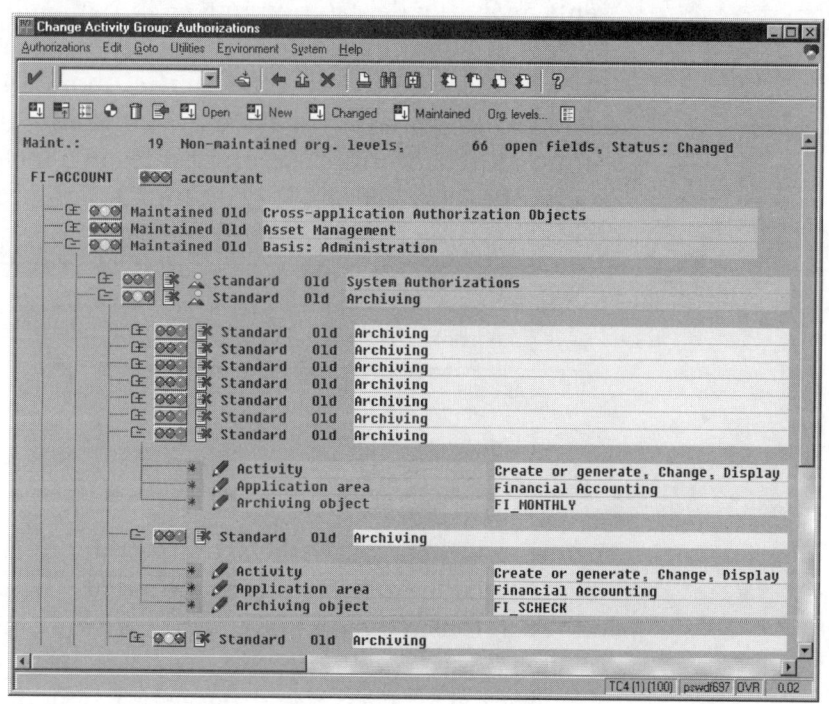

FIGURE 6.2:
Authorizations for an activity group

To administer the many authorization objects more easily, R/3 collects authorization objects into *object classes*, such as Asset Management or Basis: Administration. The tree structure in Figure 6.2 shows the hierarchical structure of the R/3 authorization concepts. The object classes form the first branch, authorization objects form the second branch, authorizations form the third branch, and authorization fields form the fourth branch.

Authorization Profiles

Once you have filled out the remaining authorization fields, you can generate an authorization profile with the customized authorizations. The authorization profile allows you to give a user the desired authorizations as one unit. An authorization profile represents a job role description in R/3. If person B has the same tasks as person A and therefore requires the same authorizations, you can give persons B and A the same authorization profile. This ensures that both people have the same authorizations. You can group multiple authorization profiles in a *composite profile*. This is useful if users need multiple authorization profiles for their work.

NOTE You can only use the profile to give a user the desired authorizations once you have generated an authorization profile.

User Master Records

Before you can allocate the activity group to its agent, you must create a user master record for the agent. The user master record allows a user to log on to R/3 and perform activities for which he or she is authorized. The user master record contains, for example, the basic data such as name, password, or address. In particular, the user master record must contain the desired authorization profile for the specific user. The Profile Generator allows you to automatically enter the required authorization profile in the user master record. You must first allocate all agents to an activity group (see Figure 6.3). Then you can adapt the user master records of the agents to this allocation, and R/3 enters the profiles in the master records.

NOTE User master records depend on the clients. A user can only work in the clients for which he or she has user master records. The user cannot log on to any other client.

FIGURE 6.3:

Agent assignment for an activity group

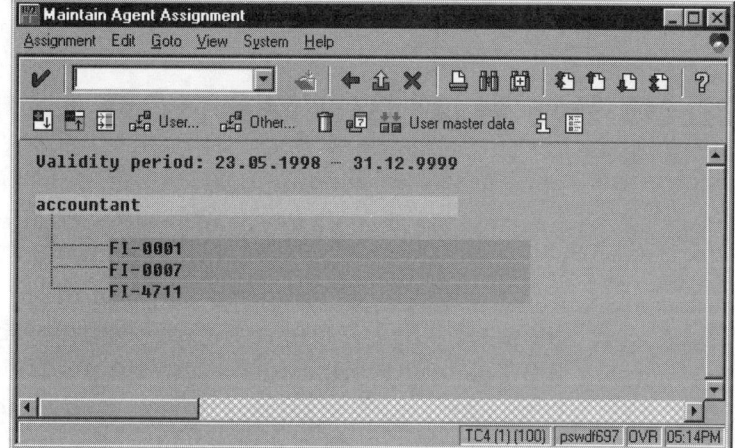

The Double-Verification Principle

In R/3, the tasks for user and authorization administration can be distributed among three administrators. The *activity group administrator* can only maintain the activity groups. The *authorization profile administrator* can only generate the existing authorization profiles. And the *user administrator* can only maintain the user master records. The three administrators must work sequentially to create a user and give the user the required authorizations. Within the sequence, the following administrator checks the preceding one, which is called the double-verification principle. With this principle, you can protect your system against abuse of authorizations or user master records.

> **NOTE** In addition to the users of the R/3 Systems, there are users on the operating-system level of every level of the client/server architecture. Only administrators have operating-system users on the application servers and the database server. However, you must ensure that all R/3 users also have an operating-system user for their front ends.

Create an Authorization Concept

During the implementation project, you'll set up many systems. Each system has different user authorization requirements. Users can perform almost all actions in the R/3 development system and the quality assurance system. In the production system, you'll frequently have more stringent security requirements and must limit user authorizations accordingly. The more complex your company's authorization concept is, the more you must plan for it. A detailed authorization concept means that data is protected against unauthorized access and users have sufficient authorizations to perform their work. For your authorization concept, consider the following points:

- Plan generic activity groups
- Standardize naming conventions for the master records
- Define secure logon procedures and password rules

The following sections describe these points in detail.

Plan Activity Groups

As described in "Activity Groups" earlier in this chapter, in an activity group, you should define the transactions and activities permitted for a job role and which users can perform them. In R/3, you can create as many activity groups as your company requires. The more activity groups you create, the more time you need for user and activity group administration. Therefore, try to find a suitable group for multiple job roles.

> **NOTE** Activity groups are client dependent. They must be created in each client or transported from one client into the other clients.

The Job Role Matrix

To define as few activity groups as possible, you should first describe all of the job roles in your company in detail. The best way to do this is to create a job role matrix. In the job role matrix, list the activities (for example, the transactions, reports, or tasks) for each job role. You can list the activities in one of two ways: You can write a *component-oriented* description of the job roles, or you can write a *business process–oriented* description of the job roles. With a component-oriented description, the job role fits one of the R/3 components used in your company, such as the Financial Accounting component or the Production Planning component. With a business process–oriented description, the job role fits a business process in R/3, such as processing a delivery or entering an order (see the sidebar "Example: Creating a Business Process–Oriented Job Role Matrix").

Example: Creating a Business Process–Oriented Job Role Matrix

The following table displays a business process–oriented job role matrix. The matrix uses a sample business process to list the tasks with the necessary transactions and some of the related job roles. The department managers can perform all of the transactions of the business process without restriction. The administrator is only responsible for some of the business processes.

Continued on next page

Business Process	Task	TCode	Job Roles	
			Administrator Sales	Department Manager Sales
Delivery process	Create delivery	VL01	Partially	All
	Change delivery	VL02	Partially	All
	Display delivery	VL03	Partially	All
	Print delivery note	VL02	Partially	All
	Process delivery due list	VL04	No	All
	Generate picking list	VL04	No	All
	Print picking list	VL16	No	All

Security Requirements

The number of job roles that you can group into an activity group essentially depends on your company's security requirements. Normally, each department or organization in your company has different requirements for data security. For example, a human resources department would want to control the access to personal data more precisely than the sales and distribution department would want to protect the access to data about available goods. Table 6.1 displays four criteria for estimating the security requirements in the departments.

Using the job role matrix and the security requirements, you can define the activity groups, the transactions used by individual business processes, and the required authorizations. The security requirements help you determine how much you have to limit the values for the authorization fields. To define specific values, you need to consult the person responsible in the department. Your decision may put data at risk of being misused; for example, you should not give uncontrolled access to personal data. To reduce this risk, first create examples of activity groups and then test them for potential security gaps.

TABLE 6.1: Security Requirements for Transactions and Authorizations

Transactions	Authorizations	Description
Perform all	Display all	Users can perform all transactions for the tasks in one department and use these transactions to access data without limitations.
Perform all	Display parts	Users can perform all transactions for the tasks in one department and use these transactions to access data, but they only have limited access to data.
Perform parts	Display all	Users can only perform some transactions for the tasks in one department and use these transactions to access data without limitations.
Perform parts	Display parts	Users can only perform some transactions for the tasks in one department and use these transactions to access data, but they only have limited access to data.

General Activity Group

If users use common resources, you should create a separate activity group with general access authorizations for resources such as printers, background processing, or SAP office functions. You can allocate this type of activity group to all users. A general activity group may not always be applicable because each department may have different printers. Therefore, you should consider creating activity groups with general access authorizations, at least for individual departments.

Standardize Master Records

The user master data in the R/3 System is grouped in the user master record. Master data is, for example, the user authorization profile or basic data such as name, password, and address. As described in "Activity Groups" earlier in this chapter, users can only log on to R/3 if a user master record has been created for them. Therefore, you must create a master record for each employee in your company who should work with R/3.

> **NOTE** User master records are client dependent. You must create them in each client for a user.

To administer the user master records faster and thus more cost-effectively, you should use uniform naming conventions for the master records. In R/3, the data in a master record is divided into six categories: Addresses, Logon Data, Defaults, Task Profile, Profiles, and Parameters. If you create or change the user master record in R/3, the Maintain User screen (transaction code SU01) displays the categories as a series of tabs (see Figure 6.4). To create a user in R/3, you must enter at least a last name and an initial password. However, most data is optional. Therefore, you must define the data that is listed in the system operation manual as required by your company in the master record. If the users and activity groups are maintained decentrally by different people, especially after the start of production, you must implement a naming convention. Otherwise, users can each choose different conventions and make master record maintenance more difficult.

Both the Defaults and Parameters tabs are important for a user's daily work. Under Defaults, you can set the default values, such as the start menu, the logon language, or the output device. In the Parameters tab, you can predefine specific values (for example, the company code or the sales organization) for a given user. If a screen with such a parameter is displayed, R/3 enters the predefined value for it. All users can enter and change this data themselves, but you should set default values for this data as much as possible.

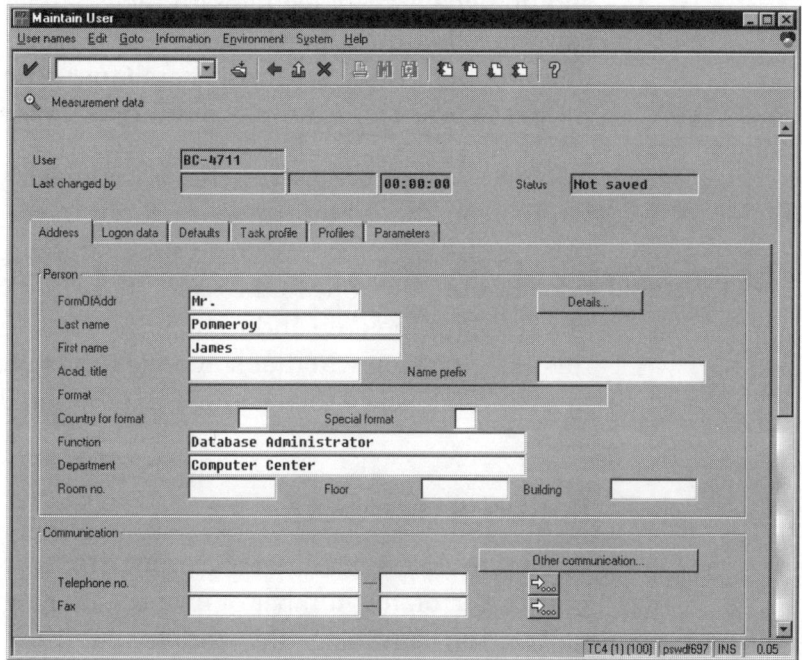

FIGURE 6.4:
Entry screen for maintaining a user

> **NOTE** Changes to master records are only effective once the user logs on to R/3 again. If a user was logged on while the changes were being made, he or she must log on again.

Define the Logon Procedure and Password Rules

To log on to R/3, a third party only needs a user name and an accompanying password. Even the most detailed authorization concept is only as secure as the users' passwords. Only passwords that are secret and difficult to guess can protect your R/3 System from unauthorized accesses by third parties. Three aspects are essential to protect against unauthorized accesses. First, all users should behave responsibly with their passwords. Second, users can enter their passwords incorrectly several times but only a limited number of times. Third, users must observe specified rules for passwords (for example, a minimum password length).

To ensure that the users behave responsibly with their passwords, you should inform them about the security risks and the rules for a safe password in a user training course. In particular, you should point out to the users that after they log on, a dialog box displays the date and time of the last logon. Users can use this to determine whether someone has logged on to the system in their name since the last time they worked in the system.

Logon Attempts

To ensure that a third party cannot discover a password through trial and error, the number of unsuccessful logon attempts is limited in R/3. You can change this number. Table 6.2 lists your options.

TABLE 6.2: Limits for the Number of Logon Attempts

Consequence of Unsuccessful Attempt	Number of Unsuccessful Attempts		Description
SAPGUI ends	Default	3	Users can start SAPGUI as often as they want. Users can attempt to log on until the user is locked.
	Possible	1 to 99	
User locked	Default	12	A locked user can no longer log on to R/3, even with the correct password. The lock is either removed at midnight or earlier by the user administrator.
	Possible	1 to 99	

Password Rules

To ensure that a password is difficult to guess, you can set up rules for passwords. Table 6.3 lists your options.

TABLE 6.3: Modifiable Password Rules

Rules	Default Values	Remarks
Length of password	Minimum of three characters	You can only increase this value and it can be a maximum of eight characters long.
Validity period	A password is valid for an unlimited time	You can set the number of days after which the password must be changed
Lock list	SAP* and PASS	Words from the lock list are rejected as passwords.

In addition to the modifiable password rules, there are some rules in R/3 that you cannot change. These mandatory rules are described in detail in the R/3 online documentation. For example, the first three characters in the password cannot be in the same order as they are in the user name, and the password cannot be PASS or SAP*.

> **NOTE** The data flow between a front end and the application server only has a simple encryption; therefore, a third party could decode the transferred user names and passwords. To protect the data flow, you can incorporate the network into a network security system by using the SAP interface Secure Network Communications (SNC). Chapter 11, "Network Administration," describes SNC in more detail.

Administer User and Activity Groups

In R/3, you can use authorizations to adapt the administration of user master records and activity groups to your organization's requirements. In companies with low security requirements, one person can do any task, such as maintain user master records and generate authorization profiles. In companies with high security requirements, you should use the double-verification principle to distribute these tasks among several people. This authorizes one person, for example, to create an activity group, yet this person is not authorized to give the users the related authorization profile.

In the following sections, you'll learn how to administer the users and activity groups. You'll learn how to implement the double-verification principle, when you should maintain the user master records centrally or decentrally, and what is important for the system operation.

Implement the Double-Verification Principle

To implement the double-verification principle in R/3 for user and authorization administration, distribute the tasks among three administrators as follows (see Figure 6.5):

Activity group administrator The activity group administrator creates activity groups, selects the R/3 transactions for an activity group, and maintains the related authorization fields. However, this administrator does not have authorization to generate authorization profiles or to maintain users.

Authorization profile administrator The authorization profile administrator generates authorizations and authorization profiles for existing activity groups. However, this administrator does not have the authorization to maintain users or activity groups.

User administrator The user administrator creates and maintains the user master record and assigns the users to one or more activity groups. However, this administrator does not have authorization to maintain authorization profiles or activity groups or to generate authorization profiles.

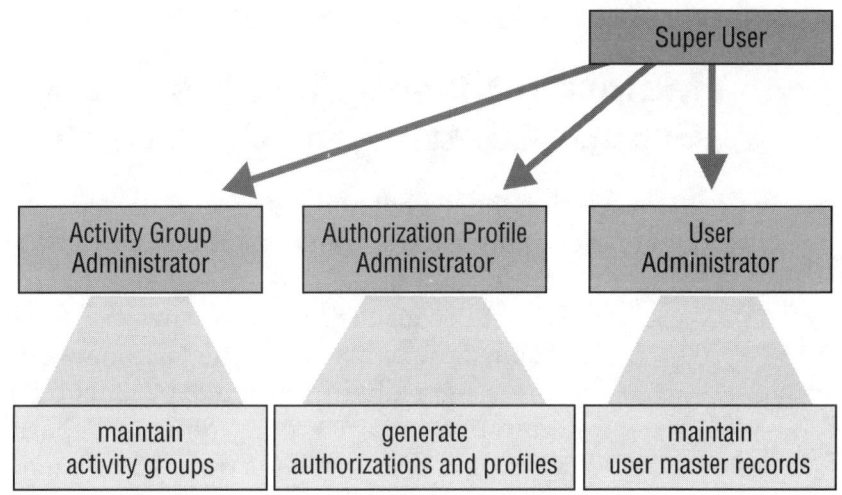

FIGURE 6.5:
Double-verification principle for administering users and their authorizations

Distributing the tasks among three administrators is the best way to protect your system from the potential abuse of authorizations and user master records. If one user had authorization for all the tasks, then that user could create activity groups and generate the accompanying authorization profile. This would allow the user to change existing authorization profiles and authorizations and generate them, thus making them effective.

Super User

As shown in Figure 6.5, the super user sets up the activity groups and user master records for the three administrators. The super user is the only user in the system who can change the user master records of the three administrators. This ensures that the administrators cannot change their own user master records, neither separately nor together. You should only set up a very limited number of super users for each system because this type of user has all the authorizations in the system. The R/3 online documentation describes how to set up the three administrators and the super users.

Maintain Master Records and Activity Groups Centrally or Decentrally

During the Realization phase, you'll decide on the strategy for user administration, and you must decide whether the user master records and the activity groups should be maintained centrally or decentrally for the production system. In particular, you must determine how to distribute the tasks between the departments and the system administration department. Since you define job roles through activity groups, only the department can decide which transactions can be performed by a job role and which authorizations are required. It is particularly beneficial for R/3 Systems with over one hundred users if each department maintains its own activity groups. For example, the departments can take over the tasks of the activity group administrator and the authorization profile administrator. To ensure that the departments do not cause each other problems, you should define naming conventions. For example, the finance department can only maintain authorization profiles that begin with the letter *F*. As shown in Figure 6.6, you can continue to divide the administrators' tasks in accordance with this naming convention. Administrators are only authorized to maintain and generate authorization profiles with a specified naming convention.

To steer the user administration procedures in the planned direction, within ASAP, it is recommended that you administer the user master records and activity groups centrally before the start of production. This ensures a uniform naming convention for the master records, groups, and authorization profiles. If you begin with a decentralized administration, all the administrators may use their own naming conventions or use different authorizations for the same job roles. To subsequently decentralize these procedures in a roll out, you should document them in a system operation manual during the implementation. The following section explains what you must take into consideration.

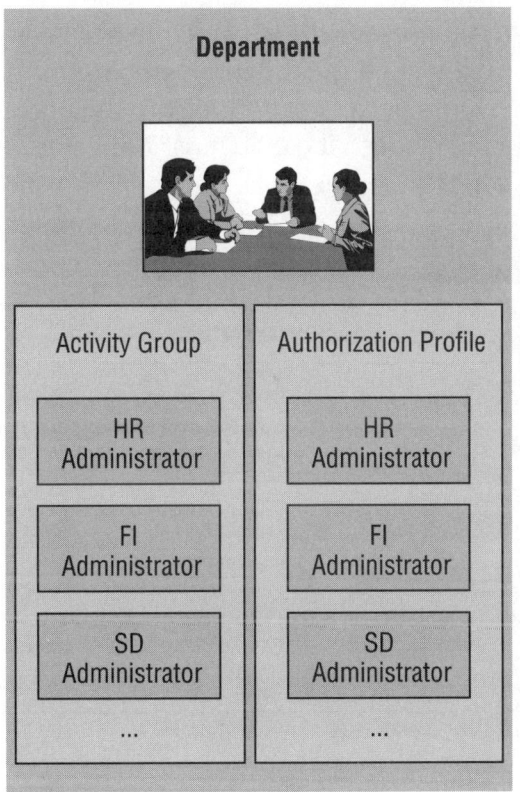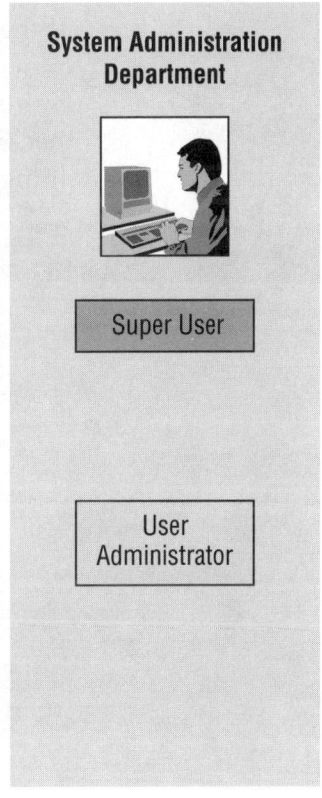

FIGURE 6.6: Decentral administration of user master records and activity groups through departments and the computer center

Define System Operation

During the Realization phase, you'll define the system operation for user administration together with the people from the department who are responsible for user administration. Then the user administrator documents this in the system operation manual. While you prepare for production, you should test the procedures and adjust the manual if any procedures have been changed. For example, the manual should document who has to take over which tasks for the user administration.

If the double-verification principle has been implemented in your company, you must define which activities each of the three administrators perform and the way they communicate with each other. Table 6.4 describes the most important activities for maintaining activity groups.

TABLE 6.4: Activities for Activity Group Administration

Activity	Role	Description
Create/change activity group	Department/ authorization administrator	Based on the job role descriptions (in the job role matrix), transactions are selected, authorization fields are maintained, and agents are allocated.
Delete activity group	Department/ authorization administrator	If users have already been allocated, the authorization profiles for the activity group are removed. The department must apply for them.
Transport activity group	Authorization administrator	The activity groups are created in the development system; the data must be recorded in change requests.

After activity groups have been created or imported into the system through a change request, you must activate the accompanying authorization profiles. The activity group administrator notifies the authorization profile administrator of the profiles that need to be activated. Table 6.5 displays the important activities for activating the authorization profiles and describes what you should take into consideration.

TABLE 6.5: Activities for Authorization Profile Administration

Activity	Role	Description
Generate authorizations	Department/ authorization administrator	An authorization that is based on the authorization object S_USER_PRO is necessary. Changes to already active profiles take effect when the user logs on to R/3 again.
Reconcile user master records	Department/ authorization administrator	A user master record must be created for all agents of a task.

The user master record is client dependent. In an R/3 System, you can copy the master records of one client into another by using the client copy tool. Transporting master records between the systems in a landscape is difficult. Therefore, you can most easily create the master records in each system manually. Table 6.6 displays the important activities for maintaining the user master records and describes what you should take into consideration.

TABLE 6.6: Activities for User Administration

Activity	Role	Description
Create/change user	R/3 System administrator	The user's department or the human resources department submits a request to create or change a user; in accordance with the naming conventions, the master records are changed or created with an initial password.
Delete user	R/3 System administrator	The human resources department notifies the R/3 System administrator about employees who have left the company; for security reasons, their master records are deleted.
Change password	Help desk	Users sometimes forget their passwords; to quickly help users, the help desk can change a password.

User Administration in ASAP

In the previous sections, you learned what to consider for user administration during the R/3 implementation. In ASAP, these points are distributed over the individual phases of the project. The following sections describe when to perform certain tasks.

Project Preparation

At the end of the Project Preparation phase, you'll define the authorization concept for the members of the Project Team. In the development system, there are essentially three roles: customizer, developer, and administrator. For smaller projects with up to 15 employees, define an activity group for each of the three roles. The larger the Project Team, the more roles are divided into roles that are more refined. You need a detailed authorization concept, and if necessary, you must create more than three activity groups. The users in the development system almost always have more authorizations than the users in the quality assurance system or the production system.

> **WARNING** For the authorization standards of the Project Team, take into consideration that nobody can have authorization to develop programs in the production system. Since all accesses to the database tables from ABAP programs are either read or change, developing programs in the production system is a security risk. Therefore, lock all the transaction codes that begin with the letters *SE*.

Business Blueprint

In the Business Blueprint phase, you'll begin to define and document the roles and tasks for users. First, plan the authorization concept for the users in the quality assurance system. During the course of the project, test the activity groups with these users. You also need to have these users train your employees in the Go Live and Support phase.

During the Business Blueprint phase, you'll install the development system. The user master records for the members of the Project Team are created in this system. In the development client, create an activity group with the authorizations that you defined during the Project Preparation phase. If necessary, copy the activity groups from the development client into the other clients of your development system.

Realization

During the Realization phase, you'll refine the complete authorization concept for your company's production system. First, describe the job roles and the related security requirements for the individual departments or organizations. In larger companies, it is beneficial to set up a security team that creates the job role matrices for each department. In a job role matrix, you should list the required transactions and authorizations for the different roles in a department. Using the job role matrix, you can then plan the activity groups. Your authorization concept is only complete once you have described how to administer the user and activity groups (see "Administer User and Activity Groups" earlier in this chapter).

After you have described your authorization concept in detail, implement it in the development system and quality assurance system. Use the Profile Generator to create the planned activity groups in the development system. Ensure that the transport system records your work in change requests. From the development system, transport an activity group into the quality assurance system. In the quality assurance system, create a user master record to test each job role, generate the authorization profiles for each activity group, and allocate test users to the activity groups. Then, together with the departments, test the defined security requirements to make sure they have been fulfilled and the test users have sufficient authorizations for their tasks.

At the end of the Realization phase, the production system should already be installed. In the production system, create a user master record for each user. If the master records should be maintained decentrally by the departments in your company after the start of production, first create the master record centrally. This is the best way to implement the defined conventions for naming and authorizations.

Table 6.7 lists the tasks from ASAP that are related to the implementation of user administration. Each task is described in accordance with the phase in which it is performed and the person who performs it.

TABLE 6.7: Tasks for User Administration in ASAP

Phase	Phase Name	Task	Role
1	Project Preparation	Define system authorization standards for Project Team	Authorization administrator, Project Team Lead
2	Business Blueprint	Define end-user roles and responsibilities	Project Manager, Business Process Team Lead
		Set up user master records for the Project Team	Authorization administrator, Technical Team Lead
3	Realization	Create detailed authorization design Implement authorization concept	Authorization administrator, Business Process Owner
		Assign system authorizations	Authorization administrator, Business Process Owner

Success Factors

To successfully implement user administration, you must especially consider the following:

- Protect special users
- Use the Profile Generator
- Create user groups

The following sections describe these points in detail.

Protect Special Users

During the implementation, three special users are created in each R/3 client: SAP*, DDIC, and EARLYWATCH. The user names and passwords are accessible to third parties. For the security of your R/3 System, you must therefore protect the special users from third parties!

SAP*

SAP* is the only user in R/3 for which no user master record is necessary. It is programmed into the R/3 System code. If no user master record has been created, its password is PASS and it has all authorizations. To ensure that third parties cannot access the data in R/3 without authorization, deactivate the user SAP* and replace it with a self-defined user. How to deactivate the user SAP* and create new super users is described in the R/3 online documentation or in *SAP R/3 System Administration: The Official SAP Guide*, by Liane Will (Sybex, 1998).

WARNING You cannot delete the user SAP*!

DDIC

You need user DDIC for specific tasks during the implementation and configuration of your system. For example, if you upgrade to a new R/3 Release, you should log on to R/3 with the user DDIC. To perform these tasks, DDIC has special authorizations for the installation, Software Logistics, and the ABAP Dictionary. The authorizations for user DDIC are defined in the system code. You must change the initial password for user DDIC, but you do not need to deactivate it.

WARNING You cannot delete user DDIC!

EARLYWATCH

The user EARLYWATCH is only created in client 066. If you wish, SAP specialists can log on to your R/3 System through a remote connection with this user. This user is especially used for the Early Watch and GoingLive Check services. The user EARLYWATCH can only access technical performance data that is required for the service. The business data in the other clients is not visible to the users of client 066. This way, client 066 protects your data from undesired access. For the user EARLYWATCH, change the initial password, and to control the access to your system, change the password after every service session.

WARNING You cannot delete the user EARLYWATCH!

Table 6.8 lists the special users and the initial password for each user in the individual clients.

TABLE 6.8: Special Users in the R/3 System

Special User	Client	User Master Record	Initial Password
SAP*	000, 001	Automatically created with authorization profiles: SAP_ALL, SAP_NEW	06071992
	066	Automatically created with authorization profiles: S_USER_ALL	06071992
	New client XXX created	Not created	PASS
DDIC	000, 001	Automatically created with authorization profiles: SAP_ALL, SAP_NEW	19920706
EARLYWATCH	066	Automatically created with authorization profiles: S_TOOLS_EX_A	SUPPORT

Use the Profile Generator

To implement the authorization concept quickly and with minimum effort, you should use the Profile Generator to automatically generate authorization profiles. The only alternative is to maintain the authorizations and profiles manually. However, you must know the existing authorizations and their interdependencies in detail. Even experienced authorization administrators cannot generate authorization profiles with the manual method more quickly than with the Profile Generator.

User Menus

If you generate an activity group with the Profile Generator, it automatically creates a user-specific menu. In the Session Manager, the user menu only displays the menu paths for the R/3 transactions that the user is authorized to perform. This allows quicker and simpler navigation of the menu for the user. Figures 6.1, 6.2, and 6.3 displayed how to create an activity group for the accountants. Figure 6.7 displays the user-specific menu that an agent of this activity group sees.

FIGURE 6.7:

User-specific menu in the Session Manager (for the accountant FI-4711)

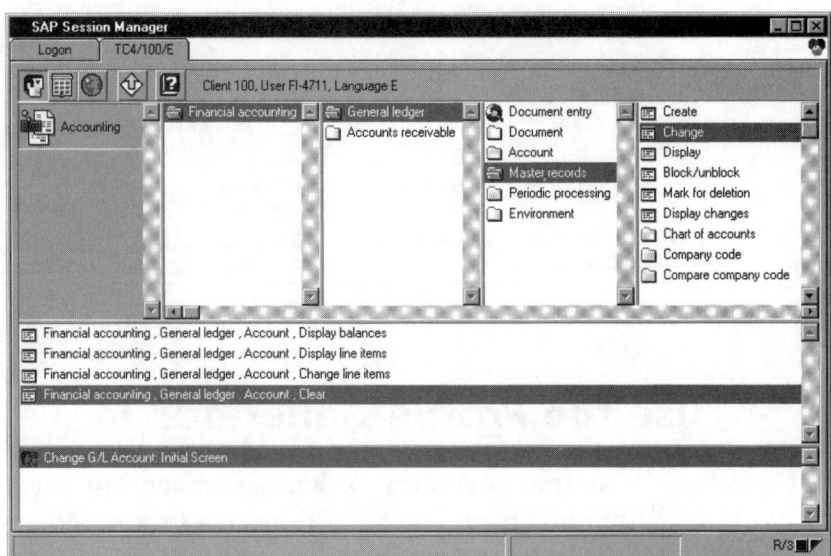

Create User Groups

If multiple user administrators administer the user master records in your company, you should set up user groups and allocate every user to one of these groups. Only give a user administrator authorization to maintain the master records of one of the user groups. Particularly for R/3 Systems with several hundred users, always group large organizational units, such as Sales and Distribution or Human Resources. Then, the administrator for the sales and distribution group can only change the master records for this group.

> **NOTE** If a user master record is not allocated to a user group, every user administrator can maintain it.

Allocate the user master records for the administrators for the user and activity groups to the special user group SUPER. This ensures that the users of the group SUPER can only be maintained by super users, who have one of two authorization profiles: S_ASYSTEM or SAP_ALL. This prevents normal administrators from changing their own user master records or those of other administrators

Review Questions

1. Which statements are correct?
    - A. User master records are client dependent.
    - B. User master records can only be created in client 000.
    - C. Activity groups are client dependent.
    - D. Activity groups cannot be transported between systems.

2. Which statements are correct?
    - A. To log on to R/3, you must know a user name and password.
    - B. A password can be used without restriction.
    - C. Users can be locked if they enter their password incorrectly too many times.
    - D. The validity period of a password is changeable.

3. What is the activity group administrator authorized to do?

   A. Create activity groups

   B. Maintain authorization fields

   C. Generate authorizations

   D. Change users

   E. Allocate agents to the activity group

4. Which special users are there in R/3?

   A. SAP*

   B. SAPDBA

   C. EARLYWATCH

   D. GOINGLIVE

   E. DDIC

   F. SUPER

CHAPTER SEVEN

Background Processing

The R/3 System can process data in the background at the same time you perform other transactions on the screen. You can plan the tasks as background jobs and define a start time or an event. When the start time is reached or the event is triggered, background processing automatically starts your job and a background work process performs the task.

Even in smaller systems, some tasks can run a long time or must be performed regularly. Background processing is the easiest way to handle these types of task. You have to plan in detail when R/3 performs these tasks for you and with which background jobs. In this chapter, you'll learn how to create a concept for background processing in your company, and then you'll learn which options you have for administering background processing.

Create Your Concept for Background Processing

During the implementation project, you'll set up multiple R/3 Systems. Each system has different requirements for background processing. Frequently, in the development system and the quality assurance system, only jobs for routine work (for example, the reorganization of old spool requests) run in the background. In the production system, you'll often have more stringent requirements for background processing and schedule jobs for business processes, such as material requirements planning. If background processing is more complex in your company, you must plan for it in greater detail. To do so, you must perform the following tasks:

- Plan the requirements and load distribution
- Define job priorities
- Set up job chains
- Consider event-driven jobs

The following sections describe these points in detail.

Plan Requirements and Load Distribution

Essentially, each department defines which tasks and how much data a job should process in the background. Specifically in R/3 Systems with a large data volume, some jobs (for example, MRP runs) eventually require many hours. In this case, the R/3 System has to make the related resources available as background work processes. In Chapter 5, "R/3 Instance Administration," you learned that a typical R/3 System requires approximately one background work process for every four dialog work processes. Whether this relationship is also appropriate for your system depends on the number of jobs and their runtimes. You should define the probable number of jobs in the Business Blueprint phase. However, you can only determine the runtimes in test runs or in production operation. Therefore, during the R/3 implementation, you should only temporarily determine how to distribute the load over the available resources. In the first weeks after the start of production, you will be able to determine the best solution.

The Job List

To be able to estimate the number of jobs, the departments work together with the application consultants to create a job list. Make sure you list the critical jobs, the jobs that are absolutely necessary to run an application. The department should at least create a schedule for these jobs. Using the schedule, you can then work together with the technical consultants and application consultants to define which jobs should run in parallel and the minimum number of background work processes you'll need for them to do so. Additionally, you should define how many background work processes run on an instance and how many work processes are switched by the operation modes. This allows you to distribute the load from background processing over the servers in your system and over the course of a day.

Parallel Background Processing

Particularly in R/3 Systems with a large data volume, an application's jobs could place a heavy load on the server's CPU for several hours. These jobs must run at night so they don't have a negative effect on the performance of dialog processing. In some cases, a background work process cannot process a time-consuming job in one night. As of R/3 Release 3.1G, you can use parallel background processing in R/3 applications for these jobs.

During parallel background processing, a job is first started in a background work process. However, processing is then distributed over dialog work processes through RFC calls. When processing is complete, the background work process collects the results from each dialog work process. As Figure 7.1 shows, you use the RFC groups to define the instances over which the load generated by this type of job is distributed.

> **NOTE** Only special Advanced Business Application Programming (ABAP) programs can be processed in parallel. The R/3 online documentation for an application contains information about which ABAP programs in that particular R/3 Release support parallel processes.

FIGURE 7.1:

An example of RFC groups for parallel background processing

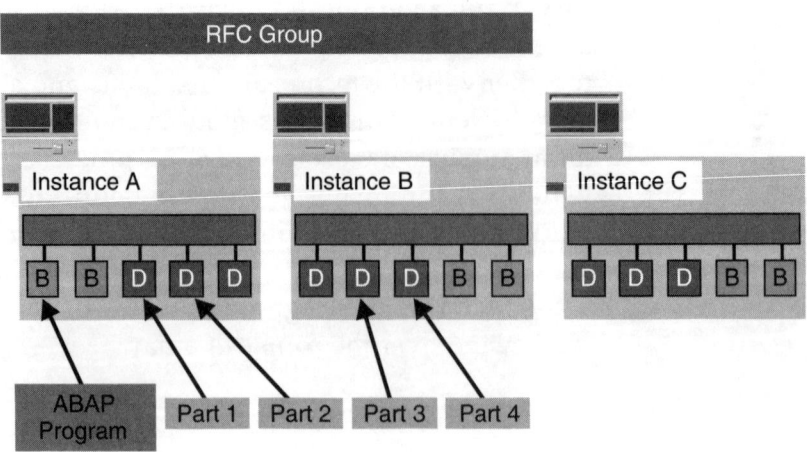

If you plan parallel background processing for your system, you can set up RFC groups in one of two ways. One way is to create an RFC group for background processing in which you include one or more instances (see Figure 7.1). However, if you start two jobs for parallel processing simultaneously, they compete for the same dialog work processes. To prevent a potential bottleneck in this case, you can create multiple RFC groups for different applications—for example, a group for Production Planning (PP) and a group for Controlling (CO).

Define Job Priorities

One of the most frequent demands on background processing is that time-critical jobs must have sufficient resources and successfully complete their tasks within the planned time period. Less important jobs should not influence the processing of time-critical jobs, although they should be processed within a reasonable amount of time. This is where problems frequently occur because the resources for background processing are limited, and to reduce costs, there are often only a few resources in reserve. To ensure that important jobs are processed with high priority, you must define priorities for the individual jobs.

Job Classes and Target Server

In R/3, you control the priority of a job by using job classes and target servers. There are three job classes: A, B, and C. Jobs in job class A have the highest priority, and jobs in job class C have the lowest priority. The target server allows you to specify the server on which a job runs. Jobs are started by R/3 according to the following rules:

- Jobs in class A run before jobs in class B.
- Jobs in class B run before jobs in class C.
- If the jobs are of the same class, jobs with specified target servers run before jobs without target servers.

- If jobs have the same priority according to these criteria, the job that has been waiting longer runs first.

Only the departments can decide which classes should be allocated to the jobs in the application. The department also should define the time and the order of the jobs when they run.

> **TIP** The only time you should specify a target server for a job is when the job can only run specifically on the target server—for example, if the job accesses data locally that it cannot access from other servers. Otherwise, you should not specify a target server; instead, allow the R/3 System to order jobs on the application servers. This way, R/3 distributes the load automatically and sensibly over the server for you.

Background Work Processes for Job Class A

The Technical Team ensures that the resources are configured optimally. Together with the departments, the Technical Team considers how to use the job class A. You have two options:

Set up multiple work processes for job class A. Reserve some of the background work processes for job class A. This ensures that at least one free work process is always reserved for jobs from job class A. You should choose this option if you have time-critical jobs that must be started at the scheduled time. These jobs should only be allocated to job class A; all other jobs are allocated to job class B or C.

Do not set up any work processes for job class A. If you do not reserve any background work processes for job class A, there may not be a free work process for jobs from job class A. A job from job class A may have to wait until another job is complete. You should choose this option if you do not have any time-critical jobs. This option still allows you to use the job classes to control the order in which the waiting jobs start.

> **NOTE** You can only reserve background work processes for job class A if you implement operation modes (see Chapter 5 "R/3 Instance Administration").

To decide between these two options, you must consider how important it is to start the job on time. If your system only has a few jobs from job class A, and if there is normally at least one background work process available, there is no advantage to reserving background work processes for job class A. More often, you would almost never use one of the background work processes and thus prevent jobs from class B or C from running, as described in the following example.

Example: Using Job Classes

In one instance, three background work processes are set up. One work process is reserved for job class A. The two situations below show in which order waiting jobs of various classes are started.

First situation All work processes are available; there is one job from each of the classes A, B, and C waiting to be processed.

The job from class A starts immediately, and R/3 reserves one of the remaining work processes for other jobs from class A. This way, only the job from class B can start immediately and the job from class C must wait. As soon as either the job from class A or the job from class B is complete, the job from class C can start.

Second situation All work processes are available; in addition to two jobs from class A, there is a job from class B and a job from class C, respectively, waiting to be processed.

Continued on next page

Both of the jobs from class A start immediately and R/3 reserves the remaining work processes for other jobs from class A. As the following graphic shows, jobs from classes B and C have to wait. As soon as one of the two jobs from class A is complete, the job from class B can start. The job from class C must continue to wait because R/3 reserves the remaining work processes again for jobs from class A. As soon as either the job from class A or the job from class B is complete, the job from class C can start.

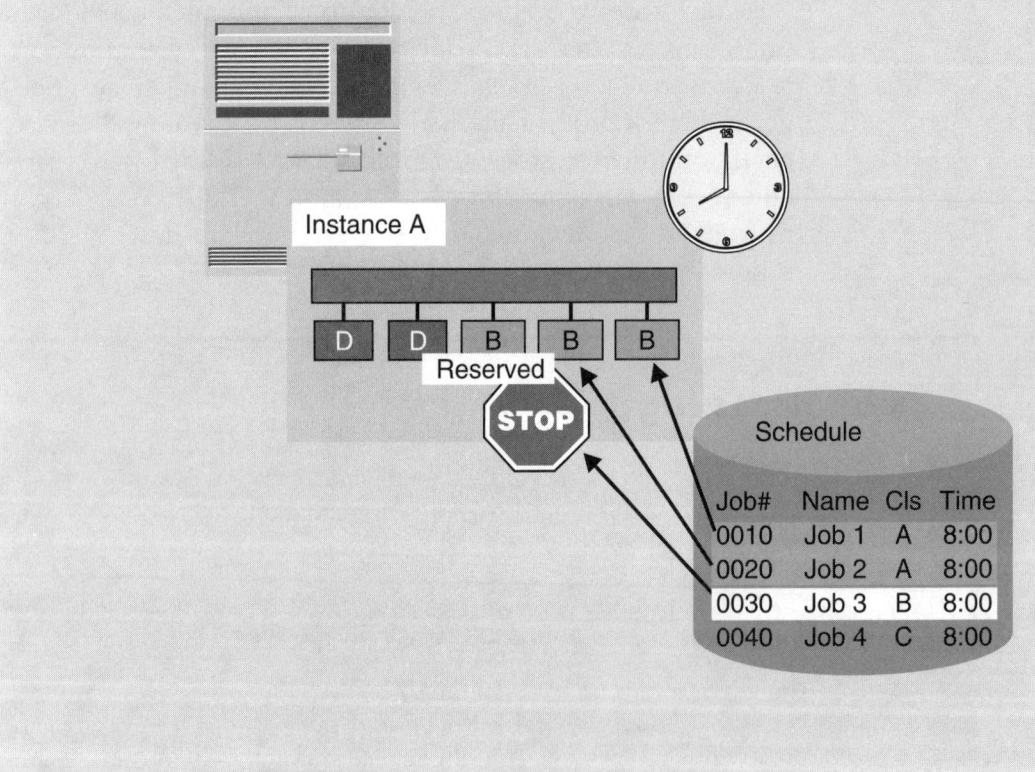

The preceding example shows you that you should reserve as few work processes as possible for job class A. This ensures that the throughput for the jobs from class B or C is not reduced. The number of work processes reserved for job class A and the number of time-critical jobs that R/3 should process at the same time should be the same. This way, you can ensure that jobs from class A start immediately and that sufficient free work processes remain for the jobs of the classes B and C.

Set Up Job Chains

For complex processes in background processing, you frequently have to ensure that jobs observe a specific order. Therefore, you must set up job chains with which you define the order in which the jobs can start and whether several different jobs should start in parallel after one job is completed. Figure 7.2 shows that you can set up simple job chains with the functions of the standard R/3 System. However, it is not possible to, for example, specify a repetition period for the entire job chain.

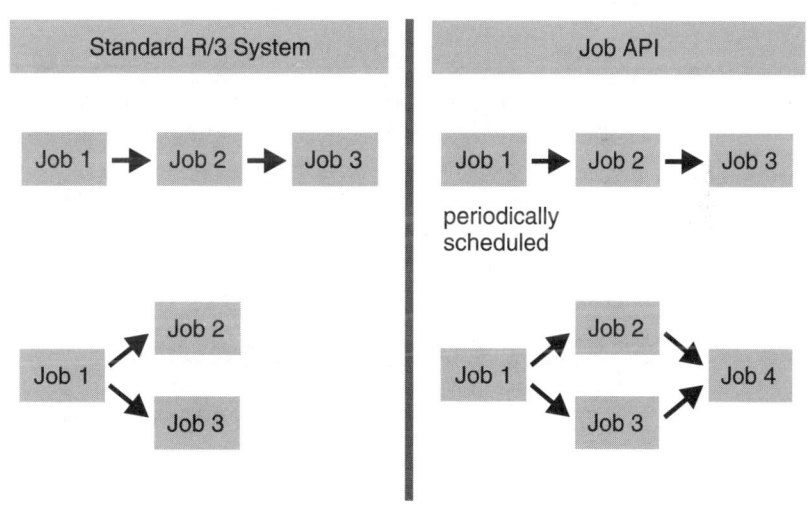

FIGURE 7.2:

Job chains in the standard R/3 System and Job API

If you require more complex job chains for your production system, you have two options in R/3. One option is to group the jobs as separate steps within a new job. This is useful if you want the successor job to start after the previous job has been processed without error. The other option is to program your own background scheduler. You can use the programming interface Job API to create the scheduler. Figure 7.2 displays the job chains that you can use with this interface.

External Job Management

Instead of programming your own background scheduler, you can access an external job management system from a third-party vendor. This type of system allows you to schedule, start, and monitor jobs outside of R/3. As of Release 3.1G, R/3 has the *XBP (eXternal Interface for Job Background Processing)* interface for this purpose. This interface allows external job management systems to call all the background processing functions and enables you to implement job chains that are more complex than those in the standard R/3 System.

> **TIP** When you select a product from a third-party vendor, make sure the product is certified by SAP. You can find information about complementary products from third-party vendors in SAPNet (`http://sapnet.sap.com/csp`) under the keyword "Complementary Solutions."

Consider Event-Driven Jobs

In R/3, you can define each job to start either at a specified point in time or after a specified event. To administer the start of jobs, R/3 uses both *time-driven* and *event-driven* background job schedulers. The time-driven scheduler runs periodically and checks to see whether there are jobs to be processed and which background work processes are available. R/3 only starts the event-driven scheduler once an event is triggered for background processing. The scheduler then starts the jobs that are scheduled for the event.

If no work processes are available at that time, the jobs are started by the time-driven scheduler.

Types of Events

If you require event-driven jobs for your background processing, R/3 has two types of events: system events and user events. The system events are contained in the standard R/3 System and are triggered by R/3. For example, R/3 triggers the event SAP_OPMODE_SWITCH when the operation mode is switched. You can define the user events yourself. You must trigger these events yourself either from an ABAP program or from an external program. For example, an external program can transfer data into the R/3 System. After the transfer has been successfully completed, an event is triggered to process the data in R/3.

> **TIP** The R/3 online documentation and *SAP R/3 System Administration: The Official SAP Guide*, by Liane Will (Sybex, 1998), describe how to define and schedule jobs.

Administer Background Processing

Background processing in R/3 enables you to organize the administration of jobs in various ways. In companies with few requirements for job scheduling, a user can schedule a job and release it for processing. In companies with a complex schedule for jobs, the tasks should be distributed among multiple employees. For example, you could distribute the tasks so that an employee can schedule a background job but cannot release it for processing. An administrator defines the start time for the jobs centrally and releases the jobs. This way, the administrator sensibly distributes the load for background processing over the day.

The following sections explain how to administer background processing with R/3. You'll learn how to release jobs centrally or decentrally and what is important for the system operation.

Release Jobs Centrally or Decentrally

When you define the authorization concept in the Realization phase, you have to decide whether you will centrally or decentrally release the background jobs in the production system for processing. In particular, you should define how to divide the tasks between the system administration department and the other departments; authorizations are useful for performing this task. A particular user requires special authorizations to release a job for processing or to access jobs that have been scheduled by other users. Figure 7.3 shows that you can define two roles for your system:

Job administrator The job administrator can perform all operations on jobs, display all the jobs in all the clients of the system, and administer and assign job classes.

Normal user Normal users can schedule a job and monitor the status and output of their own jobs. However, the normal user is not authorized to release jobs or to access the jobs of other users.

> **NOTE** Without having special authorization for jobs, all R/3 users can schedule jobs of class C, display or change the steps of their own jobs, delete their own jobs, and display the details of their own jobs.

Dividing the tasks between the job administrator and the normal users is the best way to prevent excessive load on background processing and allows you to sensibly distribute the load over the day. However, if every user can release the jobs from all job classes, too many jobs could be scheduled for the same start

FIGURE 7.3:
Decentral administration of background processing through departments and system administration

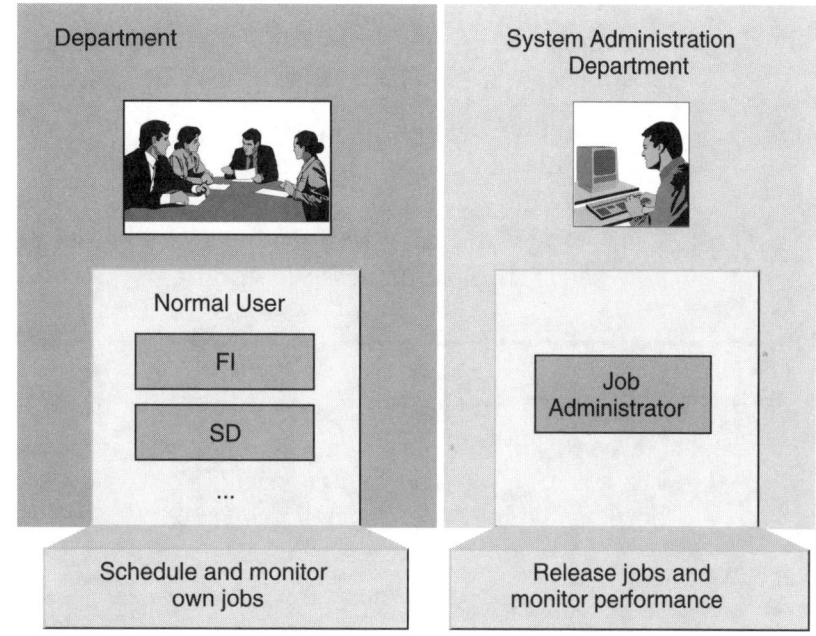

time, and thus, they would compete for resources with the important jobs from class A.

> **TIP** R/3 online documentation describes in detail which authorizations for background processing you have to allocate to the job administrator and the normal users.

Define the System Operation

At the end of the Realization phase, you should define system operation for background processing in the production system and document it in the system operation manual. Work together with the departments to create a job list of the most important jobs for the applications. Enter the priority and the start time for each job (see the table in the sidebar "Example: Creating a Job List"). In particular, you must define the person to notify in each department if an error occurs. The R/3 System administrator can see that a job is terminated; however, he or she cannot decide whether the job can be restarted once the error has been corrected. Only the department responsible for the job can decide because only the employees of the department know which business-related changes the job is performing and whether restarting the job makes sense from a business viewpoint.

Example: Creating a Job List

The following table displays an example of the job information you should document in the system operation manual.

Job	Class	Program	Client	Start	Periodic Value	Maintenance/ Problem
SAP_Reorg_Spool	A	RSPO0041	All	3:00 A.M.	Daily	Bill Smith ext. 2649
MRP run	A	RMMRP000	...			

The Job Scheduling Monitor

In R/3, there is a graphical monitor for background processing, the Job Scheduling Monitor, that allows you to monitor the load distribution over the background work processes of an R/3 System. The monitor displays the currently available background work processes and all the jobs that are already complete or are waiting for processing. Figure 7.4 shows an example of an R/3 System with seven background work processes distributed over two instances. From the Job Scheduling Monitor, you can call to a monitor that notifies you about all problems (for example, terminated jobs) that may occur during background processing.

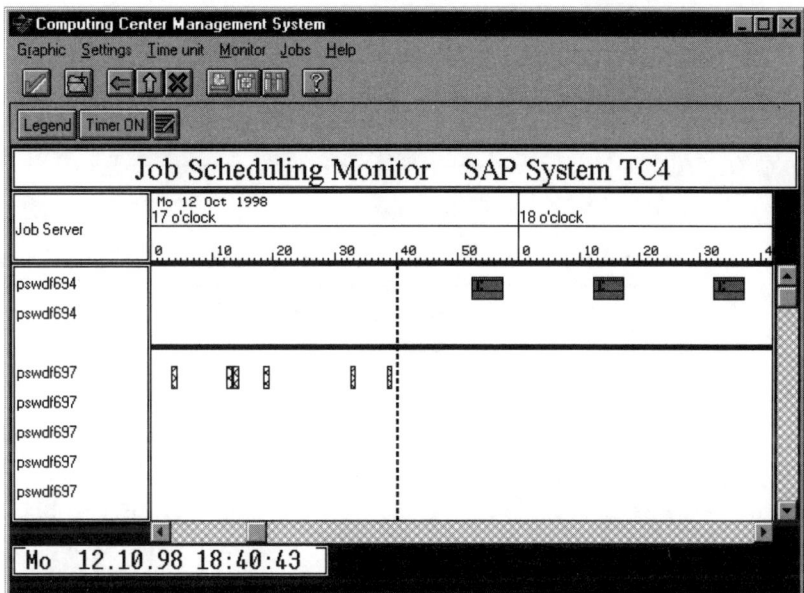

FIGURE 7.4:

A Job Scheduling Monitor for an R/3 System with three background servers

If a problem occurs with background processing and a job terminates during processing, the best way to find the error is to use the tools integrated in R/3. For each job, R/3 writes a job log that informs you about the causes of the termination.

> **TIP** The R/3 online documentation describes a procedure for analyzing a problem with background processing (see also R/3 Note 37104, "Error analysis: Background processing system").

To keep background processing running as smoothly as possible, you must check the status of the jobs regularly. Table 7.1 lists the activities for monitoring background processing. In the production system, you must check the job status at least daily. In the development system or quality assurance system, you can check the status less frequently—it is recommended that you check it at least once a week.

> **NOTE** The R/3 System does not automatically notify the users if a job terminates. Therefore, either users themselves must check or an administrator checks centrally for terminated jobs and notifies the respective user if a problem has occurred.

TABLE 7.1: Daily Activities for Monitoring Background Processing

Activity	Transaction Code	Remarks
Job Scheduling Monitor	RZ01	Monitor the runtime statistics for all jobs to harmonize the schedules for background processing of jobs. There must be a warning system for terminated jobs
Job overview	SM37	All terminated jobs must be analyzed and problems must be corrected. You must document the problems and their solutions. The procedure for resetting a terminated critical job is defined in the system operation manual.

Background Processing in ASAP

You'll set up the R/3 Systems in your system landscape in various phases of the project. For each system, define what resources you'll require for background processing and how you'll administer background processing. In a system operation manual, define who performs the activities and the procedures he or she should follow. First, define the system administration for the development system during the Business Blueprint phase. In this system, collect your first experiences with background processing, and if necessary, improve the procedures of the system operation. At the beginning of the Realization phase, you also must ensure the availability of the quality assurance system. Since the most important jobs of the application are only tested and not actually run in the development system and the quality assurance system, there are less stringent requirements for throughput and availability of background processing than there are in the production system. For this reason, the following sections describe how to implement the background processing in the production system and when to perform further tasks for background processing during the R/3 implementation.

Realization

In the Realization phase, you should prepare the throughput and system tests for the production system. Perform the tests during the Final Preparation phase. Together with the departments and application consultants, determine which jobs to include in the test; that is, which jobs are critical for running the system. The first type of jobs to include are time-critical jobs. You should test them to see whether they start and end at the specified time. The second type of jobs can be the important jobs for individual applications. In R/3 Systems with a large data volume, this type of job frequently runs for many hours and places a heavy load on the server's CPU. For these jobs, you must plan a throughput test to see whether the system resources are sufficient for the jobs and whether the jobs are completed within the planned time frame.

In addition to planning tests, define the operation of the production system at the end of the Realization phase. The experience you have gained in administering the system is important here. The administration for the restart procedure after problems occur must be fundamentally revised. If one of the applications' jobs terminates during production operation, the R/3 System administrator can use the job log to find the cause of the problem and may also be able to resolve the problem. However, the R/3 System administrator cannot decide whether and how the job can be restarted. In the system operation manual, you should define who must be notified in each department to restart the job. The R/3 System administrator must then contact this person to decide how to restart a terminated job so that no inconsistencies in the business data are caused.

Final Preparation

At the beginning of the Final Preparation phase, the Technical Team ensures the availability of the production system. First, you should configure the Computing Center Management System (CCMS), using operation modes to distribute the background work processes over the 24-hour period. Additionally, you should schedule the jobs needed for the routine system administration work. It is essential for production operation that you can depend on the procedures of the system operation; therefore, test the procedures in advance and improve them if necessary. If you have set up the role for a job administrator, you should also test whether the authorizations have been allocated as desired.

Before you can run your system in production operation, test the throughput, at least for the important jobs. These tests should tell you whether the R/3 System can process the business transactions that are important for your R/3 System in the background. If a problem occurs with the runtime or wait time during the tests, consult with the technical consultants and experts to decide whether you can improve the throughput with system settings or whether you need additional hardware.

Table 7.2 lists the tasks from ASAP that are related to the implementation of background processing. The table specifies who performs each task and in which phase.

TABLE 7.2: Background Processing Tasks in ASAP

Phase	Phase Name	Task	Role
2	Business Blueprint	Define system administration for the development system	Technical Team Lead, R/3 System administrator, technical consultant
3	Realization	Establish system administration for the development system and quality assurance system	Technical Team Lead, R/3 System administrator, technical consultant
		Develop system test plans	Technical Team Lead, R/3 System administrator, technical consultant, Business Process Team Lead
		Define production system administration	Technical Team Lead, R/3 System administrator, technical consultant
4	Final Preparation	Establish production system administration	Technical Team Lead, R/3 System administrator, technical consultant
		Conduct system tests	Technical Team Lead, R/3 System administrator, technical consultant, Business Process Team Lead

Success Factors

To successfully implement background processing, you must perform the following tasks:

- Schedule standard background jobs
- Optimize throughput

The following sections describe these points in detail.

Schedule Standard Background Jobs

Some background jobs—jobs that handle routine system administration work for you—have to run regularly in an R/3 System. For example, you can use ABAP program RSPO0041 to delete obsolete spool requests from the database. If the spool requests database were to fill, your R/3 System would not be able to function. The R/3 online documentation and *SAP R/3 System Administration: The Official SAP Guide* describe other jobs that are necessary. Table 7.3 also lists the important R/3 Notes on this topic.

TABLE 7.3: R/3 Notes about the Standard Background Jobs

Note No.	Short Text
16083	Standard jobs, reorganization jobs
98065	Spool consistency check using RSPO1043 as of Rel 40A

For the production system in particular, make sure all the necessary jobs for routine work are scheduled as recommended. Since most jobs run daily, you must also check daily to ensure that the jobs were completed successfully. For some jobs, you must also check the spool list. For example, you can use the ABAP program RSPO1043 to check the consistency of the database in the spool system. The program logs any inconsistencies in the spool list of the background job.

> **NOTE** The ABAP programs mentioned in the R/3 Notes listed in Table 7.3 only maintain and reorganize the components for the technical Basis in an R/3 System. The R/3 online documentation for each application explains which programs are required for the routine work in the applications.

Optimize Throughput

You can only achieve optimal throughput for background processing if you use a detailed schedule to distribute the jobs sensibly over the day. Before the start of production, you can simulate production operation; however, you can only create a provisional schedule this way. More often, in the first weeks after the start of production, you must analyze the performance of background processing and, if necessary, adapt your schedule. In addition to the Job Scheduling Monitor, R/3 has another monitor to analyze the performance of background jobs. Figure 7.5 shows that this monitor provides job details such as the duration of a job or the delay of a job compared to the scheduled start time. At the same time, you can also display the job history statistics, such as the number of job starts or the average runtime.

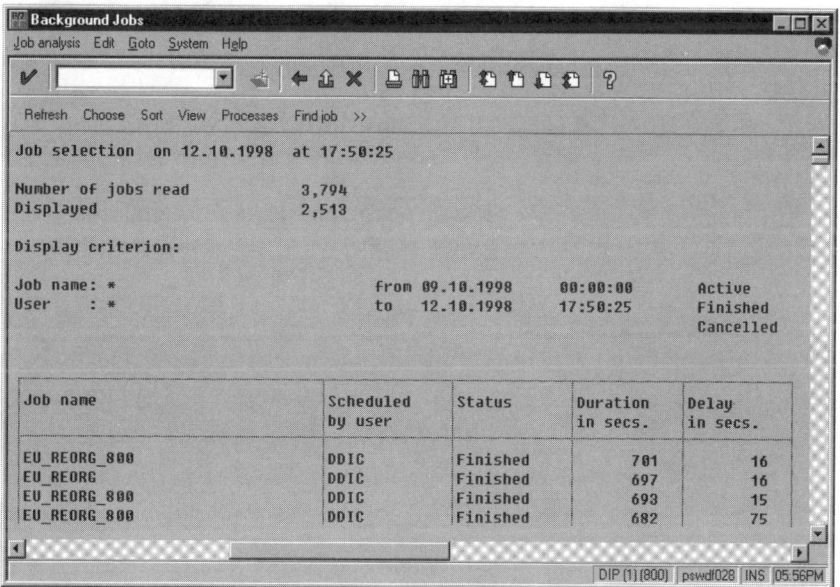

FIGURE 7.5

A performance analysis for background jobs (transaction code SM39)

The monitors in R/3 allow you to search for jobs with long runtimes and delayed start times. If you discover a problem, you may be able to distribute the load more sensibly over the day with an improved schedule and thus resolve the problem.

Review Questions

1. Which statements are correct?

    A. R/3 controls the priority of jobs with the three job classes A, B, and C.

    B. The jobs from class C have a higher priority than the jobs from class B.

    C. The jobs from one job class can only run on one instance.

    D. Work processes can be reserved for each job class.

2. Which statements are correct?

    A. In the standard R/3 System, it is possible to have job chains with jobs that can trigger multiple successors.

    B. In the standard R/3 System, it is possible to schedule a repetition period for a job chain.

    C. The Job API enables more job chains to be used.

    D. R/3 has a standardized interface through which the external job management system can connect to the R/3 System.

3. What can R/3 users do without special authorization for jobs?

   A. Schedule jobs from class B and C.

   B. Display or change the steps in their own jobs.

   C. Display or change jobs that have been planned by users in their own activity group.

   D. Release their own jobs.

   E. Display the details of their own jobs.

CHAPTER
EIGHT

Print Administration

The spool system in the R/3 System has a uniform user interface for the spool service on different operating systems. When you use dialog processing or background processing, you generate documents to be printed or faxed. The spool system stores these documents in the database or in files on the operating-system level and uses spool requests to administer the documents. To print the documents, you must connect the printer to an application server either locally or through the network. The printers in R/3 are administered with the spool system. For each printer, you must define which application server formats the data for the output. The formatted data is passed to the operating system spool.

R/3 users want to generate their printouts as easily as possible because they often need them quickly, so the Technical Team must make the required print capacity and output formats available. Printouts can be anything from simple lists to delivery notes and bar-code labels; therefore, the printer landscape in R/3 always consists of very different printers. To help you run this type of heterogeneous printer landscape cost-effectively and without excessive effort, this chapter explains how to perform the following tasks:

- Plan your print infrastructure
- Set up the print infrastructure
- Monitor the output

Plan Your Print Infrastructure

During the implementation project, you'll set up a print landscape for your entire system landscape. Each R/3 System in the landscape has different requirements. In the development system and the quality assurance system, you won't have time-critical or large-volume print jobs. In these systems, you only need to set up the printers for the Project Team and the logical structure of the server that will format the data for the output in the production system. In the production system, all the users print, and the requirements for the print infrastructure increase accordingly. You must plan this infrastructure in detail to keep the printer landscape as uniform as possible and to be able to handle all the different requirements. When you plan, you should consider the following points:

Accurately estimate the need for time-critical and high-volume print jobs. The types of devices you select and how many you need of each type depends in particular on whether the output of some documents is time critical and how many documents are printed in the course of a day.

Divide the printers into generic groups. To administer the printer landscape cost-effectively and as simply as possible, use only a small number of different printer types.

Set up high availability and load distribution for print formatting. The instance that formats the output for a printer and the number of spool work processes depends in particular on the print volume you will have and whether you need a special high availability for some printers.

The following sections describe these points in detail.

Determine the Print Requirements

If you have an R/3 System with many users, your print requirements are more complex and require more in-depth planning. This idea is not new, but it is consistently implemented in ASAP. You should begin planning in the Business Blueprint phase. The Technical Team essentially has two tasks. First, the Team analyzes the existing printer landscape and documents it. Second, together with the departments, the Team determines the print requirements and the target status for the printer landscape. You should compare the target status with your current status and then decide which of the existing printers you want to use and where you need additional printers. You can use these requirements to ask for quotations from hardware partners (see Figure 8.1). Ensure that the device type is supported by SAP. In R/3, you can create a separate device type for each device; however, you'll save time and money if you only use the device types that are already supported by the standard R/3 System.

> **NOTE** R/3 Note 8928, "List of supported printers/device types," lists the types of devices currently supported by the standard R/3 System.

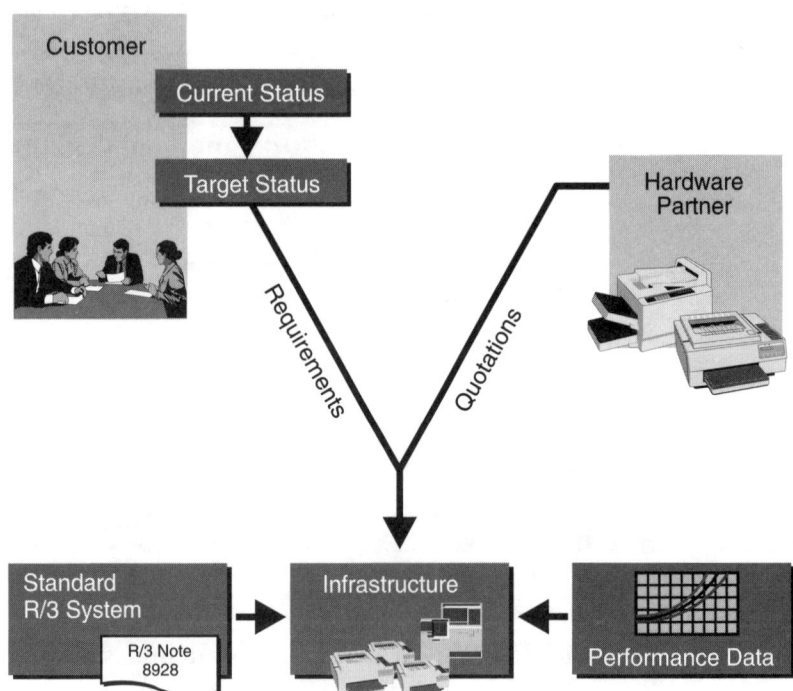

FIGURE 8.1:

Define the printer landscape

Requirements

The best way to determine the print requirements is to distinguish between the following five groups right at the beginning:

Time-critical print   For example, shipping documents

High-volume print   For example, long lists and large documents

Normal print   For example, letters and short lists

Confidential print   For example, salary lists

Special print   For example, documents with optical character recognition (OCR) fonts or bar codes

You should work with the departments to determine which size of paper is required, how many pages are printed in the course of a day or week, and what type of availability you can provide for the printers. In particular, consider whether there are unusual load peaks, such as at the end of the month. You must include this type of load peak in your print infrastructure. This ensures the system throughput for the print volume even when the spool system is heavily loaded.

Authorization Concept

You must also work with the departments to create an authorization concept for printing. Should each R/3 user be able to print an arbitrary number of print jobs on a printer or should the print volume be restricted? In R/3, you can use authorization objects to define both the printer that an activity group can access and the group's agent. You can also define the maximum number of pages a user can print with an output request. This allows you to, for example, prevent a user from occupying a printer with a long document when a time-critical print job for delivery notes should be taking place.

> **TIP** The "BC Printing Guide" in the R/3 online documentation describes which authorizations you can assign for printing, output administration, and print administration.

Classify and Standardize Printers

In R/3, you can define which R/3 instance formats the output for each printer. To allow you to control which instance processes which print requirements, SAP recommends first classifying the printers. As displayed in Figure 8.2, you should divide the printers for R/3 into the following classes:

High-volume printers A high-volume printer allows you to process large print requests such as long lists and large documents.

Production printers A production printer allows you to process print requests that are necessary for smooth production operation, for example, time-critical or special print jobs.

Desktop printers A desktop printer allows you to process smaller user print requests such as letters and short lists.

Test printers A test printer allows you to try new configurations and new device types.

> **NOTE** The printer classes are different from the print requirements listed in "Determine the Print Requirements" earlier in this chapter. For your special print infrastructure, you should determine which printer class handles which print requirements. Make sure you allocate high-volume print jobs to the high-volume printer class and time-critical print jobs to the production printer class. You should divide the other print requirements between the production printers and the desktop printers.

FIGURE 8.2:

Classify printers

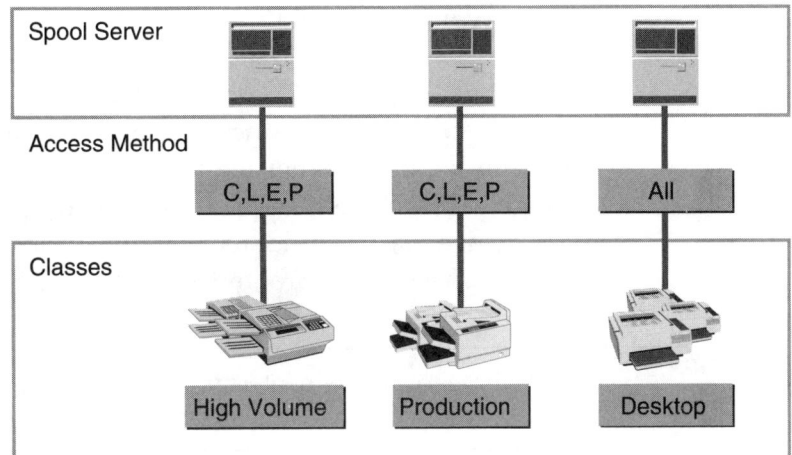

The Standard Printer

You should define a standard printer for every printer class. If the departments in your company have widely varying demands on the printer, you must select multiple printer types for a printer class. To select the appropriate printer, you should define the following technical aspects in the requirements:

- Which printer language must be supported (for example, PostScript or PCL-5)?
- What type of print technology should be used (for example, laser printer, bar-code printer, or check printer)?
- How many pages must be printed per minute or per month?
- How should the paper source be set up?
- Which paper size is required?

NOTE R/3 Note 25161 lists performance data for printers and the supported printers for which SAP has the most up-to-date product information.

Normally, you should only connect printers of one class to the spool server; you should not connect printers from different classes to a spool server (see Figure 8.2). Problems can occur if you connect high-volume printers and other printers to a single spool server. The processing time alone for large print requests could hinder all the other requests. Since the spool server works through print requests sequentially, the output requests for the other devices can be hindered if it takes a long time to process an output request or if a problem occurs during processing.

> **TIP** If you have to connect printers from different classes to a spool server, the spool server should have multiple spool work processes.

Access Modes

R/3 allows you to connect printers locally to the spool server or to a print server through a LAN or WAN. To technically implement these various options with R/3, you must configure printers in R/3 with the appropriate access mode. Table 8.1 lists all the access modes that are available in R/3 and describes the printer for which each access mode should be implemented.

TABLE 8.1: Access Modes and Printers

Access Mode	Description
C	Local printer on a Windows NT computer or AS/400
L	Local printer on a UNIX computer
S	Remote printer at LPDHOST through SAP protocol
U	Remote printer at LPDHOST through Berkeley protocol
F	Printer on front end
E	External Output Management System

Continued on next page

TABLE 8.1: Access Modes and Printers *(Continued)*

Access Mode	Description
P	Local or remote device pool
I	Archiver (for example, ArchiveLink)
X	SAP comm (for example, fax machine)
Z	IBM AFP (for example, IBM mainframe S/390)

SAP recommends the access modes you should use for each printer class. As displayed in Figure 8.2, you can choose any access mode for the desktop printer. However, you should connect the high-volume printer and production printer to the spool server locally. Production printers for time-critical print jobs should always be connected to the spool server so network problems cannot prevent the printout.

> **NOTE** You should only connect high-volume printers to the spool server as remote printers if the bandwidth of the network ensures a high throughput and the print server is reliable.

Define the Spool Server

SAP recommends setting up at least one spool work process on every application server. The spool work process formats the data for printing on its respective printer. This turns each application server into a potential spool server to which you can connect printers. As of R/3 Release 4.0, you can set up one or more spool work processes on a spool server. Whether more than one work process should run depends on the throughput you want to achieve for the printout. Currently, there are no simple rules for how many work processes you'll need for a certain print volume. If a spool work process on a spool server has a 100 percent load during the load peaks, you must set up more spool work processes in accordance with your resources.

> **NOTE** The number of spool work processes is static and is defined when R/3 is started. You cannot use operation modes to dynamically change the number as you would, for example, for dialog and background work processes.

Attributes

If your production system has multiple spool servers, you can use the attributes of the individual servers to determine the roles each server plays in the printer landscape. In R/3, you can do the following:

Classify servers You can classify servers to divide them into printer classes. You can divide the servers into the same classes as the printers. This allows you to control whether only printers of the same class are connected with a server.

Set up logical servers You can set up logical servers to administer a complex infrastructure more easily. You can use logical servers to divide the printers into groups and allocate a group to a spool server without having to allocate each printer individually.

Set up alternative servers You can set up alternative servers to achieve a higher availability. If the original server fails, an alternative server processes the print requests.

Activate load balancing You can activate load balancing to sensibly distribute the load generated by print requests over the server. If you activate load balancing, print requests will not always printed in the order in which they were generated. For this reason, the load balancing is inactive in the standard R/3 System and the print requests are statically allocated to one server.

Logical Servers

You can use a logical server to collect a group of printers into an administration unit. You must first allocate the printers to a logical server. Then you can allocate one or more logical servers to every real spool server. Figure 8.3 shows that the output is then passed from the spool server through the logical server to the printer. This type of procedure has three advantages. First, your printer landscape is more flexible. In one step, you can allocate an entire group of printers to a different spool server without having to reallocate each individual printer. Second, your printer landscape is independent of the R/3 System. You can transport the settings for the output devices and logical servers between the R/3 Systems in your system landscape. You only have to adapt the assignment between the logical server and the spool server to the R/3 System. Third, you'll increase the printer availability. If the real spool server fails for a logical server, you can allocate a new real server to the logical server or the R/3 System automatically uses the alternative server you have already specified.

The logical servers are worthwhile even for R/3 Systems with only one or two application servers. As displayed in Figure 8.3, you can group the respective printers with a logical server in accordance with your print requirements, that is, special print, time-critical print, normal print, and high-volume print. You can also divide up the output devices in accordance with various access modes. Figure 8.3 illustrates two logical servers for the high-volume printer, which separate the locally connected printers Log_4_local from the remotely connected printers Log_5_remote.

FIGURE 8.3:

Logical servers

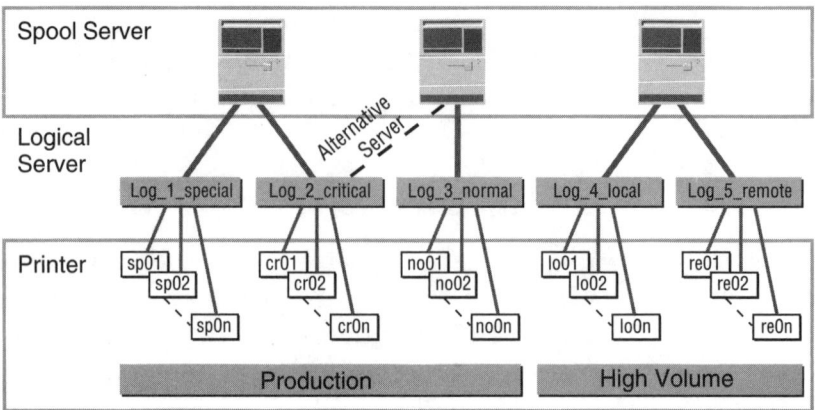

> **NOTE** In R/3, you can administer the logical servers and the real spool servers in CCMS (transaction code SPAD).

Example: Setting Up Logical and Alternative Servers

In this example, the R/3 System TC4 has two spool servers: pswdf697_TC4_00 and pswdf694_TC4_01. As displayed in the following table, one logical server is allocated to each spool server. Additionally, each logical server has an alternative server.

Logical Server	Mapping	Alternative Server
Log_Server_0	pswdf697_TC4_00	Log_Server_1
Log_Server_1	pswdf694_TC4_01	Log_Server_0

Continued on next page

To ensure that the mapping between the servers remains transparent even in more complex infrastructures, you can display the related graphical representation (transaction code SPAD). As you can see in the graphical representation for this example, the horizontal lines map the logical server to the spool servers. The vertical lines show the relationship between the servers and their alternative servers.

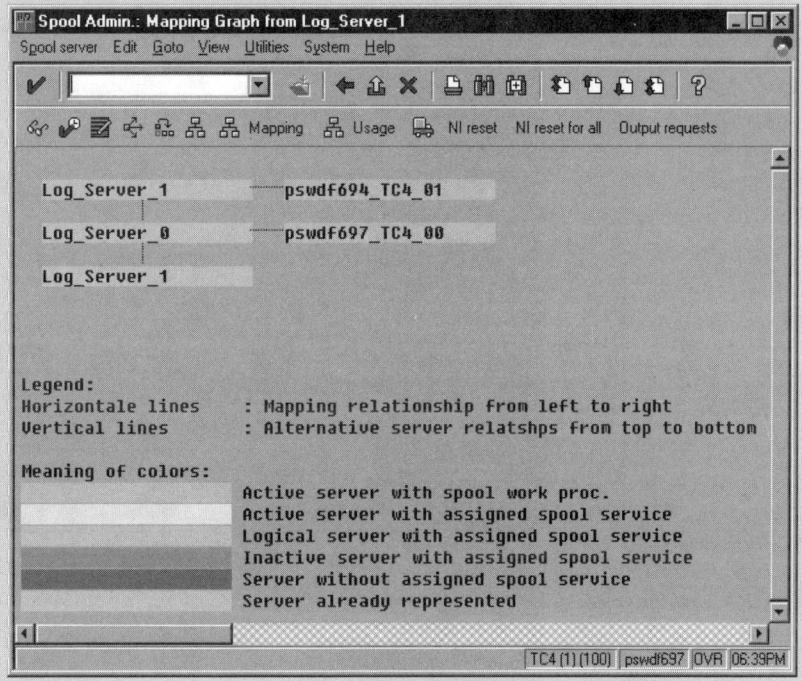

Transport System

You can display the settings for the output devices and logical servers in change requests and transport them to another system. For this reason, you should use logical servers for all the printers in your R/3 System so you can set up the same logical structure for the printers in all the R/3 Systems in your system landscape.

As displayed in Figure 8.4, you must only allocate the logical servers to the real spool servers in every system. In a three-system landscape, you should first set up all the planned logical servers in the development system. Then you can transport the settings to the quality assurance system and test them there. Subsequently, you can transport the settings to the production system and create all the required printers.

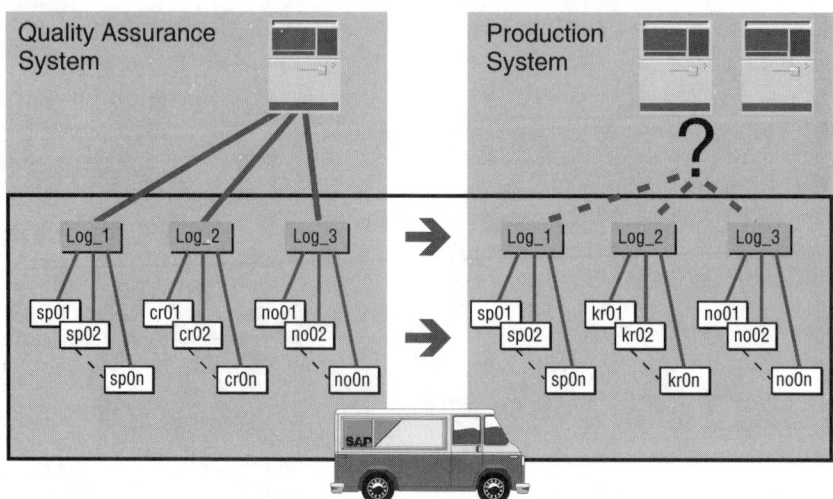

FIGURE 8.4:

Transport of the attributes and administration information for logical servers

Set Up the Print Infrastructure

After the spool work process has formatted a document for output, the data is passed to the operating system spool of the output device. Therefore, you can only print or fax from the R/3 System if the devices are installed on the operating-system level. The spool system in R/3 must also know how the output device is connected with R/3. Your print infrastructure works best if you select specific access modes for a server class. Table 8.2 lists the combinations of access modes and server classes that are recommended by SAP.

TABLE 8.2: Recommended Access Modes for Server Classes

	Access Mode				
Server Class	**Local (C, L)**	**Remote (U, S)**	**Front End (F)**	**OMS (E)**	**Pool (P)**
High-volume	Yes	Sufficient bandwidth	No	Yes	Local Pool
Production	Yes	No	No	Yes	Local Pool
Desktop	Yes	Yes	Yes	Yes	Yes
Test	Yes	Yes	Yes	Yes	Yes

The following sections describe the advantages and disadvantages of the various access modes in detail and give you hints on which access modes are appropriate in which situations.

Set Up Local Printing

For a local print from R/3, the spool work process passes the output data to the operating system spool of the spool server on which the spool work process is running. Figure 8.5 shows that the operating system spool can output the data on a locally connected printer and on a printer that is connected through the network. Table 8.3 lists two access modes that you can customize in R/3 for local printing.

In a distributed R/3 System, you can set up a print server on every application server. If you have an alternative server for local printers in your system, you must set up the printers on the operating-system level on both application servers.

FIGURE 8.5:

Local printing

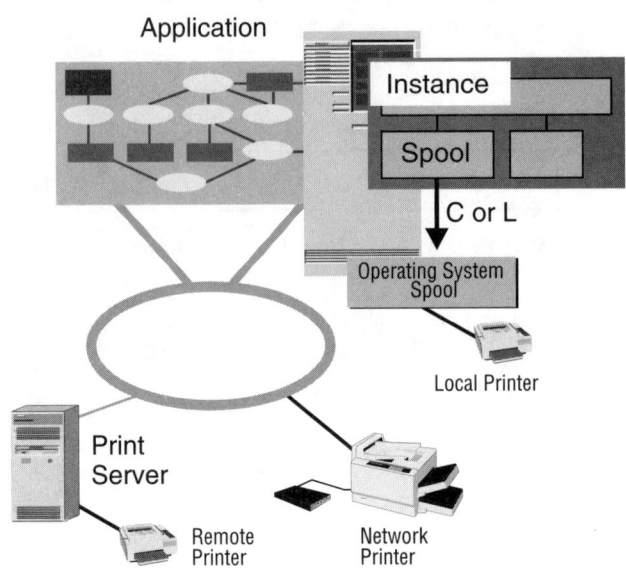

TABLE 8.3: Access Modes for Local Printing

Access Mode	Operating System Spool	Description
L	UNIX	The spool work process stores the data as operating system files and passes it to the operating system spool with UNIX commands.
C	Windows NT AS/400	The spool work process passes the data with the operating system calls directly to the print manager. The data is not stored temporarily in an operating system file.

Generally, local printing is not only the quickest way to transmit and output data to the operating system spool, it is the most reliable. For this access mode, the operating system spool of the spool server is available as a reliable communication partner. For the R/3 spool system, the availability of the printout does not depend on whether a print server or the front end can be contacted through the network. Communication does not place such a heavy load on the spool work process. If the operating system spool of the print server cannot be contacted, the spool work process is blocked until a time limit is exceeded. The spool work process can process other output requests only after the time limit is exceeded.

Set Up Remote Printing

For remote printing from R/3, the spool work process passes the output data through the network to the operating system spool of a print server or directly to the front end. Figure 8.6 shows that you can use every printer that can be contacted by the operating system spool of a print server. These printers can be connected locally and through the network. Table 8.4 lists the two access modes that you can customize in R/3 for remote printing.

FIGURE 8.6:
Remote printing

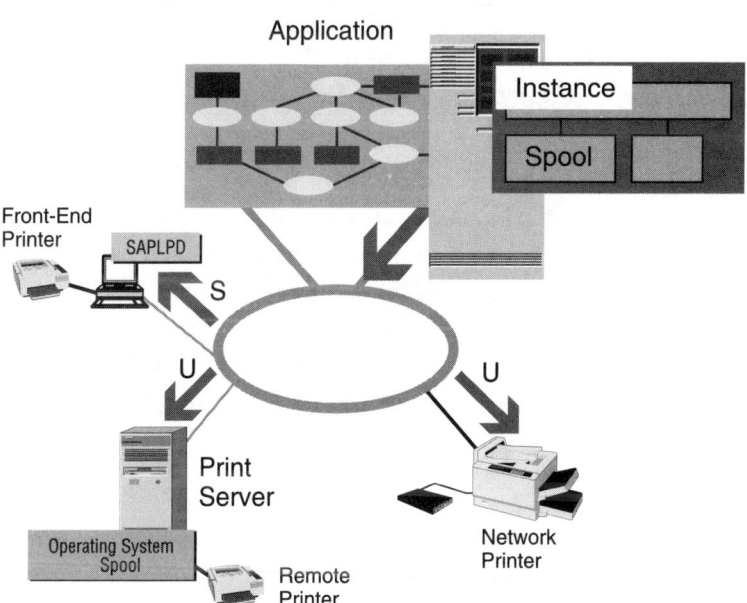

TABLE 8.4: Access Modes for the Remote Printing

Access Mode	Operating System Spool	Description
U	UNIX	Can only be used for LPD systems, that is, all UNIX systems and the IBM OS/2 LPD system. On OSF/1 systems, only local printing is possible.
	Windows NT	The spool work process passes the data to the print manager of the front ends through the SAPLPD program. Removed by access mode.
S	Windows NT	The spool work process passes the data to the print manager of the front ends through the SAPLPD program. Recommended access modes for all the output devices to the front ends.

For performance reasons, the access modes U and S are only suitable for LAN connections. If the spool work process sends the output data through a WAN connection, which is slower, it is blocked for other tasks. Normally, other output requests are hindered and the output is delayed.

To connect R/3 with the front-end printers, SAP recommends setting up the remote printing with the access mode S. If possible, you should connect the front-end printer with a spool server that does not format high-volume or production print jobs. If a problem occurs with a front-end printer, it has an effect on all the other printers that are connected with the same spool server. If you set up local and remote printing on one spool server, you should configure at least two spool work processes. If one work process is blocked by problems with the connection, the other can handle the waiting print requests.

WARNING Avoid the access mode U. As an alternative to access mode U, you can connect the print server directly to the operating system spool of a spool server. This way, you can set up the printers of the print server as local printers with access mode C or L in R/3.

Consider Front-End Printers

The front-end printers enable a special type of printing in R/3 and are set up with access mode F. With this access mode, a dialog work process passes the output data to the print control program SAPLPD on the user front end. The output data is already completely formatted. This procedure allows R/3 to remove the load on the spool work processes; however, the dialog work processes have an additional load. In problem situations, they may be completely blocked for some time.

> **NOTE** You should only use the access mode F for a few printers that are seldom used for printing from R/3. This allows you to avoid an unnecessary load on the dialog processing generated by the front-end printers. For example, you could use the access mode F for a printer in front ends of field service employees and allow them to use it to print small documents through the network.

Integrate the External Output Management System (OMS)

You can use the external Output Management System (OMS) to integrate an R/3 System into an existing printer landscape. You can connect to the products of third-party vendors through the *eXternal Output Management (XOM)* interface. Ensure that the product is certified by SAP. You must adapt all other products yourself to the XOM interface.

> **TIP** You can find information about complementary products from third-party vendors in SAPNet at `http://sapnet.sap.com/csp`. Choose Complementary Solutions. It is the third-party vendors, not SAP, who ensure product maintenance. You can only obtain a new version of a product from the third-party vendor.

It is possible to connect multiple R/3 Systems to one OMS or to connect one R/3 System to multiple OMSs. Additionally, you can connect an OMS with R/3 in various ways. For example, in R/3, it may be necessary to monitor the output on important printers. To do so, you should set up the OMS in a callback mode. Then, the OMS sends the status information about the printout to R/3. You can display this information in R/3.

LOMS and ROMS

You can divide the printers in an OMS into multiple logical groups known as the *Logical Output Management Systems (LOMS)*. All the printers in a LOMS are configured the same way. Figure 8.7 displays an example with the two groups LOMS_X and LOMS_Y. You can link each LOMS with a *Real Output Management System (ROMS)* and not directly with the OMS. You can use the ROMS to connect the OMS with R/3. For example, in Figure 8.7, both LOMS are connected with a ROMS called ROMS_1.

FIGURE 8.7:
Logical and Real Output Management System

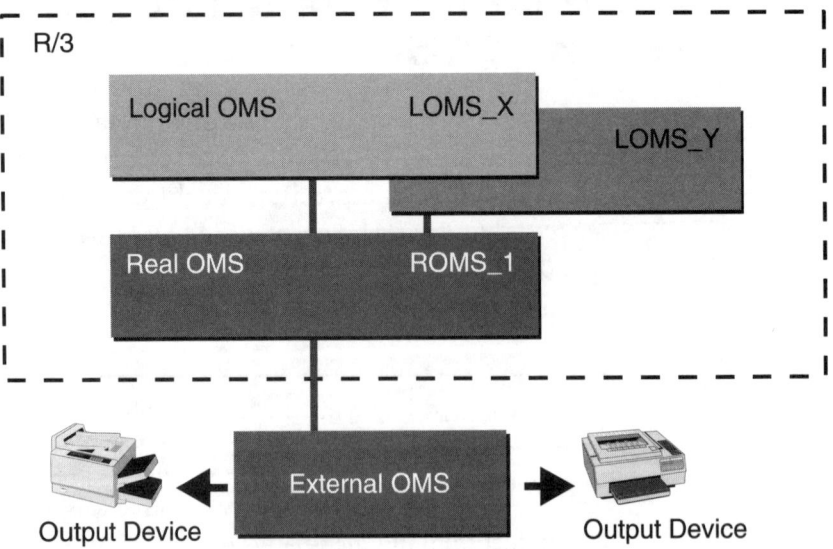

> **NOTE**
> In R/3, you can administer the LOMS and ROMS in CCMS (transaction code SPAD). The R/3 online documentation and *SAP R/3 System Administration: The Official SAP Guide*, by Liane Will (Sybex, 1998), describe the procedures.

Monitor the Output

At the end of the Realization phase, you'll define the system operation for the print infrastructure and document it in the system operation manual. To effectively monitor a heterogeneous printer landscape in particular, you should document the procedures for administration and the most important settings for each individual printer.

Example: Documenting Printer Settings

The following table uses an example to show you which settings to document for a printer in your system operation manual.

Printer	Location	Classification	Type	Logical Server	Host	Host Printer	Access Mode	Maintenance/ Problems
CR01	Sales and Distribution	Production	Laser	L_Prod_1	App1	Lp1	C	Bill Smith
DE01	Sales and Distribution	Desktop	SAPWIN	L_Desk_1	App2	Lp2	S	Bob Jones
CR02	Warehouse	Production	Laser	L_Prod_1	App1	Lp3	C	Bill Smith
DE02	Warehouse	Desktop	SAPWIN	L_Desk_1	App2	Lp4	S	Bob Jones

Continued on next page

Printer	Location	Classification	Type	Logical Server	Host	Host Printer	Access Mode	Maintenance/ Problems
CR0N	IT	High-Volume	Plotter	L_High_1	App3	Lp5	L	Carl Miller

As described in Chapter 5, "R/3 Instance Administration," R/3 has a graphical Alert Monitor that allows you to continuously monitor your entire R/3 System landscape. You can set up separate monitoring objects for each printer in the printer landscape. For example, Figure 8.8 displays three printers: CR01, CR02, and CR0N. In this example, the printers output time-critical documents. If a problem occurs, it is reported early in the Alert Monitor, which allows you to react accordingly.

The system operation of the print infrastructure is divided into nonregular activities and regular activities (for example, checking the spool system for failed print requests). In the system operation manual, you should define how frequently certain activities have to be performed. Table 8.5 displays two important daily activities for monitoring and describes situations that require special consideration.

TABLE 8.5: Daily Activities for Monitoring the Runtime Environment

Activity	Transaction Code	Description
Alert Monitor (4.0)	RZ20	If a red or yellow alert is displayed, an error has occurred.
Spool requests	SP01	Failed spool requests are displayed in red and the related error log must be analyzed.

FIGURE 8.8:

Configuring the Alert Monitor

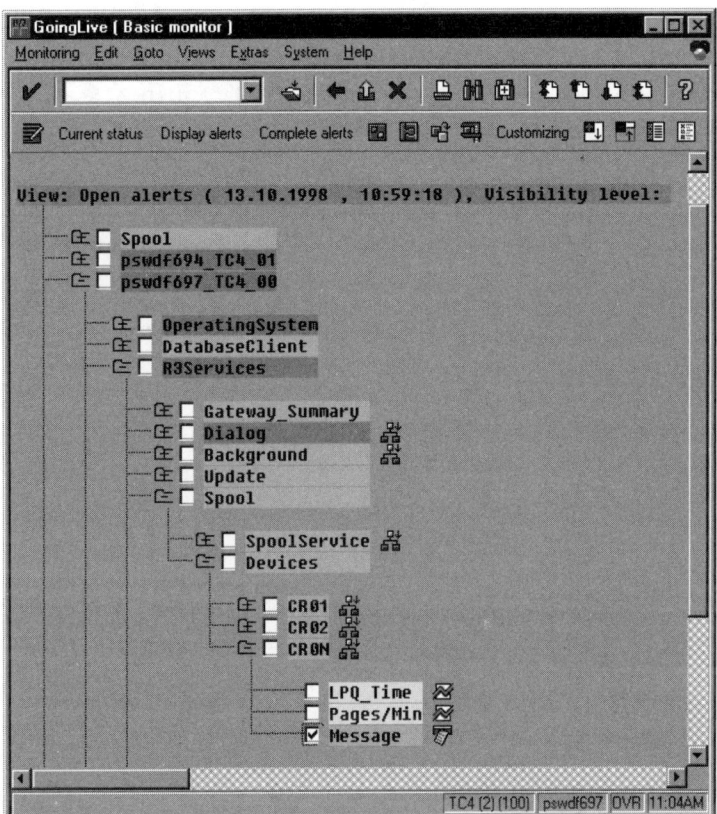

If an error occurs during a print job, it is often difficult to find the source. The source can be in any of the components that process the output data, from the R/3 application that is generating the document to the spool work process that formatted the data for the print to the operating system spool. Even the printers can cause physical errors. The R/3 online documentation describes a procedure for analyzing print errors to help you find a solution quickly. If you find other procedures that are more helpful in your system, document them in your system operation manual. For serious problems, you should also define the person to notify and which specialist can help with this type of problem.

In addition to these regular activities, the R/3 System administrator must maintain the print infrastructure when necessary. Table 8.6 displays the important activities for maintenance and describes situations that require special consideration.

TABLE 8.6: Activities for the Administration of the Print Infrastructure

Activity	Role	Description
Administer output devices	Technical Team Lead, R/3 System administrator	Every output device is classified. The settings for new or changed devices are documented in the system operation manual.
Administer spool server	Technical Team Lead, R/3 System administrator	Every server is classified. The printers' Administration units are each allocated to a logical server. In accordance with the server class, a logical server is allocated to at least one physical spool server.
Administer spool database (TemSe)	R/3 System administrator	The spool database is reorganized daily (ABAP program RSPO0041). The consistency of the spool database is checked occasionally (ABAP program RSPO1043).

Print Administration in ASAP

In the previous sections, you learned what to consider for print administration during the R/3 implementation. In ASAP, these points are distributed over the individual phases of the project. The following sections describe when to perform certain tasks.

Business Blueprint

At the beginning of the Business Blueprint phase, you'll create the technical design. Here, you should define the physical setup of the print infrastructure in your R/3 System. This also consists of the technical details, for example, the type, function, and location of the printers. To find the best possible solution for your requirements, you must first plan the infrastructure in detail with the departments. To support you, ASAP is delivered with a questionnaire and guidelines for a print infrastructure. These documents help you record the current status of your existing printer landscape and define the target status.

> **TIP** The Technical Team must work to ensure that the departments determine their respective print volumes as accurately as possible and define time frames for the output. Remember that a single R/3 module comprises additional output administrations, which are based on the print infrastructure. For example, in the Sales and Distribution (SD) module, you should decide whether you'll print delivery notes directly after creating the order or whether you'll first collect them in the NAST table and use the RSNAST00 report to print them out all at once. Each department defines the options for output administration within an R/3 module during the Business Blueprint phase. The Technical Team checks to see which print infrastructure is needed.

In addition to planning, you should set up the first system, the development system, in the R/3 System landscape in this phase. In the development system, first set up a print infrastructure that is only for the Project Team. Install, configure, and test your settings for each printer. This allows you to gain experience with the settings for the printers for the production system.

Realization

During the Realization phase, you'll set up the second system in the R/3 System landscape, the quality assurance system. In this system, you'll set up a print infrastructure for the Project Team, but more often, you'll test the infrastructure for the production system. As described in "Define the Spool Server" earlier in this chapter, you'll work in the development system to configure the settings for the output devices and the logical servers for the production system. You should record these configurations in change requests and transport them into the quality assurance system. Here, you'll only test to see if you can output the documents in the desired format for the printers. Only when you are preparing for production can you test the printers to see if they can process the planned print volume in production operation. To plan the tests, define how to control the throughput of the output devices and how to make sure all users can access the devices according to their authorizations.

At the end of the Realization phase, the Technical Team sets up the production system and its print structure at the same time. In the quality assurance system, you have already tested the configurations of the output devices and the logical servers. Transport these configurations into the production system and allocate the logical servers to the physical spool servers.

Final Preparation

At the beginning of the Final Preparation phase, you'll set up the system operation for the spool system. You should define different procedures for the various printer classes. For a time-critical print job, you need special escalation procedures because errors must be corrected quickly. For example, you should define a procedure so users can exchange a defective printer with an alternative printer. You'll need special output procedures for confidential print requests because the printout cannot be available to every user. For example, you can define the printers on which confidential documents are output and the users who can access these printers. You'll also need special output procedures for high-volume printing because it may negatively affect other print requests or dialog processing. For example, you can define the time frame during which long lists or large documents can be output through background jobs.

Table 8.7 lists the ASAP tasks that are related to the implementation of the print infrastructure. Each task is described in accordance with the phase in which it is performed and the person who performs it.

TABLE 8.7: Tasks for Print Administration in ASAP

Phase	Phase Name	Task	Role
2	Business Blueprint	Define and document printing infrastructure	Technical Team Lead, R/3 System administrator, network administrator, operating system administrator, technical consultant, Business Process Team Lead
		Install and configure printing services for Project Team	R/3 System administrator, network administrator, operating system administrator, technical consultant
3	Realization	Develop printing and fax test plan	Technical Team Lead, R/3 System administrator, network administrator, technical consultant
		Set up printing services	R/3 System administrator, network administrator, operating system administrator, technical consultant
		Define production system printing environment	Technical Team Lead, R/3 System administrator, network administrator, operating system administrator, technical consultant
		Install and configure printing services	Technical Team Lead, R/3 System administrator, network administrator, operating system administrator, technical consultant
4	Final Preparation	Configure production system printing and spool administration	R/3 System administrator, Business Process Team Lead
		Conduct printing and fax tests	R/3 System administrator, technical consultant

Success Factors

To successfully implement the print administration, you must give the following points particular consideration:

- Use standard device types
- Optimize printer throughput

The following sections describe these points in detail.

Use Standard Device Types

To create an output device in R/3, you must assign the device type. To enable the spool system to format the data for an output device without problems, the device type defines the attributes (for example, control commands for font, paper size, or character set) of the output device. To save time and money, you should only use printers that already have a device type in the standard R/3 System. Currently, the standard R/3 System supports approximately 100 device types from leading manufacturers. Table 8.8 lists the R/3 Notes that inform you about the supported device types.

TABLE 8.8: R/3 Notes about Requirements for Printers and Device Types

Note No.	Short Text
8928	List of supported printers/device types
25161	Performance data for printers
62178	Printers definition (device types) for Japanese Lang.
83502	printing support for native languages
98477	SAP R/3 device types by the company PSI

Some of the supported printers for R/3 have been so successful on the market that no-name brand printers are compatible with them. Frequently, you can use compatible no-name brand printers in R/3 if you use the device type for the printer that was originally supported. Such no-name brand printers are not supported by SAP. You may have problems if the no-name brand printer does not have exactly the same attributes as the originally supported printer. In this case, you must adapt the respective device type. This can be also valid for the successor models of a supported printer.

Optimize the Printer Throughput

To achieve an optimal throughput with the R/3 spool system, you should consider the following guidelines:

Set up at least one spool work process on each application server. This way, you can sensibly distribute the system load over the server and increase availability. If a server fails, an alternative server can process the waiting print requests. You should set up at least two spool work processes for a central R/3 System that does not have additional application servers.

Distribute the printers in accordance with the printer classes on the individual spool servers. If you do so, the print requests from different printer classes will not mutually hinder each other. If a bottleneck occurs on a spool server, you can set up additional spool work processes. Or you can activate load balancing if the print requests do not have to be output in the order in which they were generated.

Avoid using the access mode U. This allows you to prevent network problems from influencing or even blocking spool work processes.

If a bottleneck occurs, deactivate the R/3 spool system's status query to the operating system spool. This way, spool work processes can process print requests more quickly because the status notification from the operating system spool is not required. You must weigh this against the disadvantage that the spool requests in R/3 are displayed with the status "complete" as soon as the data is passed to the operating system spool.

Review Questions

1. Which statements are correct?

   A. As of R/3 Release 4.0, one or more spool work processes can run on an instance.

   B. You can use operation modes to switch the number of spool work processes.

   C. At least one spool work process should be running in the R/3 System.

2. To which classes can printers be allocated?

   A. Test print

   B. Production print

   C. Bar-code print

   D. Desktop print

   E. High-volume print

   F. Device pool print

3. Which statements are correct?

   A. Only one logical server can be allocated to each physical spool server.

   B. An alternative server can be allocated to a logical server.

   C. Logical servers are only available for production printers.

   D. You can import the settings for the logical server into other R/3 Systems by using the transport system.

4. Which access modes are not recommended for printers with time-critical output?

   A. C, local printer on a Windows NT computer or AS/400

   B. L, local printer on a UNIX computer

   C. U, remote printer on LPDHOST through Berkeley protocol

   D. S, remote printer on LPDHOST through SAP protocol

   E. F, printer on a front end

CHAPTER NINE

Database Administration

On the database layer, you can run different Relational Database Management Systems (RDBMSs) from leading vendors. In a typical R/3 System, the database layer runs on a server to which one or more application servers are connected. The database server is the most powerful server in an R/3 System. The database can contain from 20GB to several hundred GB of data.

In addition to the CPU and the main memory, you must determine what storage technology and hard disk capacity you'll need. The following section describes what you must consider to do so. To ensure that your hardware resources are available and used optimally, the subsequent sections explain how to perform the following tasks:

- Configure the database
- Define your data backup strategy
- Define your database recovery strategy
- Monitor the database

Determine the RDBMS and Hardware

You should decide which RDBMS you'll use before the R/3 implementation project begins. SAP supports different RDBMS vendors (see "Supported Hardware and Software for R/3" in Chapter 2). SAP does not provide preferential support for any particular RDBMS vendor. You should make your decision based on your requirements. Your requirements can depend on whether you already use an RDBMS and thus have special knowledge of this product. When you choose your RDBMS, make sure you implement the same RDBMS for every R/3 System in your system landscape. You can transport Customizing between different database systems, but it is difficult to do so and makes your systems more prone to errors.

Hardware Platform

You should work with your hardware partner to choose the operating system and the hardware platform on which the RDBMS will run. As described in Chapter 5, "R/3 Instance Administration," you should use the same operating system platform for the R/3 instances and the RDBMS. Currently, the only exceptions are heterogeneous R/3 Systems with the Windows NT operating system for the application servers and a UNIX derivative for the database server. As with the R/3 instances, you can use sizing to determine which CPU you need for the database server and how large the main memory must be.

Because the database stores all the data from R/3, you must decide how much storage capacity you'll require and which technology to use to store the data. Three points are important for your decision. First, you must protect the data against loss. Second, the storage capacity must be sufficiently large and expandable. And third, you must be able to access the data quickly.

Storage Technology

Based on the points discussed in the preceding section, to decide which storage technology to use, you must ask yourself the following questions:

How high should the availability be? More and more, companies want R/3 Systems to be available around the clock. You can only ensure this availability if you can switch to another database server if a serious problem occurs.

How important is high throughput? Companies in the retail industry must be able to query the database for goods as quickly as possible and to post documents. If you need this capability, the storage technology must allow you to access the hard disk with relatively short access times.

Your answers to these questions and Table 9.1 will enable you to assess your storage technology requirements. You must work together with consultants and your hardware partner to define the technology for your requirements in greater detail.

TABLE 9.1: Planning Matrix for Storage Technology

Performance	Availability	< 100 % Normal	~ 100% No Downtime
Normal		RAID 5	RAID 5, failover system
High		RAID 1 and 5	RAID 1 and 5, failover system, cluster

RAID

Using Redundant Array of Inexpensive Disks (RAID) technology can help you avoid data loss if one of your hard disks fails. RAID technology groups multiple hard disks to store data redundantly. Redundant data storage is implemented in different ways, which are distinguished by the RAID level.

Table 9.1 shows that it is advisable to use the RAID levels 1 and 5 for an R/3 System. RAID 5 stores each block once in the disk system. To keep the data redundant, a checksum is calculated and stored in the same disk system. If you update a large amount of data in the database using the R/3 System, the checksum has to be calculated frequently. This can slow the write operation, although RAID 5 is often sufficient for normal requirements. RAID 1 stores each block twice on different hard disks. Although the data is written twice, RAID 1 systems normally write data quicker than RAID 5 systems. You should use RAID 1 for database files to which blocks are most frequently written—for example, the log files. The section "Define the Disk Layout" later in this chapter explains how the disk layout should be set up.

Single systems can often achieve an availability of up to 99 percent. Despite this, the system can have approximately 100 hours of downtime each year. If your company cannot afford to have this amount of downtime, you must use either a failover system or the cluster technology.

The Failover System

A failover system often consists of one server with its own hard disk system. During normal operation, the log files in the production database are transferred to the failover system. The failover system's RDBMS recovers the log files and thus keeps the database up-to-date. The failover system is only used if a serious error occurs in the production database or if the production system is being maintained. Depending on your budget, you must decide whether you need to equip the failover system with the same hardware as the production system or whether the server can be less powerful and therefore less expensive.

The Cluster System

A cluster groups servers logically into one system. In the simplest case, two servers access the same hard disk system. The systems monitor each other, and if a problem occurs, one system takes over the functions of the system that failed. Cluster systems have better performance than a single system with an additional failover system. In normal operation, you'll benefit from the performance of the second server because you'll use it even if the other server has not failed. If necessary, an individual server can be much more powerful than a cluster (see Figure 9.1). For administration reasons, the servers in the cluster often communicate with each other, which also places an additional load on them. As shown in Figure 9.1, you can achieve a higher availability with a cluster system than with a *massively parallel processor (MPP) system* or a *symmetric multiprocessor (SMP) system*.

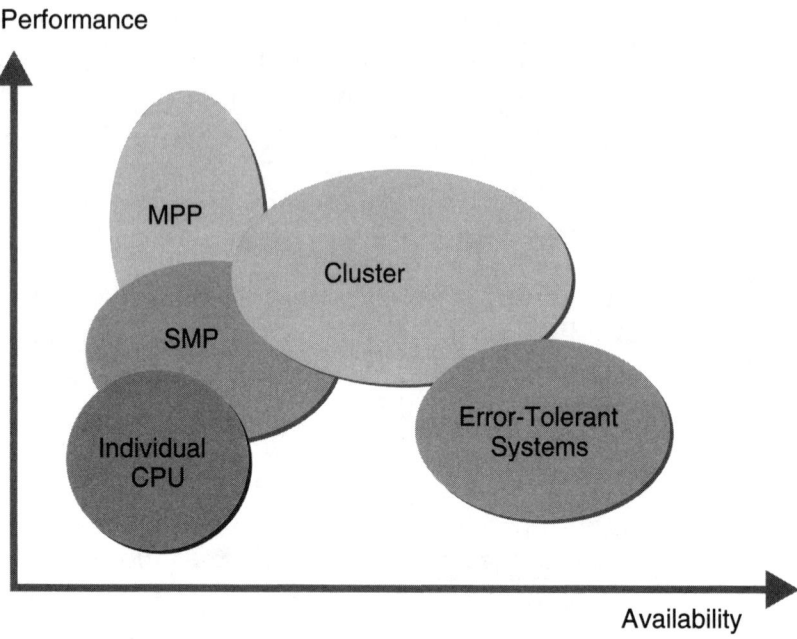

FIGURE 9.1:
Performance and availability of different computer systems

NOTE Currently, only a small number of R/3 installations run on MPP computers or cluster systems. If you require this type of installation, you should plan the implementation with your hardware partner, the SAP Competence Center, and technical consultants.

Business Framework

As of R/3 Release 4.0, the business components create an additional layer for scaling in R/3. Within the Business Framework, multiple databases can be run in parallel. This enables you to have a higher database performance than would be possible with only a single database. Despite the multiple databases, separate data storage is transparent from a business viewpoint. The R/3 business components are interconnected through business processes. R/3 uses two technologies, Application Link Enabling (ALE) and SAP Business

Workflow, to integrate the business processes. As described in the section "Distributed Component Architecture" in Chapter 2, you have two options for setting up a Business Framework with multiple databases. First, you can implement a database for each business component and distribute the entire R/3 System across multiple databases. For example, you can have an R/3 System with separate databases for Financial Accounting and Human Resources. Alternatively, you can run a central R/3 System with multiple databases. This allows, for example, companies with subsidiaries in different geographic locations to distribute their R/3 System across the subsidiaries.

> **TIP** Work with experienced consultants and specialists to decide whether one of the Business Framework solutions described in the preceding section is suited to your company and how to implement it.

Storage Capacity

The amount of storage capacity you'll require for the database depends on many factors; therefore, there are no simple rules for calculating your exact memory requirements. The SAP Quicksizer only enables you to estimate a size for the database. You should consult your hardware partner to determine your database storage capacity more precisely. When you enter data in the R/3 System, the database grows gradually until the once free storage space is completely full. Therefore, when you select your hardware, ensure that you can expand its storage space.

Archiving

It is possible to have databases with several hundred GB; however, administration is more difficult and the performance can suffer when the size of the database increases. To prevent this, you must plan early how you want to archive documents in production operation. This way, you can control the size of the database and the speed at which it is growing. Chapter 10, "Archiving," explains the options and how to organize archiving in R/3.

Configure the Database

An RDBMS physically consists of one database instance and files. Similar to the R/3 instance, the database instance consists of, from the operating system viewpoint, cooperating processes and main memory used by the processes. The processes control and organize access to the files in the database.

The following sections explains two important points about configuring the RDBMS. First, a good disk layout ensures high availability and short data access times. Second, you should run your R/3 System in production operation, with a few exceptions, so that log files are written.

Define the Disk Layout

Before you set up any of the R/3 Systems in your system landscape, you should work with technical consultants to determine a disk layout. Define which files in the RDBMS are on which hard disk or in which RAID system. In theory, you can arbitrarily distribute the files over the hard disk. A poorly distributed R/3 System can still run without reporting any errors. This section gives recommendations for the layout to help you achieve high availability and performance.

> **NOTE** The disk layout in the production system has to have the best possible design right from the beginning. To change an existing distribution, you must stop the R/3 production operation. In this case, large databases can have downtime that lasts several days.

RAID 5

The simplest option for the layout is to store all the files in the database in a RAID 5 system. This allows you to protect your data from loss (if a hard disk fails) and reduces the amount of administration. However, the access times are not optimal. The log files create a bottleneck here. Since blocks are written to these files very frequently during production operation, the RAID 5 system must frequently calculate checksums for the log files. This increases the access times and reduces the system performance.

RAID 1 and RAID 5

To improve the throughput, remove the log files from the RAID 5 system and store them in a RAID 1 system. All other files remain in the RAID 5 system. Compared with the pure RAID 5, you can reduce the access times to the log files and thus increase the performance of the system. You can achieve the highest throughput if all the files are stored in RAID 1. This is also the most expensive solution because RAID 1 requires you to double your hard disk capacity.

> **TIP** For most databases you can store the RAID 5 data files, to which blocks are often written, in a RAID 1 system. For example, for Oracle, you can store the data files for heavily used tablespaces in a RAID 1 system.

Example: Defining a Disk Layout

This example explains a recommended disk layout for an Oracle database. As shown in the graphic, every file in the database is mirrored. The mirroring is implemented as follows:

- RAID 1 for the data files (*sapdata1* ... *<n>*), the archived log files (*saparch*), and the operating system paging files

Continued on next page

To enable the shortest possible access time, the sapdata directories are stored on separate hard disks. Alternatively, the sapdata directories can also be stored in a RAID 5 system. This causes the access times to the data files to increase; however, hardware costs are lower.

- Disk mirroring without RAID 1 for the log files (origlogA, origlogB, mirrlogA, mirrlogB)

Mirroring is possible using RAID 1; however, for Oracle, SAP recommends mirroring the log files with Oracle software.

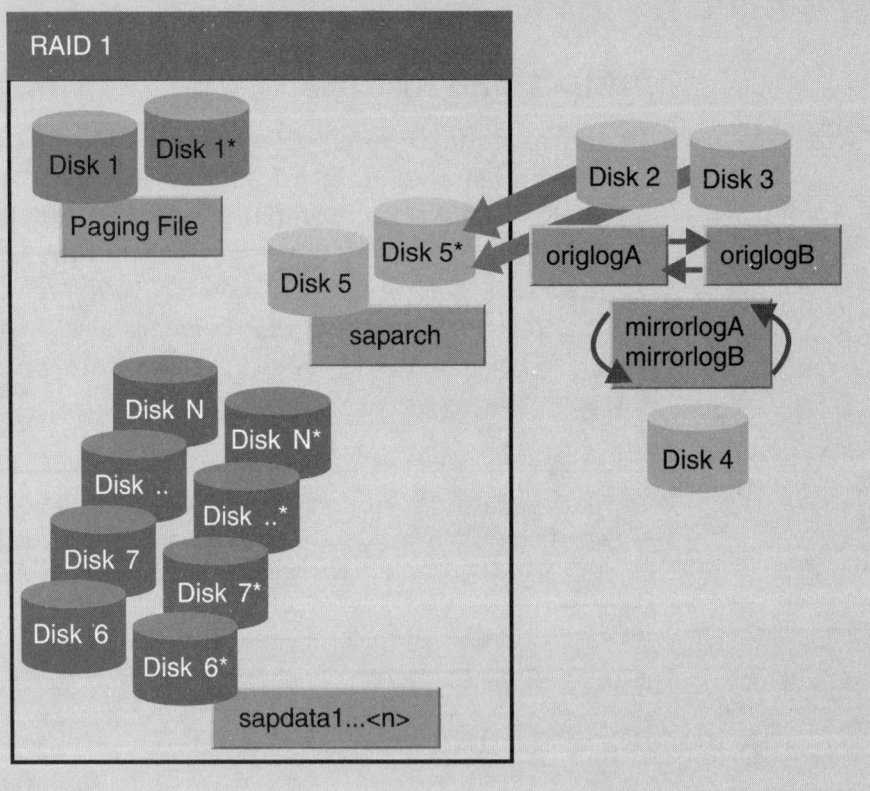

Log (File) Mode

Synchronous to processing, an RDBMS logs information about which data was changed during a transaction. You need the log files if an error occurs. After restoring the database, you need the log files to recover the database to the state it was in before the error occurred.

Ensure that log files are written and backed up for every RDBMS in your system landscape. You can use different methods to set the different database systems to write log files or to set them so they don't write log files; however, only in special situations is it advisable to set them so they don't write log files (for example, during a large data transfer or an upgrade).

TIP	The R/3 online documentation describes in detail how to set up and control the log file mode for each RDBMS.

Full Log Directory

Storing and changing data in the database each day increases the storage space requirements for the log files that are normally stored in a common log directory. Problems can occur if the storage capacity reserved for the log directory is exceeded. The RDBMS can no longer write blocks to the log directory, and thus the database fails. For Oracle, this problem situation is called Archiver Stuck (see Figure 9.2). To avoid this situation, you must store the log files on a tape during operation and subsequently delete them from the directory. This frees up sufficient storage space in the directory for the log files. The standard R/3 installation contains tools that handle this type of regular task for you.

FIGURE 9.2:
Archiver Stuck

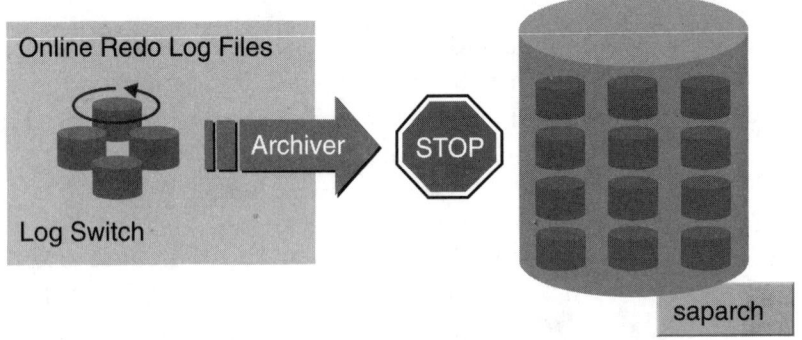

Define Your Data Backup Strategy

A good data backup strategy prevents data loss and increases the availability of the system. To decide on your strategy, consider two points. First, a data backup must not hinder the daily operation of an R/3 System. Second, the database administrator must be able to recover a database quickly after an error occurs.

Whichever strategy you define, start with this question: What is the worst problem situation that can occur for the database? Even in these situations, you have to be able to recover the database using the data backups. You must ensure both a successful recovery and the time frame in which to recover the database. To enable you to take these factors into consideration in your strategy, the following sections describe potential downtime situations and how to perform the following tasks:

- Select tools
- Define the schedule and tape administration
- Back up very large databases

Potential Downtime Situations

Although data loss is rare, experience shows that it can occur in every system sooner or later. You can minimize the negative consequences, but you cannot completely prevent data loss. Even if you resolve a problem and completely recover the data, you still have lost business and may have additional costs for external specialists. Data loss and the subsequent downtime in the R/3 System has three causes: *physical errors*, *logical errors*, and *external factors*.

Physical Errors

All hardware wears out over the course of time, and this is how physical errors such as a defective hard disk or a defective hard disk controller can occur. In these situations, you must either replace the defective hardware as quickly as possible or set up duplicates of important physical components right from the start. Frequently, RAID technology is used to secure hard disks, and a special Service Level Agreement is made with the hardware supplier for other important components. Despite these measures, there are situations in which your hardware cannot protect you from data loss. For example, you can lose data if two hard disks fail at the same time in a RAID 5 system. You can protect yourself from this type of situation by regularly backing up the data in the database to tape.

WARNING In some situations, you may have to restore the data on the operating-system level in addition to the data in the database. For this reason, you must also back up the data on the operating-system level regularly.

Logical Errors

Physical errors are not the only cause of data loss; you can also lose data because of logical errors. For example, if a user does not use the system correctly, he or she may delete data in the database or on the operating-system level. You can prevent this type of logical error with a good authorization concept, but you cannot rule it out altogether. Administrators, in particular, require such extensive authorizations in R/3 and on the operating-system level that they can potentially delete data or overwrite data with a copy. As with the physical errors, you can only protect yourself from this type of situation by regularly backing up the data on the operating-system level and in the database. This includes regularly backing up the log files. For example, if you accidentally delete one of the offline redo log files for an Oracle database, you cannot recover the database to its current status and you'll lose data if an error occurs. As displayed in Figure 9.3, you can only recover the data up to the point that all the offline redo log files in the series are intact.

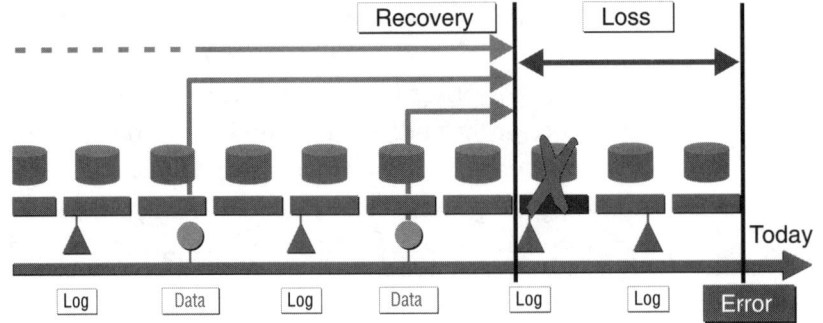

FIGURE 9.3:

The offline redo log file is in an Oracle database defective.

External Factors

Your R/3 System can be destroyed by external factors such as fire or water damage. You should also take into consideration the possibility of theft. In these types of situations, you may have to set up your entire system on completely new hardware. This is only possible if you have intact data backups of the database and of the data from the operating system level. Since external factors can also destroy your backup tapes in the computing center, you should store your data backups in a secure off-site location. You should copy the data backups each day, week, or month (depending on how critical a data loss is for your company) and store the copies separately from the other backups.

To help you protect yourself from data loss, SAP recommends that you develop your data backup strategy during the Business Blueprint phase. You can determine which strategy suits your company best with the help of technical consultants or experts from the database vendor. Your strategy must result in a plan in which you define how and when to back up the database and the data on the operating-system level. The database administrator is responsible for the data backups in all systems of the system landscape and handles any problems that occur. The following sections explain what to consider for your strategy.

Select Tools

You should always work with your hardware supplier to select your hardware for the data backup. For example, only your hardware supplier can tell you which tape drives are supported. The most important factors to consider are the capacity and the throughput of the tape drives.

Capacity

The required capacity of the tapes depends on your database's potential storage capacity. As described in "Determine the RDBMS and Hardware" earlier in this chapter, the database continually grows during operation and eventually fills the available storage capacity completely. Therefore, you must ensure that you can save the entire database when you select your hardware. Since data is usually backed up at night, for the most part, the backups should run automatically. For example, if you require multiple tapes for a data backup, you should either back up the database to multiple tapes in parallel or use a tape robot.

Throughput

The time it should take for the hardware to back up the data depends on the maximum amount of downtime you are allowed for your R/3 System during production operation if a serious problem occurs. It takes at least as long to restore your database from a data backup as it takes to perform a data backup. Normally, you should take other points into consideration for the downtime—for example, the reaction time or the time needed to deliver replacement parts. For this reason, the time frame for the data backup must be shorter that the downtime you can handle, and therefore, the storage devices must have the appropriate throughput.

> **NOTE** You should connect the storage devices to the database server locally and not through a network. Backing up data through the network places an unnecessary load on the network and the data backup takes longer.

Example: Designing Your Storage Devices

This example shows how storage devices are designed in a typical situation. The database has a data volume of approximately 40GB. To back up the data, a digital linear tape (DLT) drive is connected locally to the database server. The important technical data is as follows:

Capacity 70GB with data compression (35GB without)

Throughput 8GB each hour with all the peripheral components

Continued on next page

> Based on this information, a DLT tape station can back up the entire database to tape in approximately five hours. To shorten the backup time, backups can be performed in parallel on multiple tape drives. For a backup time of one hour, you'll need five tape drives. However, the more tape drives you run in parallel, the lower the average throughput is on each tape station. Therefore, for this example, you'll need at least six tape drives to back up the 40GB database.

Tools

The software you use for data backups and database administration depends on the RDBMS you use. Table 9.2 lists the most common tools for an R/3 System.

TABLE 9.2: Tools for Database Administration

Database	Tool
DB2/390 and DB2/400	No tools (functions are integrated into the operating system)
DB2 UDB	DB2 Control Center
Informix OnLine	SAPDBA
Microsoft SQL Server	Enterprise manager
Oracle	SAPDBA, BRBACKUP, BRARCHIVE

In R/3, you should use the Computing Center Management System (CCMS) for the simple database administration tasks. The CCMS works with the tools listed in Table 9.2. For example, you can use the CCMS database calendar to schedule the time of the database backup.

> **TIP** SAP certifies products from third-party vendors that you can use to back up Oracle databases through the BACKINT interface. You can find information about certified third-party vendors and their products in SAPNet at `http://sapnet/sap.com/csp`. Choose Complementary Solutions.

Storage Management Systems

In addition to the tools discussed in the preceding section, you can use storage management systems—for example, the *ADSTAR Distributed Storage Manager (ADSM)* from IBM. This type of system helps you back up data and restore the database if a problem occurs. For your R/3 System, you should always work with your hardware supplier and the database vendor to select the most appropriate product for your requirements.

Define the Schedule and Tape Administration

For every system in your system landscape, you must define when you'll back up the data in the database and the log files and which tapes you'll use. SAP recommends pursuing three goals. First, you should be able to recover the database for any time within the last 28 days. Second, you should always have sufficient free storage space for the log files. Third, the data should be backed up in the time frame in which the system load is lowest.

Schedule

To realize these goals for an R/3 production system, SAP recommends the following schedule for data backup:

Back up the database every night. A backup places a heavier load on the database server, which negatively affects the performance of all other queries. Ideally, you should back up the data at a time in which the R/3 System does not have to process queries in dialog or in the background. When you create your schedule for background jobs that place a heavy load on the system, take into consideration the time needed for data backups.

Back up the log files at least once daily and release the storage space. However, if you write a large volume of data to the database during daily operation, you should back up the log files more than once a day. Ensure that there is always sufficient free storage space for the log files. Otherwise, the storage space can fill up, which causes the R/3 System to fail.

Use the 28-day cycle. Every backup tape is stored for at least 28 days, after which it can be overwritten. This allows you to recover the database to the state it was in at any time within the last 28 days. It also allows you to protect yourself from data loss if a backup tape of the database is defective. If an error occurs, you should restore the last error-free data backup and all the log files that have been backed up since this backup.

Make an additional backup after each structural change. Each structural change could interrupt the data backup cycle. In some cases, the old backups from before a structural change only allow you to recover the database to the state it was in when the structural change occurred and no further.

> **NOTE** On weekends, you should back up the database and the log files on Friday night or Sunday night. If your R/3 System also processes large volumes of data in the background on the weekend, you must schedule additional backups.

Figure 9.4 shows the recommendations for an Oracle database. You can back up this database in two ways: online or offline. An online backup allows the database to remain available to the R/3 System. However, with an online backup, the data you back up will be inconsistent. To be able to restore and recover a consistent database with an online backup, you also need all the log files that were written during the data backup. An offline backup does not allow the database to remain available to the R/3 System, but it allows you to back up consistent data. As shown in Figure 9.4, you should schedule at least one offline backup for an Oracle database in the 28-day cycle.

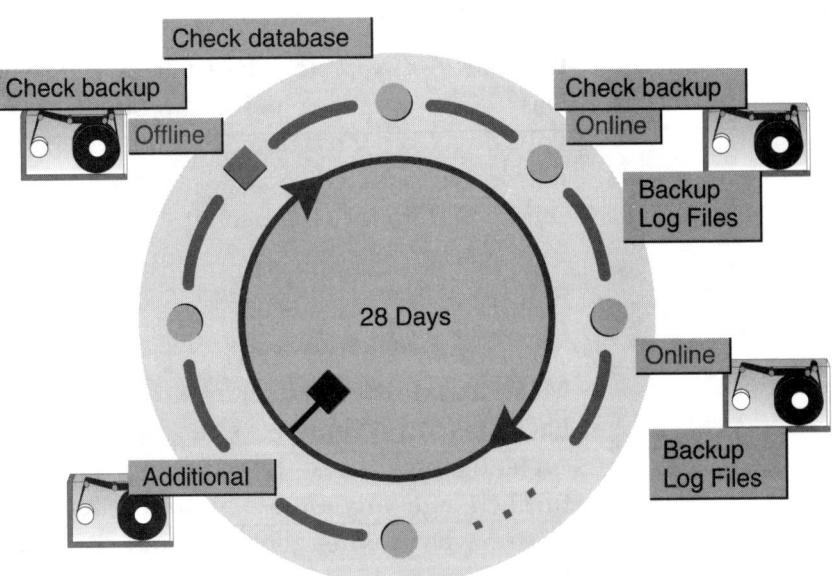

FIGURE 9.4:

A data backup cycle for an Oracle database

To save costs, you can back up the database of the development system and the quality assurance system only once a week. You should continue to back up the log files daily. You must expect a longer downtime if an error occurs when you back up the database once a week than you would expect if an error occurs with a daily backup of the database. You may have to restore all the log files from one week, which requires more time for the database restore and recovery. You also have to make sure that all the log files created since the data backup can be read without error (see Figure 9.3). The option that you choose depends on the maximum permissible downtime for the development system or quality assurance system and the reliability of the daily backup of the log files.

Tape Administration

In addition to following a schedule, you must define which and how many tapes you'll need for the data backup. The number of the tapes depends on the backup cycle you have chosen and the storage capacity of the tapes. Make sure you save the backup of the database and the log files on separate tapes. For a 28-day cycle with a daily database backup, you'll need at least 56 tapes. If the storage capacity is sufficient, you can back up the database and the log files to one tape. However, if only one tape is defective, the cycle is interrupted and data loss is more likely than if you back up to separate tapes.

> **WARNING** Do not back up any other databases or files to the backup tapes for the database and the log files of an R/3 System.

You should use the tools listed in Table 9.2 to administer the tapes. For example, you can use the SAPDBA program to define the name of each tape, how long the tape is protected from being overwritten after the backup, and how frequently a tape can be overwritten. Before beginning a backup, SAPDBA checks to see whether the correct tape for the cycle is in the tape drive. This way, the program prevents you from mixing up tapes or using them too frequently.

Back Up Very Large Databases

For an R/3 System, very large databases are between 100GB and 1000GB in size. This section explains why backing up very large databases can be difficult. You'll also learn about multiple options for quickly backing up and restoring a very large database.

Time Problem

As described in the previous sections, you should back up the databases of the production system daily. Frequently, you cannot do this for very large databases. The complete backup of a very large database takes longer than the time available in one night. You could back up data during the day, but this negatively affects dialog processing in the R/3 System. A data backup places such a load on the CPU and the I/O buses of the database server that user queries to the database take longer.

Example: Backing Up a Very Large Database

The database contains about 400GB of data. To back up the data, the same DLT drive that was used in "Example: Designing Your Storage Devices" is used. The important technical data is as follows:

Capacity   70GB with data compression

Throughput   8GB each hour

A data backup with a DLT drive takes approximately 50 hours; you need 6 DLT tapes. To shorten the backup time, you can back up in parallel to multiple tape drives. Ideally, the backup with 10 tape drives only takes 5 hours, and with 50 tape drives, only 1 hour.

In reality, the entire throughput depends on the throughput of tape drives and many other factors—for example, the time it takes to access the hard disks or the maximum throughput for the I/O and the system buses. The more tape drives you run in parallel, the more you'll load the I/O bus and reduce the throughput. Experience shows that you should use only a few tape drives with a large storage space and a high throughput for very large databases.

During a backup, you'll normally have to change the tape several times despite a large storage capacity, which means that you may have several hundred tapes to administer within a 28-day cycle. If possible, you should use a tape robot. You should only decide on the backup devices for your R/3 System with your hardware partner.

Partial Backup

For an Oracle database, you can avoid the time problem by dividing the backup of the entire database into multiple partial backups. For example, you can back up a 400GB database in five sections that are each 80GB. As Figure 9.5 shows, you can back up each section of the database on a different night. Therefore, you can save the entire database within five nights. However, you should back up the log files completely every day.

A partial backup has one important disadvantage. If you have to restore the entire database, it normally takes as long as all the partial backups combined. At worst, this includes a long downtime. You have to weigh this disadvantage against the most important advantages. You can back up sections of the database daily without negatively affecting dialog or background processing for a long period of time. Also, in many problem situations, you only need to partially restore the data backup. For example, if only one hard disk fails, you only have to restore the files on that hard disk, and you can use the log files to restore the changes that have been made since the backup.

FIGURE 9.5:

Partial backup of the database

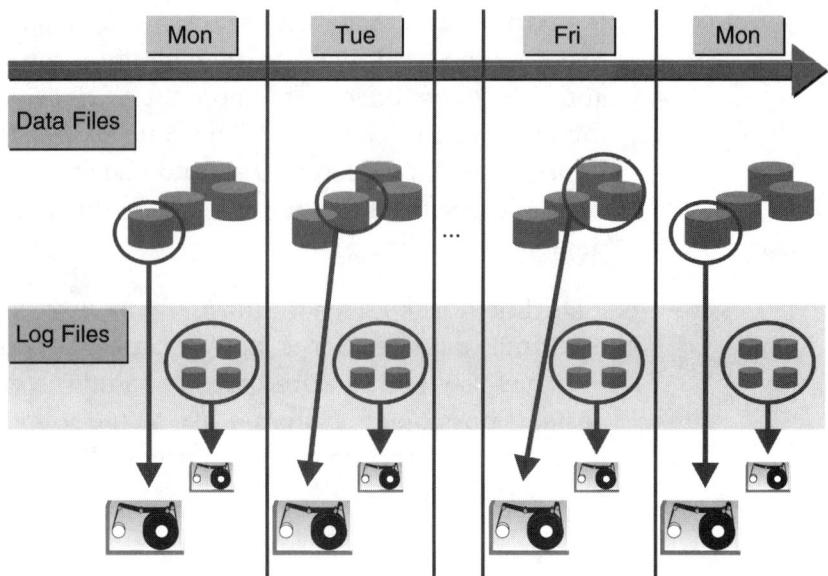

> **NOTE** If you back up your database partially, you need to plan a complete backup in your cycle. If a log file from the cycle of partial backups cannot be read without errors, none of the following partial backups can be used. You must also ensure that all the database files are backed up in a cycle.

Hard Disk Backup

A partial backup is not the only way to work around time constraints. You have the option to first back up the data to separate hard disks. Normally, this is quicker than backing up to tape and thus shortens the backup time. After you've backed up the data to separate hard disks, you can back up the data from the hard disks to tape. To avoid placing a heavy load on the database server with this step, you should connect the backup hard disks to another server. The tape drives can be connected locally to this server, and from it, the data is backed up to tape.

If a problem occurs and the data is still available on the backup hard disk, you'll shorten the downtime considerably because the data can be restored quickly. If the data is already copied to the tapes, the downtime depends on how quickly you can restore the data from the tape drives. A backup to hard disks is more expensive than a partial backup because you need additional hard disks and should also have an additional server.

Define Your Recovery Strategy

If an error causes downtime for your database, you need a detailed strategy for recovering it. For your recovery strategy, you have two goals. First, the system should be available for production operation as quickly as possible. Second, no data should be lost. To achieve these goals, determine in detail how to handle various errors and who can correct them. This is a difficult task for every database administrator. He or she must know the RDBMS in detail as well as its setting for the production system. Document your strategy in the system operation manual.

> **WARNING** If an error occurs, do not make any rash decisions. Additional mistakes will increase the downtime, and you may lose data without being able to restore it.

Downtime

You should work with the company management to determine the maximum permissible downtime for your production system when a serious problem occurs. The more expensive an hour of production downtime in the R/3 System is to your company, the shorter the maximum downtime must be and the more detailed your strategy for recovering the database must be. To estimate the maximum permissible downtime, you must be able to answer three questions: How quickly can you *react* to find the error and to potentially replace defective hardware? How quickly can you *restore* the data backup and the log files? How quickly can you *recover* the database?

React

The reaction time starts when the error occurs and ends when you have corrected the error and started to restore the data backup (see Figure 9.6). For this time period, you can plan two points in advance. First, you can define the time it should take for a specialist to analyze the problem on-site. Second, you should have a Service Level Agreement with your hardware partner for delivery of replacement components during the reaction time. However, a Service Level Agreement cannot always ensure timely delivery of a replacement for a potentially defective component. Therefore, you should store replacement parts for these components in a warehouse. For example, it would be useful to store one or more hard disks.

NOTE If you need an external specialist to handle errors, you should have an appropriate reaction time arranged with him or her. If someone in your company has sufficient knowledge of the subject, you can set up an on-call service for situations in which errors occur outside of regular working hours.

Restore

After you have corrected the error, you need to restore the data from the last data backup and all the log files that were backed up since then. To do so, you'll need the same amount of time it takes to back up the data unless you only have to restore a part of the database. As Figure 9.6 shows, if only a part of the hard disks have been damaged, frequently you only have to restore the damaged files. Therefore, the throughput of your backup devices determines the length of the restore (see "Select Tools" earlier in this chapter).

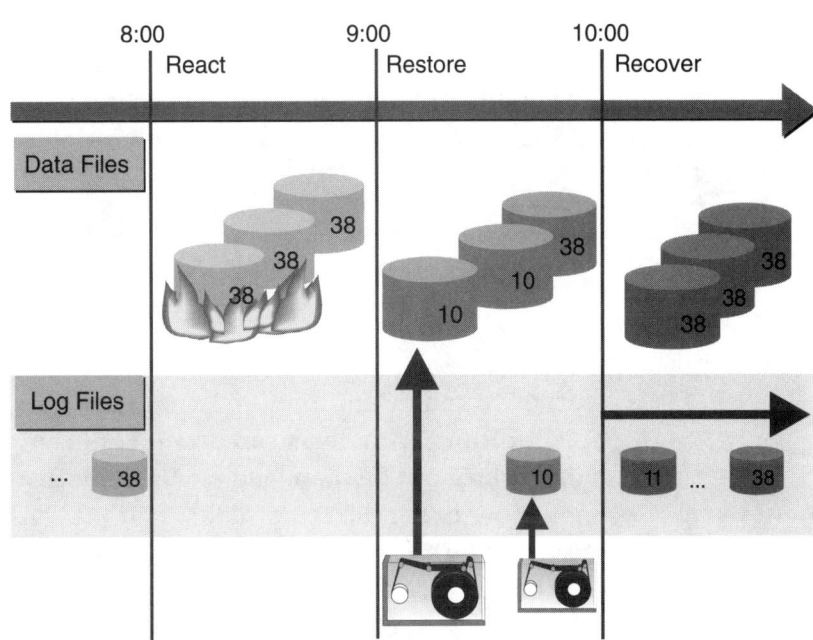

FIGURE 9.6:
A schedule for restore and recovery

NOTE It is not possible to restore a part of the database and then recover it for all RDBMSs with this partial restore. Therefore, find out whether partial restore is possible with the release of the RDBMS you are using.

Recover

After you have restored the data from the backup tapes, the database will be restored to the state it was in at the time of the backup. However, there may be inconsistencies in the data (due to an online backup of an Oracle database, for example). To achieve the most up-to-date and consistent state, you need the information from the log files that were written since the data backup. As Figure 9.6 shows, the RDBMS reads the information from the log files and changes the data in the database accordingly. This is called recovery. The amount of time you need for recovery depends on how much data the RDBMS has to read from the log files and then change in the database. Normally, it is considerably shorter than the amount of time from the data backup until the error occurred.

> **NOTE** You can recover a database to an exact point in time. You need this *point-in-time-recovery* if you use a data backup to restore a database to the state it was in before a logical error.

The total downtime can easily amount to a few hours, and at worst, it can amount to more than a day. You should consider that additional problems can occur. For example, a tape of the data backup can be damaged, or the administrators may not know how to handle the problem and may make an error themselves. To be able to perform routine tasks in these situations, you should rehearse a database recovery many times. In ASAP, this is considered part of the Final Preparation phase. You should test to make sure a restore and recovery of the production database is possible, although you should also test for this occasionally after the start of production. These tests are particularly necessary if you have changed or replaced a part of the hardware or software for the data backup.

Monitor the Database

A problem with the database affects all the users in the R/3 System. To recognize problems early and thus be able to prevent downtime, you must monitor the database regularly. The CCMS in R/3 has the required tools to do so. Make sure the data backup was successful. Additionally, monitor the growth in the log files and the database and react accordingly before the storage capacity is exceeded. To ensure that you can use the CCMS tools optimally, the following sections explain:

- What you can configure in the database calendar
- How to define the system operation

Configure the Database Calendar

You can use the database calendar in CCMS to plan the periodic tasks for the database administrator. For example, you can define when the data in the database and the data in the log files should be backed up. Every RDBMS has its specific tasks, and Figure 9.7 shows the tasks that you can schedule for an Oracle database. In addition to the data backup, the list also contains tasks for database administration, such as checking the statistics for the cost-based optimizer and generating new statistics.

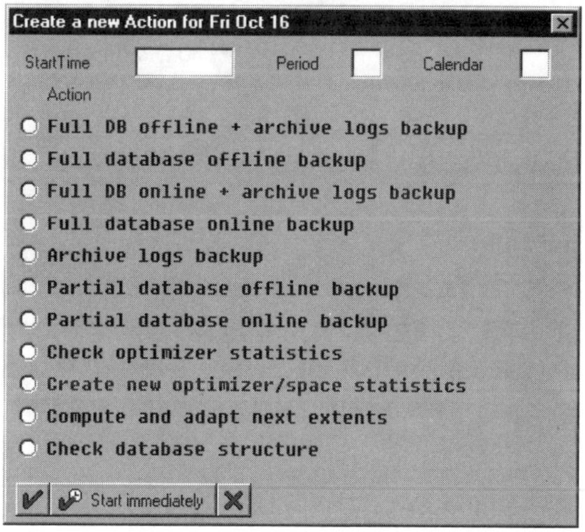

FIGURE 9.7:
Tasks that can be scheduled in the database calendar for the administration of an Oracle database

After you have set up an R/3 System in your system landscape, you should customize the CCMS. For the database administration, you can create a schedule that defines when certain tasks in the database calendar are performed. As you learned in "Define the Schedule and Tape Administration" earlier in this chapter, each system has different availability requirements. In a production system, you should back up the database every day, whereas you may only back up the databases in the development system and the quality assurance system once weekly. As shown in Figure 9.8, you can define the day and time the task should be performed. Since every customer has different requirements, there are no predefined values in the standard R/3 System.

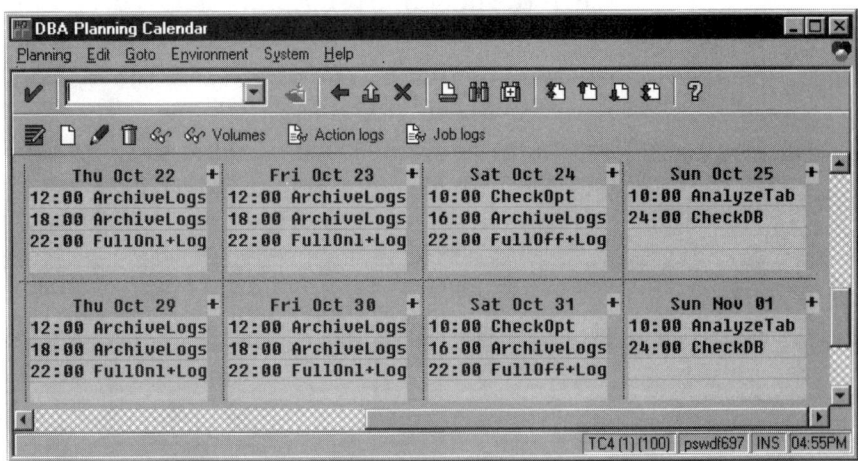

FIGURE 9.8:

An example of a database calendar for an Oracle database

In addition to using the calendar for scheduling, you can use it to monitor whether a task was completed without problems or whether an error occurred. For example, a task in data backup is marked red if a problem occurred during the backup.

Define the System Operation

During the Realization phase, you must back up the data for the development system and the quality assurance system. These two systems are the production systems for the implementation of the application. Without a regular data backup, you are in danger of losing your Customizing efforts. When you set up the development system in your system landscape, you should work with technical consultants and specialists to define the data backup strategy for all the systems in your system landscape. This is then documented by the database administrator in a system operation manual. During the Realization phase, you'll gain experience with the procedures of your system operation, and the database administrator will adapt the manual if any procedures were changed. These experiences are then used in the system operation of the other systems.

As with the R/3 instances, check the important components of the RDBMS daily. It is especially important for the production system that you check daily to see whether the data was successfully backed up or whether a problem occurred. Table 9.3 shows the checks you should perform daily. The transactions listed here are described in the R/3 online documentation.

TABLE 9.3: Daily Activities for Database Monitoring

Activity	Transaction Code	Remarks
Alert Monitor (4.0)	RZ20	If a red or yellow alert is displayed, there is a problem.
Data backup	DB12	If an error occurs when a data backup is performed, the problem must be corrected immediately and the data backup must be repeated. Make sure the data is readable with the tape station.
Storage requirements	DB02	The fill level for the log files should never be higher than 60%. The fill level for the database should never be higher than 80%.

For less serious problem situations, the solution may already be described in the system operation manual. For serious problems, define in the manual who must be notified and which specialist can help with this type of problem. SAP recommends keeping a logbook for these daily activities. In the logbook, note the time, who checked which components, and whether a problem occurred.

In addition to these regular activities, the database administrator must also perform many activities for maintaining the database if the need arises. These activities are different for each database system. SAP and its partners offer training courses for each RDBMS. Appendix B lists the training courses offered by SAP that a database administrator should attend.

Database Administration in ASAP

During the R/3 implementation, you'll set up each system in turn for your system landscape. You must protect all the systems against data loss. In the Business Blueprint phase, you should work with a technical consultant to define a data backup strategy for all the systems. Define how and when to back up the data. Additionally, define who will back up the data and monitor the data backup. When you have set up a system, the database administrator configures the database calendar in CCMS and adapts the threshold values for the Alert Monitor. To protect the system from third-party access, you should change the default passwords for the special users on the database layer. You must also protect the passwords of the operating system users on the database server. The following sections describe when to perform further tasks for database administration during the R/3 implementation.

Project Preparation

During the Project Preparation phase, define the operating system and the hardware platform that you are using for the RDBMS. You must also determine how much database storage capacity you require and the storage technology you want to use. To protect your investments, ensure that you can expand the hardware and the storage capacity. In addition, you must select the devices for the data backup. The main criteria are the storage capacity and the throughput of the devices. Normally, DLT tape drives are sufficient for the development system and the quality assurance system. If you expect to have a large data volume for your production system, you must use a relatively complex technology for the backup devices. Ensure that you can expand the capacity of the data backup as well as the storage capacity of the database.

Business Blueprint

At the beginning of the Business Blueprint phase, train the Technical Team so that they can ensure the availability of the R/3 Systems in the Realization phase. The database administrator in particular must be able to at least schedule and check the data backup after the Business Blueprint phase is completed. He or she must also be able to monitor the growth of the database and the log files.

Realization

To prepare for the implementation of the production system, you should define the disk layout for the RDBMS in detail in the Realization phase. You have two goals. First, the layout should protect against data loss. For example, important files should be backed up redundantly to separate hard disks. Second, the layout should achieve optimal throughput with the available hard disks. For example, you can distribute the database files over the hard disks in a way that all the hard disks are accessed with the same frequency.

If a problem occurs and causes downtime for your database, you must recover the database quickly and without data loss. You can only ensure that you can do so if you have defined a detailed procedure for this type of situation. Define who makes decisions and how the problem is solved in abnormal situations. To be able to guarantee a downtime, you must consider which Service Level Agreement to make with your hardware partner and consulting partner. Do you want to keep important replacement parts on hand or do you want delivery contracts with 24-hour service? You must define how to switch back to normal operation after you have resolved problems and recovered the database. If you run the system in a system group with other R/3 Systems or external systems, you must particularly consider how to restart data transfer.

Final Preparation

To prepare for production, you must test the procedures for data backup as well as for recovery in the production environment several times. In particular, this includes various tests in situations where you could lose data (for example, if you have a defective hard disk or data is accidentally deleted by users). The database recovery is one of the most difficult tasks for the database administrator. If you want to be able to recover the database without the help of external specialists, you must rehearse it during the Final Preparation phase and occasionally during production operation. Decide whether the planned downtimes are realistic for specific situations or whether you have to correct them. If you adapt the procedures, the database administrator must in turn adapt the system operation manual. Only a manual with up-to-date procedures can make the production operation easier.

Table 9.4 lists the tasks in ASAP that are related to database administration. Each task is described in accordance with the phase in which it is performed and the person who performs it.

TABLE 9.4: Tasks for Database Administration in ASAP

Phase	Phase Name	Task	Role
1	Project Preparation	Identify the technical requirements	Project Manager, Technical Team Lead, R/3 System administrator
		Procure the hardware	Project Manager, Technical Team Lead, R/3 System administrator
2	Business Blueprint	Conduct the Basis and system administration workshop	R/3 System administrator, database administrator, network administrator, operating system administrator, technical consultant
		Configure CCMS	Technical consultant, R/3 System administrator
		Define the backup strategy	Technical Team Lead, R/3 System administrator, database administrator
		Define the periodic system maintenance procedures	Technical Team Lead, R/3 System administrator, database administrator, technical consultant
3	Realization	Design the production system hard disk layout	Technical Team Lead, database administrator, technical consultant
		Define the disaster recovery procedures	Steering Committee, Technical Team Lead, Business Process Team Lead
		Verify the backup and recovery procedures	Technical Team Lead, R/3 System administrator, database administrator
4	Final Preparation	Conduct the backup and restore procedure test	Technical Team Lead, R/3 System administrator, database administrator

Success Factors

To successfully implement database administration, you must perform the following tasks:

- Size the hardware sufficiently
- Test the data backup and recovery
- Protect the special users

The following sections describe these points in detail.

Size the Hardware Sufficiently

For the database hardware, you should work with the hardware partner to define four components. First, select the required speed and thus the type of CPU. Second, determine the size of the main memory. Third, define the storage technology and the storage capacity. Fourth, plan with your hardware partner how the performance and the storage capacity can grow in the future.

> **NOTE** As with R/3 instances, you must ensure that the sizing is done for the specific R/3 Release and the RDBMS release that you will be running in production operation.

In addition to the hardware for the database server, you must sufficiently size the hardware for the data backup. This depends on the capacity you need for the storage medium and your production system's maximum permissible downtime if a problem occurs.

> **NOTE** Ensure that the capacity and the throughput of the backup devices are sufficient for the expected volume in the database. The capacity of the backup devices must be able to grow with the storage capacity of the database.

Test the Data Backup and Recovery

You can only protect yourself against data loss if you can rely on both the data backup and the recovery. The data backup is part of the routine work of a database administrator. For the production system in particular, the administrator checks daily to see whether the backup was completed successfully.

> **WARNING** R/3 receives information from the operating system about whether a data backup was successfully completed or not. In some situations, you may not be able to read the data from the tapes, even though the operating system reports to the R/3 System that the data backup was successfully completed. You can only avoid this problem situation if you check daily to see whether you can read the data from the tapes.

A data backup is only useful if you can use it to recover the database. Before the start of production, you must test the recovery several times until you achieve the desired results. The database administrator can also rehearse the procedures because they are difficult and are not part of his or her routine work. This is not a new concept; however, it is a concept that is often neglected because of lack of time before the start of production.

Protect the Special Users

After a standard R/3 installation, special users are created with which you initially log on to the database and generate other users for future work. For example, in the Oracle database, there are three users: SYS, SYSTEM, and SAPR3.

A password is predetermined for each special user; third parties also know this password. For example, the R/3 work processes log on to the database with the user SAPR3 and the predetermined password SAP. On the database layer, the user SAPR3 can access all the R/3 data. To protect yourself against third-party access to all of the R/3 data, you must change the passwords directly after the installation. SAP also recommends regularly changing the passwords and notifying very few employees. To ensure that the passwords are not lost, you should store them in a secure location. The R/3 online documentation describes how to change the password.

Review Questions

1. Which RAID level does SAP recommend for the R/3 database?

    A. RAID 1

    B. RAID 2

    C. RAID 3

    D. RAID 4

    E. RAID 5

2. Why does an RDBMS require the log files?

    A. To back up time-critical data

    B. To recover the current status of a database if an error occurs

    C. To store information about the locations of directories and files in the database

    D. To log error messages

3. Which statements are correct?

    A. For each data backup, you must stop the R/3 System.

    B. Between two data backups, you should back up the log files at least once.

    C. After each structural change, you should back up the database.

D. The data backup cycle is 28 days long.

   E. Log files and data from the database must be backed up to one tape.

4. Which options do you have to back up a very large database?

   A. Partially back up the database.

   B. Back up the database in parallel to multiple tapes.

   C. Back up only the log files of the database.

   D. Back up the database in two steps: first to a hard disk and then to a tape.

CHAPTER TEN

Archiving

The R/3 System can store data in three ways: first, in the tables of the database; second, as files on the operating-system level; and third, in a separate archive system. Normally, R/3 first saves the application data in the database. Therefore, the database continually grows in production operation. However, the larger the data volume in the database is, the lower the performance of R/3 can be and the more difficult the database administration can become. For each R/3 System, you must ask yourself how you should archive application data that is no longer needed for daily operation.

To answer this question, this section first describes how R/3 archives your application data and which archive systems can be used. To ensure that you optimally adapt the options in R/3 to your requirements, the following sections show how to:

- Define the archiving strategy
- Define the archiving procedure

> **NOTE** Archiving does not necessarily have to be implemented for the start of production. However, it is part of ASAP because its strategic importance is often recognized too late. For a detailed archiving strategy, the departments and the Technical Team should work together closely. This is easier during the implementation project because you have already brought many specialists together to work in your Project Team.

Archive Development Kit, ArchiveLink, and Hierarchical Storage Management

Depending on the industry, you must keep the records of a business transaction for an audit for several years. Accounts payable clerks or external auditors must analyze these archived records and be able to generate a report with them. If you archive R/3 application data and remove the data from the database, you must ensure that it can be displayed and analyzed in the system at any time. Therefore, archiving in R/3 is implemented in such a way that you can display and analyze archived records in R/3 even after you have upgraded the Release or your hardware.

Archiving Run

For an R/3 System, the application data is archived in three steps (see Figure 10.1). First, the *archive files* are generated. Using an *archiving object*, you select the business object and define how to archive it. The data is stored in the database and the archive files. Unlike data in the database, the data in the archive files is compressed. Normally, R/3 can compress the data to one-fifth of its original size. Second, the system checks to see whether it can read the archive files, and then, the archived data is deleted from the database. Third, you can either save the archive files to an external medium or archive them in an archive system.

> **NOTE** Before R/3 deletes the data from the database, it checks to see if it can read the archive files. This ensures that you cannot lose any data during an archiving run, so you do not need to schedule an additional data backup before archiving.

In the R/3 System, you can call archiving from an application. The R/3 System selects the appropriate archiving object. You should schedule the archiving run as a background job. Archiving can run in parallel to dialog processing, and production operation does not need to be interrupted.

> **NOTE** You cannot use archiving functions to copy and transport application data to other R/3 Systems or clients. In an archiving run, data is written only to the archive files. You can only read the archive files in the client in which you generated the archives.

FIGURE 10.1:

An archiving run

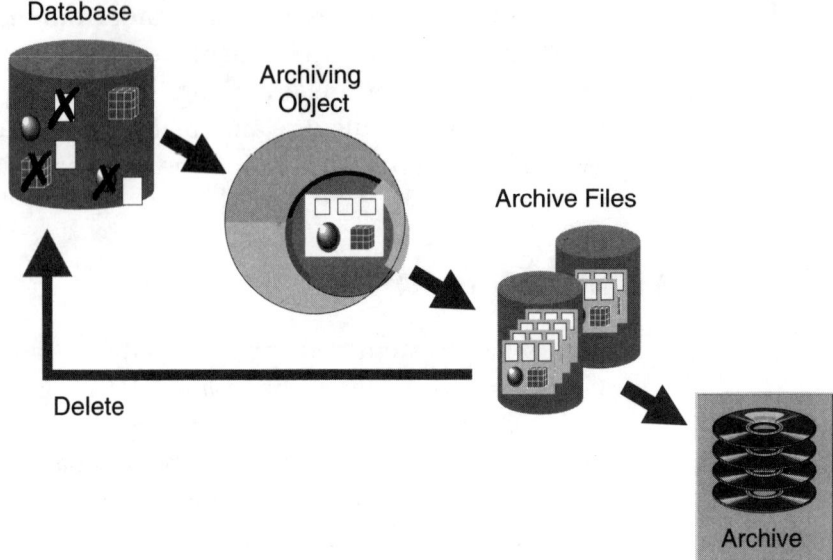

Normally, there is no danger of one user archiving documents and deleting them from the database while another user is processing them. Once generated, many types of documents cannot be processed again. These documents are automatically locked by R/3. If documents of a document type can still be processed, then a residence time is applied for them in the R/3 System. A document can only be deleted from the database when it is older than the residence time. It is not likely that you will change documents after the residence time has elapsed.

The Archive Development Kit (ADK)

The *Archive Development Kit (ADK)* is the layer between the archive files and the R/3 application. If you have, for example, upgraded your R/3 System or hardware, this layer ensures that you can read all old archive files with R/3. If data is required again, the ADK readjusts the format of the data to the current formats in the R/3 Repository.

To be able to preserve the archive files over a long period of time, you can either save the archive files to an external medium or archive them to an archive system. You can use two methods to connect archive systems from third-party vendors to an R/3 System. First, you can use the *SAP ArchiveLink* interface. Second, you can include the file system in R/3 in a *Hierarchical Storage Management (HSM)* system. The following sections describe these methods in more detail.

ArchiveLink

Through the ArchiveLink interface, you can connect optical archives and document management systems from third-party vendors with the R/3 System. In addition to archiving the archive files, you can use this type of external archive system to archive other document types. For example, you can archive scanned originals as graphics. You can use the archive system tools to display all the documents in the archive except the archive files. R/3 has all the necessary functions you need to read the data in the archive files or to search for data in the archives. These functions are based on the ADK and thus can only be called from the R/3 System.

> **TIP** When you select your third-party vendor, ensure that their product is certified by SAP. You can find information about complementary solutions by third-party vendors in SAPNet at `http://sapnet.sap.com/csp`. Choose Complementary Solutions.

The Hierarchical Storage Management (HSM) System

With a Hierarchical Storage Management (HSM) system, you can integrate the R/3 file system directly into an archive system. You won't have to manually make the files available again because, with an HSM system, the archive files are available at any time. It makes no difference to the R/3 System whether the archive files are located in a directory on the hard disk or whether the directory is included in an HSM system. Therefore, there is no SAP certification for these products. If you want to implement this type of system, you must always select a suitable product with your hardware partner.

NOTE An HSM System cannot be connected to R/3 through SAP ArchiveLink.

Define the Archiving Strategy

In an archiving strategy, you should consider the technical and business factors. From a technical viewpoint, define which data volume ensures an optimal throughput for the system. From a business viewpoint, define which application data must remain in the database and for how long. Here, you should also consider your company guidelines as well as the business and legal requirements.

There are very few cases in which you should archive application data in the first weeks after the start of production. Figure 10.2 shows how archiving should begin after the data has reached a critical volume. You can calculate in advance when you will reach this volume. In the first weeks after the start of production, measure the amount of data you enter in R/3 each day, and with this information, calculate when the critical data volume will be reached. At this point, archive regularly and keep the data volume in the database close to constant.

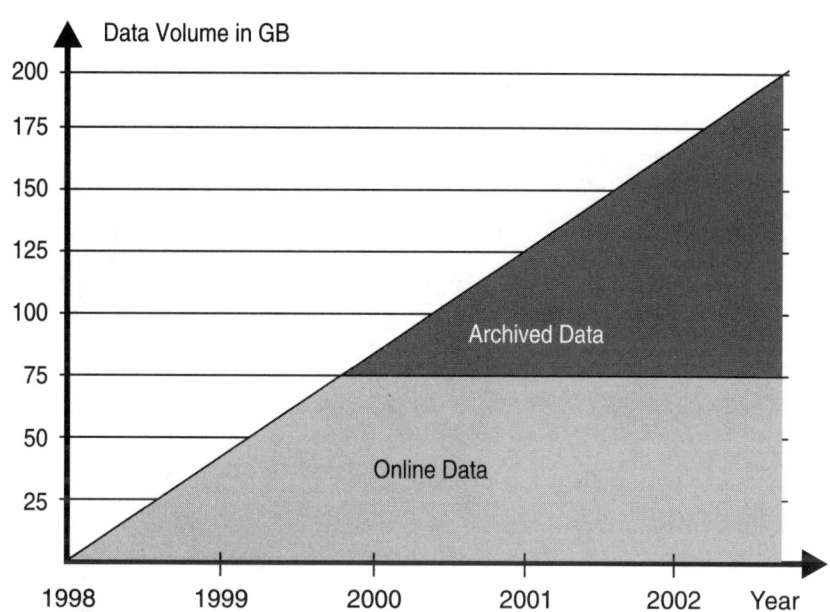

FIGURE 10.2: The balance between growth and archiving of data

Although you'll often only start to archive months after the start of production, within ASAP, it is recommended that you define the strategy and make the necessary Customizing in the Realization phase. This enables you to plan in advance the medium or archive system to which you will save the archive files. For a detailed strategy, the departments and the system administration department must work closely together as well. This is easiest during the implementation project. With each department, define a list for archiving. For each business process, enter the linked archiving objects in a table, as displayed in the table in the sidebar "Example: Creating a Business Process–Oriented Table for Archiving Objects." In particular, you must define how often you'll archive an archiving object and the minimum age of the data. Each department must include its business and legal requirements.

> ## Example: Creating a Business Process–Oriented Table for Archiving Objects
>
> The following table is an excerpt from a business process–oriented table for archiving objects. It shows a list with which you can plan the archiving runs. Based on a sample business process, two of the related archiving objects are listed.
>
> | Business Process | Archiving Object | Cycle | Residence Time | Retention Period |
> |---|---|---|---|---|
> | Process delivery | SD_VBAK Sales document SD_COND Condition record for pricing | | | |

If you want to give a part of the archiving task to a service vendor, define in detail in your strategy how the tasks are to be divided. For archiving, SAP offers a special service, the *Remote Archiving Service*. SAP specialists take on all tasks that are related to the archiving of data in your R/3 System. Through remote connections, these specialists work with integrated standard tools in the R/3 System. For example, the specialists make the necessary Customizing settings, define the size of the archive files, and schedule the background jobs. Because each company has different requirements for their archiving strategy, the Remote Archiving Service can only provide advice for the archiving strategy.

TIP You can find more detailed information about the Remote Archiving Service and how to order the service in SAPNet at `http://sapnet.sap.com/ConsultingServices`. Choose Remote Archiving. Alternatively, you can contact the SAP Local Support at the SAP office in your country.

Define the Archiving Procedure

As you learned in the previous sections, you must consider many business factors for archiving. Only the individual departments know these factors. Therefore, the departments must play an important role in the archiving procedure. The following section explains how to organize the archiving procedure. Then you will learn what is important for the system operation and which integrated R/3 tools to use.

Organize the Procedures

When you define the archiving strategy in the Realization phase, you must decide who is responsible for each archiving task. In particular, define how to distribute the tasks between the departments and the system administration department. Figure 10.3 shows how to define the following two roles for your system:

Department The department defines the Customizing settings and creates a schedule for the background jobs. At the same time, they make sure the data was successfully archived.

System administration department The administrators are responsible for the availability of the archive files or the linked archive system. In particular, they are responsible for safe data storage over a specified period of time.

> **NOTE** Ensure that you agree with the departments on procedures for exceptions and problems as well as on normal procedures.

Distributing the responsibilities is the best way for you to avoid archiving application data that you may occasionally require in dialog processing. If the R/3 System administrator is allowed to schedule the archiving runs, he or she can only base their decision about which data to archive on technical factors. However, the R/3 System administrator cannot decide which data should be archived from a business viewpoint and which data should remain in the database for dialog processing.

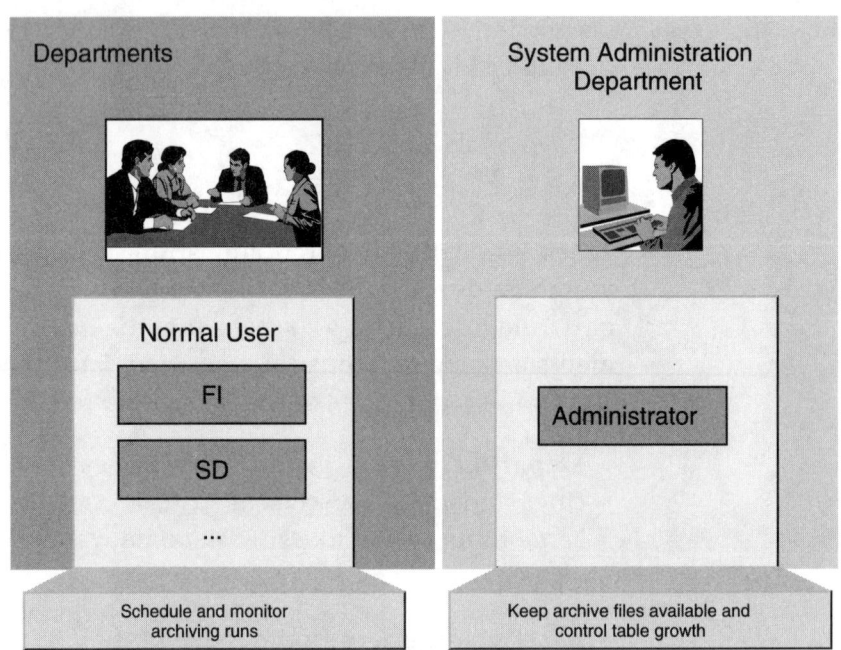

FIGURE 10.3:

Distribution of responsibilities for archiving

As part of the archiving procedure, you should work with the departments to create an appropriate authorization concept. Only a few people in the departments should be able to archive data. In particular, you must define whether these people can also schedule and release background jobs. An archiving run can place a heavy load on the database. This can then influence other background jobs or dialog processing. Therefore, you must harmonize the authorization concept for archiving with the concept for background processing (see Chapter 7, "Background Processing").

Define System Operation

In the Realization phase, you should define the future strategy for archiving and also for future system operation. Document the planned procedures and set up your schedule in the system operation manual. Together with the departments, work out a list of your business processes and the related archiving objects. As shown in the table in "Example: Creating a Business Process–Oriented Table for Archiving Objects," you should define the following for each object:

Cycle The cycles in which data is archived

Residence time The minimum age of the data stored within the R/3 System

Retention period How long archive files must be kept

For each archiving object, you should also define who is responsible for the related archiving runs and who monitors whether the data was successfully saved.

> **NOTE** During and after an archiving run, R/3 collects statistical data. This data includes the runtime, the free space in the database, and the size of the archive files. With this data, you can better plan future archiving runs.

Tables and Archiving Objects

During production operation, the Technical Team can at first only determine which tables grow quickly and thus become very large. To archive data from these tables, the Technical Team must select the appropriate archiving objects. The difficulty in this is that tables and archiving objects are linked through an n:m relationship. There can be multiple archiving objects for one table, and one archiving object can archive data from multiple tables. In the Computing Center Management System (CCMS), you can use a function (transaction code DB15) to display these relationships. You can search for archiving objects that belong to a table as well as for the tables that belong to an archiving object.

Example: Searching Archiving Objects for a Table

The Tables and Archiving Objects screen shows an example of which archiving objects are suitable for the table COEP (transaction code DB15). This table is used extensively by the controlling applications. Experience shows that this table can grow so quickly that some reports or evaluations have long processing times. If this is true for your system, you can resolve this problem by archiving the archiving objects for table COEP.

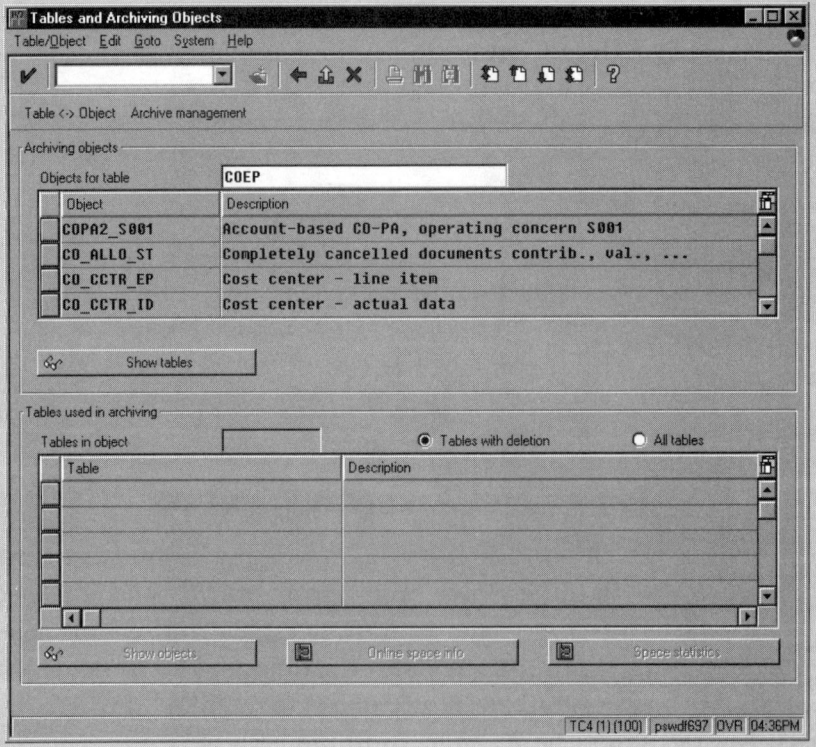

Example: Searching Tables for an Archiving Object

The Tables and Archiving Objects screen shows a second example of the tables from which you can archive data with the archiving object SD_VBAK, which includes sales documents (transaction code DB15). For individual tables, you can also display the amount of storage space you are using or how many data records the tables contain. This can help you decide whether you can archive the desired data volume with one archiving run.

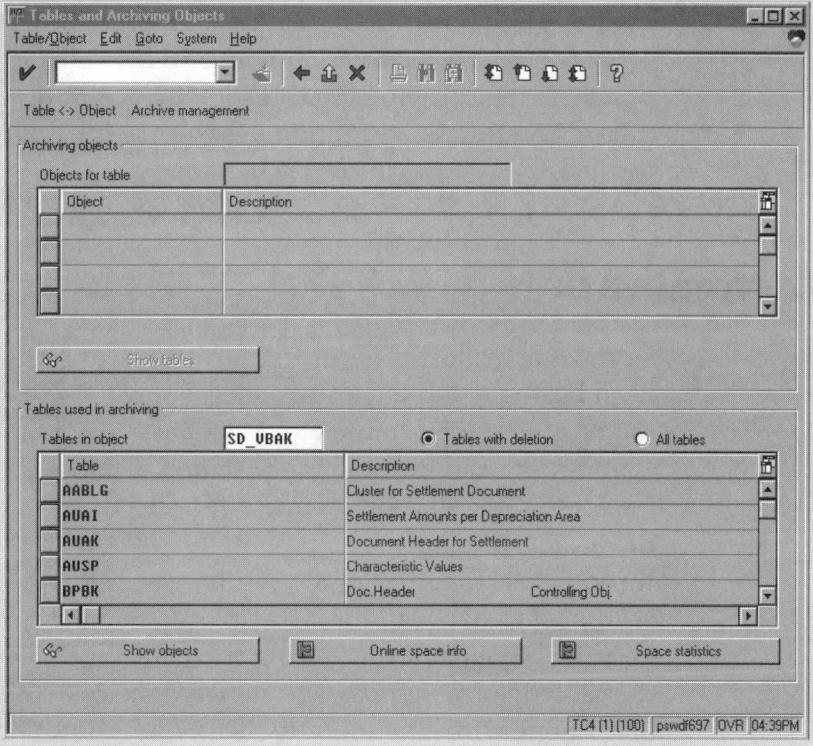

As you learned in Chapter 5, "R/3 Instance Administration," you can use a graphical Alert Monitor in R/3. SAP plans to also integrate data archiving into this monitor in the near future. You can then set threshold values for important application tables. If a threshold value is exceeded, R/3 triggers an alert. All of the related archiving objects are also referenced.

Archiving Procedure in ASAP

You often do not start archiving until some months after the start of production. Despite this, it is worthwhile to define the archiving procedures during the implementation of R/3. In the previous sections, you learned which points to consider. In ASAP, all of the points about archiving are considered in one phase, the Realization phase. The following section describes which tasks are planned for this.

Realization

First, you should define an archiving strategy with the departments. Both business and technical aspects play a role in the strategy. On the one hand, determine which business records are stored in the R/3 System and for how long. To do so, you must consider the business and legal requirements. On the other hand, you must determine which data volume in the database ensures an optimal throughput. Together with your hardware partner, specify the relationship between the data volume and the performance of your R/3 System. Considering these aspects, create the procedures to determine how, and which data, to archive. You should also define which medium to use for long-term archiving of the archive files or whether you want to use an archive system. When you have defined the procedures in a system operation manual, test the archiving procedure until you obtain the desired results. In particular, you must ensure that the departments and the computing center work well together. Subsequently, you can release the tested procedure for production operation.

Table 10.1 lists ASAP tasks that are linked to the implementation of the archiving procedure. The list shows the person who performs each task.

TABLE 10.1: Archiving Tasks in ASAP

Phase	Phase Name	Task	Role
3	Realization	Design archiving management strategy	Project Manager, Technical Team Lead, Business Process Team Lead, Business Process Owner, Business Process Team Member
		Create archiving management	Project Manager, Technical Team Lead, Business Process Team Lead, Business Process Owner, Business Process Team Member
		Test archiving procedures	Technical consultant, R/3 System administrator, Business Process Owner, Business Process Team Member
		Review archiving	Technical consultant, R/3 System administrator, Business Process Owner, Business Process Team Member, application consultant

Success Factors

To successfully implement the archiving procedure, you must give particular consideration to the following:

- Selecting a suitable storage medium
- Saving archive files

The following sections describe these points.

Select a Suitable Storage Medium

The most important criteria for selecting a storage medium are how frequently and how quickly you want to access the archived data. For example, in some companies, so much data is entered each day that you have to begin archiving at an early stage. In this situation, the archived data is required very often for evaluations in the R/3 System, so you must be able to access it quickly. You can only ensure quick access if you use a suitable storage medium. Table 10.2 lists examples of storage media and the typical access times. You should always select your storage medium together with your hardware partner.

TABLE 10.2: Access Times for Various Storage Media

Medium	Access Times	Description
HSM	Critical; about 30 seconds	Archived data is accessed frequently.
Hard disk	Critical; about 5 seconds	Archived data is accessed regularly.
Jukebox through ArchiveLink	Noncritical	Archived data is accessed rarely.
Magnetic tapes	Noncritical	Archived data is only accessed in exceptional cases.

Back Up Archive Files

When you have archived the data, you must also ensure the availability of the archive files. In particular, you must ensure that the data cannot be lost. As you learned in the preceding section, you can protect yourself against data loss with a suitable storage medium. In addition, you should back up the data twice and keep the copies in a safe place. In the worst-case scenario, your archive system or the media storing the archive files can be destroyed, for example, by fire or water damage. In this type of situation, you may have to rebuild the entire system. This is only possible if you have kept copies of your data off-site.

Review Questions

1. Which problems can be caused by database growth?

   A. Database administration becomes more difficult.

   B. R/3 performance is negatively affected.

   C. Data backup takes too long.

   D. Release upgrades take too long.

2. What do you use ArchiveLink for?

   A. To connect tape robots with the R/3 System

   B. To connect document management systems with the R/3 System

   C. To connect optical archives with the R/3 System

   D. To connect HSM systems with the R/3 System

3. Which statements are correct?

   A. You can use an archiving object only to archive the data from one table.

   B. You can use an archiving object to archive the data from multiple tables.

   C. A table can have a maximum of one archiving object.

   D. A table can have multiple archiving objects.

CHAPTER ELEVEN

Network Administration

In a typical R/3 System, the database layer, the application layer, and the presentation layer all run on different computers. The computers are linked through a network and communicate through the TCP/IP protocol. The network is divided into a front-end network and a server network. The front-end network connects the SAP Graphical User Interfaces (SAPGUIs) with the application servers through a LAN or a WAN. The server network connects the application server with the database server and it should always be a LAN.

In the course of the implementation project, you'll set up multiple systems. Each system has different network requirements. For the development system and the quality assurance system, you'll frequently only have a front-end network with few users. For the production system, you'll normally have a server network in addition to the front-end network. As the number of users working with the R/3 System increases, you'll require a more complex network topology in your company, and thus you must plan in more detail. The following sections describe what you should consider when you plan your network. The subsequent sections show you how to efficiently ensure the availability and performance of the network in production operation.

Plan Your Network

In every R/3 production system, you need at least one front-end network. Therefore, how you link the hardware components of the R/3 System with each other and the required bandwidth for the connections are relevant factors in every implementation project. The following sections first describe what you should consider for a network layout strategy and which topologies are most suitable for a front-end network or a server network. Then, you'll learn which bandwidths you need for the network in general and how to estimate the bandwidth of the front-end network. Finally, you'll learn how to assign the TCP/IP addresses and what you must consider for a remote connection.

Define the Strategy for Network Layout

Before you define a strategy for the layout of your network, you should record the current status of your network infrastructure. Based on the current status, you can work with consultants to decide how to include the R/3 System in the existing network and how far you can use the existing infrastructure for the R/3 System. In a target status, you should then document how the network should be configured in the future. The essential goal of planning is to cover your current network requirements as cost-effectively as possible. In this respect, you must consider which availability you have to ensure and which security measures you must use to secure the network against unauthorized access.

> **TIP** In addition to planning your local network when you plan your target status, you should include how you'll connect all the remote offices with the R/3 System and how you'll maintain the possible networks in these offices. In this respect, you must include the potential field service employees, who occasionally work with R/3 on their laptops through a WAN connection.

To protect your investments for the years to come, you must also consider your future requirements. For example, if you plan a step-by-step expansion of your R/3 System for the next few years, you must be able to expand the network accordingly. You must be able to ensure that the planned network infrastructure meets the common standards, such as ISO, IEEE, or ANSI. These standards allow you to create an infrastructure that is also open for solutions from other hardware vendors so you won't have to depend on the proprietary solutions of one vendor.

> **NOTE** You should work with your hardware partner or network partner to determine which network topology and technology is suitable for your requirements. This way, you can save time and compensate for a potential knowledge deficit caused by the short innovation cycles in network technology.

A good network topology allows you to meet two requirements immediately. First, a network should be easy to administer. Second, the network availability should be high. These requirements are generally limited by a budget. To help you meet the requirements with simple measures, the following sections explain which topologies are suitable. Figure 11.1 shows you a sample topology of the network at Mannaberg Inc. from Chapter 1.

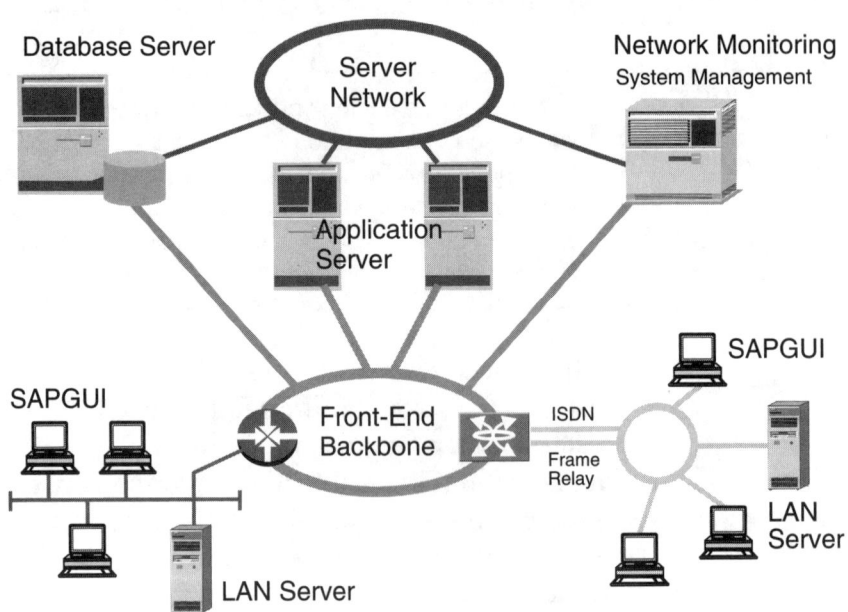

FIGURE 11.1:
Network topology at Mannaberg Inc.

Server Network

A server network essentially ensures that the application servers can use the central resources in the database. For this reason, you only need a server network in a distributed R/3 System. If a problem causes this network to fail, the R/3 System is down for all users. Therefore, you must protect the server network against potential failure. You can achieve this if you connect the servers with each other through a separate LAN subnetwork and configure the connections redundantly. You can also link important servers to the network through two network cards twice; for example, you can link the database server or the central instance with the message server and the enqueue service to the server network through two network cards.

> **TIP** The easiest way to administer the server network is to use a single LAN subnetwork and not divide it into several subnetworks.

The best way to protect the server network against potential failure is to select a current and leading LAN technology for the server network. A solution that is often implemented is an FDDI ring (FDDI stands for Fiber Distributed Data Interchange). In an FDDI ring, the connections are configured redundantly, and thus this technology inherently allows for a high availability. FDDI also has a high transfer speed of approximately 100Mbps. The server network must be the most powerful network in the entire system. You can read about this in greater detail in "Determine the Bandwidth" later in this chapter.

> **NOTE** As an alternative to an FDDI ring, you can connect the application servers and the database server to a common switch. This collapsed server network is implemented by SAP, for example, for the product Ready-to-Run R/3 (see Appendix A, "R/3 for Medium-Size Companies").

Front-End Network

The front-end network enables users to communicate with the R/3 System. If a problem occurs and this network fails, the R/3 System may continue to run, but users can no longer work with R/3 online. For the users, the R/3 System would be down. Therefore, in addition to the server network, you must also protect the front-end network against a potential failure. SAP recommends redundantly configuring the connections and the active components in the network as far as possible. Here, it is helpful to divide the front-end network into a backbone network and multiple subnetworks.

Backbone Network

The backbone network links all the subnetworks with the R/3 System. As shown in Figure 11.2, you essentially have two options. The first option is to connect the backbone directly with the server network through routers. However, if you want to separate the data stream in the front-end network from the data stream of the server network, the second option is to connect the backbone directly with the application servers. With both options, the R/3 System is down for dialog processing if the backbone network fails. To ensure that the failure of one component does not lead to this situation, you should connect the backbone network with the server network or the application servers through at least two paths. As shown in Figure 11.2, you should use at least two routers for the first option. In the second option, you should link the backbone with at least two application servers or with at least one server through two network cards.

As you learned in Chapter 5, "R/3 Instance Administration," SAP recommends using logon groups. The users first log on to the message server through a logon group. The message server passes the users to the instance from the group that has the lowest load. If the connection to the message server is broken, users cannot log on to R/3 through logon groups. For this reason, the message

FIGURE 11.2:

The connection between a backbone network and a server network

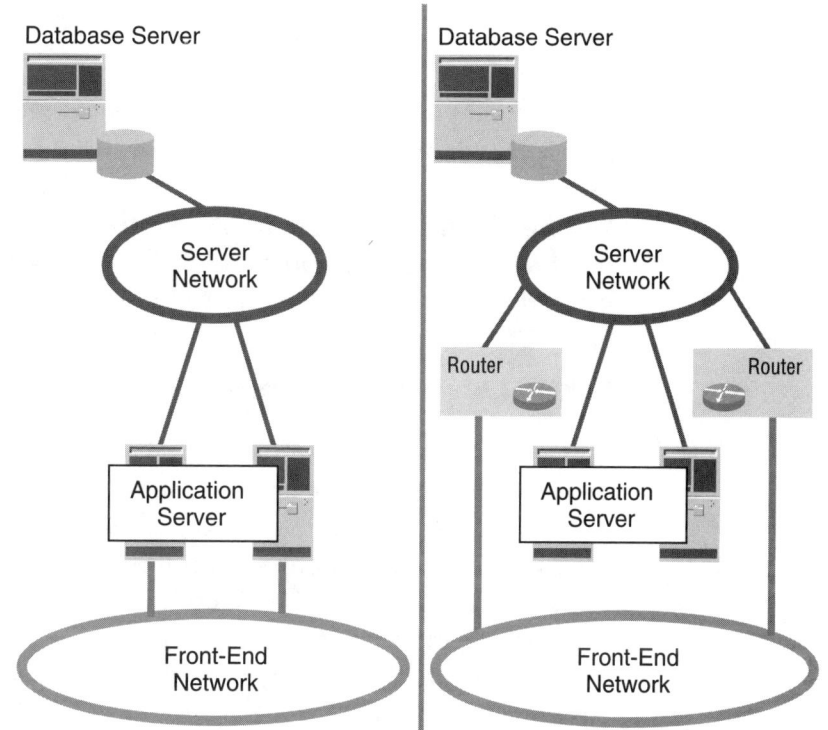

server and its network connection have to be secure against failure. As already recommended for the server network, one option is to link the computer running the message server to the network through two network cards. If you have set up an alternative computer for the message server, you must ensure that the computer is linked with the backbone network. Chapter 15, "High Availability," explains which additional measures you can use to ensure high availability in your R/3 System.

> **NOTE** You should use a backbone network exclusively for communication between subnetworks and the R/3 System.

Subnetwork

You can link the user front ends to a subnetwork. Depending on the size and number of front ends, you can set up LAN servers with which you can administer one or more subnetworks. For example, you can install the SAP front-end software either locally on each front end or centrally on the LAN server (see Chapter 4, "Front-End Administration"). From the topology viewpoint, you must define whether you set up the LAN server decentrally in the individual departments or centrally in the computing center.

Set Up LAN Servers Decentrally

The advantage of setting up all of the LAN servers decentrally is that you can reduce the data stream through the backbone network. However, in some situations, this may increase the administration work. For example, you'll need more time to regularly back up the data in the LAN server. Also, you can only set up the LAN server in rooms that meet the specific requirements for a computing center. These rooms must at least have a sufficient power supply and air-conditioning.

Set Up LAN Servers Centrally

The advantage of setting up all of the LAN servers centrally in the computing center is that you can ensure the physical security of the server and make the appropriate infrastructure available in one location. However, in some situations, this increases the data stream on the network to such an extent that you'll negatively affect the communication between the front ends and the application servers.

Often, companies combine both options. For example, in the computing center, you can set up the LAN servers that are essential for availability. You can set up the other LAN servers in the departments to relieve the backbone network and to reduce the access times.

WAN

In addition to LAN connections, you can also use WAN connections. For example, you can link subnetworks in the subsidiaries to a backbone through different types of connections, such as X.25 or ISDN. You should set up a remote connection to SAP so you can benefit from the special Service & Support offers, such as the GoingLive Check or EarlyWatch. The following sections explain which bandwidth is required for remote connection. The subsequent section, "Set Up a Remote Connection," explains the criteria for selecting connection types and what you have to consider for security.

Determine the Bandwidth

The previous section explained which topologies you can implement for your network. The next important aspect of your planning is to determine which bandwidth you require for the server network or the front-end network, which could consist of a backbone network and multiple subnetworks. As Figure 11.3 displays, with each dialog step, approximately 20KB of data flows between the database server and the application server, whereas with each screen change, approximately 1.7KB of data flows between the SAPGUI and the application server. Thus, there are very different requirements for the bandwidth for the server network and the front-end network.

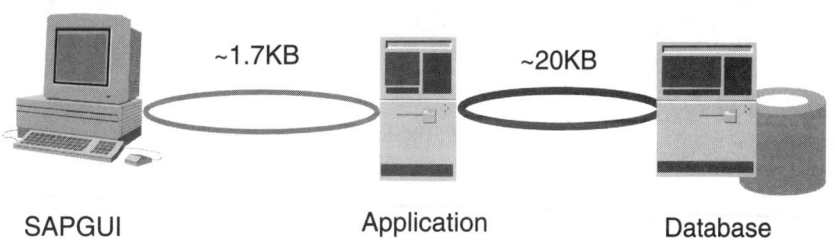

FIGURE 11.3:
The average network load for a screen change

The Bandwidth for a Server Network

In the entire network for the R/3 System, the server network must be the most powerful. If this network's transfer speed is too low, it can negatively affect the performance of the entire R/3 System because the user queries have to wait longer than necessary for data from the database. The bandwidth that you require for your system depends on many factors, and there is no simple way to calculate it. For this reason, you should define the bandwidth together with your hardware and network partner. SAP's experience shows that you need a minimum transfer speed of 10Mbps. For higher requirements, SAP recommends a high-speed network, for example, an FDDI-Ring with 100Mbps.

The Bandwidth for a Front-End Network

In addition to the server network, you have to configure a sufficiently powerful front-end network so the users can work effectively with the R/3 System. Essentially, the required bandwidth depends on the number of users working with the R/3 System through the network at the same time and the time in which the user queries should be answered. In addition to the communication between the SAPGUI and the application server, you must consider the extra amount of data that the network should transfer. For example, are printers connected to an application server through the network? If so, the network must be able to pass the printout data to the operating system spool for the printer in the desired time frame. As you learned in Chapter 8, "Print Administration," you should therefore only link the high-volume printers locally to the application server.

> **NOTE** You must also consider all the interfaces to possible external systems or field service employees as an additional load. For example, if the field service employees work in background processing through a telephone connection every night to update the day's contracts and the next day's price lists, this causes an extra load because the users are working in dialog at the same time.

The Bandwidth Formula

Using benchmarks, SAP has measured the average size of the data stream between SAPGUI and the application server, depending on the number of users. Other data streams were not taken into consideration in these measurements. From the various measurements, the following averages have been calculated. First, the required bandwidth for a network is directly proportional to the number of users working online at the same time in the R/3 System through the network. Second, the bandwidth is inversely proportional to the load on the connection and the sum of the thinking time and the response time. This empiric knowledge is considered in the following bandwidth formula:

$$C = 16.000 * N / [L * (T_{think} + T_{response})] \quad \text{bit/sec}$$

The parameters in this formula are as follows:

C   The required bandwidth measured in bits per second

N   The total number of user front ends that are used at the same time through this connection

L   The load on the connection (values are between 0 and 1)

T_{think} The thinking time (the time between two dialog steps)

$T_{response}$ The response time

With the preceding formula, you can calculate the bandwidth you'll need for a backbone network or individual subnetworks. If you also want to calculate the planned response time for the load peaks, SAP does not recommend placing a load of more than 50 percent on a connection; that is, L should be smaller than 0.5. If you also use the connection for data streams other than between SAPGUI and the application server, you should consider these data streams by selecting a smaller value for the load L accordingly.

> ### Example: Determining Bandwidth
>
> In this example, approximately 15 users are working with the R/3 System at the same time and they should only create a 50 percent load on the network. Between two dialog steps, the users need an average of 10 seconds to enter data or to select options. On average, a user query should be answered after 2 seconds at the latest. If you set these values in the preceding formula, you'll obtain the following result:
>
> C = 16,000 * 15 /[0.5 (10 sec + 2 sec)] bit/sec
>
> = 40,000 bit/sec
>
> Since there is no network technology that provides exactly 40Kbps, in this example, a minimal bandwidth of 64Kbps is required.

Minimum Bandwidth

In some situations, the bandwidth formula may allow you to calculate a smaller value than 9.6Kbps for a LAN or a WAN connection with few users. A smaller value than 9.6Kbps often underestimates the required bandwidth. Experience shows that in the course of a day, a more uneven load is placed on the network by a few users than by many users. This causes more frequent load peaks, which increase the response time. Therefore, SAP recommends using a minimum bandwidth of 9.6Kbps for each connection.

Assign IP Addresses in the Network

The individual layers in an R/3 System always communicate with each other through the TCP/IP protocol. To enable communication, each network node must have a unique IP address. If you connect a network node to the network many times, each connection is given a separate address. For example, if you connect an application server to the server network and the front-end network with a network card for each connection, the application server has two IP addresses. On a level above the network nodes, each network has a unique address that is a part of the addresses for the nodes within the network. If a local network is linked with other networks, you have to respect the conventions for which IP addresses you can assign. In principle, you have two options:

Official IP address   To connect a part of your network to the Internet, you need an official IP address area. This IP address area must be unique worldwide. You can apply for the official IP address with your Internet service provider.

Private IP address   Normally, you'll set up official IP addresses for only a few network nodes. More often, most companies implement private IP addresses in their networks. For your network, you should select the IP addresses according to the common standard, RFC 1918. This way, the addresses may not be unique worldwide, but at least they are unique within your network.

NOTE   Private IP addresses cannot be used for direct connections to the Internet.

Even in smaller networks, you have many network nodes. Therefore, you must assign many IP addresses in your network and then administer them during future production operation. A centralized administration for the addresses allows you to reduce the work and normally simplifies error analysis if an error occurs. The easiest way to control the IP addresses is from a central network server in your network (see Figure 11.1). You should also use tools with which you can automatically assign the addresses.

DHCP and WINS for Windows NT

To centrally administer the IP address in a network with the Windows NT operating system, and thus greatly simplify the administration tasks, you should implement the following protocols in the network:

- Dynamic Host Configuration Protocol (DHCP)
- Windows Internet Name Service (WINS)

If you want to implement these protocols, you must configure the network server to act as a DHCP server and a WINS server. The DHCP server automatically assigns IP addresses to DHCP clients if they connect to the network during the booting process. The WINS server allocates the computer names to the IP addresses in a network.

You can only use dynamically allocated addresses for the computers that are clients and do not have any server programs running. When a computer makes services available for other computers and can therefore be accessed from other computers, it needs a permanent address in the network. For example, the application servers and the database server in particular must have a permanent IP address in your network.

NOTE Before you implement R/3 in a DHCP environment, you must read the R/3 Notes listed in Table 11.1. These Notes explain which configurations are possible and which limitations you must take into consideration.

TABLE 11.1: R/3 Notes for Dynamic Assignment of IP Addresses

Note No.	Short Text
43403	Dynamic IP addresses and SAPLPD
47057	R/3 and DHCP

Set Up a Remote Connection

WAN connections are possible for a front-end network. You can choose between different connection types: X.25, X.31, Frame Relay, or ISDN. The costs depend on the type. For example, for an ISDN connection, the costs are the basic rate plus the cost for the length of time you use the connection. The costs for X.25 or X.31 connections depend directly on the transferred data volume. To determine which connection is the best for you, you must consider how you want to use it by asking yourself the following questions:

- How many users will use the remote connection at the same time?
- Which average response time should normally be possible?
- How many hours will the users require the remote connection each month?
- How large is the data volume that the users will transfer through the remote connection each month?

As you have already learned in "Determine the Bandwidth" earlier in this chapter, the answers to these questions can help you estimate the bandwidth for the connection. This information allows you to select the suitable connection type with the technical consultants or network specialists.

Remote Connection to SAP

You should always set up a remote connection to SAP because SAP provides much of its Service & Support services through a remote connection. This enables you to make use of these services and the expert knowledge of SAP employees without delay, and you'll also save travel expenses. Through the remote connection, SAP experts can work directly in your system to analyze and resolve problems if necessary. For example, you need a remote connection for the remote services such as the GoingLive Check and EarlyWatch. You can define the line type for the remote connection, as previously described. You must also consider how many employees will work with SAP's Online Service System (OSS) and whether SAP consultants will work in your system through the remote connection.

SAProuter and Firewalls

An official connection between SAP and you or your subsidiaries must always fulfill specific security requirements. In particular, unauthorized third parties must not be able to access your private servers and systems. To ensure this, both SAP and you must take various organizational and technical measures. Figure 11.4 shows the firewall architecture recommended by SAP. A router allows you to determine which IP addresses external users can access in your network and through which ports. Behind the router, the SAProuter utility checks again to make sure a user is authorized to access the R/3 System in the network. The SAProuter serves as a gateway for the R/3 application and runs on all the platforms that SAP supports for the application layer.

As Figure 11.4 shows, you can use private addresses for the servers in your R/3 System with the SAProuter, and you do not require official IP addresses inside your network.

> **NOTE** R/3 Note 46902, "Security aspects in remote access," describes in detail the additional security aspects that are essential for a remote connection to SAP and direct access to your system for SAP experts.

Operating Your Network

The most important task for the network administrator is to recognize and quickly resolve errors. As you learned in the previous

FIGURE 11.4:

Firewall architecture for a remote connection through SAProuter.

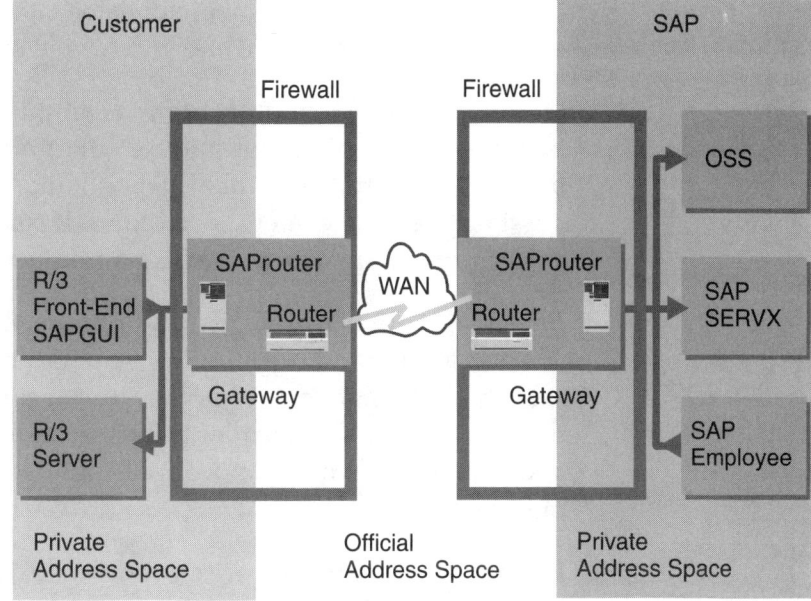

sections, an R/3 System is only available for the users as long as the front-end network and server network are operating. You can increase the availability by configuring the important components in the network redundantly. However, this does not protect you against all conceivable problem situations. More often, the network administrator must check the status of the network as a preventative measure to recognize problems in advance or to detect bottlenecks in the data transfer.

Integrated System and Network Management (ISNM)

Particularly in R/3 Systems with a complex network infrastructure, monitoring and operating the network can become very difficult in some situations. Here, it is worthwhile to set up an *Integrated System and Network Management (ISNM)* platform. Basically, the ISNM platform is divided into configuration management, error management, performance management, security management, and operating cost management. Based on these divisions, the following points are deciding factors for effective and secure network operation:

Define configuration procedures as simply as possible. Normally, not all the steps in the configuration can be automated. Therefore, the manual steps should be as simple as possible to enable even users without detailed knowledge to perform them, such as connecting a front end to the network.

Enable remote maintenance and remote check. A centralized administration simplifies operation because often it enables one network administrator to control the entire network. You must consider that you need reliable tools and connections to the appropriate subnetwork for remote maintenance.

Establish a detailed security concept. To protect yourself against internal unauthorized accesses, you should establish an authorization concept in every network—for example, a domain concept for a Windows NT network. To protect yourself against external unauthorized accesses, you should set up a firewall, at least for connections through a public network.

Measure data throughput and optimize it accordingly. Use a tool to measure the load on a specific line in detail. In the first weeks after the start of production in particular, you can use these measurements to optimally adapt the network resources to your requirements.

> **NOTE** Whether you are a service provider who makes resources available or a customer who takes advantage of a service provider's resources, the question arises as to how these services are billed. For this, you need operating costs management products with which you can determine which users have used specific resources and how much.

The Computing Center Management System (CCMS) is the system management system for the R/3 System. In addition, the CCMS performs the basic functions for network management. For example, you can check the TCP/IP connection with an operating system command. In R/3, this function is included in the R/3 transaction code OS01.

Open Interfaces

If you require additional functions and monitors for management, you should work together with your hardware partner and your network partner to decide which product is suitable for your requirements. There are various open interfaces in CCMS for creating an ISNM platform in complex R/3 Systems with heterogeneous system platforms and system management applications from third parties. The interface for network management is based on the *Simple Network Management Protocol (SNMP)* and the *Management Information Base (MIB)*. Chapter 13, "Interfaces," describes the open interfaces in CCMS in more detail.

Network Administration in ASAP

In the previous sections, you learned which points to consider for network administration during the R/3 implementation. In ASAP, these points are distributed over the individual phases of the project. The following sections describe when to perform certain tasks.

Project Preparation

During the Project Preparation phase, you should describe the technical requirements for the entire R/3 System and, thus, the requirements for the network. To do so, you should first record the current status of your existing network. Use this as a base for your target status. Make sure you use common standards in your target status. This enables you to protect your investments. Based on the standards, your network remains flexible enough to be expanded or to be equipped with new technology in the future. Therefore, you must carefully check your decisions to determine whether you can meet your current requirements and those of the foreseeable future.

SAP's Service & Support network is an important source of help and information for the entire implementation project. For this reason, ASAP recommends ordering a remote connection at the beginning of the project and setting it up early. As you learned in the section "Set Up a Remote Connection," you can create a physical network connection to SAP through a network provider. Here, it is essential that you take the required security measures, such as setting up a SAProuter, for example.

Business Blueprint

At the beginning of the Business Blueprint phase, you'll create your technical design. In the technical design, you should document all the technical aspects of the planned system landscape and thus the entire network infrastructure as well (for example, the physical network layout and the distribution of active components).

Because you'll set up the development system at the end of the Business Blueprint phase and the quality assurance system at the beginning of the Realization phase, you must set up the network for both of these systems in the Business Blueprint phase. To enable the application consultants and the software developers to work with as few disturbances as possible, the Technical Team must ensure the availability of the network. For this, you should define the temporary procedures for system operation in this early phase of the project. You should continue to develop system operation during the course of the project, and the collected experiences will influence operation of the production system. When you set up your network, you should also establish the remote connection to SAP. Ensure that the members of the Project Team and the future help desk providers can use the OSS.

Realization

At the end of the Realization phase, you'll set up the production system. Based on the specifications in the technical design, you'll also install the network. At this time, you can test whether the individual components can communicate with each other.

During the Realization phase, you should ask yourself two questions: Which situations can cause the network to fail? How does a partial failure affect the operation of the entire system? Together with network specialists, you can use the answers to these questions to determine the procedures and measures to follow to completely avoid these situations or the fastest way to resolve these types of potential problems. Document the results in the system operation manual.

Final Preparation

In the Final Preparation phase, you should test the setup of the production environment to make sure it can process the load caused by real system operation. You must ensure that you check access and throughput for the network thoroughly. However, in addition to the procedures for normal operation, you should test the procedures that are important for recovering the network if a problem occurs.

Table 11.2 lists the tasks from ASAP that are related to the implementation of the network infrastructure. Each task is described in accordance with the phase in which it is performed and the person who performs it.

TABLE 11.2: Tasks for Network Administration in ASAP

Phase	Phase Name	Task	Role
1	Project Preparation	Determine technical requirements	Project Manager, Technical Team Lead, R/3 System administrator
		Procure hardware	Project Manager, Technical Team Lead, R/3 System administrator
		Order remote network connection	Technical Team Lead, R/3 System administrator
2	Business Blueprint	Document network	Technical Team Lead, network administrator, operating system administrator, technical consultant
		Establish remote connection to SAP	R/3 System administrator, network administrator, technical consultant
3	Realization	Install and configure the network environment	Technical Team Lead, network administrator, operating system administrator, technical consultant
		Define system failure scenarios	Technical Team Lead, R/3 System administrator, database administrator, network administrator, operating system administrator, technical consultant, Business Process Owner
4	Final Preparation	Conduct system tests	Technical Team Lead, R/3 System administrator, database administrator, network administrator, operating system administrator, technical consultant, Business Process Team Lead, Business Process Owner

Success Factors

To successfully implement the network administration, you must give the following points particular consideration:

- Configure enough bandwidth
- Use supported network products

The following sections describe these points in detail.

Configure Enough Bandwidth

During the Project Preparation phase, time constraints often only allow for you to test whether the server network and the important subnetworks are sufficiently configured. However, it is only after the start of production that you can check to see whether you correctly defined the bandwidth for all the components in your network. For this reason, a detailed analysis of the current status is particularly important in the first weeks after the start of production. You can use this analysis to answer the following questions:

- Who places the heaviest load on the network?
- When do bottlenecks occur?
- Which additional services are used within the network?

To answer these questions in detail, you need applications for network management that extend beyond the basic functions in the R/3 CCMS (see "Operating Your Network" earlier in this chapter). You should select the applications with your hardware and network partners.

Use Supported Network Products

For every R/3 Release, SAP creates a list of supported network products: SAP System Requirements for Networks, Frontends and Communication Interfaces. This list specifies the exact name of the supported products and their release and contains information about the following points:

- Requirements for the front ends
- SAP communication libraries (CPI-C, RFC)
- Communication services (SAP Internet Mail Gateway, SAP Exchange Connector, SAP MAPI Service Provider Interface)
- Internet tools (Web server, Web browser)
- Interface to external security systems (Secure Network Communications [SNC])
- Requirements for the R/2 workstation software
- Communication with R/2 and external mainframe systems

You'll save time and money if you only implement the supported network products. If you want to implement another product or another version of a product, you may have to perform extensive modifications.

> **TIP** The SAP System Requirements for Networks, Frontends and Communication Interfaces list is part of each R/3 delivery package, whether it's for an installation or an upgrade. You can also receive this list through the SAP Local Support at the SAP office in your country or through SAPNet at `http://sapnet.sap.com`. To access this list in SAPNet, you need an OSS user.

Review Questions

1. Which statements are correct?

   A. A server network should consist of multiple LAN subnetworks.

   B. A backbone network should be connected with the server network or the application servers through at least two paths.

   C. A backbone network should only be used for communication between the R/3 System and subnetworks.

   D. A front-end network cannot contain any WAN connections.

2. Which factors play a role in determining the bandwidth of the front-end network?

   A. The load on the connection that is generated by the data stream between front ends and application servers

   B. The number of all the front ends in the network

   C. The number of all the users in the R/3 System

   D. The users' average thinking time between two dialog steps

3. What do you need for a remote connection to SAP?

   A. A router

   B. The SAProuter utility

   C. An official IP address

   D. An X.25, X.31, Frame Relay, or ISDN connection

CHAPTER TWELVE

Software Logistics

All standard software must be adapted to your company's requirements. The term *Software Logistics* refers to the methods and tools in R/3 that you can use to adapt the standard R/3 System. It also includes how to transport changes from one R/3 System to another R/3 System.

For an R/3 implementation, SAP recommends implementing two—or even better, three—R/3 Systems. By doing so, you can ensure that the adaptations done to the standard R/3 System were tested before you start production. While you are preparing the implementation project, you should define your strategy for Software Logistics. To enable you to optimally adapt the options in R/3 to your needs, the following sections explain how to perform these tasks:

- Plan your system landscape
- Define the system and the clients
- Maintain the system landscape

Plan Your System Landscape

The R/3 System landscape that is recommended in ASAP consists of three R/3 Systems: the development system, the quality assurance system, and the production system. You should customize the settings, develop your own programs, and document the changes in the development system. Then you should transport the changes to the quality assurance system and test them. After you have checked the quality of your work, you can transport the changes into the production system. The basic concept behind this procedure is that you perform all the changes to the standard R/3 System in only one system, and therefore, you always ensure the consistency of the changes.

The number of systems and the types of clients that you need in your company are important factors in your project preparation. You have to consider both your requirements for quality assurance and the budget for the hardware. The goal of this section is to help you with your planning by explaining how to define the following:

- The systems and clients
- The implementation strategy
- The Release strategy

Define the Systems and Clients

Although frequently only a part of the system landscape is set up in the Realization phase of an implementation project, SAP recommends defining the entire system landscape at the beginning of the project. So that it can perform its role in the system landscape, the development system is the first system you have to configure accordingly. With an appropriate configuration, you can ensure that all the Customizing settings and your own Advanced Business Application Programming (ABAP) programs are documented and marked for transport to the desired R/3 Systems in your logistics chain.

Client-Dependent and Client-Independent Data

To set up a system landscape and be able to maintain it during production operation, you must transport different data types between the R/3 Systems. As shown in Figure 12.1 (see Chapter 2, "Technology in R/3"), all the data in R/3 is divided into two categories:

Client-dependent data Customizing data, application data, and user master data

Client-independent data Special Customizing data and Repository objects

Figure 12.1 also shows that, normally, multiple clients are set up in an R/3 System. From a business and organizational viewpoint, these clients are independent. However, the clients are not independent from a technical viewpoint because the Repository and client-independent Customizing are used in all of the clients. For this reason, you cannot set up the clients in an R/3 System so that you can change Repository objects and still have a stable runtime environment for a production client. Therefore, you must set up a system landscape that consists of at least two systems.

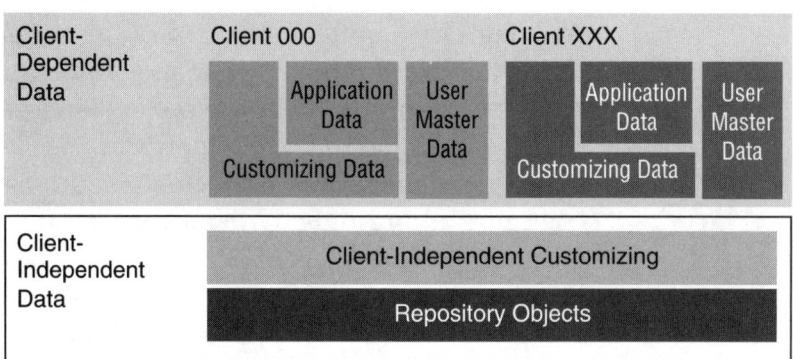

FIGURE 12.1:
The data structure of an R/3 System

A Two-System Landscape

In a two-system landscape, Customizing and production are distributed over two R/3 Systems: the development/quality assurance system and the production system. SAP recommends that you set up three clients in the development system (see Figure 12.2). In the CUST client, you can customize the settings in your system and develop your own ABAP programs. In the TEST client, you can test the settings and software developments before you release them for quality assurance. The released changes are verified and released for production operation in the QTST client, and then, the changes are transported to the production system. To ensure a stable runtime environment for production operation, you should only set up one client in the production system, the production client (called PROD in Figure 12.2).

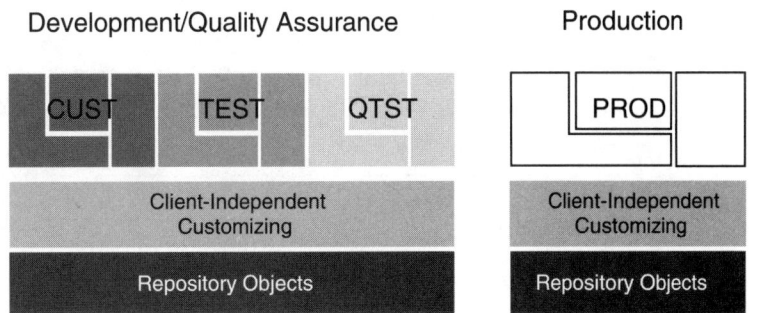

FIGURE 12.2: A two-system landscape with a typical client structure

Disadvantage of a Two-System Landscape

The main disadvantage of a two-system landscape is that you develop software and test the quality of your software developments in the same R/3 System. This can cause problems for client-independent objects, in particular. If user A changes a Repository object, the changes are automatically valid for all the clients. If user B is using this object to test previous software developments, user A has changed the end result for user B while user B is still testing, and user B may not have been notified.

Advantages of a Two-System Landscape

In a two-system landscape, you can completely separate the production operation from development and quality assurance. By doing so, you'll have a stable runtime environment in your production system. This also prevents the performance of the production client from being negatively affected by other clients. An additional advantage is that you'll protect your data against unauthorized access. If a user is authorized to change Repository objects in an R/3 System, that user can in theory bypass the authorization check and thus access all the R/3 data. To prevent this, SAP recommends that you do not assign any users authorizations that allow a user to change Repository objects in a production system (see Chapter 14, "Security").

> **NOTE** SAP implements a two-system landscape for the product Ready-to-Run R/3 (RRR). RRR is described in detail in Appendix A, "R/3 for Medium-Size Companies."

A Three-System Landscape

With a three-system landscape, you can have a separate R/3 System for Customizing, quality assurance, and production. As shown in Figure 12.3, compared with the two-system landscape, the clients are distributed differently over the systems in a three-system landscape. However, the tasks that the clients perform are the same. Both the CUST and TEST clients remain in the development system. You'll have a separate R/3 System for the QTST client and therefore a separate runtime environment. For the reasons mentioned earlier, you should only set up one client in the production system: PROD.

FIGURE 12.3:

A three-system landscape with a typical client structure

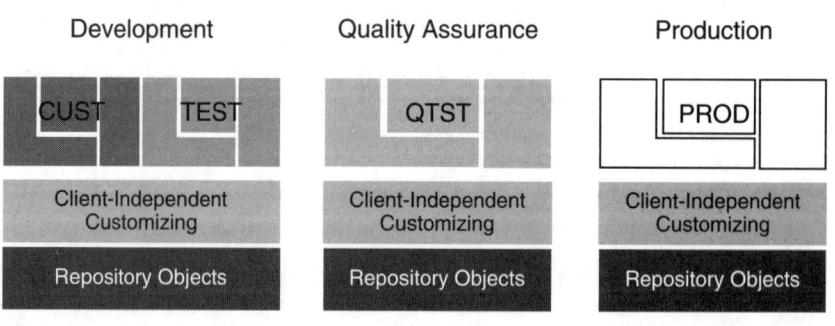

Disadvantage of a Three-System Landscape

The main disadvantage of a three-system landscape is that you need more resources in two areas. First, you have to buy additional hardware for the quality assurance system. Second, the Technical Team has to administer an additional system and ensure its availability.

Advantage of a Three-System Landscape

The main advantage of a three-system landscape is that you can test the quality of changes in a separate system. As in a production system, you must not change the Customizing or the programs in a quality assurance system. This ensures that the production system will have the same runtime environment as the quality assurance system. The two systems are the same except for the application data and the user master records.

Two- or Three-System Landscape?

You should work with consultants from SAP or SAP partners to determine which system landscape is suitable for your requirements. If you plan to use the standard R/3 installation for your R/3 System and only expand or develop a small number of programs, a two-system landscape is often less expensive and still provides sufficient opportunity for quality assurance. However, if you are planning extensive Customizing projects or if you change many client-independent objects, SAP recommends a three-system landscape.

Example: Designing a System Landscape for a Multinational Company

For some requirements, even a three-system landscape is not sufficient. In this example, a company that operates worldwide has different requirements for

Continued on next page

the production systems in R/3 for the most important areas: the U.S., Europe, and Asia. As you can see, when identical changes are made worldwide, they are made in a global development system first. These changes are then tested in a global quality assurance system. Only then is the chain for Software Logistics split and there are separate logistics chains for the development system, the quality assurance system, and the production system for each region. The settings that are specific for each region are customized and tested within this chain.

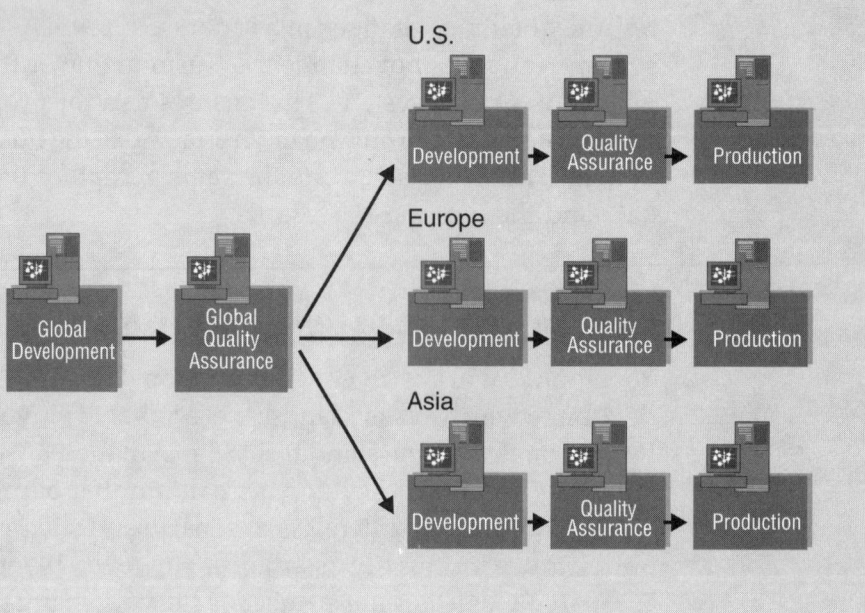

NOTE In addition to determining the number of R/3 Systems you'll need, you must also occasionally consider the following questions: Can multiple clients run in production in an R/3 System? What are the necessary conditions for this? Table 12.1 lists the R/3 Notes that provide the answer to these questions. SAP has also published a white paper, "The Multiple-Client Concept of the R/3 System," on this topic.

TABLE 12.1: R/3 Notes for Client Dependency in R/3

Note No.	Short Text
31557	The multi-client concept of R/3 – Overview
64520	Question on client-dependency R/3 - R/2

System Change Options and Client Change Options

R/3 has two options to enable you to choose the R/3 System and clients in which the standard R/3 installation can be changed. First, you can set the *system change options*. This allows you to define whether changes to client-independent Customizing and to the Repository are permissible or not. Second, you can set the *client change options*. This allows you to define whether changes to client-dependent objects are permissible or not. You can also choose whether the Customizing is automatically recorded or not.

> **NOTE** System change options do not allow you to define how to handle client-dependent objects. If you have selected Objects Cannot Be Changed from the system change options, you can still allow client-dependent Customizing data to be changed.

Figure 12.4 shows you which R/3 transaction to use to set the client change options. The steps for system change options and client administration are described in greater detail in the R/3 online documentation and in *SAP R/3 System Administration: The Official SAP Guide*, by Liane Will (Sybex, 1998).

Define the Implementation Strategy

The primary goal of an implementation strategy is to set up a consistent system landscape. Your strategy must ensure that all of

FIGURE 12.4:

Setting client change options (transaction code SCC4)

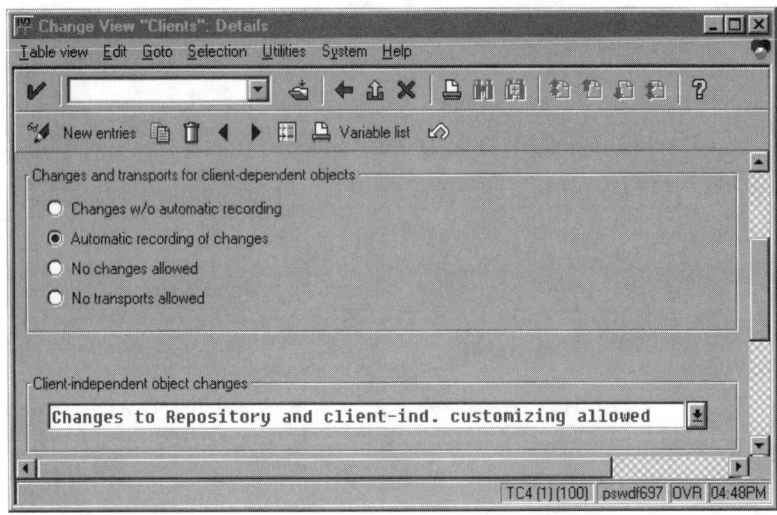

the R/3 Systems and their clients have the same Customizing settings and the same results from software developments in a logistics chain. For this, you must define how to transport the changes from the development system into the next R/3 System. The tools in R/3 make different strategies possible. ASAP recommends that you decide on a strategy during the Project Preparation phase.

> **TIP** As far as possible, you should use the same procedure to implement the system landscape and to maintain the landscape. This way, you can avoid switching tools and establishing new procedures in the course of the implementation project.

A good implementation strategy allows you to meet two requirements. First, all the changes should be transported from one R/3 System to the next R/3 System as easily and securely as possible. Second, the changes should be documented and thus controllable. In accordance with these requirements, this section describes how to implement the recommended three-system landscape in the course of the implementation project. If you are planning to implement a different system landscape in your company, you can use this procedure as a model.

The Change and Transport Organizer (CTO)

Regardless of which system landscape you selected, as soon as you have installed an R/3 System, you should set up the Change and Transport Organizer (CTO). With it, you can determine the system change options, the system landscape, and the status of the system, whether it is newly installed or a copy of another R/3 System. The R/3 online documentation and *SAP R/3 System Administration: The Official SAP Guide* describe in detail how to do this.

The Transport Management System (TMS)

The Transport Management System (TMS) enables you to centrally configure and administer the transport of changes from one system in your system landscape (see "The Transport System" in Chapter 2). The way you physically transport the change requests on the operating-system level from one R/3 System to the next R/3 System is fundamental for the TMS. In most cases, a transport directory that all the systems in the landscape can access is set up. Figure 12.5 uses an example of the three-system landscape to show that you can logically connect the systems in your landscape through a transport domain. Within the transport domain, you should configure an R/3 System as the transport domain controller (TDC). From the TDC, you can administer the transport domains centrally. Within the transport domains, you must define the transport path. By doing so, you can define the system to which the TMS marks and transports a released change request.

Development

At the beginning of the Business Blueprint phase, you'll install the development system. You should configure this system so that

FIGURE 12.5:

Transport domain for a three-system landscape

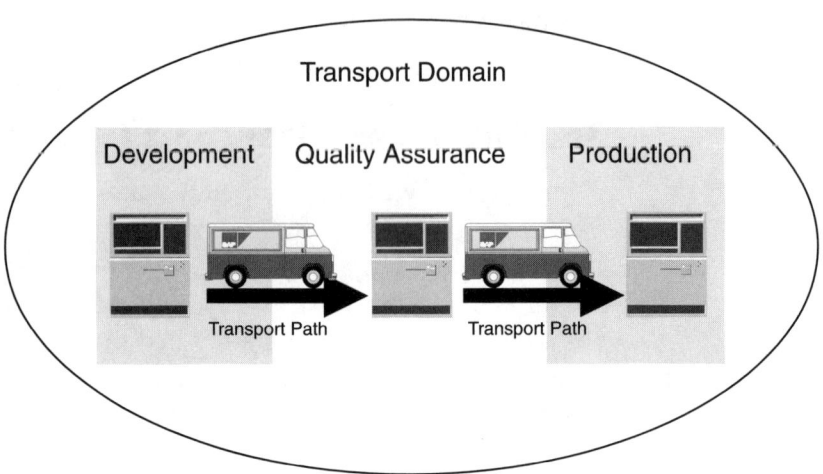

client-independent data can be changed. As shown in Figure 12.3, SAP recommends both of the following for the development system:

CUST In the CUST client, you can perform Customizing and develop all your own programs. Client-dependent and client-independent objects can be changed, and the changes are automatically recorded as change requests.

TEST In the TEST client, you can test the Customizing and development efforts before you release the change requests. You can use the client copy to regularly copy the changes from CUST to TEST. In TEST, objects cannot be changed. This way, you can ensure that all the changes are only performed in CUST.

As shown in Figure 12.6, you can use the client copy to create both of the clients from client 000 in the standard R/3 System. When you perform Customizing and develop software in CUST, you should copy the results into the TEST client regularly (transaction code SCC1). To transport the data along the transport route into the quality assurance system, release the change requests in the development system and R/3 exports them automatically to the transport directory.

FIGURE 12.6:
Setting up the development system in a three-system landscape

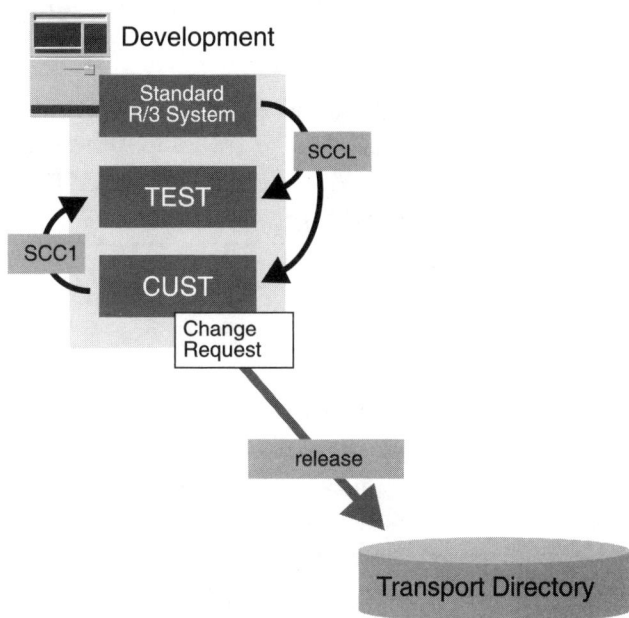

Quality Assurance

At the beginning of the Realization phase, you'll set up the quality assurance system. In this system, only the released change requests from the development system are tested, but you cannot change an object manually. This ensures that the originals, including all their versions, reside in the development system, which simplifies the administration of the versions.

As shown in Figure 12.7, you can use the client copy to create the QTST client in the quality assurance system. In this client, verify the Customizing settings and your own software development.

The change requests released from the development system are imported from the transport directory. As of R/3 Release 4.0, you can control the transport of the change requests from R/3 by using the TMS. In the TMS, you can see, for example, which change requests are waiting to be imported from a system.

> **NOTE** In addition to the quality assurance client, you'll often set up a training client, TRNG. To ensure that this client is identical to the production client, you can use the client copy to copy the client-dependent changes from QTST to TRNG on a regular basis.

Production

At the end of the Realization phase, you'll set up the production system. As you did for the other systems, you should start by using the client copy tool to create the production client PROD from the client 000. This client is at the end of the logistics chain. Import the change requests that were successfully verified in and released from the QTST client into the PROD client.

> **NOTE** In the production system, you must change the settings for the system change options to Objects Cannot Be Changed and the settings for the client change options to No Changes Allowed. By doing so, you'll prevent users from manually changing Customizing settings or your software developments. If changes are necessary, the changes must go through the entire logistics chain.

Production Operation

When you start the Final Preparation phase, you will have completely set up your system landscape. You should only use change requests to transport the changes from one R/3 System to another R/3 System in the logistics chain. Use the client copy tool to copy the changes from one client to the next client within an R/3 System. Figure 12.8 shows each step that you perform in production operation.

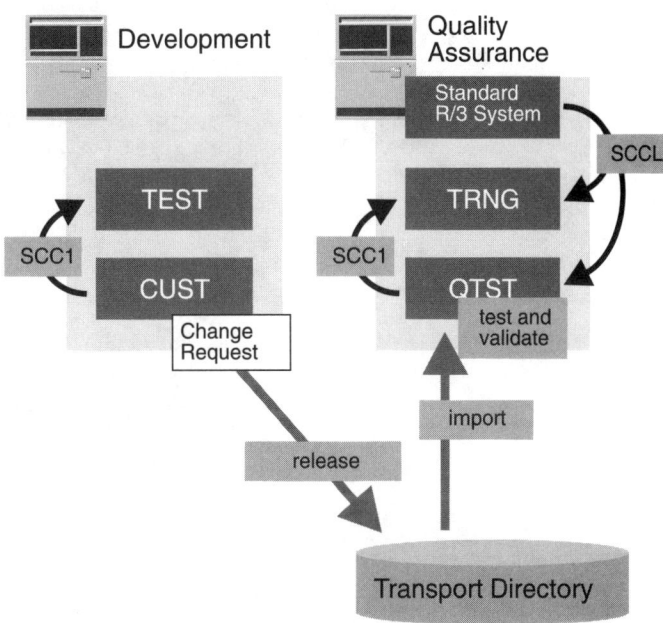

FIGURE 12.7:
Setting up the quality assurance system in a three-system landscape

Advantage of the Three-System Landscape's Implementation Strategy

The main advantage of the implementation strategy for a three-system landscape is that you'll use the same transport procedure to implement the system landscape and to run the systems in production operation. Since you do not change the procedure, you'll save time because you don't need to notify or train the Project Team about the new procedure. Additionally, you can use the processes in this strategy to upgrade the R/3 Release or to implement additional R/3 modules on a step-by-step basis.

FIGURE 12.8:

Production operation for Software Logistics in a three-system landscape

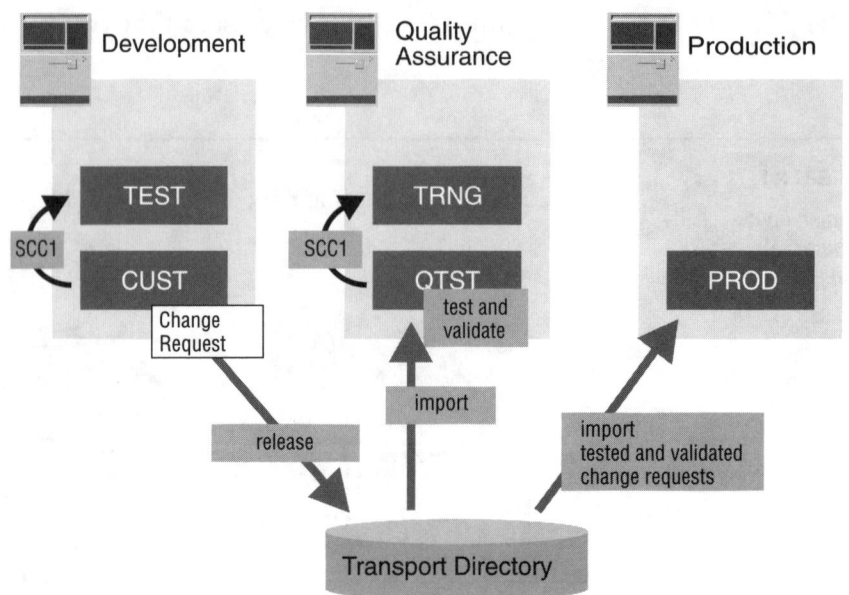

Restrictions of the Three-System Landscape's Implementation Strategy

As long as you are implementing the system landscape, you cannot upgrade the R/3 Release with this implementation strategy. You can only upgrade the R/3 System when you have set up the entire logistics chain and have imported the change requests in each system. This restriction exists because the data structure of the change requests depends on the R/3 Release. For example, you cannot transport the change requests from an R/3 System with the Release 3.1H to an R/3 System with the Release 4.0B.

NOTE SAP recommends that you keep the same R/3 Release during the implementation project. A Release upgrade during the implementation project can postpone your start of production.

An additional restriction is that you cannot transport most master records from one system to the next. You must either manually import the master records or import them through interfaces into the systems (see Chapter 13, "Interfaces").

> **TIP** The SAP Basis training course BC325, Software Logistics, describes additional implementation strategies and their restrictions (see Appendix B, "Training Courses for the Technical Team").

Define the Release Strategy

Before you begin the implementation project, SAP recommends defining a Release strategy for your R/3 System landscape. Essentially, your strategy must answer the following questions:

- Which R/3 Release will you be using when you start production operation?
- In which time frame after the start of production are you planning to perform an R/3 Release upgrade?

To be able to answer these questions in detail, you should find out about SAP's current Release planning and which business functions you can use in which R/3 Release.

Functional Release and Correction Release

SAP's Release planning is based on two types of Releases: *functional Release* and *correction Release*. The two Release types alternate. A correction Release always follows a functional Release and vice versa. A functional Release expands on and improves the functions of the previous correction Release both from a business viewpoint and from a technical viewpoint. The primary goal is to work with customers to verify and, if necessary, improve the quality of the expanded functions in the functional Release. SAP teams from Software Development, Service & Support, and Consulting support customers who are using a functional Release in production operation. All the experiences and improvements to a functional Release are collected and become part of the next correction Release. The goal of the correction Release is to improve the quality of a functional Release. For this reason, the functions available in the functional Release are improved in a correction Release, and no new functions are added.

> **NOTE** Every R/3 customer receives a correction Release. SAP only provides a functional Release upon request, and SAP provides you with special support with the First Customer Shipment (FCS).

Customer and Partner System (CPS)

To get to know and to test the new functions in an R/3 Release before a delivery, you can use SAP's Customer and Partner System (CPS). If you are a customer or a partner of SAP, you can log on through a remote connection. If you are interested in having access to CPS, you can write a request in OSS under the component XX-SER-SWFL-CPS.

> **TIP** You can find the current information on SAP Release planning in the OSS under the component XX-SER-SWREL. Table 12.2 also lists the relevant R/3 Notes. In addition, SAP regularly publishes the brochure *Release Planning R/3 System*. All customers automatically receive this brochure. You can also order the brochure through OSS or the dispatch department at SAP.

Patches

SAP regularly offers release-specific patches that contain important corrections to the R/3 software. For the most part, you can automatically import these patches into each of your R/3 Systems. More details are given in "Import Patches" later in this chapter.

TABLE 12.2: R/3 Notes for R/3 Release Planning

Note No.	Short Text
8039	R/3 Release Strategy
52505	What support does SAP offer at end of maint.?
65074	New Release Strategy for R/3 (starting 3.0D)
72483	Reserving namespaces/naming conventions at SAP
80475	Terms: Release, Hot Package, kernel patch ...
85123	R/3 Customer and Partner System (CPS)
101126	Shipment and Maintenance Strategy

Release Upgrade

The goal of a Release strategy should be to perform as few Release upgrades as possible, but as often as necessary. For a Release upgrade, you must consider two important points. First, the newest R/3 Release has additional and improved functions in comparison to the previous R/3 Release. Second, a Release upgrade incurs costs. When you import the new R/3 software, your R/3 System is down for some time. The length of the downtime depends on the size of your system. Furthermore, you must then adapt your settings and your own software developments to the new Release.

To ensure that you can perform an R/3 Release upgrade cost-effectively and with little effort, you need a detailed strategy. For example, you should define how you'll upgrade to a new R/3 Release within a system landscape and in which order you'll upgrade the systems; normally, you'll begin with the development system and continue along the logistics chain. The Technical Team can only estimate how long the production system will be down from a technical viewpoint, and you can only determine how long the business activities will take at the end of the upgrade by working with the departments and consultants. To consider all the factors,

SAP recommends starting a separate project for a Release upgrade. The section "Plan an Upgrade" covers this in more detail.

Remote Upgrade

If you assign part of the tasks for the Release upgrade to a service vendor, your strategy should include detailed instructions on how the tasks are to be distributed. For a Release upgrade, SAP offers a special service, the Remote Upgrade. SAP specialists handle almost all the tasks that are related to the Release upgrade of your system landscape.

> **TIP** You can find more detailed information about Remote Upgrade and how to order it in SAPNet at `http://sapnet.sap.com/ConsultingServices` under the keyword Remote Upgrade. If you don't have an Internet connection, you can contact SAP Local Support at your local SAP office.

Define Strategies for Customizing and Software Development

In the R/3 System with R/3 Release 4.0, you can adapt more than 800 business processes and their related functions to your company's requirements. R/3 has tools for performing the modifications as well as tools for organizing the multitude of necessary tasks. In addition, you need procedures to use the R/3 transport system to transport the results of the modifications to the next systems in the logistics chain. To ensure that you use the R/3 tools that are suitable for your strategy, the following sections explain how to perform these tasks:

- Organize a Customizing project
- Organize a software development project
- Determine a transport procedure

Organize a Customizing Project

To organize the Customizing project, you can use two R/3 tools: the *Implementation Guide (IMG)* and the *Customizing Organizer (CO)*.

The Implementation Guide (IMG)

The IMG is the central tool for Customizing. You can use it to generate a hierarchical list of the Customizing transactions in R/3. You can use the Customizing transactions to make settings for the desired modules or business processes. SAP delivers a complete IMG for all the modules in R/3, the *SAP Reference IMG*. Normally, you'll only completely implement some of the modules in a project, not all of them. For this reason, you can generate an IMG that is specific to your company, the *Enterprise IMG*. In complex implementation projects in particular, multiple subprojects are started for the application. The subprojects are divided in accordance with modules or business processes. To also support this from an organizational viewpoint, you can divide the Enterprise IMG into multiple *Project IMGs*.

Usually, the departments and the application consultants define the IMGs. For the technical implementation of R/3, only a small number of points in the IMG are relevant for R/3 Release 4.0. These points (for example, the implementation of user and authorization administration) are listed under the keyword Basis. Figure 12.9 shows an example of topics in the IMG that relate to users and authorizations.

The Customizing Organizer (CO)

When you make a Customizing setting from the IMG, you branch into the related Customizing transaction in R/3. The Customizing Organizer (CO) enables you to record your Customizing settings in change requests. In the CO, you can release a change request and pass it on to the TMS. The change request then becomes a

FIGURE 12.9:

Excerpt from the SAP Reference IMG with subtopics about Basis

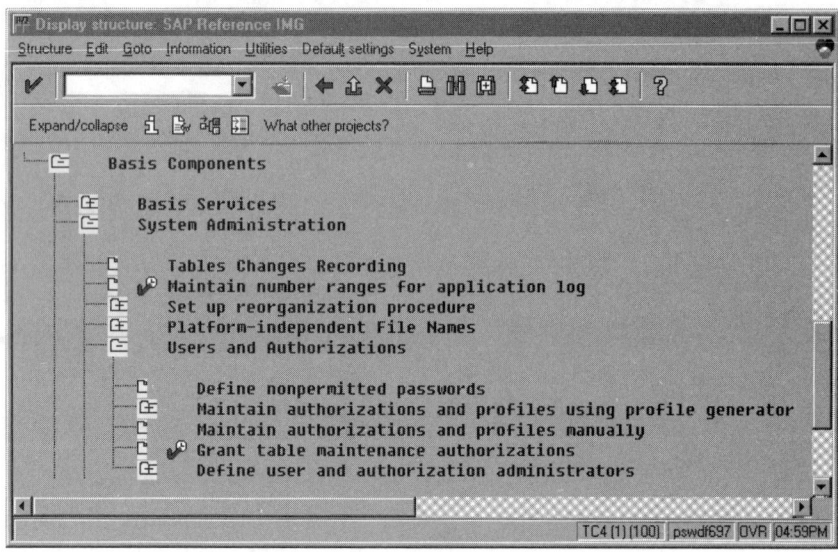

transport request, which you control with the TMS and transport along your logistics chain to the next systems.

Roles for the Customizing Project

The goal of your project organization must be to divide the large number of activities among the Project Team so the team members don't interfere with each other's work. Figure 12.10 shows how to divide the tasks in a Customizing project among three roles. As the following list shows, each role is responsible for certain tasks:

Project Manager The Project Manager creates the change requests and assigns the appropriate Customizers to them. For every Customizer, R/3 creates a task; the settings of each Customizer are recorded in his or her task. For the transport to other systems, the Project Manager can release change requests that he or she created.

Customizer The Customizers perform their Customizing from the IMG and allocate their settings to a change request and thus to their individual task, which is within the change request. The Customizers test their settings in the TEST client. They are authorized to release their own tasks in a change request. However, they are not authorized to release the change request with all the tasks.

R/3 System administrator The R/3 System administrator uses the TMS to transport the released change requests to the next R/3 Systems in the logistics chain.

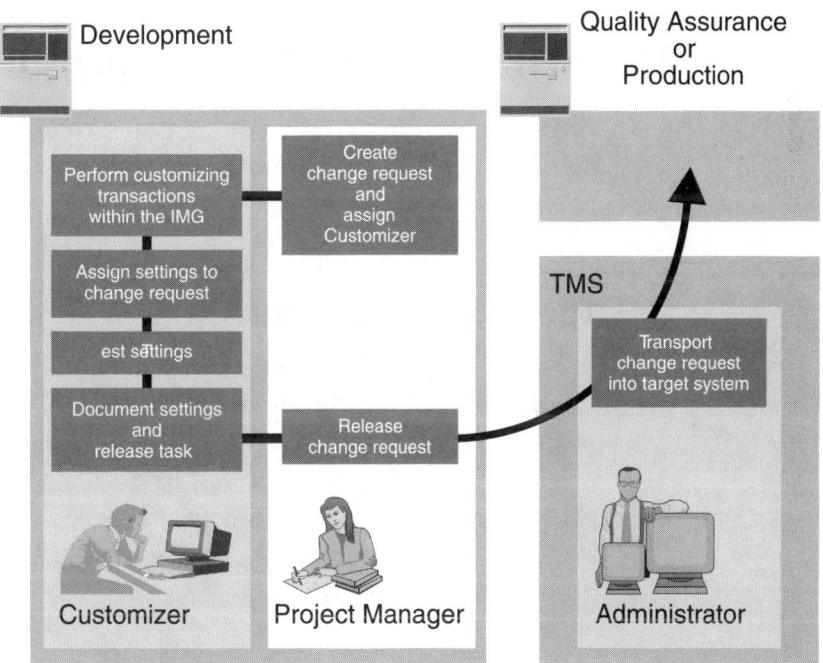

FIGURE 12.10:
The procedure for a Customizing project and the associated roles

Normally, the application consultants and employees in the department handle the roles of the Project Manager and the Customizers. Only these team members can decide, based on the Business Blueprint, which Customizing settings to perform and how to divide them among the Project Team members. The R/3 System administrator is responsible for the transport between the systems along the transport path. The R/3 System administrator has no authority to decide when to transport the released change requests. In smaller implementation projects with few members, the R/3 System administrator is verbally informed about released change requests and transports them as required. In larger implementation projects, this is not practical. You should create a schedule for transports and notify every person about the schedule. In large projects, the R/3 System administrator only transports when he or she receives verbal information as required in exceptional cases.

Organize a Software Development Project

There are two R/3 tools you can use to organize the software development project: the *ABAP Workbench* and the *Workbench Organizer (WBO)*.

The ABAP Workbench

Through the ABAP Workbench, you can access all the tools in R/3 you'll need to completely develop a business application. You can use these tools to create your own Repository objects and expand or modify the objects delivered by SAP. For example, if a business process that is important for your company is not covered by the standard R/3 System, you can use the ABAP Workbench to program your own solution.

Development Classes

So that you can administer the large number of Repository objects more easily, they are divided into development classes. Therefore, at the beginning of each implementation project or development project, you should set up one or more development classes. You can only assign a name that begins with Y or Z to a development class. These names are not used by SAP, so this enables you to avoid conflicts during a Release upgrade. If you don't use these conventions, your programs may be overwritten by a standard SAP program during a Release upgrade. If you implement a complex system landscape with multiple development systems, you must avoid name conflicts within your customer namespace. In this situation, you should name the classes and objects uniquely and, in the name, include the name of the R/3 System in which the original object resides.

> **NOTE** Table 12.3 lists the most important R/3 Notes about existing naming conventions and namespaces.

TABLE 12.3: R/3 Notes for Naming Conventions and Namespaces

Note No.	Short Text
16466	Customer namespace for SAP objects
38781	Partner namespace SAP objects
84282	Development namespaces for customers and partners

The Workbench Organizer (WBO)

As with the CO, you can use the Workbench Organizer (WBO) to create, administer, release, and analyze change requests. You should use the WBO to record your software development results in the change request. To ensure that two software developers do not change a Repository object at the same time or choose the same name for an object, WBO automatically locks on Repository objects that are allocated to a change request. If a Repository object is assigned to a change request, the object can only be changed by the software developers for whom tasks were created in the request. If a software developer processes the object, the editor locks the objects for the other software developers who are authorized to change it.

Versions Database

When you release a change request in the WBO, R/3 creates a new version of the Repository objects that are allocated to it. The versions database stores the most recent version of an object, and only the differences between the older versions and the most recent version are saved. This allows you to have a complete history of the Repository objects, and if necessary, you can return to an older version.

Roles for the Software Development Project

As it is for the Customizing project, the goal of your project organization is to divide the large number of activities among the Project Team so the team members don't interfere with each other's work. Compared to a Customizing project, the tasks in a software development project are also divided among three roles: Project Manager, software developer, and R/3 System administrator. Essentially, these roles have the same tasks they have in the Customizing project. A major difference is the role of the software developer. If you manually modify SAP Repository objects, you must register with SAP through the SAP Software Change Registration (SSCR).

The SAP Software Change Registration (SSCR)

As of R/3 Release 3.0A, SAP uses SSCR to record which users are authorized to modify SAP Repository objects in your R/3 System and which objects a specific user has modified. SAP matchcodes and tuning measures, such as creating a database index, are not registered.

You can benefit from SSCR in many ways. First, you can correct errors faster in (and thus ensure a higher availability of) modified R/3 Systems. All changed objects are logged by SAP. Using this information as a base, SAP Service & Support employees can limit the possible causes for errors and resolve problems faster. Second,

SSCR also makes it less likely that unintentional modifications will be made. Therefore, it simplifies an R/3 Release upgrade. Before you modify an object, you must register it.

> **NOTE** Table 12.4 lists the most important R/3 Notes that explain what SSCR means and, in particular, how to register.

TABLE 12.4: R/3 Notes about SSCR

Note No.	Short Text
13809	SAP enhancement concept: support for cust. modif.
27532	SAP Software Change Registration (SSCR)
29236	Registration (SSCR) without remote connection
29237	Registration (SSCR) with temporary license
40850	OSS: SSCR key does not work
86161	Registering developers and objects

Determine a Transport Procedure

When you set up your R/3 System landscape, you'll use change requests to transport the Customizing settings and the software changes from one R/3 System to the next. For a three-system landscape, the transport procedure consists of four steps:

1. Release the change request in the development system.

   When you release a change request, R/3 exports the change request data from the database into the transport directory on the operating-system level. You can use the log to determine whether the data was exported without errors.

2. Import the change request into the quality assurance system.

    You must check the transport log for errors after the TMS was used for an import.

3. Test and verify settings and software developments in the quality assurance system.

    Once you have tested the settings and software developments, either release the objects for the production system or correct the errors. You should only correct errors in the development system. To do so, you must correct the errors in a new change request and redo steps 1 and 2.

4. Import the change request into the production system.

    Using the TMS, import the transport requests in the same sequence they were in when you released them from the development system so you can be sure corrections are not overwritten by old requests. As in step 2, you must check for errors after the import.

In every implementation project, you have to transport a large number of change requests (and, in particular, corrections for errors in requests) between the systems. To simplify the administration of requests and assure quality at the same time, you should define who will be responsible for each step in the transport procedure (do this at the beginning of the project). The goal of your transport procedure is to ensure that new functions are only imported into the production after they have been successfully tested.

Roles for the Transport Procedure

You should always make several people responsible for the transport. They must work together to transport a change request along the transport route to the production system. These people check each change request and make it less likely that a setting or program with errors is transported to the production system. You can distribute the tasks for the transport over three roles:

Project Manager   The Project Manager controls the contents of a change request and is the only person authorized to release a change request. After each export or import, he or she checks the transport log for errors.

R/3 System administrator   The R/3 System administrator uses the TMS to transport the released change requests along the transport route. However, he or she is not authorized to release change requests or to test their contents.

Quality Assurance Team   The Quality Assurance Team consists of people from the departments. This team tests all the settings and software developments that are released for quality assurance. The team tells the Project Manager which change requests have to be corrected. The members of this team are not authorized to transport or release change requests in the development system.

Schedule for the Transport Procedure

SAP recommends creating a schedule to define when you will transport released change requests to a specific system. Each system has different requirements for such a schedule. You'll transport more frequently from the development system to the quality assurance system than from the quality assurance system to the production system. If an error occurs during the test in the quality assurance system, you may require several additional change requests with corrections until the error is corrected. In the meantime, you cannot transport these change requests separately into the production system because they must be together for error-free Customizing or error-free software development.

> **WARNING** Imports to the production system should only be made when the system has a low load in dialog and in background. Even if you import verified and corrected objects, you can negatively affect system performance.

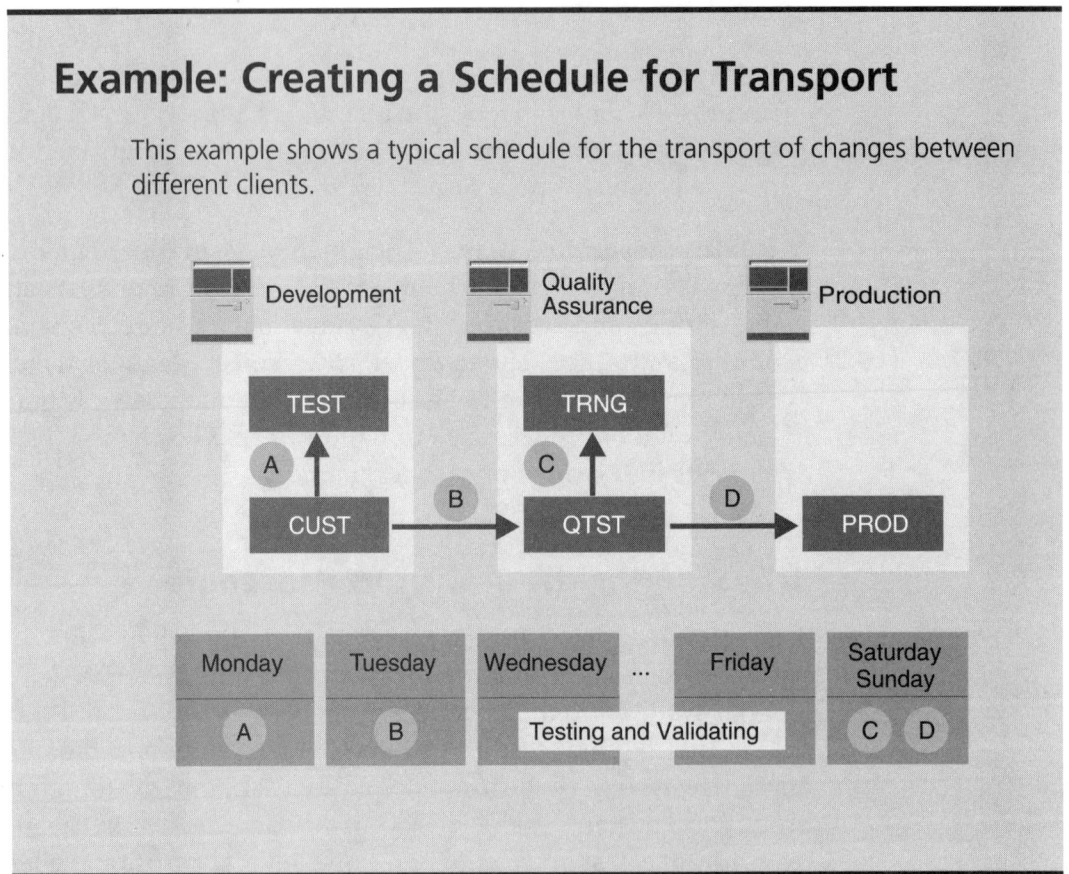

Maintain the System Landscape

From the viewpoint of Software Logistics, two requirements are important for production operation in an R/3 System. First, to avoid potential problems with the delivered R/3 software, important corrections should be applied as quickly and cost-effectively as possible. Second, a Release upgrade should run quickly and efficiently to shorten the downtime and thus achieve a cost-effective upgrade. To help you meet the requirements for your system, the following sections explain these important points:

- Which patches you can import
- How to plan an upgrade

Import Patches

During the life of a functional Release or a correction Release, SAP offers release-specific patches. Patches contain important corrections that help you avoid potential problems. SAP makes patches available in three ways: in the SAP Online Service System (OSS), in SAPNet, or on Patch Collection CDs. Table 12.5 lists the different types of patches.

TABLE 12.5: Different Types of SAP Patches

Patch	Meaning
SPAM Update	Improves and enhances the SAP Patch Manager (SPAM)
Hot Package	Corrects errors in the ABAP Repository
Conflict Resolution Transport (CRT)	Resolves conflicts between a Hot Package and an industry solution; only valid for one industry solution
FCS Final Delta Patch (FFDP)	Upgrades an FCS System to its final status before Hot Packages can be imported
HR Legal Change Patch (LCP)	Adapts the HR components to irregular legal changes and regulations in their respective countries

Online Correction Support and SAP Patch Manager

Online Correction Support (OCS) has tools you can use to import patches into your R/3 System. For example, with the tools from OCS, you can download patches from OSS through a remote connection and use the SAP Patch Manager to import them into your system. This way, you don't have to correct errors in the ABAP Repository manually.

SAP recommends regularly importing the latest patches to an R/3 Release; that is, you should continually import the latest patches during the implementation project. To do so, you should follow your transport path for Software Logistics. As shown in step 1 in Figure 12.11, first you import a patch into the development system. In step 2, you determine whether the patch will change Repository objects that you have modified. To record the affected objects and compare the modifications with the corrections, use R/3's SPAU transaction. Within this transaction, you can decide whether an affected object has to be replaced by the new object in the patch or whether it should remain modified. The result of this so-called adjustment is a change request that you release from the development system for transport.

> **NOTE** You can use transaction code SPAM to see if you have to adjust modifications with the corrections. You only have to create a change request for the adjustment if you have modified Repository objects that the patch will change.

In step 3, you import the patch into the quality assurance system. Only after this do you import the change request, which you use in step 4 to adjust your potential modifications. Then, you proceed for the production system exactly as you did for the quality assurance system (see Figure 12.11, steps 5 and 6). You only import the patches into the production system during the time frames in which the system has a low load in dialog and in background.

FIGURE 12.11:

Importing patches into a three-system landscape

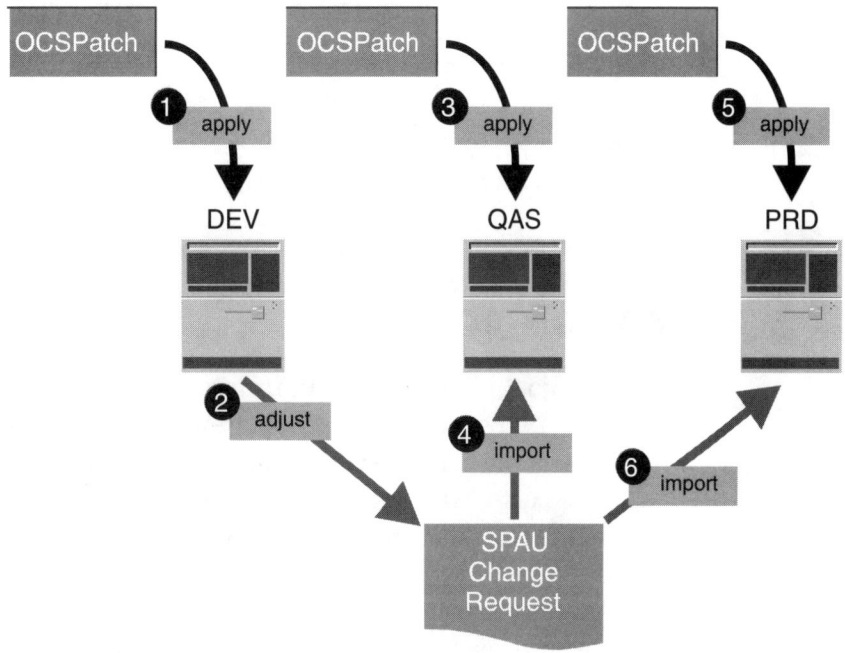

> **NOTE** Table 12.6 lists the important R/3 Notes on patches. These Notes contain the most current information about available patches and how to import them.

TABLE 12.6: R/3 Notes on Patches

Note No.	Short Text
33525	Important information about Hot Packages (3.0B-3.1G)
37617	ONLINE CORRECTION SUPPORT (OCS)
42763	Hot Packages for systems without OSS access
53902	Conflicts between Hot Packages Laps & Add-Ons

Continued on next page

TABLE 12.6: R/3 Notes on Patches *(Continued)*

Note No.	Short Text
60419	Display modifications before applying a patch
63974	'HOT PACKAGE/LC COLLECTION' delivery on CD-ROM

Plan an Upgrade

The goal for planning an upgrade is to make sure all the R/3 Systems in a system landscape are upgraded quickly and efficiently. This is the only way you can keep the downtime short and thus save costs. Although every system landscape has different requirements for an upgrade, SAP's experiences show that a standardized upgrade project is possible. Therefore, as of R/3 Release 4.0, ASAP integrates the upgrade project in addition to the implementation project. The upgrade project consists of four phases:

- Upgrade Project Preparation
- Realization of Development and Quality Assurance
- Realization of Production
- Go Live and Support

The following sections explain which tasks should be performed in each phase.

Upgrade Project Preparation

As with an implementation project, a deciding factor for how effective and secure the Release upgrade will be is whether you plan the upgrade in great detail. ASAP takes this into consideration in a separate phase, Upgrade Project Preparation. In this phase, you should define the schedule for the upgrade project, organize the Technical Team, assign the necessary resources and the budget, plan the technical requirements, and prepare the necessary technical steps for an upgrade.

> **NOTE** You should read the *Upgrade Manual* for your future R/3 Release. This document contains all the important information for a secure Release upgrade and is part of every R/3 upgrade delivery package.

Only after you have recorded the current technical status of your system landscape and compared it with the technical requirements of the new R/3 Release can you begin with an upgrade. This way, you can determine whether your existing hardware is sufficient or whether you have to expand it. You can also check to see whether you have to upgrade the front-end software, the operating system, or the Relational Database Management System (RDBMS) in addition to the R/3 Release.

> **NOTE** When you plan your upgrade, you must consider all external applications that are connected to the R/3 System. You should consider the following questions: Do interfaces have to be adapted to the new R/3 Release? Does an external system have to be adapted? Which versions of office applications does the new R/3 Release support?

During the upgrade, the runtime environments in all systems in your system landscape have to be identical. For this reason, you must ensure that the change requests are consistent within your system landscape. Therefore, you must notify the respective Project Teams and tell them they cannot change any Customizing settings or any ABAP programs during the two Realization phases.

> **NOTE** The same patches must be imported into all of the R/3 Systems in your system landscape.

Realization of DEV & QAS

The goal of the second phase, Realization of Development (DEV) and Quality Assurance (QAS), is to complete the upgrade for all the nonproduction systems. As shown in Figure 12.12, you must begin with the development system. The upgrade consists of eight steps:

1. Import new SAP front-end software to all the front ends.

   Versions of the SAP front-end software are backward compatible. For example, with SAPGUI Release 4.0B, you can work with an R/3 Release 3.1G but not vice versa. You decided how you would maintain your front-end software during the implementation of R/3 (see "Plan Front-End Maintenance" in Chapter 4).

2. Install the R/3 Upgrade Assistant.

   To help you upgrade to R/3 Release 4.0, SAP offers a new graphical interface, the R/3 Upgrade Assistant. It can be started from any front end and is easier to use than the previous command-mode procedure.

3. Use the PREPARE script to check the requirements.

   The PREPARE script tests the technical settings in the system and writes the results in a log. You can analyze the log and adapt the incorrect settings.

4. Perform a complete data backup.

   In the worst-case scenario, you must be able to restore and recover the entire system. This includes the data in the database and in the operating system.

5. Upgrade the versions of non-R/3 software.

   You must consider the interfaces in addition to the operating system or the RDBMS.

6. Upgrade the Release of R/3 software.

In the course of the Release upgrade, call R/3 transaction SPDD. Use this transaction to define the modified Data Dictionary objects that the new standard R/3 System replaces and the objects that remain modified. R/3 records the results in a change request that you import into the quality assurance system and the production system during the upgrade of these systems.

7. Adjust ABAP programs.

   After the Release upgrade, you must call the transaction code SPAU. Use this R/3 transaction to define the modified ABAP programs that have to be replaced by the new standard R/3 System and the programs that remain modified. R/3 records the results in a change request, which you import into the next systems during their upgrade.

> **NOTE** SAP recommends that you replace modified objects with objects from the new standard R/3 System as often as possible. This simplifies future upgrades and you'll need fewer resources for the adjustment.

8. Perform a complete data backup.

   A Release upgrade changes the data in the database and the data on the operating-system level, such as operating-system parameters and executable programs.

Once the steps are completed, all the Customizers and software developers can work in the development system again. However, you cannot import change requests from the new R/3 Release into the systems with the previous R/3 Release.

When you have completed the Release upgrade for the development system, you should upgrade the quality assurance system (see Figure 12.12). To do so, follow the same eight steps you followed to upgrade the development system. The difference is that you have already adjusted the modifications and recorded your results in change requests. These change requests are imported in step 6, and R/3 verifies that the objects to be adjusted match those in the change requests.

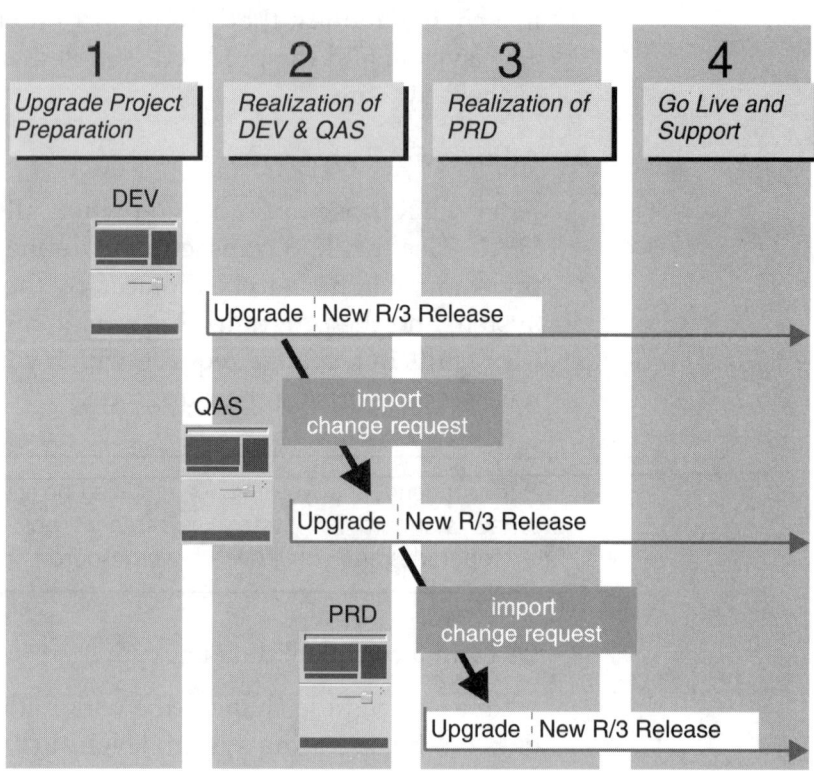

FIGURE 12.12:
Schedule for an upgrade in a three-system landscape

> **TIP** To test the upgrade of the production system with the upgrade of the quality assurance system, you can first copy the production system and use the copy to set up a new quality assurance system. Then you can switch the R/3 Release for a copy of the production system.

Realization of PRD

In the Realization of Production (PRD) phase, you should complete the upgrade of the production system. Follow the steps you followed to upgrade the quality assurance system and adjust the modifications with the change requests from the development system. However, compared to the nonproduction R/3 Systems, there are more tasks to complete after the upgrade of the production system before you can begin production operation. For example, you must schedule the necessary background jobs again. In the new R/3 Release, additional authorization checks may have been added and you must adapt the activity groups or authorization profiles accordingly.

Go Live and Support

In the next phase, Go Live and Support, you'll switch from production operation in the previous R/3 Release to the new R/3 Release. In the first weeks after the upgrade in particular, users have the most questions about the new functions. For this reason, you must prepare your help desk. Members from the Upgrade Project Team may have to support the help desk.

Software Logistics in ASAP

In the previous sections, you learned which points to consider for Software Logistics during the R/3 implementation. In ASAP, these points are distributed over the individual phases of the project. The following sections describe when to perform certain tasks.

Project Preparation

To prepare for the project, you should work with consultants to design the entire system landscape for your company. Define how many R/3 Systems you need, which clients you need, and how to distribute these clients over the systems. In addition, you must define how to implement the system landscape. To do so, create a schedule that defines when to implement each system and how to set up the planned clients within the systems. For a three-system landscape, ASAP recommends a schedule and a detailed implementation strategy. If you plan to use a different landscape or a step-by-step implementation, you can use the three-system landscape as a model, as explained in the sidebar "Example: Planning a Step-by-Step Implementation Strategy."

Example: Planning a Step-by-Step Implementation Strategy

A company implements the R/3 modules on a step-by-step basis; that is, first they implement the Financial Accounting (FI) and Sales and Distribution (SD) modules. After their start of production, they begin the Customizing project for the Production Planning (PP) module.

How would you distribute the clients in this situation? The company chose a three-system landscape for the step-by-step implementation. After the first partial start of production, they copied the development client and the quality assurance client, locked the original clients against changes, and started the Customizing project for PP in the copied development client. They set up a second logistics chain between the copied clients. They only transported all the changes into the production client at the end of the Customizing project for PP. This way, they combined the two development clients in a new production client. However, with this strategy, the new development clients must be locked against changes to the client-independent objects to protect the maintenance of the production client.

NOTE In the development system, you must record the Customizing settings and the developed programs in change requests and document them so you will be able to transport them to the next systems in the logistics chain. Therefore, you should define your system landscape in detail before you start the implementation of the development system.

Keep the number of modifications to the standard R/3 Systems as low as possible. By doing so, you can avoid problems and reduce the amount of work involved in a Release upgrade. To avoid unnecessary modifications, you should use an approval procedure. Every modification must be formally applied for, and the Project Manager must decide whether the standard R/3 System should be modified or not.

Before you start the implementation project, you should define the R/3 Release that you are using for production operation and the R/3 Release you want to use in one or two years. Essentially, your hardware sizing depends on this factor because different R/3 Releases have different hardware requirements. You should begin your implementation project with the R/3 Release that you will run in production operation. An upgrade during the implementation project prolongs the project unnecessarily. Upgrades are only worthwhile if the new Release has new functions that you would have otherwise programmed yourself, but with a large amount of effort.

Business Blueprint

At the beginning of the Business Blueprint phase, you'll set up the development system. Set up the Change and Transport Organizer (CTO) and configure the Transport Management System (TMS). First, set up the development system as the transport domain controller (TDC). When you have set up the production system in the Realization phase, set it up as the TDC and the development system becomes the backup domain controller (BDC). Also, generate the development client with the client copy.

In addition to these technical points, it is important to define the procedures for how to transport and who is responsible for specific steps. The Technical Team is essentially responsible for transporting the change requests between the clients and the systems.

However, the departments organize the Customizing project and the software development project. To ensure that these different groups can work together effectively, you should define communication paths and escalation paths. Who tells the R/3 System administrator when specific change requests should be transported to a specific system? Who does the R/3 System administrator notify if requests are imported incorrectly?

> **TIP** You should continually import the newest patches for an R/3 Release so you always have the most current corrections to potential errors.

Realization

At the beginning of the Realization phase, you'll set up the quality assurance system the same way the development system is set up. You should connect the two systems physically through a common transport directory on the operating-system level (see "The Transport System" in Chapter 2).

The R/3 System administrator transports the already released change requests from the development system into the quality assurance system. This enables the Project Team to start to check the results of the Customizing settings and software development. In the course of this phase, you should regularly transport the released change requests. In a change request, group the Customizing settings or changed objects that you can test together so you won't need information from other requests.

At the end of the Realization phase, you'll set up the production system. You'll also physically connect this system with the transport directory and set up the production clients. In the production system, lock every option to change objects, whether they are client-dependent or client-independent objects.

Final Preparation

To prepare for going live, transport the successfully tested Customizing settings and software developments from the quality assurance system into the production system. Only after you have successfully imported the released change requests can you transfer data from your legacy system.

Go Live and Support

In the first week after the start of production in particular, you should transport change requests with corrections to your settings into the production system. You should schedule imports into the production system for times when the system has a low load in dialog and in the background. You should only deviate from this schedule for urgent corrections. If you import objects every day, you can negatively affect the system performance. In addition to your own corrections, you should continue to import the latest patches from SAP into your R/3 Release. This enables you to run a secure and consistent system landscape.

In the course of system operation, you will also upgrade the R/3 System sooner or later. During this type of upgrade, your production system will be down for a period of time. Detailed planning enables you to keep the downtime as short as possible and save costs. SAP recommends planning the upgrade as an independent project with its own Project Management. Therefore, ASAP has an integrated upgrade project that allows you to upgrade all of the R/3 Systems in your system landscape to the new R/3 Release in four phases.

Table 12.7 lists the tasks from ASAP that are related to the implementation of Software Logistics. Each task is described in accordance with the phase in which it is performed and the person who performs it.

TABLE 12.7: Tasks for Software Logistics in ASAP

Phase	Phase Name	Task	Role
1	Project Preparation	Define system landscape strategy	Project Manager, Technical Team Lead, technical consultant
		Define system enhancement and modification approval process	Project Manager, Technical Team Lead, technical consultant
2	Business Blueprint	Perform initial setup of system landscape (DEV)	Technical Team Lead, R/3 System administrator
		Define change request management	Project Manager, Technical Team Lead, R/3 System administrator
3	Realization	Set up client management and transport system (QAS)	Technical Team Lead, technical consultant
		Test and migrate enhancement programs	Technical Team Lead, technical consultant
4	Final Preparation	Transport to production environment	Technical Team Lead, R/3 System administrator, technical consultant
5	Go Live and Support	Upgrade the production system landscape	Upgrade Team, technical consultant

Success Factors

To successfully implement Software Logistics, you must give the following points particular consideration:

- Define guidelines for modifications
- Create an authorization concept
- Plan Customizing and software development in detail

The following sections describe these points.

Define Guidelines for Modifications

The principle of the guidelines for modifications is that you should only modify the standard R/3 System when it is absolutely necessary and you have no other option.

By keeping the number of modifications as low as possible, you'll save time and money when you upgrade your system in the future. During an upgrade, you have to decide whether each modified object should be replaced in the new standard R/3 System or whether the object should remain modified. Only the relevant departments or the developer can make this decision, which is frequently very time consuming.

To help you decide whether you have to modify the standard R/3 System for the new R/3 Release, you must ensure that you document each modification. You must set up guidelines for what needs to be documented. For example, you should formalize the application for the recommended approval procedure. The formal criteria help the Project Manager make decisions easier and faster.

> **NOTE** If you modify an SAP program, errors may occur when you process other programs. The programs in the standard R/3 Systems may have interdependencies that may not be obvious to you. In this case, SAP cannot guarantee that you can run your system without serious problems.

Create an Authorization Concept

You can use authorizations to map the organization of your Customizing project and development project in the R/3 System. You have to plan your concept in more detail, depending on the size of your Project Teams. As shown in Figure 12.13, you can use authorizations to define the following four roles:

Super user (R/3 System administrator) The super user has all the authorizations for the Change and Transport System (CTS).

Project Manager The Project Manager is responsible for the change requests. The Project Manager creates the requests, allocates the tasks in the request to the Customizer or the software developer, releases the requests, and controls the transport into the next systems.

Customizer/software developer The Customizer or software developer is responsible for his or her task within a change request. The Customizer or software developer can only release his or her own task.

Normal user The normal user can read the information in the change requests but cannot change them.

The R/3 online documentation contains more detailed information on this topic.

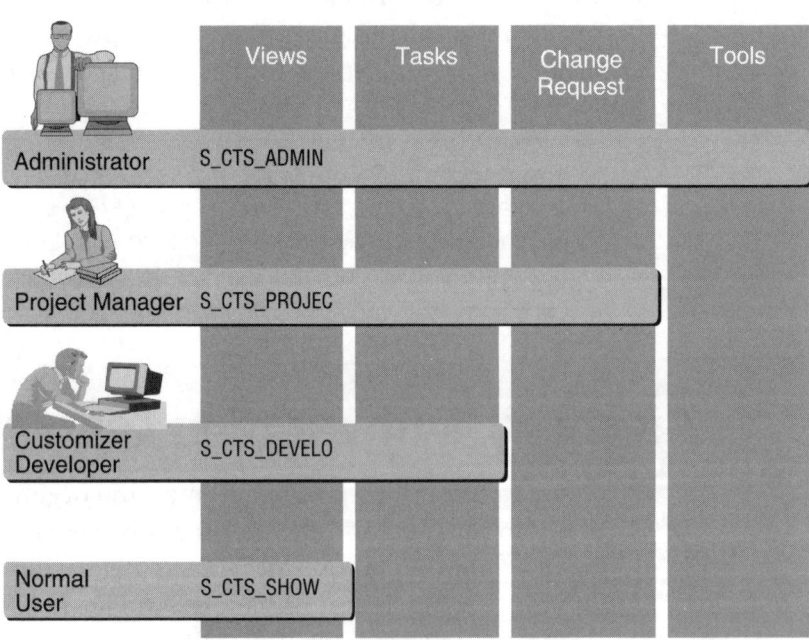

FIGURE 12.13:
Authorizations for the CTS

Plan Customizing and Software Development in Detail

SAP recommends that you perform Customizing and develop your own programs in the same client. This ensures right from the start that your settings do not interfere with each other. You must ensure that you can only change objects in the development system and specifically only in the client in which you perform Customizing and develop your own programs; this is valid for client-dependent objects and for client-independent objects. In addition, you must activate automatic logging for the development clients. You should not change objects in any other clients. In the quality assurance system and the production system, set system change options so that you cannot change any client-independent objects.

Before you can release a task or a change request in CO or WBO, R/3 requires that you document your changes in a template. You should use this function, and you can expand the template to suit your guidelines. If you are implementing R/3 on a step-by-step basis, these documents can help you make decisions about how to harmonize the existing Customizing with the new functions or modules. You must ensure that you thoroughly document each of your own ABAP programs. Only in this way can you keep a part of the knowledge about the program in your company.

Review Questions

1. What are the advantages of a two-system landscape?

    A. A stable runtime environment for production operation.

    B. A stable runtime environment for quality assurance.

    C. The production data is protected against unauthorized access by developers.

2. For which data can you allow or deny changes using the system change options?

   A. All R/3 data

   B. All client-dependent data

   C. All client-independent data

   D. All Repository objects

   E. All Customizing data

3. Why do you require an SCCR key?

   A. To be able to develop your own programs in the R/3 System

   B. To be able to modify standard R/3 programs in the R/3 System

   C. To be able to import patches into an R/3 System from the OSS

   D. To be authorized to use the transactions SPDD and SPAU

4. Which tools does ASAP recommend for organizing a Customizing project?

   A. Change and Transport Organizer

   B. Customizing Organizer

   C. ABAP Workbench

   D. Workbench Organizer

   E. Implementation Guide

5. Which statement is correct?

   A. The SAP front-end software Release has backward compatibility and therefore can be newer than the R/3 Release.

B. The SAP front-end software Release must be the same as the R/3 Release.

C. The SAP front-end software Release has upward compatibility and therefore can be older than the R/3 Release.

CHAPTER THIRTEEN

Interfaces

The R/3 System has interfaces to other systems on all the layers of its client/server architecture. As of R/3 Release 4.0, SAP recommends using Business Application Programming Interfaces (BAPIs) as your central interface technology. SAP ensures stable interface specifications for the BAPIs for different R/3 Releases. BAPIs allow you to integrate long-term external applications into the R/3 business processes. If no suitable BAPIs are available for your requirements, R/3 offers other technologies. For example, you can use Object Linking and Embedding (OLE) to link office applications to the front ends, or you can use Remote Function Call (RFC) to call a function in a remote R/3 or R/2 System.

This chapter will help you choose a technology that is suitable for your requirements. The following sections explain how to perform these tasks:

- Plan the interface infrastructure
- Monitor the interfaces

Plan the Interface Infrastructure

At the beginning of every interface infrastructure, the following questions arise: After R/3 has been implemented, which business processes have to be operated over multiple systems? Where can you set up interfaces within a business process? Which data has to be transferred from the legacy systems for the business processes? You need to consult with the departments to answer these questions. The Technical Team ensures that the most suitable interface for a solution is chosen. The goal of this section is to help you with planning and selection by explaining how to perform the following tasks:

- Determine the interface requirements
- Implement the Interface Adviser

- Plan the data transfer
- Use the Legacy System Migration (LSM) Workbench

Determine the Interface Requirements

In a *requirements catalog*, you should define the business requirements you must meet for the interfaces and the technical points that are essential for their implementation. Your company's system topology is the starting point for the requirements catalog. In your company, which systems will be replaced by R/3, which systems will operate in parallel to R/3, and with which external systems (such as customers' and suppliers' systems) will you exchange data? The Business Process Team creates the Business Blueprint for the planned system topology during the Business Blueprint phase. In the Business Blueprint, you should first define how to map the organizational structure in your company to the organizational units (such as company codes or sales organizations) in R/3. Second, you should determine how certain business processes from your company are mapped in R/3. For technical or functional reasons, business processes are often distributed over different application systems. You should set up interfaces for these processes. Together with the Business Process Owner and the application consultants, create the requirements catalog for the interfaces. The following points are important for the requirements catalog:

- At what point do the processes have to be interrupted between different application systems?
- What technology can be used to connect the external system?
- When do data objects have to be exchanged with an external system and in what volume?
- Which requirements must the interface meet for throughput and performance?
- If a problem occurs, how should the interface be documented to enable quick reaction and enable you to then restart?

- Do solutions—for example, a distribution using Application Link Enabling (ALE), suitable BAPIs, or certified third parties—already exist in the standard R/3 System for the data objects to be exchanged?

Example: Determining Interface Requirements

A company operates two systems in parallel. The company uses the non-R/3 System for financial accounting and the R/3 System for controlling. At the end of each day, controlling requires the postings from financial accounting in order to create a current report. As shown here, the data must be transferred overnight within a time frame of four hours. This way, a report from the preceding day is available every morning.

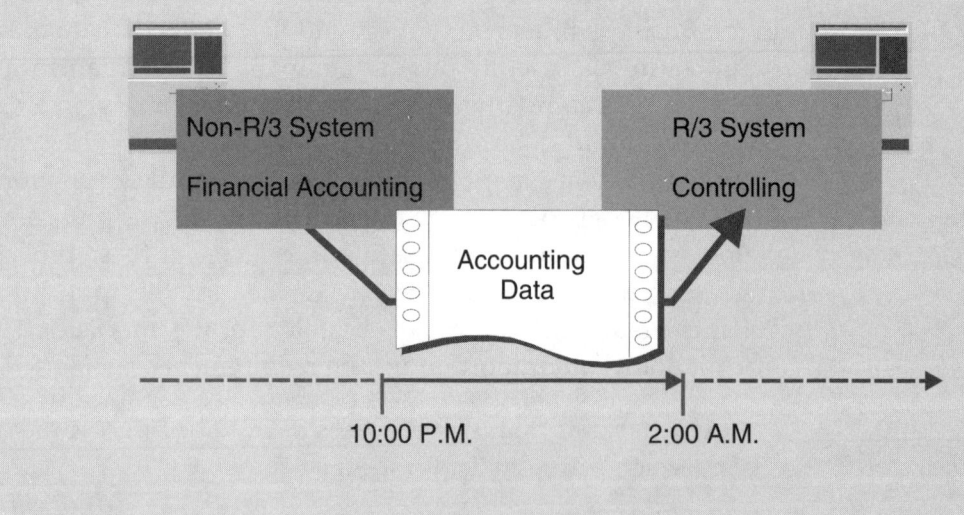

| TIP | Keep the number of interfaces as low as possible. Each additional interface increases the administration, and when you upgrade the R/3 Release, you may have to adapt each interface to the new Release. |

Technical Design for the Interfaces

After the Project Management has agreed to the requirements in the requirements catalog, you should create the technical design for the interfaces. The following factors are important:

Data consistency throughout the system Define logical units of work (LUWs). An LUW is either processed fully or not processed at all. If an error occurs during processing, the only way to ensure a consistent database rollback is to use LUWs.

Error tolerance Divide the process of writing application data in the source system and transferring data to the target R/3 System into two LUWs. If the network or the target system fails, you only have to reset the data transfer and not the data written in the source system. In the target R/3 System, separate the data receipt from the process of writing data into two LUWs. If the data object is locked by another program, you only have to reset the writing and not the data receipt.

Simplified error solutions Set up global monitoring and plan for experts to be automatically notified if an error occurs.

Authorization concept To ensure that the authorization concept is not bypassed by the use of an interface, you must secure the target system and the source system. The target system must determine which authorizations the source system has, and the source system has to authenticate itself accordingly for the target system.

Scalability If you need to transfer a large data volume through an interface in a growing R/3 System, design a growth path for this interface at the very beginning. For example, you can configure this type of interface now for a future parallel data transfer.

Before you can run the interfaces in production operation, you must test them during the Final Preparation phase to determine whether they all work as desired. In the technical design, you should define which criteria the interfaces must meet in order to operate smoothly and effectively. This way, you can prepare the future test processes in advance.

Implement the Interface Adviser

To help you plan and realize a separate interface structure, SAP developed the R/3 Interface Adviser. The Interface Adviser is on CD-ROM. The information is presented through HTML documents (see Figure 13.1). The Interface Adviser will make it easier for you to design interfaces for your requirements, to select an effective interface technology, and to use examples to implement the design.

> **TIP** You can find out more information about the Interface Adviser and order it in SAPNet at `http://sapnet.sap.com/int-adviser`.

Figure 13.1 shows that the Interface Adviser introduces different scenarios that demonstrate which typical interfaces you can include in your business processes. Each scenario contains detailed information about the best way to divide the entire process into subprocesses. In addition, you'll learn about the restrictions for each scenario, and thus, what you cannot do. The Interface Adviser describes which implementation strategies are suitable for each scenario. For example, you'll learn which data must be available in the R/3 System for the interface to work without problems. As shown in Figure 13.2, these scenarios should help you during the Business Blueprint phase when you write the requirements catalog for the requirements in your company. These detailed scenarios help you estimate in advance what resources you need and the time frame you must schedule to implement the interfaces.

FIGURE 13.1:

The R/3 Interface Adviser

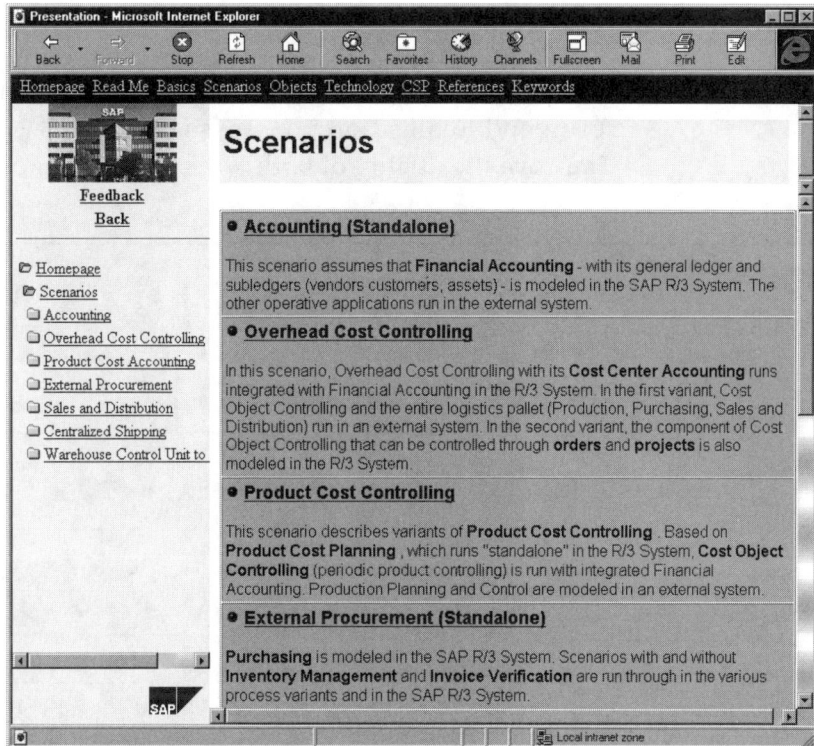

The Interface Adviser links each scenario with the business objects that can be exchanged between the systems. For each scenario, the Interface Adviser informs you about the interface technologies that you can use to export or import data. The Interface Adviser contains checklists that enable you to decide which interface technology is suitable for your requirements. This information is especially helpful for the technical design of your interface infrastructure.

During the Realization phase, implement the interface by using the selected interface technology. You can use the many sample programs the Interface Adviser has for the various technologies as models. In addition, the concepts and functions of the individual technologies—for example, BAPI, ALE, RFC, Batch Input, Intermediate Documents (IDocs), and Common Programming Interface-Communication (CPI-C)—are described in detail. For this reason, the Interface Adviser supports you throughout the Business Blueprint and Realization phases (see Figure 13.2) and enables you to improve the quality of both your planning and the implementation.

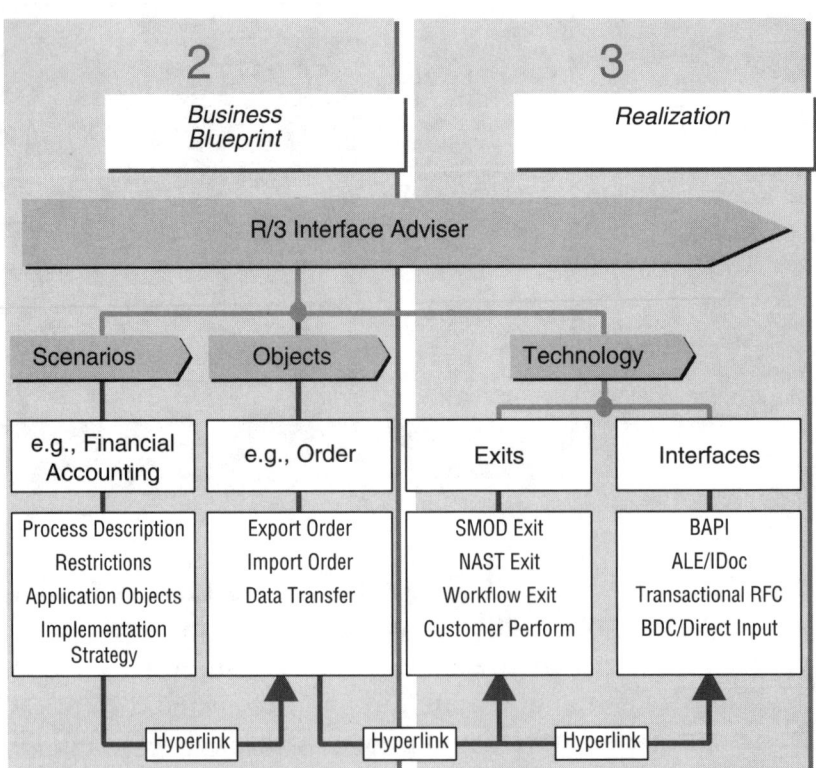

FIGURE 13.2:

Integration of the Interface Adviser in ASAP

Plan the Data Transfer

From a technical viewpoint, the data is transferred in two steps (see Figure 13.3). During the first step, the data from your legacy system is converted to a format that the R/3 System can process.

For the conversion, the data is exported from the legacy system and stored in a data transfer file on the operating-system level in a way that the R/3 System can interpret the data. In the second step, the data is transferred from the data transfer file into the R/3 System. There are three different processes for data transfer: Batch Input, Call Transaction, and Direct Input (see the section "Communication through Sequential Files" in Chapter 2).

FIGURE 13.3:

The steps for data transfer

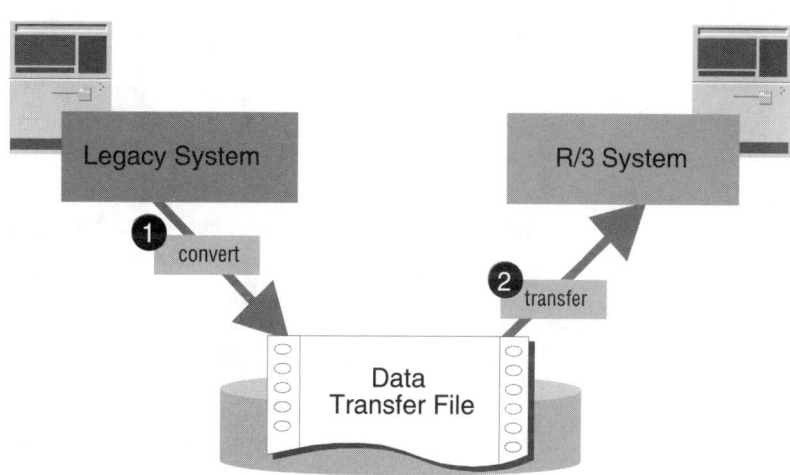

TIP If you only have a small volume of data to transfer, it may be easier to transfer it manually into the R/3 System. If you transfer the data manually, you should prepare the data of the legacy system in a format that enables the users to quickly enter it into the R/3 transactions in dialog.

Target Concept for the Data Transfer

In the Realization phase, you should define a target concept in which you determine which data you must transfer from your legacy system into the R/3 System and which processes you'll use to do so. The starting point for this concept is your existing system topology and, particularly, the systems and the parts of systems that must be replaced by the R/3 System. Together with the departments, you should specify the business processes for which you must transfer data into the R/3 System. The following questions are important for your target concept:

- What is the data volume that must be transferred for the individual business processes?
- How quickly does the data have to be transferred?
- What technology should be used?
- Can you transfer the data in any order or must it be transferred in a specified order?

Technical Design for the Data Transfer

After the Project Management has approved your target concept, the next step is for you to create a technical design for the data transfer. In the technical design, document the data format in which the business objects must be transferred, the functions that the transfer program must have, and how the transfer is organized.

Data Format

In the target concept, you have defined which business objects will be transferred. For the technical design, you must first analyze the business objects to determine which data fields require specific formats and which data fields are optional. This information allows you to define the data structure for the data transfer files on the operating-system level and decide how to map the data of the existing system on the desired data structure.

Data Transfer Program

The standard R/3 System has special programs that allow you to transfer data for many business objects. These programs are based on the Batch Input process or the Direct Input process. If none of these programs are suitable for your requirements, you should document the functions that the program should offer in your technical design. For example, to create a transfer program for the Batch Input process, you can use a Batch Input Recorder to record one or more transactions in R/3. Based on the recording of the transactions, R/3 creates a transfer program for the Batch Input process. By executing this program, you can create a Batch Input Session. To transfer the values from the data transfer file into the Batch Input Session, you must modify the programs accordingly.

> **NOTE** In the R/3 online documentation, the section "BC Programming Interfaces" describes how to use a Batch Input Recorder to create a transfer program in R/3.

Data Transfer Workbench

For some business objects, you can use the Data Transfer Workbench in R/3 Release 4.0. The Workbench has a standard user interface for the different application-specific transfer programs in the standard R/3 System. For example, you can generate and edit a data transfer file or trigger the actual data transfer from this user interface. Figure 13.4 displays the selection list for the data transfer objects for R/3 Release 4.0B.

> **NOTE** In the R/3 online documentation, the section "CA Data Transfer Workbench" describes the Data Transfer Workbench in detail.

Transfer Organization

In addition to the technical points described in the previous sections, you should describe how you want to organize the data transfer in your technical design. Before you can finally transfer data into the production system, the Customizing must be completed and transported to it. Customizing influences the data format for the data transfer objects. If you change the system settings after the data transfer, you may have to transfer the data again because you require additional data fields for a data transfer object. In addition, you should define the order in which you'll transfer the business objects. From a business viewpoint, dependencies can occur that you can only determine with the departments. When you begin the data transfer, you should not enter any new data in your legacy system. This allows you to simplify the process and shorten the duration of the data transfer because the resources of your legacy system can be used for data transfer. In all, these considerations are part of the detailed Cut Over Plan, which is described in Chapter 3 in the section "Plan the Cut Over and the Help Desk."

FIGURE 13.4:

Data transfer objects in the Data Transfer Workbench

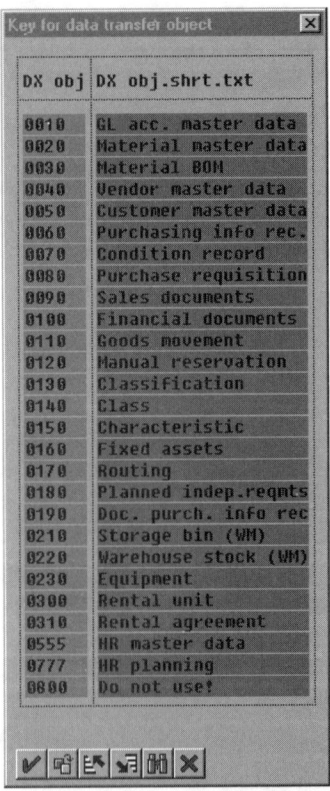

> **NOTE** The guide *Initial Data Transfer Made Easy* informs you about data transfer from non-SAP systems. This document is delivered with the ASAP CD-ROM and is part of the so-called Implementation Accelerators. You can find out more information about additional guides and order them via `http://www.saplabs.com` (choose SAP Books & Publications).

Use the Legacy System Migration (LSM) Workbench

To help you through all the steps of the data transfer from non-R/3 Systems to R/3 Systems, SAP developed the Legacy System Migration (LSM) Workbench. In particular, this tool supports the conversion of the data from your legacy system into a data format that R/3 can process. In addition, the LSM Workbench is linked with the Batch Input Recorder so you can use the LSM Workbench to create the data transfer program. You can transfer the data with either the Batch Input process or the Direct Input process.

> **NOTE** The LSM Workbench is not yet a part of the standard R/3 System and is delivered on request on a CD-ROM free of charge. SAP plans to include the LSM Workbench in the standard R/3 System, but currently, no date has been set. The best way to receive the tool is to send a request by e-mail to `lsm@sap-ag.de`. You can find additional information in the R/3 Note 101014, "Legacy System Migration Workbench – LSM Workbench."

Monitor and Restart the Interfaces

At the end of the Realization phase, you'll define the system operation for the production system and thus how you want to monitor the interfaces. In your system operation manual, you should document all the important interfaces in the R/3 System. The following points are important for the system operation:

- Which task does the interface perform?
- In the department, who is responsible for the interface?
- Which data volume is transferred, and is a time frame defined?
- Which technologies are used to transfer the data?
- How is the interface restarted after a problem has occurred?
- How is the interface dependent on the R/3 Release? What do you have to consider for a Release upgrade?

It is important that the R/3 System administrator has tools to monitor the interfaces. For many interfaces, SAP delivers the appropriate tools with the standard R/3 System. For example, for the Batch Input process, there is an R/3 transaction that displays all the waiting or already processed Batch Input Sessions in a detailed overview. As Figure 13.5 shows, the Sessions overview shows you whether a Batch Input Session has errors or was successfully processed.

FIGURE 13.5:

An example of an overview of the Batch Input Sessions in the R/3 System (transaction code SM35)

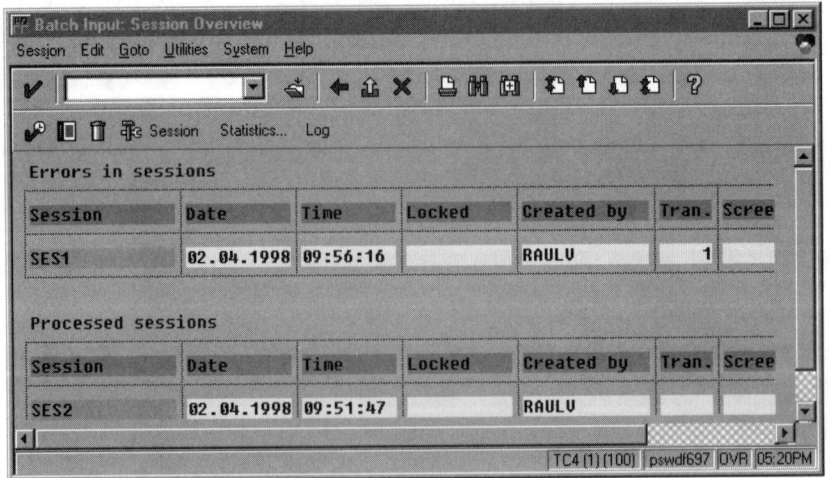

If a problem causes the interface to run with errors or to terminate, the Technical Team must first ensure that the error is resolved from a technical viewpoint. Then the R/3 System administrator can ensure that data transfer is technically possible. However, to restart the data transfer, you often require a detailed restart procedure that also contains business viewpoints. You should work with the departments to define your restart procedure in your technical design for the interfaces. For example, when you divide the entire data transfer into multiple LUWs, you'll often only have to repeat parts of the entire process and thus simplify the restart procedure. Often, the R/3 System administrator can restart the interfaces (for example, the Batch Input process) without additional help from the departments. In other cases, only a specialist from the departments can restart the interface. SAP recommends that you always document the restart procedure in detail in the system operation manual and test it during the Final Preparation phase.

Interfaces in ASAP

In the previous sections, you learned what to consider when you are planning your interfaces during the R/3 implementation. In ASAP, these points are distributed over the individual phases of the project. The following sections describe when to perform certain tasks.

Business Blueprint

During the Business Blueprint phase, the Project Team determines which business processes are implemented in your company's R/3 System. In this planning phase, you should determine which interfaces you'll require for your R/3 System. Often, the business processes extend across multiple systems in your company, although currently, they extend more frequently to customers and suppliers.

Define the business processes for which you require interfaces and work with consultants to decide where you should set up an interface in a business process and which interface technologies you can implement. In particular, determine whether BAPIs are available for your requirements.

Normally, the implementation of an R/3 System requires that you replace your legacy system partially or sometimes even completely. In every case, you should transfer the data from your legacy system into your R/3 production system before the start of production. In your Business Blueprint, document the business processes for which you'll transfer data. From a technical viewpoint, you should estimate the volume of data to be transferred and the extent to which the existing data format must be adapted to meet the format of the standard R/3 System. Often, you do not have much time between the deactivation of the legacy system and the start of production of the R/3 System. The earlier you plan your data transfer, the easier it is for you to estimate the required time frame and the resources you'll need for it. With the technical consultant, determine which technology allows you to transfer data most quickly and effectively.

Realization

In the course of the Realization phase, you'll develop the programs and procedures for transferring the data from the legacy system. In most projects, the majority of the data is transferred automatically through Batch Input processes or Direct Input processes. Only a small part of the data is transferred manually. Before you can go into the Final Preparation phase, you must complete the data transfer programs and test them in the quality assurance system. You should also check how quickly you can transfer data. This is the only way you can estimate whether you can transfer the data volume within the planned time frame. Otherwise, you must additionally optimize the data transfer programs.

If you require one or more interfaces for some business processes, develop the required programs during the Realization phase. When you develop the programs, you must ensure that the planned data volume can be imported or exported within the planned time frame. To do so, transport the interface programs into the quality assurance system to test them.

Final Preparation

To prepare for production, plan the Cut Over in detail and transfer the data from the legacy system during the Cut Over. As described in the section "Plan the Cut Over and the Help Desk" in Chapter 3, you should switch from the legacy system to the R/3 System at the end of the Final Preparation phase. Often, the time frame for the switch should be as short as possible. Therefore, you should create a detailed plan for the order in which the data will be transferred. At the beginning of the Cut Over, transport the released Customizing settings and Repository objects from the quality assurance system to the production system. Subsequently, transfer the master records and transaction data in the order defined in the technical design. The Cut Over ends when the Project Management has signed off the production system and released the start of production.

Table 13.1 lists the tasks from ASAP that are related to the implementation of the interfaces. Each task is described in accordance with the phase in which it is performed and the person who performs it.

TABLE 13.1: Tasks for Implementing Interfaces in ASAP

Phase	Phase Name	Task	Role
2	Business Blueprint	Determine required interfaces	Application consultant, Business Process Owner, technical consultant

Continued on next page

TABLE 13.1: Tasks for Implementing Interfaces in ASAP *(Continued)*

Phase	Phase Name	Task	Role
2	Business Blueprint	Determine data transfer requirements	Application consultant, Business Process Owner, technical consultant
		Document interface topology	Technical Team Lead, R/3 System administrator, technical consultant
3	Realization	Develop data transfer programs	Technical Team Lead, R/3 System administrator, technical consultant, Business Process Owner
		Develop application interface programs	Technical Team Lead, R/3 System administrator, technical consultant, Business Process Owner
4	Final Preparation	Refine Cut Over and production support plan	Project Manager, Business Process Team Lead, Technical Team Lead
		Perform conversions	Technical Team Lead, R/3 System administrator, technical consultant

Success Factors

To successfully implement the interfaces, you must consider how to perform the following tasks:

- Define guidelines for the interfaces
- Test the throughput
- Consider open interfaces in the Computing Center Management System (CCMS)

The following sections describe these points in detail.

Define Guidelines for the Interfaces

The goal of the guidelines for interfaces is to implement interfaces only when it is absolutely necessary.

By keeping the number of interfaces as low as possible, you can save time and costs. You must monitor each interface, and you may have to adapt them to the new Release during a Release upgrade. Only the responsible departments or the respective developers can make these decisions. You also need a detailed procedure for restarting the interface in case one of the systems is down, whether planned or unplanned.

To implement only necessary interfaces, you should set up an approval procedure. Each interface must be formally applied for. Set up guidelines for what the application must contain. The Project Management must consider the costs against the usefulness and then determine whether or not to give approval for the interface. In this respect, if you develop an interface, ASAP recommends documenting the interface and the programs that were developed for it in detail. Detailed documentation enables you to decide before a Release upgrade whether or not you have to adapt the interface for the new R/3 Release.

Test the Throughput

Often, a specified data volume is supposed to be imported or exported through an interface within a specific time frame. Particularly, the transfer of large data volumes before the start of production is time critical. Despite time constraints, the data should be as error free as possible and completely exchanged. The Project Management has typical requirements for the throughput and the quality of the interfaces, which you can only meet if you constantly test the new work done in your system.

For time-critical interfaces in particular, you should determine for the technical design which interface technologies allow for the highest throughput. The most important factors for this are the data volume, the size of the system, and the system performance. For example, the Data Input process is normally the quickest way to transfer data.

Consider Open Interfaces in CCMS

Especially in large R/3 implementations with heterogeneous system platforms, various additional network services, and interfaces to external applications, system management services are often used. CCMS has various open interfaces. You can select from a series of products for global system management. The interfaces are divided into the data collector interface, the service interface, and the management interface. External products can query and process management data in the R/3 System in dialog from a special Simple Network Management Protocol-Management Information Base (SNMP-MIB), the SAP Private Enterprise MIB 649. For specific exceptional situations in the R/3 System, the R/3 System generates SNMP alerts.

All interfaces are in the standard R/3 System. Third-party vendors that use these interfaces can have their products certified by SAP. You can find information about the certified products from third-party vendors in SAPNet at `http://sapnet.sap.com/csp` under the keyword Complementary Solutions.

Review Questions

1. On which layers of the client/server architecture does R/3 have interfaces?

    A. Presentation layer

    B. Application layer

    C. Database layer

2. Which interface technology can you implement on the application layer?

   A. BAPI

   B. OLE

   C. ALE

   D. RFC

   E. Batch Input

   F. CPI-C

   G. ODBC

3. Which procedures and tools can you use to transfer data from an external system into the R/3 System?

   A. Legacy System Migration Workbench

   B. Batch Input

   C. Direct Input

   D. SAP Automation

CHAPTER FOURTEEN

Security

The security of the data in your R/3 System is seldom threatened, yet threatening situations can arise in every system. For example, data that is read or changed without authorization may cause transaction downtime or, at worst, data loss. No system can provide you with complete protection against these types of risks. However, R/3 has many options to help you protect yourself from the majority of security risks. Two such options are the user and authorization concept and Secure Network Communications (SNC).

> **NOTE** Before you define your security strategy, read the security guidelines from SAP documented in the guide called "R/3 Security Guide." Customers and partners can find the guidelines in SAPNet at `http://sapnet.sap.com/securityguide`.

What type of security do you want to implement to protect against internal and external accesses? You should ask this question at the beginning of your implementation project. The answer determines how you should provide complete security for your system landscape. To help you find the answer, the following sections explain how to perform these tasks:

- Define your strategy
- Define the system operation

Define Your Strategy

When you define your strategy for data security, you must give consideration to two areas. First, the security mechanisms must not negatively affect the daily operation of an R/3 System. Second, it must be possible for the R/3 System administrator to control accesses and log unauthorized access attempts. To enable you to consider these aspects in your strategy, the following sections explain how to:

- Control access
- Secure the network
- Secure the operating-system level

Control Access

Essentially, you can access all the system data from every level in the R/3 client/server architecture. On every level, users are created that have to be authenticated at logon.

Special Users

During the R/3 implementation, special users are set up on almost every level with the exception of the presentation layer. Figure 14.1 shows that the various special users have different tasks for R/3 System operation. For this purpose, almost every special user is equipped with wide-reaching authorizations that enable them to access all of the R/3 data. After installation, these special users are required to log on to a level for the first time. The passwords are predetermined and thus are also known to third parties. For this reason, you should change the passwords directly after the installation.

SAP*, DDIC, SAPCPIC, and EARLYWATCH

On the application layer, four special users are created: SAP*, DDIC, SAPCPIC, and EARLYWATCH. In "Success Factors" in Chapter 6, you learned that you must protect the special users in the R/3 System against unauthorized access. Chapter 6 also contains a detailed description of what to take into consideration when you are working with the special users.

FIGURE 14.1:

Special users on the individual levels in R/3

	Component	Special User
Presentation	SAPGUI, Front End	Operating System Specific User
Application	Application Module, Work Processes, Message Service	SAP*, DDIC, SAPCPIC, EARLYWATCH
Database	RDBMS	SAPR3, Manufacturer-Specific User
Operating System	UNIX, Windows NT, OS/400, OS/390	<SAPSID> adm, <DB><SAPSID>, SAP service <SAPSID>, <Dbservice> Manufacturer-Specific User

SAPR3

On the database layer, every Relational Database Management System (RDBMS) uses separate special users whose name and initial password are known to third parties. In addition to the special users for the RDBMS, only one database user is created during the implementation of the standard R/3 System: SAPR3. Every work process logs on to the database as user SAPR3 and can access all the R/3 data. In "Success Factors" in Chapter 9, you learned that you must change the initial password for the special users for the RDBMS and SAPR3.

> **NOTE** In addition to protecting against technical access, you must protect the data backup tapes against theft. A thief can use a data backup to re-create the status of your R/3 database on their own hardware and thus access your data.

root and <SAP System name>adm

On the operating-system level, each vendor uses its own special users with wide-reaching authorizations; for example, the user root is for UNIX systems. In addition, more special users are created for an R/3 System on the application servers and on the database server—for example, <SAP System name>adm. SAP recommends that you do not set up any further users on these servers. The administrators can use these users to do all the necessary tasks for the operating system. Since you can use these users to stop and start the R/3 System, ensure that only the administrators know the passwords.

> **NOTE** You should document the passwords for the special users and keep them in a secure location, such as a safe. This way, the password can be accessed if, for example, the responsible administrators are sick or have left the company.

R/3 Users

Every R/3 user must be able to access the application layer. These users should be created in accordance with the security requirements. You can control the access to data and transactions with the R/3 authorization concept (see Chapter 6 "User Administration"). On the application layer, users enter their user names and passwords to authenticate themselves. Ensure that the passwords are difficult to guess; "Define the Logon Procedure and Password Rules" in Chapter 6 describes the options available in R/3 for the logon procedures and password rules. For example, you can determine the minimum number of characters a password must contain or which passwords cannot be used.

Front-End Users

On the presentation layer, you can use the security functions of the front-end operating system. It is becoming more common to use operating systems or screen savers with password protection on front ends. This allows you to largely rule out the risk of third parties accessing the system through the front ends unnoticed. You should inform the users about the security risks and the password rules that apply to them. Normally, the users handle their passwords responsibly and lock their front ends when they leave their office.

Developers

Users should not have authorization to develop programs in R/3 production systems. Therefore, you should lock all the transaction codes that begin with the letters *SE*.

Developing programs is a security risk because you can use an ABAP program to read and change the data in all the database tables. For this reason, you should develop programs in a separate R/3 System, the development system. Before you transport these programs to the production system, make sure they meet your security requirements and that you are not transporting a Trojan horse. To check your programs, SAP recommends the separate quality assurance system. If an exceptional situation arises and you need to immediately correct a program in the production system, you should only issue development authorization temporarily. While the correction is being made, ensure that another employee checks the work.

Secure the Network

A network has many points where third parties can gain unauthorized access other than only the one R/3 System. Only with network specialists can you define a security concept that meets your requirements. The following sections describe the most important measures to take.

Topology

Depending on the size of your system, the topology can vary from simple networks with few subnetworks to complex networks. As described in Chapter 11, "Network Administration," in a distributed R/3 System with a database server and multiple application servers, the network is divided into a front-end network and a server network. Normally, the server network requires a higher security level than the front-end network.

TIP To ensure a high level of security, separate the server network as a single subnetwork.

Network Services

Some network services—for example, the Network File System (NFS) and the Network Information System (NIS) in a UNIX network—enable you to access servers directly on the operating-system level. If you have this type of service in a server network, a third party may be able to gain unauthorized access to the operating-system files. Every network service listens to a specific port for queries that are waiting to be processed. The more services implemented in your network, the more ports there are available and the more access points there are. Therefore, in secure networks, you should keep the number of ports as low as possible. The "R/3 Security Guide" (see http://sapnet.sap.com/securityguide) describes the ports required for the R/3 network services.

NOTE Use only the network services that you require for your R/3 System operation.

Firewall and SAProuter

WAN connections in particular can allow third parties to gain access to the network without stepping on company premises. Normally, the WAN connection does not belong to you but to an official provider, which does not allow you to influence the security against outside monitoring and unauthorized access. To be able to protect yourself against unauthorized access to your internal network, SAP recommends setting up a firewall and a SAProuter. As described in Chapter 11 in the section "Set Up a Remote Connection," SAP uses the same configuration on the other end of the connection (see Figure 11.4).

> **NOTE** To control the access to your network, combine the SAProuter and firewall.

Secure Network Communications (SNC)

In addition to using the measures already mentioned, you can increase the security on the protocol level by encrypting the data. The data stream between the presentation layer and the application layer is compressed and is therefore not easily interpreted by third parties. However, this does not provide security if someone monitors the data from outside and then decompresses it with the appropriate equipment. To rule out this security risk as much as possible, you can integrate external security products in the front-end network of the R/3 System. Based on the standardized interface GSS-API v2, SAP has developed an interface called Secure Network Communications (SNC).

> **TIP** You can find information about certified third-party vendors and their products for SNC in SAPNet at `http://sapnet.sap.com/csp`. Choose Complementary Solutions.

> **WARNING** Before you implement a security product, you should take the legal conditions for your country into consideration. Not all products can be implemented in every country.

As Figure 14.2 displays, the SNC interface does not allow you to encrypt the communication between the application layer and the database layer. As already mentioned, SAP recommends using a separate and secure server network between these layers. If a separate and secure server network does not meet your requirements for security, you must see if your database vendor offers an appropriate security product.

> **TIP** SNC can also be implemented between two SAProuters. This allows you to establish a secure connection for either a LAN or a WAN connection between networks.

FIGURE 14.2:

SNC in a LAN or a WAN

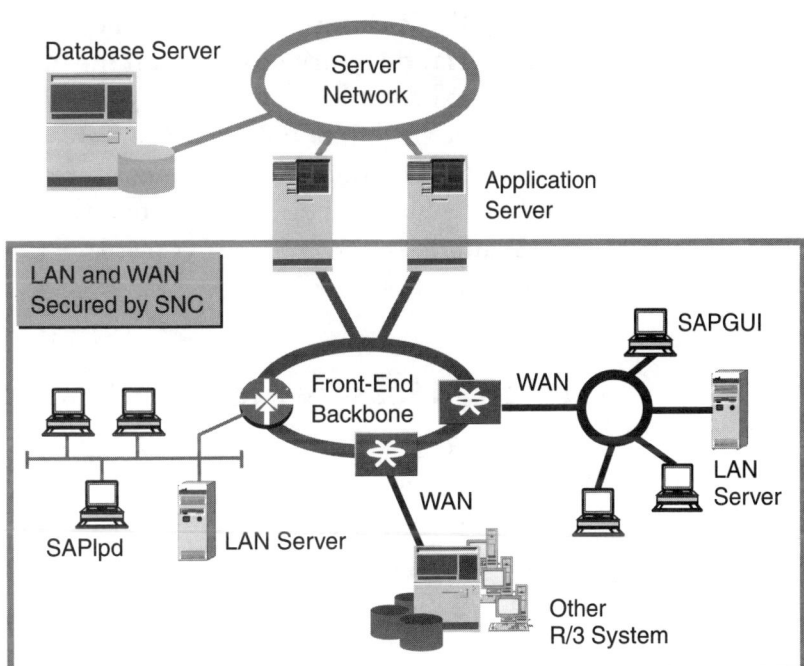

Secure the Operating-System Level

For the R/3 System, SAP supports the following operating systems: the leading UNIX derivatives, Windows NT, OS/400, and OS/390. Each operating system has different requirements for a security concept. The vendors can tell you the details about the options in each operating system. SAP cannot guarantee the security of the operating system. SAP can only recommend concepts that are suitable for system operation with R/3. The following sections explain which aspects are important for the UNIX and Windows NT operating systems.

Security Measures for UNIX

You should take security measures for some files and services in UNIX, for example, the password file passwd, the Network Information System (NIS), and the Network File System (NFS). The "R/3 Security Guide" (see `http://sapnet.sap.com/securityguide`) describes in detail the measures that SAP recommends.

During the R/3 implementation, the installation program creates a special directory structure on the operating-system level to store the executable programs or parameter files. For security reasons, the installation program assigns different access authorizations to each file. These settings correspond to the SAP recommendations and you do not need to change them. Ensure that the access authorizations for files you create also correspond to the recommendations.

Security Measures for Windows NT

The domain concept is essential for the security in a network with Windows NT as a network operating system. A domain logically collects a group of computers that use common resources and work with a common database for user accounts. The user account allows you to define the resources that an NT user can and cannot access. Every user account has a name and a password. You should administer the user accounts centrally from the primary domain controller. A backup domain controller serves as an alternative system.

SAP Domain and USER Domain

In the Business Blueprint phase, you should define which resources are grouped in which domains in the technical design. You should plan this in detail because, once you have established a solution, it is very difficult to switch to another solution. SAP recommends that you generate two separate domains for your R/3 System: the SAP Domain and the USER Domain. In the SAP Domain, group the resources of the application layer and the database layer. You should only create Windows NT users for the individual administrators in this domain. In the USER Domain, group the resources of the presentation layer and the network administration. Create Windows NT users for all the R/3 users in this domain.

> **NOTE** Do not configure a domain controller on an application or database server in the R/3 System. If you set up a local NT user on a domain controller, this user is known on all the domain controllers of the domain.

Example: Defining a Domain Concept

This example displays the domain concept that SAP has chosen for Ready-to-Run R/3 (RRR) for a Windows NT platform. This example's graphic shows that two domains are set up:

SAP Domain   Contains the application server and the database server

USER Domain   Contains the LAN server and all the front ends

Continued on next page

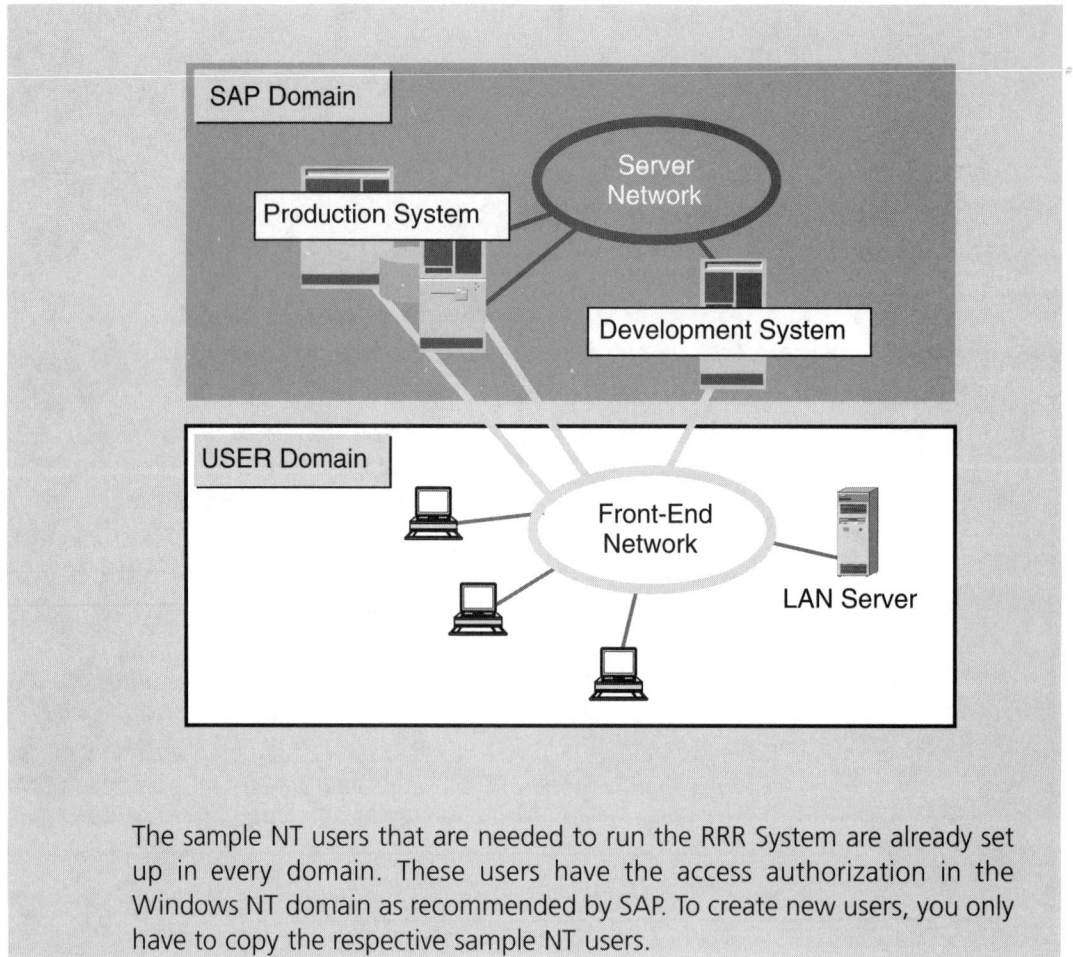

The sample NT users that are needed to run the RRR System are already set up in every domain. These users have the access authorization in the Windows NT domain as recommended by SAP. To create new users, you only have to copy the respective sample NT users.

NOTE The guidelines in the "R/3 Security Guide" (see `http://sapnet.sap.com/securityguide`) describe in detail how to secure the operating system.

Define the System Operation

After the start of production, you should regularly check to make sure your security guidelines are being followed and to see if third parties have attempted to gain access to your system without authorization. The R/3 System has tools for monitoring the R/3 users. The two most important tools are the user list and the information system.

The User List

You can use the user list to see which users are logged on to the R/3 System. As Figure 14.3 shows, the overview allows you to display the terminal from which the user is logged on, the last transaction called, and when it was called. In R/3, you can choose between two lists. One list allows you to see only the users of the application server to which you are logged on (transaction code SM04, see Figure 14.3). You can also use another list that displays all the users logged on to the individual application servers (transaction code AL08).

FIGURE 14.3:
Overview of users (transaction code SM04)

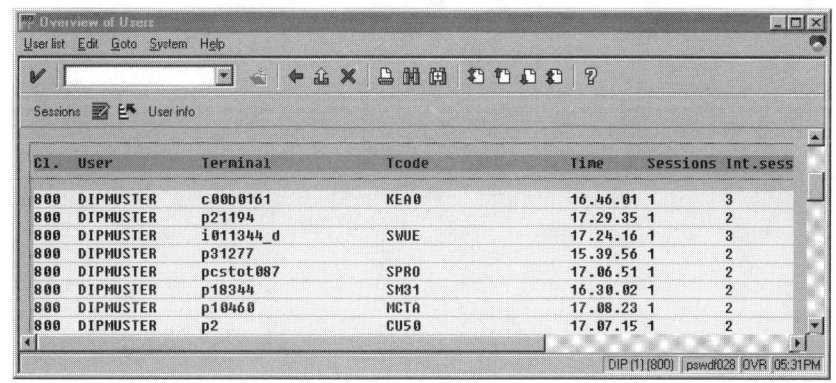

The Information System

The information system allows you to centrally control, for example, which users have developer authorizations that are a security risk for a production system. Figure 14.4 shows that the information system displays authorization objects as well as complex selection criteria. In this way, you can make sure your guidelines for the authorization concept are being followed.

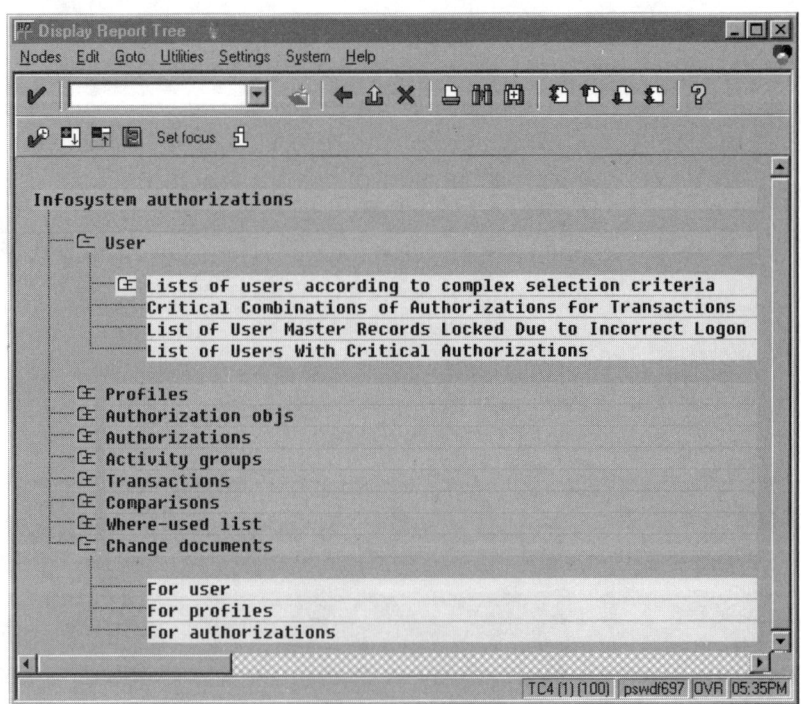

FIGURE 14.4:

The information system for user administration (transaction code SARP)

As you learned in "Control Access" earlier in this chapter, there are users on every level of an R/3 System that can access all of the R/3 data. Both of the tools introduced here only take the R/3 users into consideration. You have to use tools from the operating system vendor or the database vendor to control the other users.

Security in ASAP

Normally, you'll implement the R/3 Systems of your system landscape on a step-by-step basis during the implementation project. The various systems also have different requirements for the security concept. The development system and the quality assurance system require a lower level of security than the production system does. However, you should change the predefined passwords for the special users in all of the R/3 Systems directly after the implementation. In addition, you must define which users are authorized to access the database level and operating-system level in all of the systems. For example, to develop an interface that uses data on the operating-system level, a developer requires the appropriate authorizations for the development system and the quality assurance system. In a production system, these authorizations would be a security gap. You should define an authorization procedure to document the users and their authorizations on the operating-system level and the database level in your R/3 System. The following sections describe when to perform certain tasks for security measures during the R/3 implementation.

Business Blueprint

As soon as you have set up the development system in the Business Blueprint phase, you should use the security guidelines to take the necessary measures for protecting your system internally and externally against unauthorized accesses. You should also establish the remote connection to SAP in this phase. To be able to use the SAP Online Service System (OSS), you must install a SAProuter. SAP also recommends that you combine the SAProuter with a firewall (see "Set Up a Remote Connection" in Chapter 11).

Realization

At the beginning of the Realization phase, you'll set up the quality assurance system. Essentially, you should take the same measures for this system as you did for the development system. You should also define the procedures and guidelines for ensuring the security of the production system in this phase. In a system operation manual, document who can assign authorizations and who can create users. Chapter 6, "User Administration," describes how to set up the double-verification principle in R/3 for user and authorization administration. When you use the double-verification principle, different team members can check on each other, and you can protect your system against authorization abuses. Make sure you can also set up a similar procedure for the non-R/3 users.

At the end of the Realization phase, you'll set up the production system. Change the passwords for the special users directly after the installation and document the new passwords of the most important users (for example, SAP* or root). If a problem occurs and the administrator is not available, you can fall back on the documented password.

Final Preparation

While you prepare the project, you should implement and test the procedures and guidelines for the security of the production system. The SAP security guidelines contain a checklist. You can use it to decide whether you have given consideration to the most essential security risks.

Table 14.1 lists the tasks from ASAP that are related to the implementation for security measures. Each task is described in accordance with the phase in which it is performed and the person who performs it.

TABLE 14.1: Tasks for Security in ASAP

Phase	Phase Name	Task	Role
2	Business Blueprint	Secure the development system	Technical Team Lead, R/3 System administrator, network administrator, database administrator, operating system administrator, technical consultant
		Configure remote network connection	R/3 System administrator, network administrator, technical consultant
3	Realization	Secure quality assurance system	Technical Team Lead, R/3 System administrator, network administrator, database administrator, operating system administrator, technical consultant
		Define production system security	Technical Team Lead, R/3 System administrator, network administrator, database administrator, operating system administrator, technical consultant, authorization administrator, Business Process Team Lead
		Secure operating system and database	Database administrator, operating system administrator, technical consultant
		Establish authorization concept	Authorization administrator, Business Process Owner
4	Final Preparation	Secure the production environment	Technical Team Lead, R/3 System administrator, network administrator, database administrator, operating system administrator, technical consultant

Success Factors

To rule out security risks as much as possible, you must give the following points considerable consideration:

- Read and implement the security guidelines
- Train users

The following sections describe these points in detail.

Read and Implement Security Guidelines

In the security guidelines, SAP has documented the security aspects that you must consider for various components in an R/3 System. In addition to this, the guidelines inform you of the measures you can take to protect yourself internally and externally from unauthorized accesses. The security guidelines are regularly updated to include the latest developments and are presented in three documents:

VOLUME I: An Overview of R/3 Security Services The first document informs you of the essential aspects of the R/3 Security Services and will help you set up an appropriate security strategy for your R/3 System landscape.

VOLUME II: R/3 Security Services in Detail The second document will help you realize your security strategy for R/3. It explains the technical measures and options available in the R/3 Security Services (for example, user authentication, R/3 authorization concept, Secure Network Communications, protection for the operating system, protection for database access, and Internet connections).

VOLUME III: Checklists The third document contains checklists for the topics listed in VOLUME II. These checklists enable you to make sure you have taken the essential aspects of your security strategy into consideration.

> **NOTE** Table 14.2 lists important R/3 Notes on the topic of security.

TABLE 14.2: R/3 Notes on Security

Note No.	Short text
23611	FAQs concerning R/3 security
28175	Questions regarding the authorization concept
30724	Data protection and security in R/3
35493	Secrecy and Data Security Obligations
46902	Security aspects in remote access
77503	Audit Information System (AIS) Version 1.5.1

If the security guidelines don't provide sufficient information for your requirements, the SAP technical consulting services can help you. Specialists can give you advice on topics such as the following:

- Detailed security analysis or simple security check
- Customer-specific security guidelines
- Workshop about the R/3 authorization concept
- Customer-specific Windows NT domain concept
- Security aspects for using the Internet Transaction Server

> **NOTE** You can request these SAP services through your respective technical consulting service.

Train Users

Users are the essential factor for security in your system landscape. If the users are poorly trained, malicious, or not reliable, even the best security concept cannot help you. For example, if users disclose their passwords to others or write their passwords on a piece of paper and hang them on their PCs for everyone to see, a third party can easily gain unauthorized access into the system.

To ensure that the users follow the planned security strategy, you can create a special security guideline for them. In it, document the rules for passwords and set up the organizational guidelines. With regard to the guidelines, you should train the users and explain the considerable security risks. This way, you can often make the users aware of the security risks that arise through improper behavior and how to sensibly implement the security mechanisms.

Review Questions

1. Which special users are there for each RDBMS on the database layer?

    A. SAP*

    B. SAPDBA

    C. DDIC

    D. SAPR3

    E. EARLYWATCH

2. How can you secure your network?

   A. Make the server network into a separate subnetwork.

   B. Only use the network services that you require to operate an R/3 System.

   C. Combine the SAProuter and a firewall.

3. Which statement is correct for a Windows NT environment?

   A. Configure the database server as primary domain controller.

   B. Configure an application server as primary domain controller.

   C. Do not configure any of the R/3 servers as a domain controller.

CHAPTER FIFTEEN

High Availability

In every client/server architecture, a client component needs to be able to use the services of the server component. If a server component fails, the dependent client components are also affected. The more clients that depend on one server, the more the services have to be protected against failure. The services that are particularly affected are those that cause the entire system to fail; such a service is called a single point of failure (SPOF). For example, the Relational Database Management System (RDBMS) counts as an SPOF for the R/3 System.

While you prepare the project, you must answer the following questions: What level of availability does the production R/3 System need? What is the maximum allowable downtime for the R/3 production system as defined in possible internal Service Level Agreements in your company? An essential criterion for your answers is the cost. If the R/3 System fails, lost business and external specialists incur costs. However, you must invest more in additional hardware and software or external Service Level Agreements to achieve higher availability. The goal of this chapter is to help you with this decision. The following sections explain how to perform these tasks:

- Define a strategy for high availability
- Define the system operation

Define a Strategy for High Availability

Every strategy for high availability starts with the following questions: Which downtime situations can occur? How long do they last in the worst situation? Detailed answers to these questions depend on how the R/3 System landscape was implemented in your company. General answers can be given to some points. The following sections explain more about downtime situations. The subsequent sections explain some strategies for how to protect yourself against system failure. You'll learn how to:

- Encapsulate redundant subsystems
- Integrate switchover solutions

Potential Downtime Situations

Normally, when you make your calculations, you should take into consideration times when each component in a system group can fail. You must make a distinction between planned and unplanned downtime.

Planned Downtime

You should maintain the hardware and software for each R/3 System at regular intervals. To maintain essential services of your R/3 System, you must stop the entire R/3 System. Such maintenance periods are called *planned downtime* because you determine when you will stop the R/3 System and when you will start it again. This gives you the advantage of maintaining your system when the dialog processing and background processing load is low.

Unplanned Downtime

In every system, a component may fail sooner or later. Hardware and software problems can affect individual front ends, the Web server, the front-end network, the application servers, or the RDBMS. You cannot predict when problems will occur, which is why the periods in which they do occur are called *unplanned downtime.*

Today, high-quality servers can reach an availability of up to 99 percent. By using alternative systems, mirroring disk systems, and additional software, you can increase this value to 99.9 percent or even up to 99.999 percent. The ideal situation for a high-availability solution is when the system remains available for the users when an error occurs. To be able to come as close as possible to this ideal, you must protect all the components of your R/3 System against failure. Table 15.1 lists typical downtime situations for individual components. It also displays which high-availability solutions can help you avoid an R/3 System failure. It does not take into consideration all of the solutions. Instead, it is intended to illustrate that the availability of the entire system is determined by the weakest link in the chain. For example, a database with high availability cannot help you if the front-end network frequently fails and is therefore not available for the users of the entire R/3 System.

TABLE 15.1: Potential Downtime Situations and Their Respective High-Availability Solutions

Component	Failure	High-Availability Solution
Presentation	Front end	SAPGUI reconnect
Front-end network	Topology Active components (for example, LAN server, router, hubs)	Redundant network layout Standby systems
Application	Message service, enqueue service Dialog service, update service, background service, gateway service, spool service	Standby server Distribute services over multiple computers, logon groups
Server network	Network layout Network card	FDDI Ring Connect important server redundantly to the network
Database	Server Hard disks	Standby server, DB reconnect RAID Technology, technical software redundancy, for example, Logical Volume Manager (LVM)
Hardware/operating system	CPU, hard disks, power supply, etc.	Cluster technology and storage technology, Uninterrupted power supply (UPS)

Performance

Unplanned downtime is not only caused by a component failure. You can also reduce availability by placing too heavy a load on the resources. For example, if the CPU of the database server is overloaded, the users must wait a long time for their queries to the R/3 System. This reduces availability to almost zero. For this reason, the availability of a system is a deciding factor in optimizing the performance, and during the implementation project, sizing is important (see Chapter 5, "R/3 Instance Administration," and Chapter 9, "Database Administration"). Particularly in the first weeks after the start of production, you can still improve the performance of the R/3 System. You can use the tools in R/3 to measure the load on individual components. Using the results of your measurements, you can optimize the settings of the system parameters. To help you with your performance analysis, SAP offers a special service, the EarlyWatch Service (see Appendix C).

Encapsulate Redundant Subsystems

A good high-availability solution is to encapsulate the entire system into redundant subsystems. This allows you to avoid single points of failure (SPOFs) as much as possible.

Services in R/3

The R/3 System has many options to configure the services redundantly and thus inherently achieve high availability. One such option is logon load balancing through logon groups. If an instance is not available for the users within the logon group, the message service recognizes this and, at logon, only connects the users to the available instances. Table 15.2 lists the important services in the R/3 System and displays which services you can distribute redundantly over multiple servers and which services can only be configured once in the entire system.

TABLE 15.2: R/3 Services and Single Points of Failure

R/3 Component or Service	Possible Number	Systemwide SPOF
RDBMS	1 in each R/3 System	Yes
Enqueue service	1 in each R/3 System	Yes
Message service	1 in each R/3 System	Yes
Dialog service	From 2 to N on each instance	No
Update service	From 0 to N on each instance	No
Background service	From 0 to N on each instance	No
Spool service	From 0 to N on each instance	No
Gateway service	1 on each instance	No
SAProuter	From 0 to N in each R/3 System	No
NFS Service (UNIX)	1 in each R/3 System	Yes

> **NOTE** SAP recommends that you configure the enqueue service and the message service together on one server. It is essential for the performance of the entire system that these two services can communicate with each other as quickly as possible.

Non-SPOFs

In a distributed R/3 System, the following question presents itself for all of the non-SPOFs: How many of a service's work processes should be configured and on which instance? There is no universal answer to this question. The answer depends on your hardware resources and how you use the R/3 System. In Chapter 5, the section "Distribute Work Processes" describes which relationships result between the number of work process types. In the first weeks after the start of production in particular, you must check to see if the recommendations in Chapter 5 also apply to your R/3 System. You can refer to the high-availability guide for the advantages and disadvantages of the various configurations for distributed R/3 Systems.

> **TIP** The high-availability guide is a part of the R/3 online documentation and is called "BC SAP High Availability."

SPOFs

When you need to protect the SPOFs in the R/3 services against failure, consider the following question: Which technology allows you to achieve a redundancy for the SPOFs? You can also only give a concrete answer to this question based on your system configuration. For your RDBMS in particular, you should work with the database vendor and your hardware partner to create a high-availability solution. For example, if you want to use a cluster technology, you must find out which options are supported by your hardware. As displayed in Figure 15.1, you can choose whether two servers use the same hard disk physically or logically.

FIGURE 15.1:
Possible cluster technology for application servers and a database server

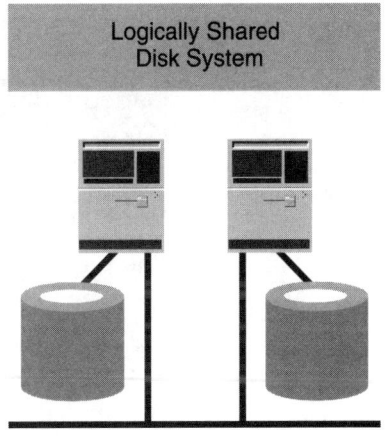

Integrate Switchover Solutions

A switchover solution protects you against unplanned downtime if a hardware problem occurs. If a server with services that are important to the R/3 System operation fails, the switchover software automatically transfers the services to a standby server and the users can continue with their work after a short interruption.

> **NOTE** To integrate a switchover solution, you need extensive knowledge about the technology of the selected product. For the implementation, you therefore need technical consultants who are familiar with the switchover software.

Because of costs, you should only implement a switchover solution for distributed R/3 Systems for the servers that are systemwide SPOFs (see Table 15.2). SAP recommends that you divide the systemwide SPOFs into two components:

- RDBMS
- Central instance, which contains the enqueue service and the message service

This division is sensible for high availability and for the performance of the entire R/3 System. In a distributed R/3 System, the RDBMS and the central instance are often set up on different servers to avoid taking away the central instance resources from a heavily loaded database server.

RDBMS

There are two conceivable switchover solutions for the database. First, you can set up an additional database server, which accesses the same hard disk. Second, you can set up a complete mirror of the database that also has a separate disk system in addition to the server. As displayed in Figure 15.2, you must replicate all the changes in the active database to the alternative database. Only your database vendor can tell you which solutions are supported for your database.

FIGURE 15.2:
Potential standby systems for the database

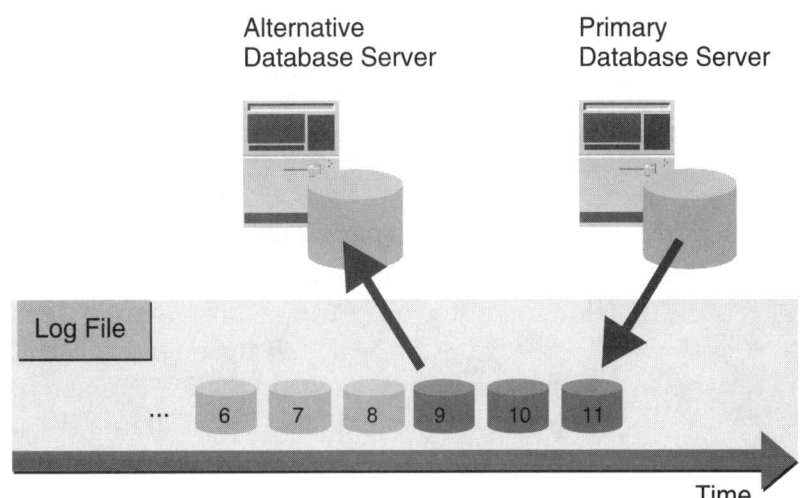

Database Reconnect

If the active database fails and the switchover software has to transfer the services to the standby system, the connection to the database is interrupted for all the work processes for a short time period. During this time, the work process is not terminated; instead, it attempts to reconnect itself to the database. This is called *database reconnect*. Using database reconnect, the database can switch without having to first stop the R/3 System and then start it again. The manual *SAP R/3 in Switchover Environments* describes how to configure the database reconnect for switchover software.

> **TIP** The manual *SAP R/3 in Switchover Environments* explains switchover solutions for an R/3 System in detail. You can find the manual in SAPNet at http://www.sap.com/systemmanagement under the keyword High Availability.

> **NOTE** Database reconnect ensures that the R/3 System can be run in production operation without significant interruptions. However, in practice, data in dialog processing and background processing can be lost for individual users. The transactions that are affected are those that have not been completed from the database viewpoint.

Central Instance

If the central instance fails, the lock table in the main memory is lost, and thus, there are no longer any locks on business objects for any of the open transactions (see the section "The Enqueue Service" in Chapter 2). If the enqueue service is down, users cannot call transactions in the R/3 System. When you make the enqueue service available on an alternative server with the switchover solution, you must ensure that all transactions that were open before the failure were reset. Otherwise, the data in the database may be inconsistent because of the missing locks. As of R/3 Release 3.0E, R/3 automatically resets the open transactions under certain conditions after restarting the enqueue service. You must consult with specialists to determine whether this applies to your solution in every situation. You must test your switchover solution with regard to this before you start production.

Define the System Operation

A critical factor for high availability in your system landscape is system operation. If your system operation is not sufficiently organized or if the administrators are not reliable, even the best technical solution for high availability will be of no benefit. For example, if the R/3 database administrator does not know that he or she must consult specialists in specific problem situations, he or she may use the RDBMS incorrectly and thus unintentionally increase the downtime.

The System Operation Manual

To achieve a high degree of availability, SAP recommends formalizing the system operation as far as possible. You should define which administrator regularly checks specified components for their functions. If the administrator determines a serious problem in the R/3 System, he or she will need concrete instructions on how to resolve the problem alone or who must be notified. In addition to these regular checks, there are many tasks for maintaining the R/3 System. Formalized procedures also help you to coordinate the R/3 System operation. As explained throughout this book, document all the procedures, communication paths, and escalation paths centrally in a system operation manual.

The CCMS

The Computing Center Management System (CCMS) is the central tool for system operation in the R/3 System. The monitoring functions in the CCMS enable you to recognize problem situations early and thus prevent a system failure for users in many situations. For example, the Alert Monitor triggers an alert as soon as the fill level in the database has exceeded the threshold value you defined. By regularly checking this alert, you can avoid filling up the database. The R/3 online documentation and *SAP R/3 System Administration: The Official SAP Guide*, by Liane Will (Sybex, 1998), describe how to use the CCMS optimally for your requirements.

High Availability in ASAP

During the implementation project, you must not only prepare for the availability of the production system; more often, you must also ensure for the availability of the development system and the quality assurance system in the course of the project. In addition to the technical aspects of availability, you cannot forget system operation. You should define procedures that can help you recognize and resolve problems early. For example, you should check daily to see whether the Alert Monitor displays errors or whether the data backup was successful. Ensure that the administrators know how to resolve problems themselves or tell them which specialist can help them if a problem occurs. Each system has different requirements, and accordingly, you should document the procedures centrally in a system operation manual (see "Define the System Operation" earlier in this chapter). The following sections describe when to perform certain tasks for high-availability solutions during the R/3 implementation.

Project Preparation

To prepare for the project, define the required technical infrastructure for your system landscape. Your hardware configuration will depend on, among other things, the availability that you want to ensure for the system. Should an alternative system be available for the database server? How should the message service and the enqueue service be backed up? Should you use a switchover solution and which additional hardware is required? You should discuss these questions with your hardware partner. Only your hardware partner can tell you, for example, which switchover solutions are supported.

Business Blueprint

If your database fails because of a hardware or software error, a RAID 5 system or an standby system may not protect you against data loss in every situation. In any situation, you need a strategy for backing up the data in the R/3 System. In the Business Blueprint phase, work together with a technical consultant to define how and when to back up data. Select your tools for data backup in accordance with the maximum downtime permitted for your system if a problem occurs. Chapter 9, "Database Administration," describes what you should take into consideration to determine the maximum allowable downtime.

Realization

Before you start production operation, you should test the technical configuration and all the procedures that you defined in the system operation manual. For this reason, you must prepare the system tests during the Realization phase. In the Final Preparation phase, conduct these tests in accordance with your planning. In the system test, you should simulate critical downtime situations and make sure the administrators can complete the regular tasks and use the system operation manual to resolve errors.

You can resolve many problem situations yourself; however, for some problems, you need help from your hardware and software partners. In accordance with your requirements for availability of the system, create Service Level Agreements with your partners. For example, agree on a reaction time with your hardware partner. If a hardware error occurs, your hardware partner must be able to react within the agreed-upon time frame. For problems with the software, SAP provides a worldwide R/3 Service & Support network, which is available around the clock and includes SAP's partner companies. The central contact for questions about R/3 is R/3 Support. If a problem occurs and you need additional advice, SAP offers a variety of consulting services. Appendix C describes the recommended services from a technical viewpoint.

Final Preparation

To run R/3 securely in production operation, you should test the production system extensively during the Final Preparation phase. You have already established the test plans in the Realization phase. During the Final Preparation phase, use these tests to find out if the configuration of the production system is suitable for your requirements for availability. For example, if you have implemented a switchover solution, you can simulate a downtime situation and make sure the standby system takes over the production operation as planned.

Before you can go live, you must set up the help desk. The help desk is essential for production support. For the help desk, you need to define how to report, process, and resolve problems. A well-organized help desk reduces the costs of running R/3 and improves user acceptance of the new system. In Chapter 3, the section "Plan the Cut Over and the Help Desk" describes how to set up a help desk.

Go Live and Support

During the subsequent Go Live and Support phase, you should make the production support available. Experience shows that the majority of problems occur and that the users have the most questions about using R/3 in the first weeks after the start of production. You must consider making extra resources available for the help desk during this time.

Table 15.3 lists the tasks from ASAP that are related to the implementation of high-availability solutions. For each task, the table specifies the phase in which it is performed and the person who performs it.

TABLE 15.3: Tasks for High-Availability Solutions in ASAP

Phase	Phase Name	Task	Role
1	Project Preparation	Plan the technical requirements	Project Manager, Technical Team Lead, R/3 System administrator

Continued on next page

TABLE 15.3: Tasks for High-Availability Solutions in ASAP *(Continued)*

Phase	Phase Name	Task	Role
2	Business Blueprint	Define backup strategy	Technical Team Lead, R/3 System administrator, database administrator
		Define periodic system maintenance procedures	Technical Team Lead, R/3 System administrator, technical consultant
3	Realization	Develop system test plans	Technical Team Lead, Business Process Team Lead, R/3 System administrator, technical consultant
		Define Service Level Agreement	Technical Team Lead, R/3 System administrator, database administrator, network administrator, operating system administrator, technical consultant
		Create system operation manual	Technical Team Lead, R/3 System administrator, database administrator, network administrator, operating system administrator, technical consultant
4	Final Preparation	Conduct system tests	Technical Team Lead, R/3 System administrator, technical consultant
		Refine production support plan	Project Manager, Technical Team Lead, Business Process Team Lead
5	Go Live and Support	Provide production support	Help desk provider

Success Factors

To successfully implement a high-availability solution, you must give the following points particular consideration:

- Read the high-availability guide

- List potential downtime situations
- Conclude a Service Level Agreement

The following sections describe these points in detail.

Read the High-Availability Guide

For the various layers in an R/3 System, SAP has published a high-availability guide to document the situations in which the R/3 System can fail and how you can protect yourself against this. In the high-availability guide, SAP recommends how to set up a high-availability solution for your system landscape.

> **NOTE** The high-availability guide is a part of the R/3 online documentation and is called "BC SAP High Availability." You can find it in the R/3 Library in the directory Computing Center Management System (see Figure 15.3).

List Potential Downtime Situations

Before you create a detailed plan for high availability in your R/3 System, you should first list all the potential downtime situations for your system configuration. In addition to the "normal" situations, also consider situations in which individual devices are defective as well as exceptional situations such as fire damage or water damage. You should also consider the potential for logical errors if the users do not use the R/3 System correctly. You should especially consider all the interfaces in the R/3 System through which errors can occur.

For each situation, you should specify how R/3 users are affected. Is the problem a SPOF and has the entire R/3 System failed? Or, has the R/3 System only partially failed and is it therefore performing poorly?

FIGURE 15.3:

Table of contents in the high-availability guide

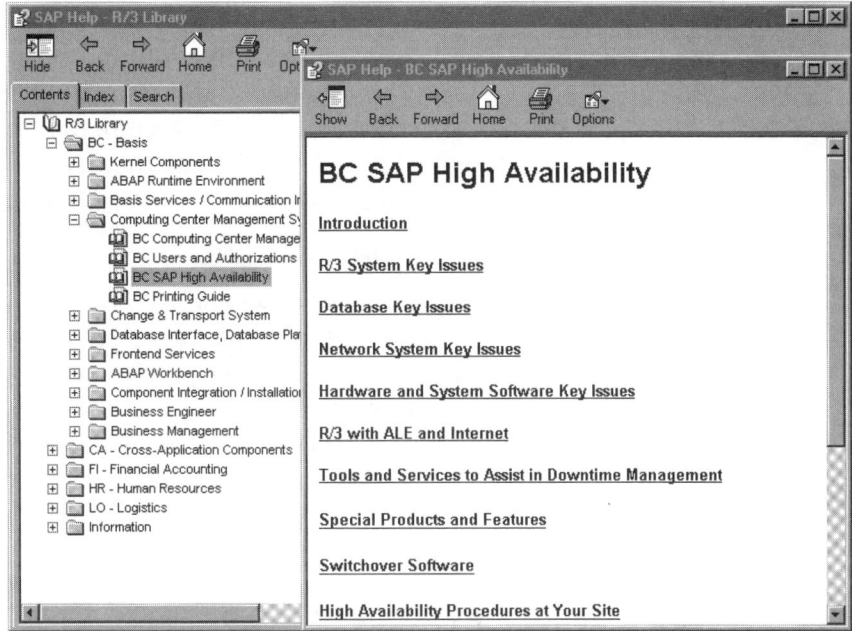

Based on the downtime situations that are possible for your R/3 System, you should decide with experienced technical consultants how you can protect yourself against specific downtime situations—whether you should invest in additional hardware and software or whether you can accept the risk of downtime. Document the result of your strategy in the system operation manual. In particular, ensure that you generate reports about the downtime situations that have occurred. To do so, define in your system operation manual the person who decides how to solve and log a serious system failure.

Conclude a Service Level Agreement

How quickly can you replace defective hardware? Or how quickly can a specialist be on-site to analyze your problem situation? These questions are also deciding factors for the availability of your system. Before you conclude a Service Level Agreement, consult your list and decide which downtime situations will require the quick help of your hardware and software partners. On this basis, you can conclude the Service Level Agreements. If you have defined a maximum acceptable downtime in the production system, ensure that the hardware and software partners can react with corresponding speed.

> **TIP** Occasionally, parts such as hard disks, CPU boards, and cables fail. Therefore, it is advisable to keep replacement parts on hand. For high availability, it can be particularly useful to have delivery contracts with 24-hour delivery service for your hardware and software.

Review Questions

1. Which services are always SPOFs for the entire R/3 System?

    A. RDBMS

    B. Dialog service

    C. Update service

    D. Enqueue service

    E. Background service

    F. Message service

    G. Gateway service

    H. Spool service

    I. SAProuter

2. What can you use to help reduce unplanned downtime?

   A. Switchover software for the database server

   B. One logon group for each R/3 instance

   C. Switchover software for the central instance

   D. Logon groups over multiple R/3 instances

3. What does database reconnect mean?

   A. The work processes attempt to reestablish an interrupted connection to the database.

   B. The database processes attempt to reestablish an interrupted connection to the R/3 System.

   C. The connection to the database can be interrupted for a short time without having to stop and restart the R/3 System.

APPENDIX A

R/3 for Medium-Size Companies

Many medium-size companies have decided to implement R/3. To enable even more to do so, SAP supports them with a special program. This program combines the standard R/3 software with special system solutions and additional services and is called Ready-to-Run R/3 (RRR).

Ready-to-Run R/3 (RRR)

To implement R/3 faster and more effectively from a technical viewpoint, SAP offers the new system solution RRR as a complement to the ASAP method. In RRR, SAP experts and partners have already created and configured a hardware and software infrastructure for you. This infrastructure contains a complete two-system landscape with a development system and a production system. RRR also offers a one-system landscape. This one-system landscape is suitable for R/3 Systems with few users and for companies with many subsidiaries, each of which wants to set up a separate R/3 System. There is no difference between a typical on-site R/3 implementation and an already configured RRR System except for the advantages of RRR that you receive free of charge.

> **TIP** You can find more detailed information about Ready-to-Run R/3 and how to order RRR in SAPNet at http://sapnet.sap.com/rrr. Alternatively, you can write directly to the e-mail address rrr@sapag.de, or you can contact the SAP Local Support at the SAP office in your country.

The hardware in the RRR system landscape is sized for R/3 Systems that are typical for medium-size companies. Currently, you can select from 7 RRR packages that have hardware that can support R/3 production operation for 15 to 200 users at the same time. You should work together with your hardware partner to decide which package is suitable for your requirements. Table A.1 lists the operating systems, RDBMSs, and hardware partners that are supported for R/3 Release 3.1H.

TABLE A.1: Supported Operating Systems, RDBMSs, and Hardware for RRR (as of R/3 Release 3.1H)

	UNIX	Windows NT		Middleware
Hardware	SUN	Bull Compaq Digital	HP IBM NCR SNI	IBM AS/400
Operating System	SOLARIS	Windows NT		OS/400
RDBMS	Informix OnLine Oracle	DB2 UDB Informix OnLine MS SQL Server Oracle		DB2 for AS/400

NOTE The RRR Systems based on R/3 Release 4.0B will be delivered in the fourth quarter, 1998.

Implementation Project

An RRR System relieves you of many tasks during the technical implementation of an R/3 System landscape. RRR provides you with answers to the basic questions about the technical design during the Project Preparation phase in ASAP, for example:

- How should the hardware be sized?
- How should the main memory be configured and which disk layout is suitable for the database?
- What should the network infrastructure be like?

- How should the transport system be configured?
- How should the R/3 front-end software be installed?

In addition to helping you with the technical design, RRR shortens the time required to implement the R/3 Systems. Additionally, with a two-system landscape, you can choose to have your hardware partner deliver the entire RRR package with all of the hardware at the beginning of the Business Blueprint phase, or you can buy the development system first and then implement the production system at the end of the Realization phase.

The Front End

The RRR package contains a front-end PC that is ready to operate, and depending on your requirements, you can order additional front-end PCs. The SAP front-end software and the network are already configured for the front ends. As soon as you connect the PC with the RRR network, you can access the R/3 System from it by calling the SAPGUI through its icon. The PC selection depends on your hardware partner.

The Network

RRR also has a solution for the network. The concept for the network infrastructure is based on establishing stable communication paths between the computers, administering the network centrally, and being able to easily link the network to an existing network. RRR uses a separate network server for central administration. Depending on the RRR package, administration is set up on a separate computer or on the development system server. For example, from the network server, you can centrally administer the users in the network or assign IP addresses to the front ends.

Remote Connection

To benefit from the SAP online services for R/3, you need a remote connection to SAP. RRR allows you to establish a connection more easily than before. The service partners offer a complete complementary package for RRR. This package contains the required WAN hardware, the complete configuration services, and registration with an external communication provider.

Software Logistics

As described in Chapter 12, "Software Logistics," the technical implementation includes your plans for the system landscape and the number of clients you will have as well as how to configure this infrastructure. The two-system landscape in the RRR System offers a practical solution. In the development system (R3T), you can customize your settings and verify the quality of your changes. Then you can transport the released change requests into the production system (R3P). Table A.2 shows which clients are created in RRR in addition to the clients in a standard R/3 System.

TABLE A.2: Client Structure in the RRR System

System	R3T	(Development System)	R3P	(Production System)
Client	010	Customizing client for the implementation project	001	Production client
	020	Test client for the implementation project		
	030	Test and training client		

The change options in the clients and systems are set according to SAP's recommendations. In addition, all the transport paths for Customizing and development changes are set up.

> **NOTE** In a one-system landscape, all the clients listed in Table A.2 are created in an R/3 System.

System Operation

In the RRR System, many procedures are already implemented for secure operation of an R/3 System landscape. For example, the operation modes for day and night operation are created in the Computing Center Management System (CCMS), and the required background jobs are scheduled for the routine tasks for system administration. The data backup strategy is defined. Each RRR package includes appropriate data backup devices that are installed and configured in the operating system and in the R/3 System. Figure A.1 shows the CCMS DBA Planning Calendar set up according to the data backup strategy.

FIGURE A.1:

The DBA Planning Calendar for RRR with an Oracle database.

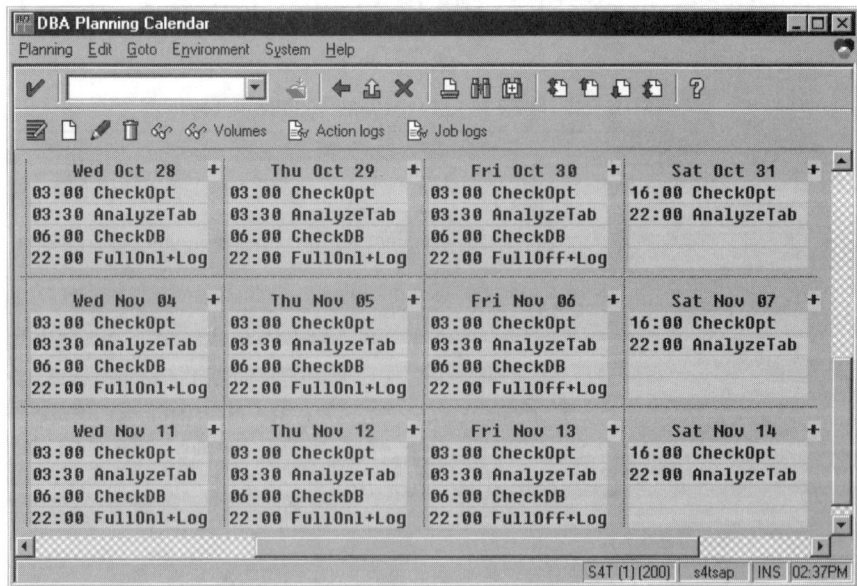

System Administration Assistant

To ensure high system availability for low operating costs, SAP developed a special tool, the System Administration Assistant. The Assistant is a hypertext checklist that displays your regular tasks for administering your R/3 Systems, the operating system, and parts of the network infrastructure (see Figure A.2). The tasks in the checklist branch into separate transactions for the CCMS or for system administration. You can also administer the two-system landscape from one system. Using a Remote Function Call (RFC), the Assistant in one system calls the selected transaction from the other system. The Assistant supports you with online help tailor-made for the RRR System. The System Administration Assistant also displays in red the tasks that are still to be processed. When you complete a task, it is displayed in green. This prevents you from overlooking any of the regular tasks.

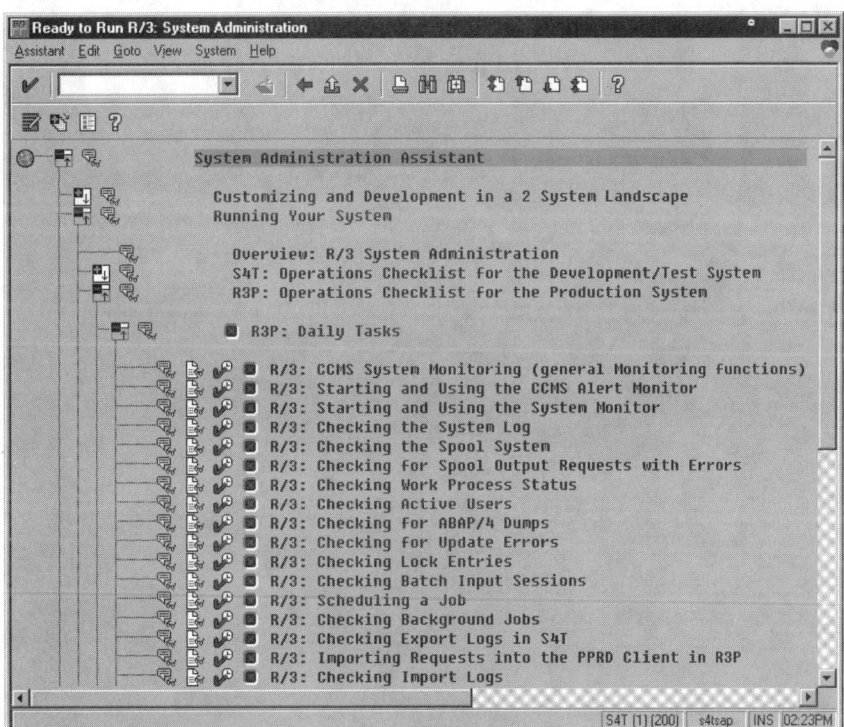

FIGURE A.2:

An excerpt from the RRR System Administration Assistant

APPENDIX B

Training Courses for the Technical Team

If a project is going to be successful, it needs a well-trained Project Team. SAP offers a broad spectrum of training courses for the entire Project Team. These courses cover a range of topics, from a general overview of the technology of R/3 to an in-depth look at R/3 System administration and performance optimization. The training courses are divided into three levels of difficulty:

Level 1 One- to two-day training courses introducing R/3 technology

Level 2 Three- to five-day training courses providing initial specialization in an area

Level 3 Three- to five-day training courses providing in-depth knowledge of an area covered by a Level 2 training course

The following three sections explain which courses are recommended for which role in the Technical Team:

- Management training courses
- Foundation training courses (Level 1)
- Basis training courses (Level 2 and Level 3)

These sections are part of the training catalog for R/3 Release 4.0. Training courses are only listed if they are relevant to the technical implementation project of an R/3 System.

> **TIP** The complete SAP training catalog and up-to-date information on the training offering can be found in SAP Online Service System (OSS) or in SAPNet at `http://sapnet.sap.com/training40`.

Management Training Courses

The management training courses are intended for decision-makers in an implementation project. SAP recommends that you attend these training courses before the start of the project. Table B.1 contains the courses, which are particularly intended for Technical Team Leads.

> **TIP** The content of the management training courses will be more easily accessible to you if you have first completed the foundation course SAP50, "Basis Technology"—see also "Foundation Training Courses (Level 1)."

TABLE B.1: Management Training Courses for R/3 Release 4.0

SAP Course	Description	Duration	Intended For
MBC20	Business Framework	2 days	Technical Team Leads
MBC30	R/3 Technical Implementation and Operation Management	2 days	Technical Team Leads
MBC40	Managing ABAP Development Projects	2 days	Technical Team Leads

Foundation Training Courses (Level 1)

The foundation training courses are intended for all the members of the Technical Team. These courses are Level 1 courses and provide an overview of R/3 technology. Table B.2 contains the relevant SAP courses from the training catalog. SAP recommends that you attend these courses at the beginning of a project.

TABLE B.2: Foundation Training Courses for R/3 Release 4.0

SAP Course	Description	Duration	Intended For
SAP50	Basis Technology	2 days	Technical Teams
SAP80	R/3 Service and Support	2 days	Technical Team Leads
SAP81	OSS Online Service System	1 days	Team members, who use OSS frequently
SAP82	Network Technology	1 days	Technical Team Leads, network administrators

Basis Training Courses (Level 2 and Level 3)

The Basis training courses include Level 2 and Level 3 courses. The following topics are of particular interest for the Technical Team:

- Administration
- Business Process Technology
- Integration Technology

Administration

The training courses for administration are divided into *core competence* (Level 2) and *expert competence* (Level 3). The core competence courses are intended for all the members of the Technical Team. These Level 2 training courses cover technical issues such as how to administer an R/3 System and ensure secure production operation. Many system administration tasks depend on the operating system and the Relational Database Management System (RDBMS) with which you are running the R/3 System. As Table B.3 shows, each course is based on a combination of operating system and RDBMS.

TABLE B.3: Level 2 Training Courses for Administration (R/3 Release 4.0)

SAP Course	Description	Duration	Intended For
BC310	Technical Core Competence Windows NT/Oracle	5 days	Technical Teams
BC312	Technical Core Competence Windows NT/Informix	5 days	Technical Teams
BC314	Technical Core Competence Windows NT/MS SQL Server	5 days	Technical Teams
BC317	Technical Core Competence Windows NT; AIX/DB2 UDB	5 days	Technical Teams
BC360	Technical Core Competence UNIX/Oracle	5 days	Technical Teams
BC361	Technical Core Competence UNIX/Informix	5 days	Technical Teams
BC362	Technical Core Competence UNIX/ADABAS	5 days	Technical Teams
BC370	Technical Core Competence AS/400	5 days	Technical Teams
BC390	Technical Core Competence OS/390	5 days	Technical Teams

The expert competence courses provide in-depth coverage of specific areas from the core competence courses. As Table B.4 shows, the training courses address the different roles within the Technical Team. Courses for database administration are available for each RDBMS supported.

TABLE B.4: Level 3 Training Courses for Administration (R/3 Release 4.0)

SAP Course	Description	Duration	Intended For
BC305	Advanced R/3 System Management	3 days	R/3 System administrators, authorization administrators
BC315	Workload Analysis	3 days	R/3 System administrators, performance specialists
BC325	Software Logistics	3 days	R/3 System administrators, database administrators
BC340	Going Live	2 days	Technical Team Leads, R/3 System administrators, database administrators
BC505	Database Administration/ Oracle	3 days	Database administrators
BC511	Database Administration/ Informix	5 days	Database administrators
BC515	Database Administration/ ADABAS	2 days	Database administrators
BC520	Database Administration/ SQL Server	3 days	Database administrators
BC525	Database Administration/ DB2/400	3 days	Database administrators
BC530	Database Administration/ DB2/390	3 days	Database administrators
BC535	Database Administration/ DB2 UDB	3 days	Database administrators

Business Process Technology

If you are implementing the functions of SAP Business Workflow, the courses on Business Process Technology will be of particular interest for your Technical Team. Table B.5 shows the Level 2 training course on this topic. This course teaches you the fundamental concepts of Business Workflow and how to work with the available functions.

TABLE B.5: Level 2 Training Course for Business Process Technology (R/3 Release 4.0)

SAP Course	Description	Duration	Intended For
BC600	SAP Business Workflow Introduction	2 days	Technical Team Leads, Technical Teams

The Level 3 training courses teach you in detail about the individual products. You'll learn how to configure the standard R/3 System for your specific Business Process Technology requirements and how to administer the R/3 System after the start of production. As Table B.6 shows, the training courses address the different roles within the Technical Team.

TABLE B.6: Level 3 Training Courses for Business Process Technology (R/3 Release 4.0)

SAP Course	Description	Duration	Intended For
BC601	SAP Business Workflow— Definition and Usage	3 days	System administrators, authorization administrators
BC602	SAP Business Workflow— Integrating Forms with SAPforms	2 days	Software developers
BC610	SAP Business Workflow— Programming	3 days	Software developers
BC615	Archiving Technology	3 days	Technical Team Leads, R/3 System administrators
BC616	SAP ArchiveLink—Applications	2 days	R/3 System administrators, software developers

Continued on next page

TABLE B.6: Level 3 Training Courses for Business Process Technology (R/3 Release 4.0) *(Continued)*

SAP Course	Description	Duration	Intended For
BC620	SAP IDoc Interface (Standard)	2 days	R/3 System administrators, software developers
BC621	SAP IDoc Interface (Development)	1 days	Software developers
BC630	SAP Business Communication	3 days	R/3 System administrators, network administrators

Integration Technology

Training courses for technical aspects of the interfaces are grouped under Integration Technology. In these courses, you'll learn how to design, implement, and maintain the interfaces between individual R/3 components or to external systems. The Level 2 courses on this subject are replaced by the two Knowledge Product CDs:

- SAP Integration Technology
- Interface Adviser

> **TIP**
> To find out about SAP's Knowledge Product CDs offering and how to order your CDs, visit SAPNet at `http://sapnet.sap.com/EducationServices` and choose R/3 Knowledge-Products.

The Level 3 training courses give you in-depth information about the individual interface technologies. You'll learn how to develop interface programs for your requirements. Table B.7 lists the training courses and shows the roles within the Technical Team to which they are suited.

TABLE B.7: Level 3 Training Courses for Integration Technology (R/3 Release 4.0)

SAP Course	Description	Duration	Intended For
BC210	Interface Programming in C/C++	3 days	Software developers
BC215	Interface Programming with SAPAutomation	3 days	Software developers
BC415	Interface Programming in ABAP	3 days	Software developers
BC420	Interfaces for Data Transfer	2 days	R/3 System administrators, network administrators
BC440	Developing Internet Application Components (IAC)	5 days	Software developers
BC925	Programming BAPIs with Visual Basic	5 days	Software developers
BC926	Programming BAPIs with Java	5 days	Software developers
BC927	Programming BAPIs with C++	5 days	Software developers

APPENDIX C

SAP Service & Support for the Technical Team

SAP Service & Support is available worldwide 24 hours a day. It offers you all the support you need to ensure optimal R/3 operation. *SAP Local Support* for each subsidiary is your first point of contact. Here, your questions are received in the local language. If you report a problem, Local Support processes it first. If Local Support cannot provide a solution, the problem is passed to one of the *Regional Support Centers* that have been set up in each region of the world. If a conclusive solution still cannot be provided, the problem is passed on to the SAP development department in one of the *Development Support Centers*. In addition to support, SAP offers Consulting Services. These services are delivered by SAP experts to enable you to further improve the quality of the implementation project and production operation.

The following three sections explain which SAP Service & Support offerings play an important part for the Technical Team during the implementation project and at the start of production:

- Online Service System and SAPNet
- GoingLive Check
- EarlyWatch Service

> **TIP** The complete SAP Service & Support offering and up-to-date information can be found in SAPNet at `http://sapnet.sap.com` under the keyword Service.

The Online Service System (OSS) and SAPNet

The *Online Service System (OSS)* is an interactive connection between SAP and its customers and partners. Customers can search for solutions in a comprehensive Notes database, download patches such as Hot Packages, and create problem messages and send them immediately to SAP Support.

In addition to OSS, customers and partners can access detailed information about SAP and SAP software through *SAPNet*. SAPNet also allows you to download online corrections to your system or to participate in forums with other customers. For example, you can access Self Service to order brochures or book training courses.

Remote Connection

To be able to use OSS and SAPNet, you need a remote connection to SAP. Table C.1 lists the function brochures that explain how to set up a remote connection and what points you need to consider.

TABLE C.1: Function Brochures for a Remote Connection to SAP

Brochure	Order Number
Remote Connection to the R/3 Online Services	5000 9179 (English)
	5000 9178 (German)
SAProuter	5001 1968 (English)
	5001 1967 (German)
SAP Network Security for Remote Services	5001 2924 (English)
	5001 2925 (German)

If you already have a remote connection, Table C.2 lists some R/3 Notes that cover this topic in greater depth.

TABLE C.2: R/3 Notes for Remote Connections to SAP

Note No.	Short Text
14716	Questions about X.25, ISDN, remote connection to SAP
28976	Remote Connection Data Sheet
30289	SAProuter Documentation
31515	Service Connections
33953	Network Providers for OSS Connection
35010	Service Connections: Composite Note (overview)
46902	Security Aspects in Remote Access
48243	Integrating SAProuter into a Firewall
50430	Official IP Addresses for SAP Access
66687	Use of Network Security Products

Using OSS

Two brochures explain in detail how to work with OSS. Table C.3 contains their titles and order numbers.

TABLE C.3: Function Brochures for Using OSS

Brochure	Order Number
Logging on to OSS	5001 1970 (English)
	5001 1969 (German)
Function brochure	5001 2923 (English)
	5001 2922 (German)

Table C.4 shows the R/3 Notes that can assist you with specific questions about using OSS.

TABLE C.4: R/3 Notes about Working with OSS

Note No.	Short Text
17285	Logon to OSS (Transaction OSS1)
18554	Registration Form: New OSS users
22072	New Logon Procedure for OSS
29501	General Procedure for Note and Message Search OSS
64410	What is the OSS Corporate Function?
64417	OSS Corporate Function: Collective Note
69378	Inbox BIBO in OSS/O01
78040	New OSS Inbox: History of Problems, Substitution...
74313	Customer Messages in OSS
75686	OSS - Deleting or Changing Users/Installations
80618	Access to OSS Services via the Internet
86657	Filter Definition in a Message Search in the OSS
94569	Note Search
105625	Add. Info on OSS User Administration for CCCs

SAP Service & Support

Table C.5 contains R/3 Notes with further information and contacts for SAP Service & Support. These Notes explain how to contact the SAP Local Support of your subsidiary and how Consulting and Support are separated.

TABLE C.5: R/3 Notes for R/3 Service & Support

Note No.	Short Text
23128	Form for Reporting Production Dates
38054	Information on Production Customer Services
38373	Local Support (HelpDesk): Telephone and Fax
39507	Customer Check List for Production Startup
46742	Priority 1 Support Generally Available
83020	What is Consulting - What is Support?

The GoingLive Check

The goal of the GoingLive Check is to help you ensure that your start of production is trouble-free and efficient. SAP experts check the settings and situations that can cause problems with many users in production operation. Through a remote connection, the experts log on to client 066 of your production system and ensure that you can start production without any problems. You are sent detailed reports that include recommendations on how to further optimize your technical settings.

> **NOTE** Detailed information about the GoingLive Check and how you can request it is available in SAPNet at `http://sapnet.sap.com/GoingLiveCheck`. If you do not have access to the Internet, SAP Local Support for your region's SAP subsidiary will be able to assist you.

Analysis, Optimization, and Verification

The GoingLive Check consists of three sessions: Analysis, Optimization, and Verification (see "Perform the GoingLive Check" in Chapter 1). As Figure C.1 shows, the Analysis session occurs during the Final Preparation phase and thus about eight weeks before the actual start of production. You should schedule the subsequent Optimization session for about four weeks before the start of production. In the final session, Verification, the experts check to determine whether all the recommendations from the previous sessions will be effective for production operation. SAP recommends that you schedule this session for four weeks after the start of production.

FIGURE C.1:

Schedule for the GoingLive Check in ASAP

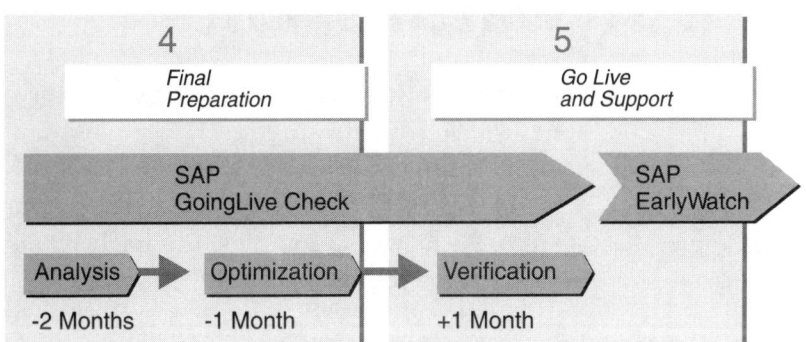

Requirements

To be able to take advantage of the GoingLive Check, you need a remote connection to SAP that is secured with an SAProuter. SAP recommends that you request the GoingLive Check at least three months before the start of production. This enables SAP to ensure that the required resources are available.

Data Security

The security of your data is ensured at all times throughout the sessions. You control the connection to SAP and decide when to open the connection and for what period of time. For a GoingLive session, an SAP expert logs on to client 066 of your production system with the EARLYWATCH user. You control the password for this user. SAP recommends that you change the password after each session. During the session, you can track the R/3 transactions the EARLYWATCH user is calling on your screen. This user cannot access your production data because application data from other clients is not visible in client 066.

The EarlyWatch Service

The EarlyWatch Service aims to continuously improve the response behavior of your production R/3 System and thus increase the user acceptance for the R/3 System. This service combines a technical analysis of both the Basis and the applications of your R/3 System. As Figure C.2 shows, the EarlyWatch Service experts analyze the Basis to make sure the operating system parameters are set correctly, the database is configured correctly, and the workload is optimally distributed over the available resources.

In a technical analysis of the applications in your R/3 System, the SAP experts focus on your most important business processes. For example, from a technical viewpoint, important background jobs such as Material Requirements Planning are analyzed and processing is gradually improved if necessary. After an EarlyWatch session, you are sent a detailed report, which includes recommendations on how to further optimize your technical settings.

FIGURE C.2:

Components of the EarlyWatch Service Basis analysis

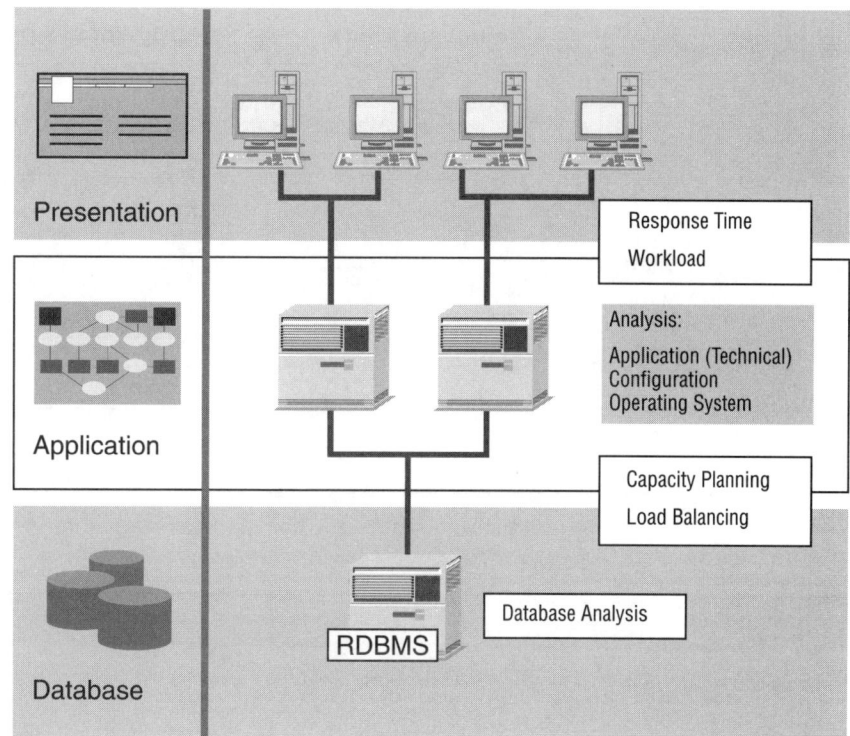

> **NOTE** Detailed information about the EarlyWatch Service and how to request it is available in SAPNet at `http://sapnet.sap.com/EarlyWatch`. If you do not have access to the Internet, SAP Local Support for your region's SAP subsidiary will be able to assist you.

Unlike the GoingLive Check, the EarlyWatch Service consists of individual sessions. You can request the sessions individually or as a package consisting of several sessions held at regular intervals. Whereas the GoingLive Check prepares you for the start of production, the EarlyWatch Service is aimed at the subsequent production operation. Table C.6 shows the differences between the two services.

TABLE C.6: Differences between the GoingLive Check and the EarlyWatch Service

	GoingLive Check	**EarlyWatch Service**
Application	Optimizes the central business processes (for example, Create Sales Document)	Optimizes the central background processing (for example, Material Requirements Planning) on a step-by-step basis Optimizes the most frequent requests to the database on a step-by-step basis
Basis	Performs a plausibility check for sizing Optimizes the system configuration for the start of production	Optimally distributes the workload on the R/3 System over the resources Plans capacity Analyzes bottleneck and performance

> **NOTE** As with the GoingLive Check, to take advantage of the EarlyWatch Service, you need a remote connection to SAP.

APPENDIX D

Glossary

ABAP

Advanced Business Application Programming. The programming language of the R/3 System.

ABAP Dictionary

Central metadata of all objects in the R/3 System. (The term *metadata* refers to data about the data.)

ACID

Describes the basic attributes of transaction management for the database and R/3: Atomic, Consistency, Isolation, and Durability.

activity group

Subset of actions from the set of actions that were defined in the Enterprise IMG. From the activity group, you can use the Profile Generator to generate the authorizations needed by R/3 users for these actions.

ADK

Archive Development Kit. Contains tools to define related business data to a logical archiving unit (archiving object), methods for transferring the data to be archived to an archive file in the form of function modules, example programs, documentation, archive administration to start programs, data transfer, and network graphics representing the interdependencies between data that can be archived.

ADO

Application-defined object.

ALE

Application Link Enabling. ALE is a technology for building and operating distributed applications. The basic purpose of ALE is to ensure a distributed—but integrated—R/3 installation. It comprises a controlled business message exchange with consistent data storage in non-permanently connected SAP applications.

Applications are integrated not through a central database but through synchronous and asynchronous communication. ALE consists of three layers: application services, distribution services, and communication services.

Alert Monitor

Graphical monitor for analyzing system states and events.

ANSI

American National Standards Institute.

API

Application Programming Interface. The software package used by an application program to call a service provided by the operating system, for example, to open a file.

APPC

Program-to-program communication within the IBM world. Based on the LU6.2 protocol.

application server

A computer on which at least one R/3 instance runs.

ArchiveLink

Integrated into the Basis component of the R/3 System, a communications interface between the R/3 applications and external components. ArchiveLink has the following interfaces: user interface; interface to the R/3 applications; and interface to external components (archive systems, viewer systems, and scan systems).

archiving object

A logical object comprising related business data in the database that is read from the database using an archiving program. After it has been successfully archived, a logical object can be deleted by a specially generated deleting program.

ASAP

AcceleratedSAP. Standardized procedural model to implement R/3.

background processing

Processing that does not take place on the screen. Data is processed in the background, while other functions can be executed in parallel on the screen. Although the background processes are not visible for a user, and run without user intervention (there is no dialog), they have the same priority as online processes.

BAPI

Business Application Programming Interface. Standardized programming interface that provides external access to business processes and data in the R/3 System.

Batch Input

Method and tools for rapid import of data from sequential files into the R/3 database.

button

Element of the graphical user interface. Click a button to execute the button's function. You can select buttons using the keyboard as well as the mouse. Place the button cursor on the button and select Enter or choose the Enter button. Buttons can contain text or graphical symbols.

CATT

Computer-Aided Test Tool. You can use this tool to generate test data and to automate and test business processes.

CCMS

Computing Center Management System. Tools for monitoring, controlling, and configuring the R/3 System. The CCMS supports 24-hour system administration functions from within the R/3 System. You can use it to analyze the system load and monitor the distributed resource usage of the system components.

CET

Client Components Enabling Technology.

client

From a commercial law, organizational, and technical viewpoint, a closed unit within an R/3 System with separate master records within a table.

CO

Customizing Organizer. Tool to administer change and transport requests of all types in an R/3 System.

Control Panel

Central tool for monitoring the R/3 System and its instances.

CPI-C

Common Programming Interface-Communication. Programming interface, the basis for synchronous, system-to-system, program-to-program communication.

CTO

Change and Transport Organizing Method used to manage changes and development in the R/3 System, as well as their transport to other R/3 Systems.

Customizing

Adjusting the R/3 System to specific customer requirements by selecting variants, parameter settings, etc.

DAS

Data Striping Array (RAID 1).

data archiving

Removing data that is currently not needed from the R/3 database and storing it in archives (see also *archiving object*).

database

A database is made up of files that are needed for permanently storing data on the hard disk and one or more database instances. Each R/3 System has only one database. There is normally only one database instance for each database. DB2/390 and Oracle Parallel Server are database systems for which a database can be made up of multiple database instances. In an R/3 System a database instance can either be alone on a single computer or together with one (or theoretically more) R/3 instance(s).

database instance

An administrative unit that allows access to a database. A database instance consists of database processes with a common set of database buffers in the shared memory.

database server

A computer with at least one database instance.

DBA

Database administrator.

DCL

Data Control Language. Language commands to control user transactions.

DDL

Data Definition Language. Language commands to define relationships.

deadlock

Blocking of multiple transactions that are each waiting for locked objects to be released.

DIAG protocol

The communication protocol between SAPGUI and dialog work processes on the instance.

dialog work process

R/3 work process used to process requests from users working online.

Dispatcher

The process that coordinates the work processes of an instance.

DML

Data Manipulation Language. Language commands to query and change data.

Dynpro

The DYNamic PROgram that consists of a screen and the underlying process logic.

EDI

Electronic Data Interchange. Intercompany electronic interchange of structured data (for example, business documents) between business partners in the home country and abroad who may be using different hardware, software, and communication services.

Enterprise IMG

Company-specific Implementation Guide.

entity

Uniquely identifiable real or imaginary. The connections between entities are described by relationships.

FDDI

Fiber Distributed Data Interchange.

firewall

Software to protect a local network from unauthorized access from outside.

front-end computer

A computer or CPU that generates and manipulates data before that data is passed to another process.

GUI

Graphical User Interface. The medium through which a user can exchange information with the computer. You use the GUI to select commands, start programs, display files, and perform other operations by selecting function keys or buttons, menu options, and icons with the mouse.

high availability

Property of a service or a system that remains in production operation for most of the time. High availability for an R/3 System means that unplanned and planned downtimes are reduced to a minimum. Good system administration is decisive here. You can reduce unplanned downtime by using preventive hardware and software solutions that are designed to reduce single points of failure in the services that support the R/3 System. You can reduce the planned downtime by optimized scheduling of necessary maintenance activities.

Hot Package

Delivered by SAP, software corrections or enhancements for a specific R/3 release.

HSM

Hierarchical Storage Management. Software and hardware for archiving data.

HTML

HyperText Markup Language.

HTTP

HyperText Transfer Protocol. Protocol used between a Web server and the Web client.

IAC

Internet Application Components.

IDA

Independent Disk Array (RAID 5).

IDES

International Demo and Education System. IDES contains multiple model companies, which map the relevant business processes of the R/3 System. Using simple user guidelines and different master and transaction data, scenarios with large data volumes can be tested. IDES is therefore well suited as a training tool to assist in instructing project teams.

IDoc

Internal Document. An IDoc type filled with real data.

IDoc type

Internal Document SAP format, into which the data of a business process is transferred. An IDoc is a real business process formatted in the IDoc type. An IDoc type is described by the following components:

- A control record. Its format is identical for all IDoc types.

- One or more records. A record consists of a fixed administration segment and the data segment. The number and format of the segments differs for different IDoc types.

- Status records. These records describe stages of processing that an IDoc can go through. The status records have the same format for all IDoc types.

IMG

Implementation Guide. A tool for making customer-specific adjustments to the R/3 System. For each application component, the Implementation Guide contains:

- All steps to implement the R/3 System

- All default settings and all activities to configure the R/3 System

- A hierarchical structure that maps the structure of the R/3 application components

- Lists of all the documentation relevant to the implementation of the R/3 System

instance

R/3 instance. Administrative unit that groups together components of an R/3 System that offer one or more services. An R/3 instance can provide the following services:

D—Dialog

V—Update

E—SAP lock management (Enqueue)

B—Background processing (Background)

S—Printing (Spool)

G—SAP Gateway

An R/3 instance consists of a Dispatcher and one or more work processes for each of the services, as well as a common set of R/3 buffers in the shared memory.

The Dispatcher manages the processing requests. Work processes execute the requests. Each instance provides at least one dialog service and a gateway. An instance can provide further services. Only one instance can be available that provides the service SAP lock management. In accordance with this definition, there can be two (or more) R/3 instances on an application server. This means that if there are two or more instances on one server, there are the same number of Dispatchers.

IPC

Interprocess Communication.

IS

Industry Solution. Industry-specific applications for R/3, for example, IS-H (IS Hospital), IS-RE (IS Real Estate), or IS-PS (IS Public Sector) are ISs.

ISAPI

Microsoft Information Server API.

ITS

Internet Transaction Server. The gateway between the R/3 System and the World Wide Web.

LAN

Local area network.

LUW

Logical unit of work. From the viewpoint of R/3, an indivisible sequence of database operations that conform to the ACID maxims. From the viewpoint of a database system, this sequence represents a unit that plays a decisive role in securing data integrity.

MAPI

Messaging Application Programming Interface.

MIME

Multipurpose Internet Mail Extensions.

NSAPI

Netscape Server API.

OLE

Object Linking and Embedding.

OLTP

Online Transaction Processing.

OMS

Output Management System.

Operation mode

Defined number and type of work processes of one or more instances in a particular time period. Operation modes can be switched automatically.

OS

Operating system.

OSS

Online Service System. OSS is SAP's central service and support system. OSS can be used by all SAP's customers and partners.

PAI

Process after Input. Technical program processes after data is entered in a screen in R/3.

PBO

Process before Output. Technical program processes before a screen is output in R/3.

performance

Measurement of the efficiency of an IT system. The synonym for this is *throughput*.

pop-up window

A window that is called from a primary window and that is displayed in front of that window.

port

Term used for the channel through which the R/3 System exchanges data with an external system.

Profile Generator

Automatically generates an authorization profile based on the activities in an activity group.

Q-API

Queue Application Programming Interface. The interface to buffered, asynchronous data transfer between decentralized applications and R/2 and R/3 SAP systems, based on CPI-C.

R/3

Runtime System 3.

RAID

Redundant Array of Inexpensive Disks. Hardware-based technology that supports disk redundancy through disk mirroring and related methods.

RDBMS

Relational Database Management System.

RFC

Remote Function Call. RFC is an SAP interface protocol, based on CPIC. It allows the programming of communication processes between systems to be simplified considerably. Using RFCs, predefined functions can be called and executed in a remote system or within the same system. RFCs are used for communication control, parameter passing, and error handling.

SAPGUI

SAP Graphical User Interface. (*See* GUI.)

SAProuter

A software module that functions as part of a firewall system.

server

The term *server* has multiple meanings in the SAP environment. It should therefore only be used if it is clear whether it means a logical unit, such as an R/3 instance; or a physical unit, such as a computer.

session

A user session in a SAPGUI window.

Session Manager

The tool used for central control of R/3 applications. The Session Manager is a graphical navigation interface used to manage sessions and start application transactions. It can generate both company-specific and user-specific menus. The Session Manager is available from R/3 Release 3.0C under Windows 95 and Windows NT.

shared memory

Main memory area, which can be accessed by all work processes in an instance. Also used in the RDBMS. The term *shared memory* is used to also mean the main memory area shared by the RDBMS processes.

SID

SAP System Identifier. Placeholder for the three-character name of an R/3 System.

SQL

Structured Query Language.

SSCR

SAP Software Change Registration. A procedure for registering manual changes to SAP sources and SAP Repository Objects.

SUSE

Self-Upgrading Software Environment.

system landscape

A real system constellation installed at a customer site. The system landscape describes the required systems and clients, their meanings, and the transport paths for implementation and maintenance. Of the methods used, client copy and the transport system are particularly important. For example, the system landscape could consist of a development system, a test system, a consolidation system, and a production system.

TCP/IP

Transmission Control Protocol/Internet Protocol.

TDC

Transport domain controller. Application server of an R/3 System in the transport domain, from which transport activities between the R/3 Systems in the transport domain are controlled.

TemSe

Temporary sequential objects. Data storage for output management.

TMS

Transport Management System. Tool for managing transport requests between R/3 Systems.

TO

Transport Organizer. Tool for managing all the change and transport requests with more extensive functionality than the CO and the WBO.

transaction code

Code (consisting of four alphanumeric characters) that is used to call an R/3 Transaction directly.

transport

Term from software logistics in R/3: Data export and import between R/3 Systems.

transport domain

Logical group of R/3 Systems between which data is transported in accordance with fixed rules. The transport domain controller exercises control over the transport domain.

tRFC

Transactional RFC. Remote Function Control to which the ACID principles are applied.

URL

Uniform Resource Locator.

WAN

Wide area network.

WBO

Workbench Organizer. Tool for managing change and transport requests that are generated from the use of the ABAP Workbench.

WORM

Write Once, Read Multiple. Storage medium that can be written once and read any number of times. WORM ensures that data stored cannot be changed and that it will be intact for many years. It is primarily used for data archiving.

WP

Work process. The application services of the R/3 System have special processes, for example, for dialog administration, updating change documents, background processing, spool processing, and lock management. Work processes can be assigned to dedicated application servers.

APPENDIX E

Review Questions and Answers

Chapter 2: Technology in R/3

1. Which work processes exist in R/3?

    A. Dialog

    B. Update

    C. Message

    D. Enqueue

    E. Background

    F. Gateway

    G. Spool

   Answer: A, B, D, E, G

2. Which statements are correct?

    A. The update service allows users to work more quickly in dialog.

    B. Each dialog work process requires its own update work process.

    C. A dialog step in a transaction marks the data for the update.

    D. The update service requires the necessary locks from the enqueue service so that no other user can change the same data.

   Answer: A, C

3. Which work processes have direct access to the lock table?

    A. All work processes

    B. All work processes on the enqueue server

    C. Only the enqueue work process

    D. All dialog work processes

   Answer: B

4. Which statements are correct?

    A. A job consists of one or more steps. Each step is scheduled to start automatically at a specified time.

    B. A job consists of one or more steps. Each step calls either an ABAP program or an external program.

    C. The background scheduler starts the scheduled jobs automatically. A background work process processes a job's steps.

    D. Only special ABAP programs can be scheduled as jobs. For example, ABAP programs that generate large lists cannot be scheduled as jobs.

Answer: B, C

5. Which work processes log on to the database when R/3 is started?

    A. All work processes

    B. All work processes except the enqueue work process

    C. Only the work processes of the central instance

    D. Only the dialog, background, and update work processes

Answer: A

6. Through which protocol do front ends and application servers communicate?

    A. UUCP (UNIX to UNIX Copy Protocol)

    B. IPX/SPX (Internet Packet Exchange/Sequential Packet Exchange)

    C. TCP/IP (Transmission Control Protocol/Internet Protocol)

    D. NetBIOS (Network Basic Input Output System)

Answer: C

7. Through which protocol does an R/3 System communicate with an R/2 System on an MVS/VSE Mainframe?

   A. SNA LU6.2
   B. TCP/IP
   C. DCAM

   Answer: A

8. Which statements are correct?

   A. A client has its own users and its own tables in the database. You can change them from other clients through application functions.
   B. All R/3 data is divided into client-dependent and client-independent data.
   C. A client has its own ABAP programs and ABAP Dictionary data.
   D. A client is an independent unit, from a business viewpoint as well as from an organizational viewpoint.

   Answer: B, D

9. Which statements are correct?

   A. At the beginning of a Customizing project, the Project Manager creates a change request and assigns the Project Team members to it. Tasks are only generated for the assigned team members.
   B. To correct errors, you can reverse the release of a task and change your settings in the old task.
   C. Employees with developer authorization may change all ABAP programs in a development system.
   D. Each Repository object is linked with the name of the system in which it is generated. For example, all Repository objects that SAP delivers belong to one system called SAP.

   Answer: A, D

Chapter 3: Project Administration

1. Which roles must be occupied in a Technical Team?

    A. Operating system administrator

    B. Technical Team Lead

    C. Training Manager

    D. Network administrator

    E. R/3 System administrator

    F. Database administrator

    G. Authorization administrator

    Answer: A, B, D, E, F, G

2. Which consulting service helps you find potential performance bottlenecks in your R/3 System?

    A. Remote Archiving

    B. EarlyWatch

    C. Remote Upgrade

    D. Conversion Service

    Answer: B

3. When do you begin planning the Cut Over?

    A. During the Project Preparation phase

    B. At the end of the Business Blueprint phase

    C. During the Realization phase

    Answer: C

Chapter 4: Front-End Administration

1. Which operating systems are supported by SAP for SAPGUI Release 4.0?

    A. Microsoft Windows 95

    B. Microsoft Windows NT 4

    C. Unix/Motif

    D. OS/2

    E. Linux

    F. Windows emulations

    G. Windows NT (Alpha Processor)

    H. Apple Macintosh

    Answer: A, B, C, D, H

2. Which statements are correct?

    A. As of R/3 Release 4.0, you can include OLE-enabled office applications through ABAP objects on all supported platforms.

    B. You can start an office application from R/3 or react to the results of the application in R/3.

    C. You can directly access the tables of the R/3 database from office applications through the ODBC interface. SAP recommends read-only accesses to tables through ODBC.

    D. You can bypass the authorization check in R/3 and the processing logic in R/3 with the office applications that are integrated through ABAP objects.

    Answer: B, C

3. Which options do you have to install the front-end software?

    A. Install the software locally on the front ends.

    B. Install the software centrally on a file server.

C. Install all components of the front-end software without selecting individual options.

D. Install the software on the front ends without dialog using system management tools.

Answer: A, B, D

4. Which statements are correct?

   A. As of Release 4.0A, SAP has HTML-based online documentation.

   B. The HTML files in the online documentation must reside on every front end.

   C. For the installation of the online documentation, you can choose between two types of help: PlainHtmlFile and HtmlHelpFile.

   D. You can use a Web browser to display the HTML-based online documentation on all supported front-end platforms.

Answer: A, D

Chapter 5: R/3 Instance Administration

1. What are the important things to consider when you select your hardware?

   A. The minimum hardware requirements must be met.

   B. You must be able to expand your hardware.

   C. The instances in an R/3 System should run on different hardware platforms.

   D. Hardware sizing is the same for all R/3 Releases.

Answer: A, B

2. Which statements are correct?

   A. At least two dialog work processes must run on each instance.

   B. At least one enqueue work process must run on each instance.

   C. Only one spool work process can run on each instance.

   D. At least one update work process must run in each R/3 System.

   Answer: A, D

3. Which statements are correct?

   A. You can only monitor the R/3 instances with the Alert Monitor.

   B. You can divide the entire monitoring object tree structure into partial tree structures.

   C. You can monitor all the systems in your system landscape from one system with the Alert Monitor.

   D. The Alert Monitor only displays two statuses for a monitoring object: a red alert for an error and a green alert if everything is okay.

   Answer: B, C

Chapter 6: User Administration

1. Which statements are correct?

   A. User master records are client dependent.

   B. User master records can only be created in client 000.

   C. Activity groups are client dependent.

D. Activity groups cannot be transported between systems.

Answer: A, C

2. Which statements are correct?

   A. To log on to R/3, you must know a user name and password.

   B. A password can be used without restriction.

   C. Users can be locked if they enter their password incorrectly too many times.

   D. The validity period of a password is changeable.

Answer: A, C, D

3. What is the activity group administrator authorized to do?

   A. Create activity groups

   B. Maintain authorization fields

   C. Generate authorizations

   D. Change users

   E. Allocate agents to the activity group

Answer: A, B

4. Which special users are there in R/3?

   A. SAP*

   B. SAPDBA

   C. EARLYWATCH

   D. GOINGLIVE

   E. DDIC

   F. SUPER

Answer: A, C, E

Chapter 7: Background Processing

1. Which statements are correct?

    A. R/3 controls the priority of jobs with the three job classes A, B, and C.

    B. The jobs from class C have a higher priority than the jobs from class B.

    C. The jobs from one job class can only run on one instance.

    D. Work processes can be reserved for each job class.

    Answer: A

2. Which statements are correct?

    A. In the standard R/3 System, it is possible to have job chains with jobs that can trigger multiple successors.

    B. In the standard R/3 System, it is possible to schedule a repetition period for a job chain.

    C. The Job API enables more job chains to be used.

    D. R/3 has a standardized interface through which the external job management system can connect to the R/3 System.

    Answer: A, C, D

3. What can R/3 users do without special authorization for jobs?

    A. Schedule jobs from class B and C.

    B. Display or change the steps in their own jobs.

    C. Display or change jobs that have been planned by users in their own activity group.

    D. Release their own jobs.

    E. Display the details of their own jobs.

    Answer: B, E

Chapter 8: Print Administration

1. Which statements are correct?

    A. As of R/3 Release 4.0, one or more spool work processes can run on an instance.

    B. You can use operation modes to switch the number of spool work processes.

    C. At least one spool work process should be running in the R/3 System.

   Answer: A, C

2. To which classes can printers be allocated?

    A. Test print

    B. Production print

    C. Bar-code print

    D. Desktop print

    E. High-volume print

    F. Device pool print

   Answer: A, B, D, E

3. Which statements are correct?

    A. Only one logical server can be allocated to each physical spool server.

    B. An alternative server can be allocated to a logical server.

    C. Logical servers are only available for production printers.

    D. You can import the settings for the logical server into other R/3 Systems by using the transport system.

   Answer: B, D

4. Which access modes are not recommended for printers with time-critical output?

   A. C, local printer on a Windows NT computer or AS/400

   B. L, local printer on a UNIX computer

   C. U, remote printer on LPDHOST through Berkeley protocol

   D. S, remote printer on LPDHOST through SAP protocol

   E. F, printer on a front end

Answer: C, D, E

Chapter 9: Database Administration

1. Which RAID level does SAP recommend for the R/3 database?

   A. RAID 1

   B. RAID 2

   C. RAID 3

   D. RAID 4

   E. RAID 5

Answer: A, E

2. Why does an RDBMS require the log files?

   A. To back up time-critical data

   B. To recover the current status of a database if an error occurs

   C. To store information about the locations of directories and files in the database

   D. To log error messages

Answer: B

3. Which statements are correct?

   A. For each data backup, you must stop the R/3 System.

   B. Between two data backups, you should back up the log files at least once.

   C. After each structural change, you should back up the database.

   D. The data backup cycle is 28 days long.

   E. Log files and data from the database must be backed up to one tape.

   Answer: B, C, D

4. Which options do you have to back up a very large database?

   A. Partially back up the database.

   B. Back up the database in parallel to multiple tapes.

   C. Back up only the log files of the database.

   D. Back up the database in two steps: first to a hard disk and then to a tape.

   Answer: A, B, D

Chapter 10: Archiving

1. Which problems can be caused by database growth?

   A. Database administration becomes more difficult.

   B. R/3 performance is negatively affected.

   C. Data backup takes too long.

   D. Release upgrades take too long.

   Answer: A, B, C, D

2. What do you use ArchiveLink for?

   A. To connect tape robots with the R/3 System

   B. To connect document management systems with the R/3 System

   C. To connect optical archives with the R/3 System

   D. To connect HSM systems with the R/3 System

   Answer: B, C

3. Which statements are correct?

   A. You can use an archiving object only to archive the data from one table.

   B. You can use an archiving object to archive the data from multiple tables.

   C. A table can have a maximum of one archiving object.

   D. A table can have multiple archiving objects.

   Answer: B, D

Chapter 11: Network Administration

1. Which statements are correct?

   A. A server network should consist of multiple LAN subnetworks.

   B. A backbone network should be connected with the server network or the application servers through at least two paths.

   C. A backbone network should only be used for communication between the R/3 System and subnetworks.

   D. A front-end network cannot contain any WAN connections.

   Answer: B, C

2. Which factors play a role in determining the bandwidth of the front-end network?

    A. The load on the connection that is generated by the data stream between front ends and application servers

    B. The number of all the front ends in the network

    C. The number of all the users in the R/3 System

    D. The users' average thinking time between two dialog steps

    Answer: A, D

3. What do you need for a remote connection to SAP?

    A. A router

    B. The SAProuter utility

    C. An official IP address

    D. An X.25, X.31, Frame Relay, or ISDN connection

    Answer: A, B, C, D

Chapter 12: Software Logistics

1. What are the advantages of a two-system landscape?

    A. A stable runtime environment for production operation.

    B. A stable runtime environment for quality assurance.

    C. The production data is protected against unauthorized access by developers.

    Answer: A, C

2. For which data can you allow or deny changes using the system change options?

    A. All R/3 data

    B. All client-dependent data

C. All client-independent data

D. All Repository objects

E. All Customizing data

Answer: C, D

3. Why do you require an SCCR key?

   A. To be able to develop your own programs in the R/3 System

   B. To be able to modify standard R/3 programs in the R/3 System

   C. To be able to import patches into an R/3 System from the OSS

   D. To be authorized to use the transactions SPDD and SPAU

   Answer: B

4. Which tools does ASAP recommend for organizing a Customizing project?

   A. Change and Transport Organizer

   B. Customizing Organizer

   C. ABAP Workbench

   D. Workbench Organizer

   E. Implementation Guide

   Answer: A, B, E

5. Which statement is correct?

   A. The SAP front-end software Release has backward compatibility and therefore can be newer than the R/3 Release.

   B. The SAP front-end software Release must be the same as the R/3 Release.

C. The SAP front-end software Release has upward compatibility and therefore can be older than the R/3 Release.

Answer: A

Chapter 13: Interfaces

1. On which layers of the client/server architecture does R/3 have interfaces?

    A. Presentation layer

    B. Application layer

    C. Database layer

    Answer: A, B, C

2. Which interface technology can you implement on the application layer?

    A. BAPI

    B. OLE

    C. ALE

    D. RFC

    E. Batch Input

    F. CPI-C

    G. ODBC

    Answer: A, C, D, E, F

3. Which procedures and tools can you use to transfer data from an external system into the R/3 System?

    A. Legacy System Migration Workbench

    B. Batch Input

C. Direct Input

D. SAP Automation

Answer: A, B, C

Chapter 14: Security

1. Which special users are there for each RDBMS on the database layer?

    A. SAP*

    B. SAPDBA

    C. DDIC

    D. SAPR3

    E. EARLYWATCH

   Answer: D

2. How can you secure your network?

    A. Make the server network into a separate subnetwork.

    B. Only use the network services that you require to operate an R/3 System.

    C. Combine the SAProuter and a firewall.

   Answer: A, B, C

3. Which statement is correct for a Windows NT environment?

    A. Configure the database server as primary domain controller.

    B. Configure an application server as primary domain controller.

    C. Do not configure any of the R/3 servers as a domain controller.

   Answer: C

Chapter 15: High Availability

1. Which services are always SPOFs for the entire R/3 System?

    A. RDBMS

    B. Dialog service

    C. Update service

    D. Enqueue service

    E. Background service

    F. Message service

    G. Gateway service

    H. Spool service

    I. SAProuter

    Answer: A, D, F

2. What can you use to help reduce unplanned downtime?

    A. Switchover software for the database server

    B. One logon group for each R/3 instance

    C. Switchover software for the central instance

    D. Logon groups over multiple R/3 instances

    Answer: A, C, D

3. What does database reconnect mean?

    A. The work processes attempt to reestablish an interrupted connection to the database.

    B. The database processes attempt to reestablish an interrupted connection to the R/3 System.

    C. The connection to the database can be interrupted for a short time without having to stop and restart the R/3 System.

    Answer: A, C

INDEX

Note to the Reader: Throughout this index **boldface** page numbers indicate primary discussions of a topic. *Italic* page numbers indicate illustrations.

NUMBERS

2-system landscape.
  See two-system landscape
3-system landscape.
  See three-system landscape
16-bit platforms, R/3 support for, 151
24-hour dialog operation, **193**
28-day cycle, for backup, 319

A

ABAP (Advanced Business Application Programming), 66, 530
  connecting office application to R/3 system through, 154
ABAP Dictionary, 76, 530
ABAP Native SQL, 78
ABAP Open SQL, 78
ABAP Workbench, 92, **408–409**
AcceleratedSAP. *See* ASAP (AcceleratedSAP)
access modes
  for printing, **276–277**, 297
    front-end, 287
    local, 284
    remote, 286
  for server classes, 283
access to networks, ensuring for front end, **171–172**
ACID, 530
activity group administrator, 219, 228
activity groups, 34, **215**, 530
  administration, **228–233**
  activities list, 232
  planning, **220–223**
ADK (Archive Development Kit), **344–345**, 530
administrators
  expertise and high availability, 488
  super user to change master records, 229–230
  training courses for, **510–512**
ADO, 530
ADSM (ADSTART Distributed Storage Manager), 318
Advanced Business Application Programming (ABAP), 66, 530
  connecting office application to R/3 system through, 154
agents, creating user master record for, 218
ALE (application link enabling), 88, 306, 531
Alert Monitor, 29–30, 199, 531
  Basic monitor, *198*
  configuration, **195–198**
  customizing, **209–210**
  and data archiving, 353–354
  and high-availability, 489
  for printers, 290, *291*
  structure, *196*
alert threshold values, 204
alternative spool servers, example of setup, **280–281**
analysis, in GoingLive Check, **523**
ANSI, 531
ANSI X12 standard, 88
API (Application Programming Interface), 531
APPC, 531
Apple Macintosh
  as front end, 153
    recommended hardware, 148
  web browsers for online documentation, 164

Application gate, 63
Application layer, 51, **65–75**
    instances in, 176
    R/3 transaction, **65–66**, *67*
    R/3 user access to, **461**
    server network between database layer and, 465
    services, 51
    supported platforms, 18
application link enabling (ALE), 88, 306, 531
Application Programming Interface (API), 531
application servers, 531
    background scheduler on, 72
    connecting backbone directly with, 364
    data stream between SAPGUI and, 369
    maximum work processes on, 184, 185
    print server on, 283
    for printers, 270
    and server network, 363
    spool work process (SPO) on, 277, 297
    work processes per, 58
application servers per database server, 59
applications
    calling archiving from, 343
    critical jobs for, 247
    high-availability solution to prevent downtime, 482
approval procedure, for implementing interfaces, 453
Archive Development Kit (ADK), **344–345**, 530
archive files, 343
ArchiveLink interface, 345, 532
Archiver Stuck (Oracle), 311, *312*
archiving, 342
    in ASAP, **354–355**
    database, **307–308**
    procedure definition, **349–354**
        organization, **349–350**
    remote, 128
    strategy definition, **346–348**, *347*
    success factors, **355–357**
    system operation, **351–354**
Archiving authorization object, 217
archiving objects, 343, 532
    creating business process-oriented table for, **348**
    searching for table in, **352**
    searching in table for, **353**
    tables and, **351–354**
archiving run, **343–344**, *344*
ASAP (AcceleratedSAP), 335, 532
    archiving procedure, **354–355**
    tasks, 355
    background processing, **260–263**
    Business Blueprint, **6**. See also Business Blueprint
    database administration, **332–335**
    tasks, 335
    Final Preparation phase, **6**.
        See also Final Preparation phase
    front end administration, **166–169**
    tasks, 169
    Go Live and Support phase, **7**. See also Go Live and Support phase
    high-availability strategy, **489–493**
    tasks, **492–493**
    how it can help, **2–7**
    instances in, **201–207**
    Interface Adviser integration in, *442*
    interfaces, **449–452**
    tasks, **451–452**
    network administration, **377–380**
    tasks, 380
    print administration, **292–295**
    tasks, 295
    project administration, **135–140**
    tasks, **139–140**
    Project Preparation phase, **5, 7–21**. See also Project Preparation phase
        implementation strategy, **8–9**
        project organization, **10–11**
        system landscape, **12–16**
        technical requirements, **18–21**
    R/3 Services integration in, *128*
    Realization phase, **6**. See also Realization phase
    security in, **471–472**
    software logistics in, **423–428**
    technical requirements, sizing, **20**
    upgrade projects, 418
    user administration, **234–236**
        table, 236
asynchronous RFC, 85

attributes, of spool servers, 278–279
audit, recordkeeping requirements, 342
authorization
    for special users, 459
    in user master record, **214–220**
authorization administrator, 108
authorization concept, **34–36**, 458
    creating, **220–227, 429–430**
    and data loss from logical errors, 314
    interface and, 439
    for printing, **273**
    in Project Preparation phase, 234
    in Realization phase, 235
authorization fields, security and, 222–223
authorization groups, 214
authorization objects, 216
authorization profile administrator, 219, 228
authorization profiles, 214–215, **218**
    activities for administering, 232–233
    Profile Generator to create, 239
availability. *See also* high availability strategy
    of database, 303

B

backbone network, **364–365**, *365*
background processing, 246, 532
    administration, **255–260**
        releasing jobs centrally or decentrally, **256–257**
        system operation definition, **257–260**
    in ASAP, **260–263**, 263
    concept creation, **246–255**
    daily activities for monitoring, 260
    Final Preparation phase and, **262**
    job priorities definition, **249–253**
    optimizing throughput, **265–266**
    order of job processing chains for, 253
    parallel, *248*, **248–249**
    performance analysis, *265*, 265–266
    scheduling standard jobs, **264**
    and sizing, 181
    start time for, 246
    success factors, **263–266**

termination of, 259
background scheduler, 72
Background service, 51, **71–72**
    and single point of failure, 484
background work process, 57
    defining number for instance, 247
    for job class A, **250–253**
    minimum number of, 186
    rules for number allowed, 185
backup domain controller (BDC), 99
    development system as, 425
backup strategy definition, **312–325**
    downtime and, **313–315**
    hardware selection, **315–318**
    partial backups, **323**, *324*
    in Ready-to-Run R/3, 504
    schedule and tape administration, **318–321**
    for very large databases, **322–325**
backups
    of archive files, **356–357**
    of data, **31–32**, *33*
    of database and operating system, 29
    on hard disk, **324–325**
    and high-availability strategy, **490–491**
    system operation definition, **331–332**
    testing, **337**
bandwidth
    example of determining, 370
    formula, **369**
    in network planning, **367–370**
    and network success, **381**
BAPI (Business Application Programming Interface), 86, 90, 436, 532
Basic monitor, **197–198**
Basis Knowledge Products, **114–115**
Basis training courses, 114
Batch Data Communication (BDC) tables, 82
Batch Input procedure, **37, 82**, *83*, 532
    for data transfer, 444
    tools to monitor, 448
Batch Input Recorder, 445
Batch Input Sessions, *448*
BDC (backup domain controller), 99
BDC (Batch Data Communication) tables, 82
Big Bang migration, 9

BOR (Business Object Repository), 90
bottlenecks
    from log files, 309
    on spool server, 297, 298
    testing production system for, 208
browsers. *See* Web browsers
budget plan, **133–134**
buffer, 58, 188, *189*
Business Application Programming Interface (BAPI), 86, 90, 436, 532
Business Blueprint phase, 26, 106
    background processing, table, 263
    data backup strategy definition, 332
    database administration, **333**
        tasks, 335
    front end administration in, **167–168**
        table, 169
    high-availability strategy, **490–491**
        tasks, 493
    installing development system during, **395–396**
    instances administration, **202–203**
        table, 206
    interfaces, **449–450**
        tasks, 451–452
    mapping organizational structure to R/3 organization units, 437
    network administration, **378–379**
        tasks, 380
    print administration, table, 295
    print infrastructure definition, 292–293
    project administration tasks in, **137–138**
        table, 140
    project planning for, 130
    quality checks in, 135
    resources grouping in domains, 467
    security guidelines, **471**
        tasks, 473
    software logistics, **425–426**
        tasks, 428
    users' roles and tasks definition, 234–235
business components, **86–88**
Business Framework, 86, **306–307**
business integration, **88–89**
Business Object Repository (BOR), 90
business objects, **89–90**

business process-oriented description of job roles, 221
Business Process Team, 437
    role of, 10
Business Process Technology, courses on, **512–514**
button, 533

C

Call Transaction procedure, 37, **82–83**, *83*
capacity, of tape drives, **315–316**
CATT (Computer-Aided Test Tool), 533
CCMS (Computing Center Management System), 29–30. *See also* Computing Center Management System (CCMS)
CDs, Patch Collection, 415
central instance
    in distributed R/3 system, 53
    failure and lock table, 488
central R/3 systems, 8–9, 53, **54**
central user administration, 36
CET, 533
Change and Transport Organizer, **395**, 425
Change and Transport System, authorization for, 429, *430*
change request, 94
    for Development project, 95
    from patches, 416
    R/3 Release and data structure of, 400
    releasing in development system, 411–412
    schedule for transporting released, 413
    steps to transport, 16, *17*
    Technical Team responsibility for transporting, 425
    Workbench Organizer for, 409
changes, transport between systems, 395
checksum, in RAID, 304
client change options, 393, *394*
    in production system, 398
client copy tool, 233, 398–399
client-dependent data, **387–388**
client-independent data, **387–388**
client/server architecture
    layers in, 2, 50, 51
    multilayer, 52

clients, 12, 91, 533
    creating, 396
    defining, **387–393**
    in development system, 388–389, *389*
    structure in Ready-to-Run R/3, 503
    in system landscape, **14–15**
    in three-system landscape, *390*, **390–391**
cluster system, **305**
CO (Customizer Organizer), **405–406**, 533
COMMIT WORK ABAP statement, 68
Common Programming Interface-Communication (CPI-C) protocol, 73, 79
communication
    defining path for project team, **110–111**
    program-to-program, **84–86**
    through sequential files, **82–84**, *83*
communication layers, 79
completed transaction data, from legacy system, 37
component-oriented description of job roles, 221
composite profile, 218
compression of archive data, 343
Computing Center Management System (CCMS), **29–30**, 195, 553
    configuration, 203
    customizing, 330
    for database administration, 317
    database calendar in, 329
    to display table/archiving objects relationship, 351–352
    distributing background work processes by, 262
    and high-availability, 489
    to manage logon groups, 190
    and network management, 377
    open interfaces, **454**
    in Ready-to-Run R/3, 504
confidential print jobs, 273
    output procedures for, 294
configuring hardware
    printers, **23**
    standardizing for front ends, **149**
Conflict Resolution Transport patch, 415
connections, external to network, 81
Control Panel, 534
conversion services, 129

cooperative operation, 9
core competence, training courses for, 510–511
correction Releases, 44, **401–402**
    patches, 415
CPI-C (Common Programming Interface-Communication) protocol, 73, 79, 534
CPS (Customer and Partner System), **402**
CPU
    for database server, 303
    selecting for database, 336
    and work process distribution, 184
critical path tasks, **132–133**
CTO (Change and Transport Organizing), 534
currency conversion, 129
CUST client, for Customizing and program development, 396
Customer and Partner System (CPS), **402**
customer application data, database to store, 76
Customizer Organizer (CO), **405–406**, 533
Customizer role, 406–407
    authorization to define, 430
customizing, 534
Customizing project, **94**
    and data transfer, 445–446
    organizing, **405–408**
    planning, **431**
    procedure for, *407*
    roles for, **406–408**
Customizing transactions, generating hierarchical list, 405
Cut Over, **122–123**, *123*
    data transfer during, 451
    plan for, 138

D

DAS, 534
data archiving, 534
data backups, **31–32**, 33. *See also* backups
Data Dictionary objects, transaction to define modified, 421
data files, security and distribution of, 28

data loss, and downtime, 313–315
data stream, average size between SAPGUI and application server, 369
data structure of change requests, R/3 Release and, 400
data transfer plan, **442–446**, *443*
　format and, 444
　manual transfer, 443
　organizing, 445
　target concept, **443–444**
　technical design, **444**
Data Transfer Workbench, 445, *446*
database, 534–535. *See also* RDBMS (Relational Database Management System)
database access agent, **77–78**
database administrator, 108
database calendar, configuration, *329*, **329–330**, *330*
database instance, 535
Database layer, 51, **76–78**
　Repository, **76**
　SAPR3 user, **77**
　server network between application layer and, 465
　supported platforms, 18
database reconnect, **487**
database server, 535
　application servers per, 58
day operation mode, **193**
DB2, administration tools, 317
DBA, 535
DCL, 535
DDIC user, **238**, 239, 459
DDL, 535
deadlock, 535
default values, for users, 225
departments
　activity groups maintenance by, 230
　decision on job classes, 250
　job list from, 257
　print requirements, 273
　role in archiving procedure, 349, *350*
desktop printers, 274
developer authorizations
　controlling users with, 470
　and security, **462**
development classes, 95, **408–409**

development clients, automatic logging for, 431
Development project, **95–96**
Development Support Centers, 518
development system, 12, *13*, 92
　authorization concept implementation, 235
　background processing in, 246
　backups in Realization phase for, 331
　component check in, 203
　database backup, 320–321
　defining system operation for instances, 199
　installing during Business Blueprint, **395–396**
　network requirements, 360
　print jobs in, 270
　recording Customizing settings, 424
　releasing change request in, 411–412
　role of, 386
　security for, 471
　setup in Business Blueprint, 202–203
　in three-system landscape, *397*
　upgrades, 420–421
device types for output, **296–297**
DHCP (Dynamic Host Configuration Protocol), 371–372
DIAG protocol, 535
Dialog service, 51, **66–68**
　and single point of failure, 484
dialog work process (DIA), 536
　minimum number of, 186
　rules for number allowed, 185
digital linear type (DLT) drive, 316
Direct Input procedure, **37**, *83*, **83–84**
　for data transfer, 444
disk layout for RDBMS, **308–309**
　defining in ASAP, 333
　example of defining, **309–310**
Dispatcher, 56–58, 536
　in instance, 183
distributed component architecture, **86–90**
　business components, **86–88**
　business integration, **88–89**
　business objects, **89–90**
distributed R/3 system, 53, **54–55**
　print server on, 283
distributed user administration, 35
DLT (digital linear type) drive, 316

DML, 536
documentation. *See also* system operation manual
    installation of online, **162**, *163*
domain concept
    example of defining, **467–468**, *468*
    for Windows NT network security, 466–467
double-verification principle, **34–35, 219–220**
    implementing, **228–229**, *229*
downtime. *See also* high availability strategy
    and backup hardware throughput, 316
    and backup strategy definition, **313–315**
    potential situations, **481–483**
        and high-availability solutions, 482
        listing, **494–495**
    procedure for, 334
    protecting server network from, 363
    recovery strategy and, **325–328**
    for Release update, 44
    testing with simulation, 491
    from upgrades, 427
dump analysis, for monitoring runtime environment, 200
Dynamic Host Configuration Protocol (DHCP), 371–372
Dynpro (Dynamic Program), 65, 536

E

EarlyWatch, **43–44**, 128, **524–525**
    components of Basis analysis, *525*
    GoingLive Check vs., 526
    remote connection for, 374
EARLYWATCH user, **238**, 239, 459
EDI (Electronic Data Interchange), 536
EDIFACT standard, 88
encryption of data, at protocol level, 464
Enqueue service, 51, 52, **70**, *71*
    configuration with message service on one server, 484
    and single point of failure, 484
enqueue work process (ENQ)
    minimum number of, 186
    rules for number allowed, 185

Enterprise IMG, 405, 536
entity, 536
error indicator, in database calendar, 330
error tolerance, interface technical design and, 439
escalation path, defining for project team, **110–111**
event-driven jobs, **254–255**
example company. *See* Mannaberg Inc.
expansion of hardware, 182
expert competence, training courses for, 511–512
exporting data, 84
extended memory, 58
external connections, to network, 81
external factors, and downtime, **314–315**
eXternal Interface for Job Background Processing (XBP) interface, 254
external job management, **254**
external Output Management System, **287–289**

F

failover system, **305**
failure. *See* downtime
fax, spool service to format data for, 23
FCS Final Delta Patch, 415
FDDI (Fiber Distributed Data Interchange), 363, 536
file server
    front end software on, *159*, **159–160**
    on subnetwork, 160
Final Preparation phase
    background processing, **262**
        table, 263
    Cut Over in, **451**
    database administration, **334**
        tasks, 335
    front end administration, **168–169**
        table, 169
    high-availability strategy, **491–492**
        tasks, 493
    instances administration, **204–205**
        table, 207
    interfaces, tasks, 452
    network administration, **379**
        tasks, 380

print administration, table, 295
production operation, **398–399**
project administration tasks, **138**
    table, 140
project planning for, 130
quality checks in, 135
security guidelines, **472**
    tasks, 473
software logistics, tasks, 428
system operation setup for spool system, **294–295**
Finance component, 87
firewall, 537
firewall architecture, 374, *375*, 376, 464
format, for data transfer from legacy system, 444
foundation training courses, **509–510**
Frame Relay, for WAN connection, 373
front-end network, 79, 360
    bandwidth for, **368**
    high-availability solution to prevent downtime, 482
    planning, **364–367**
front ends, 537
    access modes to connect printers, 286
    administration in ASAP, **166–169**
    hardware standardization, **147–149**
        configuration, **149**
        pools for resource grouping, **148–149**
        recommended system requirements, 148
    importing software upgrades, 420
    maintenance plans, **165–166**
        strategy definition, 167
    office applications, **154–156**, *155*
    in R/3 setup, 28
    for Ready-to-Run R/3, **502**
    for SAPGUI, 54
    security, **461–462**
    software installation, **156–165**
        on file server, *159*, **159–160**
        local, **157–158**, *158*
        online documentation, **162–165**
        remote connections to subnetworks, **160–162**, *161*
    software standardization, **149–153**
        supported platforms, **150–153**, *151*
    strategy definition, **146–156**
    success factors in administration, **170–172**

and system costs, 146
    WAN to connect, 61
full log directory, for RDBMS, **311**
full migration, 9
functional Releases, 44, **401–402**
    patches, 415

G

Gateway service, 51, **73**, *74*
    and single point of failure, 484
general activity group, **223**
Go Live and Support phase, 41
    after upgrade, **423**
    high-availability strategy, tasks, 493
    instances administration, **205–206**
        table, 207
    project administration tasks, **139–140**
        table, 140
    project planning for, 130
    quality checks in, 135
    software logistics, **427**
        tasks, 428
GoingLive Check, **39–41**, 127, **183**, **522–524**
    analysis, **40**
    vs. EarlyWatch, 526
    optimization, **40**
    remote connection for, 374
    requirements, **523**
    schedule, *41*
    schedule for, *523*
    and security, **524**
    verification, **41**
graphics card, SAP recommendation for, 149
GUI (graphical user interface), 35, 537

H

hard disk
    for archiving, 356
    for backup, **324–325**

hardware, **54–60**, *55*
   front end
      requirements for, 160
      standardization, **147–149**
   high-availability solution to prevent downtime, 482
   life cycle for, 27
   Quicksizer to estimate, **21**
   for R/3 releases, 425
   R/3 system support of, 59–60
   for RDBMS (Relational Database Management System), **303**
   in Ready-to-Run R/3, 500, 501
   requirements catalog, **177–178**
   selecting, **176–183**
      criteria for, 182
      in Project Preparation phase, 202
      simplicity in, **181–182**
   selecting in backup strategy, **315–318**
      example, **316–317**
   sizing, 178
      for database, **336**
   for step-by-step implementation, *119*
   switchover solutions for problems with, 486
   and unplanned downtime, 481–482
help desk, 42–43, **123–126**, *125*
   after upgrade, 423
   and high-availability strategy, 492
   planning, 138
   problem processing, 124–125, *125*
   problem reporting, 124, *125*
   problem resolution, 126
   role of, 10
   service level agreement, 126
   setup, 7
help, types of, **163–165**
Hierarchical Storage management (HSM), **346**
   for archiving, 356
high availability, 537
high-availability strategy, **480–488**
   in ASAP, **489–493**
      tasks, 492–493
   encapsulating redundant subsystems, **483–485**
   success factors, **493–496**
   switchover solutions, **486–488**
   System Administration Assistant, **505**, *505*
   system operation and, **488–489**
high-volume print jobs, 271, 273
   output procedures for, 294
high-volume printers, 274
   connection for, 277
homogeneity, of front ends, **147**
Hot Package patch, 415, 537
HR Legal Change Patch, 415
HSM (Hierarchical Storage management), **346**, 537
   for archiving, 356
HTML, 538
HTML documents
   for Interface Adviser, 440
   for online documentation, 162
HtmlHelpFile, 163, 164
HTTP, 538
Human Resources component, 87

I

IAC, 538
IDA, 538
IDES (International Demo and Education System), 538
IDoc type, 538–539
IDocs (Intermediate Documents), **88–89**, 538
IMG (Implementation Guide), 91–92, 162, **405**, 539
Implementation Accelerators, 447
Implementation Assistant, *4*
implementation strategy, **8–9**, **117–120**
   advantage in three-system strategy, **399**
   defining, 136
      and system landscape, **393–401**
   restrictions in three-system landscape, **400–401**
   roll-out, **119–120**
   step-by-step, **118–119**, *119*
      planning, **424**
implementing R/3, **22–36**
   ASAP for, 2
   authorization concept, **34–36**
   categories of complexity, 111–112
   checking progress, **129–135**
   Cut Over, **122–123**, *123*
   hardware, **54–60**, *55*

personnel costs, 106
Ready-to-Run R/3 (RRR), **501–502**
standards definition, **120–122**
system operation definition and setup, **29–34**
system setup, **25–29**
technical design creation, **22–25**
importing data, 84
    from legacy system, **36–37**
importing patches, **415–418**
information system, **470**, *470*
Informix OnLine, administration tools, 317
Initial Data Transfer Made Easy, 447
installation
    online documentation, **162**, *163*
    software. *See* software installation
instances, *53*, **53–54**, 176, 539–540
    activities for administering, 201
    in ASAP, **201–207**
        Business Blueprint, **202–203**
        Final Preparation phase, **204–205**
        Go Live and Support phase, **205–206**
        Project Preparation phase, **202**
        Realization phase, **204**
        tasks in implementing, 206–207
    checking components in, 203
    configuration, **183–194**
        logon groups, **187–191**
        work processes distribution, **184–187**
    defining system operation for, 199
    monitoring, **195–201**
    operation modes definition, **191–194**, *192*
    physical parts of, **56–59**, *57*
    success factors in implementing, 207–210
Integrated System and Network Management (ISNM), **375–377**
integration technology, training courses for, **514–515**
Interface Adviser, implementing, **440–442**, *441*
interfaces, **81–86**
    in ASAP, **449–452**
        tasks, 451–452
    guidelines, **453**
    infrastructure planning, **436–447**
        requirements, **437–440**
    minimizing number, 438
    monitoring and restarting, **447–449**

success factors, **452–454**
technical design, **439–440**
testing throughput, **453–454**
Intermediate Documents (IDocs), **88–89**
internet application, as user interface, 150
Internet-enabling layer, 51, **63–64**
Internet, official IP address for connection, 371
Internet service, SAP TechNet, **115**, *116*
Internet Transaction Server (ITS), 63, *65*
introductory training courses, 114
invitation to tender, **178**
IP addresses
    administration in Windows NT, **371–372**
    assigning, **370–372**
IPC, 539–540
IS (Industry Solution), 540
ISAPI, 540
ISDN, for WAN connection, 373
ISNM (Integrated System and Network Management), **375–377**
ITS (Internet Transaction Server), 63, *65*, 540

J

Java, 63, *64*
    as front end, **152**
job administrator, and background processing, 256
job chains, *253*, **253–254**
job classes, 72
    example using, **251–252**
    reserving for work processes, 252
    and target server, **249–250**
job list, **247**
    from departments, 257
job log, 259
job priorities, defining, **249–253**
job role matrix, **221**, 235
job roles, 214
    activity group for, 35
    security and, **222–223**
job scheduling monitor, **258–260**, *259*
jukebox, for archiving, 356

K

Knowledge Product CDs, 514

L

LAN (local area network), 540
    access modes for remote printing, 286
    centralized server setup, 366
    decentralized server setup, 366
    printer communication through, 276
    for server network, 80
    temporary link for installing SAP front-end software, 162
laptops, connection through WAN, 361
last logon, dialog box display of, 226
layers in R/3 client/server architecture, 2, 50, 51
    hardware distribution over, *19*
    supported platforms for, 18
legacy system
    Cut Over from, **122–123**, *123*
    importing data from, **36–37**
    migration, 9–10
    in step-by-step implementation, 118
    transferring data from, 120, 427, 450
        planning, **442–446**, *443*
Legacy System Migration Workbench, **447**
life cycle, for hardware, 27, 182
linked R/3 systems, 8
load on R/3 system
    from archiving run, 350
    balancing for spool servers, 278–279
    distribution, 30, **208–209**
        background processing and, **247–249**
        operation modes to adapt resources to, 192
    logon balancing, **73**, 187, 188, 483
    monitoring during production, 206
    peaks in print infrastructure, 273
    statistics on, 41
    Technical Team monitoring of, 43
    and unplanned downtime, 483

local area network (LAN). *See* LAN (local area network)
local installation of front end software, **157–158**, *158*, 162
local printing, setup, **283–285**, *284*
lock entries, for monitoring runtime environment, 200
lock list, for password, 227
lock table
    central instance failure and, 488
    for enqueue service, 70
locking mechanism, for R/3 transaction, 66
log (file) mode, **311**
log files
    backups of, 32, 319
    data recovery from, **327–328**
    during online backup, 320
    in RAID disk layout, 309
logbook, of daily monitoring, 332
logged-on users, listing current, 469
logical errors, downtime from, **313–314**
Logical Output Management Systems (LOMS), 288
logical servers, 278
logical services, **50–54**
logical spool servers, **279–280**, *280*
    example of setup, **280–281**
logical unit of work (LUW), 65, 439, 541
Logistics component, 87
logon groups, 30, 364
    central control of user logons with, 188
    configuration of one, **189**
    defining, **187–191**
    multiple, **190**
    setup example, **190–191**
logon load balancing, **73**, 187, 483
logon procedure
    defining, **225–227**
    unsuccessful attempts, 226
LOMS (Logical Output Management Systems), 288
LUW (Logical unit of work), 65, 439, 541

M

magnetic tapes, for archiving, 356
Maintain User screen, 224, *225*

maintenance
    logon groups to manage, 188
    and planned downtime, **481**
    plans for front ends, **165–166**
Management Information Base (MIB), 377
management training courses, 113, **509**
Mannaberg Inc. (fictitious company)
    authorization concept for user administration, 35
    change requests, 17
    client definition, 15
    data backup and recovery, 33–34
    data transfer from legacy system, 37
    legacy system migration, 9–10
    network topology, 24–25, *25*, *362*
    printers, 24
    project team, 11
    system landscape, 13–14
    system operation manual, 31
    system topology determination, 8–9
    technical needs, 19–20
    technical requirements, 22
    test system for correction Release, 46
MAPI, 541
massively parallel processor (MPP) system, 305
master data, from legacy system, 36
Master IDoc, 89
master records. *See also* user master records
    importing, 401
    maintaining centrally or decentrally, **230**, *231*
medium-sized companies. *See* Ready-to-Run R/3 (RRR)
memory
    selecting for database, 336
    work process use of, 58
menus
    customized for job role, 35
    Session Manager to navigate tree, 215, *216*
message server, 72
Message service, 51, 52, **72–73**
    configuration with Enqueue service on one server, 484
    and single point of failure, 484
MIB (Management Information Base), 377
Microsoft SQL Server, administration tools, 317

migration, **9**
MIME, 541
minimum bandwidth, **370**
modules in R/3, 2
monitoring
    instances, **195–201**
    for interface errors, 439
    interfaces, **447–449**
    performance of background jobs, 265
    print infrastructure output, **289–292**
    RDBMS (Relational Database Management System), **328–332**
    runtime environment, 199–200
monitoring objects, 195–196, *196*
MPP (massively parallel processor) system, 305
multinational company, system landscape design example, **391–392**

N

names
    for development classes, 408–409
    for R/3 system, **96–97**
    uniform conventions, 230
        for master records, 224
    for user, 214
network administration, success factors, **381–382**
network administrator, 108
network planning, **360–374**
    bandwidth, **367–370**
    front-end network, **364–367**
    IP address assignment, **370–372**
    layout strategy, **361–364**
    remote connection setup, **373–374**
    server network, **363**
    topology, *362*, 362
network services, and security, **463**
networks
    administration in ASAP, **377–380**
    architecture, **78–81**
        external connections, 81
        for three-tiered R/3 system, *80*

ensuring access by front end, **171–172**
load, software storage on file server and, 160
operations, **374–377**
for Ready-to-Run R/3, **502**
security for, **462–465**
supported products, **382**
topology, **24**
night operation mode, **193**
no-name brand printer, 297
non-SPOFs, **484–485**
nonregular activities
    in print infrastructure, 290
    for system operation, 199
NSAPI, 541

O

object classes, for authorization objects, 217
ODBC (Open Database Connectivity), **156**
office applications, **154–156**, *155*
offline backup, 320
offline redo log files, for Oracle database, 314
OLE (Object Linking and Embedding), 79, **85–86**, **154**, 436, 541
OLTP, 541
OMS, 541
on-site consulting, 127
online backup, 320
Online Correction Support, **416–417**
online documentation
    installation, **162**, *163*
    on print error analysis, 291
    Web browsers available for, 164–165
Online Service System (OSS), **518–522**, 542
Open Database Connectivity (ODBC), **156**
open interfaces, 377, **454**
open transaction data
    automatic reset on switchover, 488
    from legacy system, 36
operating system
    access to servers, 463
    high-availability solution to prevent downtime, 482
    R/3 system support of, 60

in Ready-to-Run R/3, 501
security for, **466–467**
selecting, **176–183**
special users, 461
spool for spool server, 284–285
system hardware requirements, 148
operating system administrator, 108
operating system spool, 282
operation modes, 30, 541
    defining, **191–194**, *192*
    example of setting, 194
    exception operation, **194**
optimistic approach to security, 214
optimization, in GoingLive Check, **523**
optimizing technical settings,
    SAP recommendations, 522
Oracle database
    administration tools, 317
    data backup cycle for, *320*
    offline redo log files, 314
    recommended disk layout, **309–310**, *310*
    special users, 337
organization, defining, **106–115**
OS, 542
OS/2
    as front end, 153
        recommended hardware, 148
    web browsers for online documentation, 165
OS/390, SAP support for, 466
OS/400, SAP support for, 466
OS/DB Migration Service, 129
OSF/Motif
    as front end, 153
    web browsers for online documentation, 165
OSS (Online Service System), **518–522**, 542
Output Management System, external, **287–289**

P

paging, work process and, 184
PAI (Process after Input), 67, 542
parallel background processing, *248*, **248–249**
parameters, for users, 225

partial backups, **323**, *324*
partial tree structure, for monitoring, 197
password
    changing after system implementation, 471
    defining rules, **225–227**
    for operating system users, 332
    for SAP* user, 237
    for special users, 239, 337, 459, 461
    for users, 225, 461
patches for SAP, **402**
    importing, **415–418**
    importing into three-system landscape, *417*
    for Release maintenance, 46
PBO (Process before Output), **68**, 542
performance, 542
    importing objects and, 427
pessimistic approach to security, 214
physical errors, downtime from, **313**
PlainHtmlFile, 163, 164
PlainHtmlHttp, 163, 164
planned downtime, **481**
platforms, supported by R/3, 18
point-in-time recovery, 328
pools for resource grouping, **148–149**
pop-up window, 542
ports, 542
    in secure networks, 463
PREPARE script, for upgrade, 420
Presentation layer, 51, **60–63**
    supported platforms, 18
print administration
    in ASAP, **292–295**
    success factors, **296–298**
print infrastructure
    ASAP tasks related to, 295
    monitoring output, **289–292**
    planning, **270–282**
        determining requirements, **271–274**, *272*
        printer classification and standardization, **274–277**, *275*
    setup, **282–289**
        external Output Management System integration, **287–289**
        front-end printers, **287**

print jobs
    remote, *285*, **285–286**
    source of, 291
print requests, for spool request, 75
printer classes, 278
printer landscape, **23**
    logical spool services on, 279
    recording current status, 293
printers
    access modes, **276–277**
    activity group to access, 223
    application servers for, 270
    defining standard, **275–276**
    no-name brand, 297
    optimizing throughput, **297–298**
    setup for local, **283–285**, *284*
    spool service to format data for, 23
priorities, defining for job, **249–253**
private IP address, 371
Process after Input (PAI), 67, 542
Process before Output (PBO), **68**, 542
Process overview, for monitoring runtime environment, 200
PROD client, 398
production, **27–29**
    preparation, **36–41**
    support availability, **42–44**
production printers, 274
    connection for, 277
production system, 12, *13*, 93
    background processing in, 246
    change objects and, 426
    client in, 389
    component check in, 203
    disk layout, 308
    importing change request to, 412
    importing patches in, 416
    logical spool servers, 282
    maximum permissible downtime for, 325
    network requirements, 360
    print infrastructure in, 271
    role of, 386
    setup in Realization phase, 204, 398
    testing for bottleneck, 208

testing upgrade, 422
throughput and system tests for, 261–262
user master records in, 236
Profile Generator, 215, **239–240**, 542
    search for authorizations, 216
program-to-program communication, **84–86**
project administration
    in ASAP, **135–140**
    in Business Blueprint phase, **137–138**
    control of project scope, **141–142**
    in Final Preparation phase, **138**
    Go Live and Support phase, **139–140**
    procedures determination, **116–129**
        implementation strategy, **117–120**
    in Realization phase, **138**
    success factors, **141–142**
    tasks in ASAP, **139–140**
Project IMGs, 405
project management, 10
    tools, **131**, *132*
Project Manager
    administrative duties, 135–140
    authorization to define, 430
    for Customizing project, 406
    role in project kickoff, 5
    for software development project, 410
    for transport procedure, 413
project plan, preparing, **130–134**
Project Preparation phase
    authorization concept definition, 234
    database administration, **333**
        tasks, 335
    front end administration, **167**
        table, 169
    high-availability strategy, **490**
        tasks, 492
    implementation strategy decisions during, 394
    instances administration, **202**
        table, 206
    network administration, **377–378**
        tasks, 380
    project administration tasks in, **136–137**
        table, 139–140

project planning for, 130
quality checks in, 134
software logistics, **423–425**
    tasks, 428
project team
    defining communication and escalation paths, **110–111**
    determining, **107–111**
    organization chart for, 107, *109*
    preparing, **141**
    roles in, 10
    training, **113–115**
    training courses, **508–515**
    working environment, 110
protocol, 79
protocol level, data encryption for security, 464
prototype, during Realization phase, 27

Q

Q-API, 543
QTST client, creating, 397
quality assurance system, 6, 12, *13*, **27**, 93
    authorization concept implementation, 235
    availability of, 261
    background processing in, 246
    backups in Realization phase for, 331
    component check in, 203
    database backup, 320–321
    importing change request to, 412
    logical spool servers, *282*
    network requirements, 360
    print jobs in, 270
    in Realization phase, **397–398**, *399*
    Release upgrade for, 421
    role of, 386
    security for, 471
Quality Assurance team, 413
quality check, **134–135**
Quicksizer, **21**, **178–181**, *180*

R

R/3
  characteristics, 2–3
  maintenance releases, 44–46, *45*
R/3 Notes
  about operating systems for R/3 Release 4.0, 177
  about printers and device type requirements, 296
  about SAP Software Change Registration, 411
  about using Online Service System, 521
  for client dependency, 393
  for dynamic assignment of IP addresses, 372
  "Legacy System Migration Workbench", 447
  for naming conventions and namespaces, 409
  on patches, 417–418
  for R/3 Release planning, 403
  for R/3 Service and Support, 522
  for remote connection to SAP, 520
  on security, 475
  on security aspects in remote access, 374
  on standard background jobs, 264
R/3 releases
  correction or functional, 44, **401–402**
  hardware requirements, 425
  strategy, **401–404**
  upgrades and interfaces, 453
R/3 Security Guide, 458, 468
R/3 system, 543. *See also* load on R/3 system; Ready-to-Run R/3 (RRR)
  archiving steps, 343
  configuration, **121**
  connecting office application through ABAP, 154
  data structure, 387–388, *388*
  modifications to standard, 425
    guidelines, **429**
  modifying programs in, **121–122**
  name for, **96–97**
  online documentation installation, 162, *163*
  redundant services, **483–484**
  resource requirements, **58–59**
  services and single points of failure, 484
  size of, 118
  steps to setup, 28–29
  testing operation, **38–39**
  transporting data types between different, 387–388
  upgrades to, 400
R/3 System administrator, 108
  authorization to define, 429
  for Customizing project, 407
  for software development project, 410
  for transport procedure, 413
R/3 transport domain, 15, *16*
R/3 transport system, 15, *16*
RAID (Redundant Array of Inexpensive Disks), **304–305**, 543
  for RDBMS, **309**
RDBMS (Relational Database Management System), 76, 302, 543
  administration in ASAP, **332–335**
  administration tools, **317**
  archiving, **307–308**
  backup strategy definition, **312–325**
    downtime and, **313–315**
    hardware selection, **315–318**
    partial backups, **323**, *324*
    schedule and tape administration, **318–321**
    for very large databases, **322–325**
  backups, 32
    testing, 38
  configuration, **308–311**
    disk layout definition, **308–309**
  daily activities for monitoring, 331
  hardware for, 303
  high-availability solution to prevent downtime, 482
  log (file) mode, **311**
  monitoring, **328–332**
  in Ready-to-Run R/3, 501
  recovery strategy, **325–328**
  and single point of failure, 484
  special users, 460
  storage capacity requirements, 307
  storage technology for, **303–307**
  success factors in administration, **336–338**
  switchover solutions, **486–487**, *487*
reaction time
  in Service Level Agreement, 491
  to system error, 326

Ready-to-Run R/3 (RRR), **500–505**
    backup strategy, 504
    DBA Planning Calendar, 504
    front ends for, **502**
    implementation project, **501–502**
    networks for, **502**
    remote connection for, **503**
    software logistics for, **503**
    system operation, **504**
Real Output Management System (ROMS), 288
Realization of Development and Quality Assurance phase, for upgrade, **420–422**
Realization phase
    archiving strategy definition, 349–350, **354–355**
    authorization concept, 235
    availability of quality assurance system, 261
    background processing, **261–262**
        table, 263
    data backup in, **331–332**
    data transfer from legacy system, **450–451**
    database administration, **333–334**
        tasks, 335
    documenting system operation procedures, 199
    front end administration in, **168**
        table, 169
    high-availability strategy, **491**
        tasks, 493
    instances administration, **204**
        table, 207
    interface
        implementation, 441
        tasks, 452
    network administration, **379**
        tasks, 380
    print administration, table, 295
    production system setup in, 398
    project administration tasks in, **138**
        table, 140
    project planning for, 130
    prototype during, 27
    quality assurance system, **397–398**, *399*
        setup, 204, **293–294**, 426
    quality checks in, 135
    security guidelines, **471–472**
    tasks, 473
    software logistics, tasks, 428
    throughput and system tests for production system, 261–262
    user administration strategy decisions, 230
recovery strategy
    for database, **325–328**
    testing, **337**
Redundant Array of Inexpensive Disks (RAID), **304–305**, 543
    for RDBMS, **309**
Regional Support Centers, 518
regular activities
    in print infrastructure, 290
    for system operation, 199
relational database management system. *See* RDBMS (Relational Database Management System)
release strategy, **401–404**
    upgrades, **403–404**
remote archiving, 128
Remote Archiving Service (SAP), 348
remote check, of network, 376
remote connection
    for Online Service System and SAPNet, **519–520**
    for Ready-to-Run R/3, **503**
    setup, **373–374**
remote consulting, 127
Remote Function Call (RFC), 79, **84–85**, 436
    to distribute processing, **248–249**
remote maintenance, of network, 376
remote printing, *285*, **285–286**
    access modes for, 286
remote upgrades, 129, **404**
replacement parts, 496
    storage of, 326
Repository, ABAP Workbench to change, 92
Repository objects
    development classes for, 408–409
    new version of, 410
    tools to create, 408
requirements catalog, **177–178**
    Interface Adviser scenarios and, 440
    for interfaces, 437–438
    in Project Preparation phase, 202

residence time
    in archiving strategy, 351
    and document deletion, 344
resource plans, 133
resources
    activity group to access, 223
    pools for grouping, **148–149**
Repository objects, user authorization to change, 390, 410
restart procedure, 261
    for interfaces, **447–449**
restoring data, time requirements, 316, **326–327**, *327*
retention time, in archiving strategy, 351
RFC (Remote Function Call), 79, **84–85**, 436, 543
    to distribute processing, **248–249**
Roadmap, 4–5
roll-in, 57, 67
roll-out, 58, 68
    implementation strategy, **119–120**
ROMS (Real Output Management System), 288
root users, 461
routers, to connect backbone with server network, 364
runtime environment
    daily activities for monitoring, 199–200, 290
    Repository to describe, 76
    stability in two-system landscape, 389–390
    in system landscape during upgrade, 419
runtime object, 92

S

S_ASYSTEM authorization profile, 241
SAP
    consulting services, 127
    EarlyWatch, **43–44**, 128, **524–525**
    GoingLive Check, **39–41**. *See also* GoingLive Check
    high-availability guide, 494, *495*
    Reference IMG, 406
    Release Planning R/3 System brochure, 402
    Remote Archiving Service, 348
    remote connection to, **373–374**
    Service & Support network, 378
    technical consulting on security, 475
    white paper on Multple-Client Concept, 392
SAP Business Workflow, 88, 306–307
SAP Domain, 467
SAP jobs, background service to process, 71
SAP Local Support, 518
SAP Online Service System, 471
    patches from, 415
SAP R/3 in Switchover Environments manual, 487
SAP R/3 Services, 127
SAP Reference IMG, 405
SAP Service & Support, 518, **521–522**
SAP Software Change Registration, **410–411**
<SAP System name>admn user, 461
SAP System Requirements for Networks, Frontends and Communication Interfaces, 382
SAP TechNet, **115**, *116*
SAP* user, 459, **237**, 239
SAP_ALL authorization profile, 241
SAPCPIC user, 459
SAPGUI (SAP Graphical User Interface), 61, **62**, 146, 543
    data stream between application server and, 369
    front end for, 54
    as user interface, 150
SAPLPD print control program, 287
SAPNet. *See also* Quicksizer
    patches from, 415
    third-party vendors in, 287
SAPR3 user, **77**, **460**
SAProuter, **81**, 374, *375*, 464, 471, 543
    and single point of failure, 484
scalability, of interface, 439
scalable hardware, 182
schedule, for transport procedure, **413–414**, *414*
scheduling jobs, 71–72
    for data backup, **318–321**
    for database calendar, 329
    standard background, **264**
scope of project, **141–142**
Secure Network Communications (SNC), 81, 458, **464–465**, *465*
security
    in ASAP, **471–472**

backups and, 32
central LAN server setup and, 366
for connection with SAP, 374
and distribution of data files, 28
front ends, **461–462**
GoingLive Check and, **524**
and job roles, **222–223**
for network, 376, **462–465**
network topology and, **463**
for operating system, **466–467**
R/3 system tools for monitoring users, **469–470**
SAP documents for guidelines, 474–475
strategy definition, **458–468**
  control access, **459–462**
success factors, **474–476**
and system access to transport directory, 97
user authorization to change Repository objects, 390
user training and, **476**
sequential files, communication through, **82–84**, *83*
server, 544. *See also* application servers; spool server
  database, 535
    application servers per, 58
  file
    front end software on, *159*, **159–160**
    on subnetwork, 160
  target, job classes and, **249–250**
server classes, access modes for, 283
server component, availability to client component, 480
server network, 80, 360, **363**
  between application layer and database layer, 465
  bandwidth for, **368**
  high-availability solution to prevent downtime, 482
server programs, and permanent IP addresses, 372
Service Level Agreement, 126, 182, **495–496**
  for delivery of replacement components, 326
  reaction time in, 491
service provider, for Technical team roles, 109
service strategy, **127–129**
session, 544
Session Manager, **61–62**, *62*, 146, 544
  job role menu in, 35
  to navigate menu tree, *216*

as user interface, 150
and user menus, **239–240**
shared memory, 544
SID, 544
Simple Network Management Protocol (SNMP), 377
single point of failure, 52, 480
  R/3 services and, 484
  redundancy for, **485**
sizing hardware, 178
  for database, **336**
  of instances, **208**
  requirements, **20**
SMP (symmetric multiprocessor system), 305
SMS (System Management Server), 165–166
SNC (Secure Network Communications), 81, 458, **464–465**, *465*
SNMP (Simple Network Management Protocol), 377
software
  R/3 system support of, 59–60
  requirements for front-ends, 160
software developer
  authorization to define, 430
  for software development project, 410
software development project
  organizing, **408–411**
  roles for, **410–411**
software installation
  on file server, *159*, **159–160**
  for front ends, **156–165**
  local for front ends, **157–158**, *158*
  remote connections to subnetworks, **160–162**, *161*
software logistics, **90–100**, 386
  in ASAP, **423–428**
    tasks related to, 427–428
  production operation in three-system landscape, *400*
  for Ready-to-Run R/3, **503**
  success factors, **428–431**
  system landscape, **91–93**
source of print job, 291
SPAM Update patch, 415
special print jobs, 273
special users, 239
  protecting from third parties, **237–239**, **337–338**
  and security, **459–462**, *460*

spool requests, 75
    deleting obsolete, 264
spool server
    attributes of, **278–279**
    bottlenecks on, 297, 298
    connecting printers to, 276
    defining, **277–282**
    example of setup for logical and alternative, **280–281**
    local and remote printing on single, 286
    logical, **279–280**, *280*
Spool service, 23, 51, **74–75**, *75*
    and single point of failure, 484
    transport system, **281–282**, *282*
spool system, 270
spool work process (SPO)
    on application servers, 297
    minimum number of, 186
    operating system spool and, 285
    in remote printing, **285–286**
    rules for number allowed, 185
SQL (Structured Query Language), 77, 156, 544
SSCR, 545
standard printers, defining, **275–276**
standards, and network infrastructure, 361
start time, for background processing, 246
statistics
    on archiving run, 351
    on system load, 41
status query, by spool system, 298
steering committee, role of, 10
step-by-step implementation strategy, **118–119**, *119*
    planning, **424**
step-by-step migration, 9
storage devices
    for archiving, **356**
    for database, **303–307**
        selecting, 336
    example of defining, **316–317**
    management systems, 318
strategic goals, and R/3 implementation, 8
strategy. *See also* implementation strategy
    defining for front ends, **146–156**
    for support, **127–129**

structural changes to database, backups after, 319
Structured Query Language (SQL), 77, 156
subnetworks
    to link user front ends, 366
    remote connections for front end software, **160–162**, *161*
super user, *229*, **229–230**
    authorization to define, 429
SUPER user group, 241
support strategy, **127–129**
SUSE, 545
switchover solutions, **486–488**
symmetric multiprocessor system, 305
synchronous RFC, 84
System Administration Assistant, *505*, **505**
system administration department, role in archiving procedure, 349, *350*
System administrator, print infrastructure maintenance, 292
System Architect, 107. *See also* Technical Team Lead
system change options, 393
    in production system, 398
system error, reaction time to, 326
system events, 254
system landscape, **12–16**, **91–93**, 545. *See also* three-system landscape; two-system landscape
    clients, **14–15**
    defining technical infrastructure for, 202
    design in Project Preparation phase, **423–424**
    documenting plans for, 378
    implementation strategy definition, **393–401**
    maintenance, **414–423**
        patches import, **415–418**
    technical status vs. upgrade requirements, 419
    transport system, **15–16**
system landscape planning, **386–404**
    design example for multinational company, **391–392**
    release strategy, **401–404**
    system and client definition, **387–393**
    two- or three-, 391
system load. *See* load on R/3 system
system log, for monitoring runtime environment, 200
System Management Server (SMS), **165–166**

System Monitor, 199
system operation definition, **199–201**
    for background processing, **257–260**
    for user administration, **232–233**
system operation manual, 29, **38–39**
    archiving procedures and schedule, 351, 354
    background processing in, 257
    backup strategy definition, 331
    in Business Blueprint phase, 203
    creating for production, 204
    front end information in, 171
    help desk use of, 43
    and high-availability, **489**
    interfaces documentation, 448
    print infrastructure documentation, 289
    user administration documentation, 232
system parameters
    to define number of work processes, 185
    optimally customizing, 206
    testing, 39
system topology, in implementation strategy, **8–9**
Systems Network Architecture Logical Unit 6.2 protocol (SNA LU6.2), 79

T

tables
    and archiving objects, **351–354**
    searching archiving objects for, **352**
    searching for archiving objects in, **353**
Tables and Archiving Objects screen, *352, 353*
tape drives
    administration of tapes, **321**
    capacity, **315–316**
    example of defining, **316–317**
    throughput for backup, **316**
tape robot, 323
tapes, testing, 337
target concept, for data transfer, **443–444**
target server, job classes and, **249–250**
target status
    for local network, 361
    for network, 378

TCP/IP, 19, 24, 79, 360, 545
    to communicate between network nodes, 370
TDC (transport domain controller), 99, 545
technical consultant, 108
technical design, 6
    creating, **22–25**
    documenting plans for system landscape, 378
technical infrastructure, defining for system landscape, 202
Technical Team, 6, 106
    estimating required number of members, **111–113**
    involvement in user problems, 205
    load monitoring by, 43
    part-time vs. full-time member requirements, 112
    planning for print requirements, 271
    and print infrastructure, 293
    project rooms for, 137
    recommended courses, 508–515
    responsibility for transporting change requests, 425
    role of, 10
    service provider for roles of, 109
Technical Team Lead, 107
    management training courses for, **509**
TemSe (Temporary Sequential Objects), 75, 545
terminated jobs
    administrator check for, 260
    procedure for restarting, 261
termination, of background processing, 259
TEST client, 396
test printers, 274
testing
    database backup and recovery, **337**
    database restore and recovery, 328
    downtime with simulation, 491
    production system upgrade, 422
    R/3 system operation, **38–39**
    throughput, 262
    throughput for interfaces, **453–454**
theft, of data backup tapes, 460
Thin Client, 60–61
third-party vendors
    interface use by, 454
    for job scheduler, 254
    in SAPNet, 287

three-system landscape, 12, *13*, 13–14, **92–93**
   advantage of implementation strategy, **399**
   clients in, *390*, **390–391**
   development system in, *397*
   implementing, 394–399
   importing patches into, *417*
   restrictions of implementation strategy, **400–401**
   setup schedule, *26*
   transport of requests in, 97
   transport procedure, 411–412
   upgrade schedule, *422*
three-tier configuration, **55–56**
threshold values, for alerts in monitor, 209–210
throughput
   for data backup, **316**
   of database storage, 303
   measurement for network, 376
   optimizing for background processing, **265–266**
   optimizing for printer, **297–298**
   for tape backup, 323
   testing, 262
   testing for interfaces, **453–454**
time-critical interfaces, 453–454
time-critical jobs
   print jobs as, 271, 273
   resources for, 249
time requirements
   restoring data, **326–327**, *327*
   for very large database backups, **322–323**
TMS (Transport Management System), **100**, 545
TO (Transport Organizer), 546
topology of network, 362, *362*
   and security, **463**
training
   Basis Knowledge Products, **114–115**
   project team, **113–115**
   SAP TechNet, **115**, *116*
   for team members, 137, **508–515**
     basic courses, **510–515**
     foundation courses, **509–510**
     management courses, **509**
   users, 168–169, **171**
     and security, **476**

Training and Documentation team, role of, 10
transaction code, 546
transaction code AL08, 469
transaction code DB02, 331
transaction code DB12, 331
transaction code DB15, 353
transaction code PFCG, 215
transaction code RZ01, 260
transaction code RZ02, 199
transaction code RZ20, 199, 290, 331
transaction code SARP, *470*
transaction code SE*nn*, locking, 462
transaction code SM04, *469*
transaction code SM12, 200
transaction code SM13, 200
transaction code SM21, 200
transaction code SM35, *448*
transaction code SM37, 260
transaction code SM50, 200
transaction code SM66, 200
transaction code SP01, 290
transaction code SPAU, 421
transaction code SPDD, 421
transaction code ST22, 200
transaction code SU01, 225
transaction code VL*nn*, 222
transaction data, from legacy system, 36–37
transactional RFC, 85
transport, 546
transport directory, **97–98**
transport domain, **98**, *99*, 546
transport domain controller (TDC), 99, 395
   development system as, 425
transport group, **98**, *99*
Transport Management System (TMS), **100**, 395
   in Business Blueprint phase, 425
transport procedure
   determining, **411–414**
   roles for, **412–413**
   schedule for, **413–414**, *414*
transport route, **99–100**
transport system, **15–16**, **96–100**
   spool service, **281–282**, *282*

tRFC, 546
triggering events, 254
two-system landscape, 13, **93**, **388–390**, *389*
    advantages and disadvantages, 389–390
    in Ready-to-Run R/3, 500
two-tier configuration, **54–55**

U

unauthorized access. *See* security
UNIX
    SAP support for, 466
    security for, **466**
unplanned downtime, **481–482**
unsuccessful logon attempts, 226
update processes, for monitoring runtime environment, 200
update record, for dialog service, 68
Update service, 51, **68–70**, *69*
    and single point of failure, **484**
update work process (UPD)
    minimum number of, 186
    rules for number allowed, 185
Upgrade Project Preparation, **418–419**
upgrades
    downtime from, 427
    modifications and, 429
    planning, **418–423**
    to R/3 system, 400
    Realization of Production phase, **422–423**
    in Release strategy, **403–404**
    remote, 129, **404**
URL, 546
user administration
    activities for, 233
    in ASAP, **234–236**
    central, 36
    defining system operation for, **232–233**
    distributed, 35
    success factors, **237–241**
user administrator, 219, 229

user, authorization to define, 430
USER domain, 467
user events, 254
user groups
    administration, **227–233**
    creating, **240–241**
    for software setup, 150
user list, **469**
user master records, **218–219**
    allocating to user groups, 240–241
    authorization in, **214–220**
    authorization to adapt administration, **228–233**
    client dependence of, 233
    for special users, 239
    standardized, **224**
user menus, **239–240**, *240*
user name, 214
users. *See also* logon groups
    access to application layer, **461**
    authorization to change Repository objects, 390, 410
    and background processing, 256
    multiple administrators for authorization, **34–35**
    protecting special from third parties, **237–239**
    in R/3 setup, 29
    and required bandwidth for network, 369
    security and training of, **476**
    super user, *229*, **229–230**
    supervising, 205
    training, 168–169, **171**
users per dialog work process, 58

V

V1 components, 69
V2 components, 69
validity period, for password, 227
verification, in GoingLive Check, **523**
versions database, 95
    from change request, 410

W

WAN, 367, 546
   for front-end network, 61, 373
   for installing SAP front-end software through remote connection, 162
   laptop connection through, 361
   printer communication through, 276
   and security, 464
WBO (Workbench Organizer), **409–410**, 547
Web browsers
   availability for online documentation by platform, 164–165
   as front end, 61, **152**
   Java-enabled, 63
Web Gate, 63
web sites
   Quicksizer, 179
   SAP about EarlyWatch, 525
   SAP about High Availability, 487
   SAP about Interface Adviser, 440
   SAP about Remote Archiving Service, 348
   SAP on Ready-to-Run R/3, 500
   SAP TechNet, **115**, *116*
   third-party vendors in SAPNet, 287, 345
Web transactions, 63–64
Windows 3.1
   as front end, **151–152**
      recommended hardware, 148
   web browsers for online documentation, 164
Windows 95
   as front end, recommended hardware, 148
   web browsers for online documentation, 164
Windows NT
   DHCP and WINS for, **371–372**
   as front end, recommended hardware, 148
   SAP support for, 466
   security for, **466–467**
   web browsers for online documentation, 164
WINS (Windows Internet Name Service), 371–372
work plan and schedule, **131–132**
   recommended status for tasks in, 132
work processes
   Dispatcher requests to, 57
   distributing, **184–187**
   in instance, 183
   minimum number of, 186
   monitor to display available background, 258
   multiple for job class A, 250
   rules for number allowed, 185
   typical relations for, 187
   users per, 58
work processes per application server, 59
Workbench Organizer, 95
   and development project, 95
workload, scheduling, 133
WORM (Write once, Read multiple), 547
WP (work process), 547

X

X/Open standard, 73
X.25 connection, for WAN connection, 373
X.31 connection, for WAN connection, 373
XBP (eXternal Interface for Job Background Processing) interface, 254
XX-SER-SWFL-CPS component, 402
XX-SER-SWREL component, 402

Testing Your R/3 Knowledge with the CD-ROM

The CD that comes with this book includes a test engine designed to familiarize you with the Certified Technical Consultant (CTC) exam format. The test questions are taken from the pages of the book and can help you gauge your preparedness for the real world of SAP R/3 Implementation with ASAP and for the CTC test.

The test contains proprietary software components and information of SAP AG and AsseT GmbH Assessment and Training Technologies.